S0-BHT-972

PROUST

BETWEEN TWO CENTURIES

PROUST

BETWEEN TWO CENTURIES

Antoine Compagnon

Translated by Richard E. Goodkin

Columbia University Press
New York

Columbia University Press wishes to express its appreciation of assistance given by the government of France through Le Ministère de la Culture in the preparation of this translation.

Earlier versions of some chapters of the present work originally appeared as follows:

Chapter 1: *Equinoxe* 2 (1988): 9–28, under the title "Le dernier écrivain du xixe et le premier du xxe siècle."

Chapter 2: *Romanic Review* 78, no. 1 (1987): 114–21, under the title "Fauré, Proust, et l'unité retrouvée."

Chapter 3: *Revue des sciences humaines* 196 (1984): 39–64, under the title "Proust sur Racine." A revised version was published in English in *Yale French Studies* 76 (1989): 21–58.

Chapter 4: André Guyaux, Christian Heck, and Robert Kopp, eds., *Huysmans: Une esthétique de la décadence* (Paris: Champion, 1987): 227–35, under the title "Huysmans, Proust, et la lecture pervers de la Renaissance italienne."

Chapter 6: *Nouvelle Revue de psychanalyse* 33 (1986): 117–39.

Columbia University Press
New York Oxford

Library of Congress Cataloging-in-Publication Data

Compagnon, Antoine, 1950–
[Proust entre deux siècles. English]
Proust between two centuries / Antoine Compagnon ; translated by Richard E. Goodkin.
p. cm.
Translation of: Proust entre deux siècles.
Includes bibliographical references and index.
ISBN 0-231-07264-3
1. Proust, Marcel, 1871–1922. A la recherche du temps perdu.
I. Title.
PQ2631.R63A784413 1992
843'.912—dc20 92-16681
CIP

Casebound editions of
Columbia University Press books
are Smyth-sewn and printed on
permanent and durable acid-free paper.

Book design: Teresa Bonner
Printed in the United States of America
c 10 9 8 7 6 5 4 3 2 1

Contents

Acknowledgments

A portion of this book was a part of the thesis I defended in June 1985. I would like to express my gratitude to those who evaluated the thesis: Julia Kristeva, Pierre Brunel, Jean-Claude Chevalier, and Michel Raimond. I also wish to acknowledge Jean-Yves Tadié, to whom special thanks are due, as he also gave me my start in the field of Proustian studies by offering me the opportunity to prepare the Pléiade edition of *Sodome et Gomorrhe*.

Several chapters have been published in a different form in various journals and collected volumes. All these chapters have been reworked, sometimes expanded and sometimes shortened, particularly material related to philological and genetic considerations.

I am grateful to all those who invited me to speak at the following institutions and whose criticisms have been very helpful: Saint-Louis, Brussels; Edinburgh University; Institut français, London; Université de Paris VII; Accademia di Belle Arti, Venice; Institut des textes et manuscrits modernes, CNRS; Universität Tübingen; New York University; University of Pennsylvania; Yale University; Université de Montréal; Columbia University; Louisiana State University; University of California, Berkeley and Santa Cruz; Ecole polytechnique; Musée d'Orsay; Wellesley College; University of Pittsburgh; and Société des amis de Marcel Proust.

I was the recipient of a John Simon Guggenheim Memorial Foundation Fellowship in 1988, and I would like to take this opportunity to express my thanks to the Guggenheim Foundation: the fellowship I was awarded allowed me to put this book into its final form.

Finally, thanks to Peter Consenstein, who typed a portion of the manuscript, and especially to my friends Alain Ferry, André Guyaux, and François Wahl, who took great care in reading the manuscript.

Introduction

It's not very pleasant to think that just about anyone (if people are still interested in my books) will be allowed to pore over my manuscripts, to compare them to the definitive text, to draw suppositions from them that will always be wrong about my working habits, the evolution of my thought, etc. All of that rather annoys me.

—Proust, in letter to Monsieur and Madame Sydney Schiff, 1922, Correspondance générale

Like most of the early readers of *Du côté de chez Swann,* Paul Souday, the literary critic for the daily newspaper *Le Temps,* as early as 1913 blamed the novel for an absence of construction: "It seems to us that Monsieur Marcel Proust's thick volume has no composition, that it is as limitless as it is chaotic, although it does contain invaluable elements from which the author could have put together an exquisite little book."[1] In his own defense, Proust stated that *A la recherche du temps perdu* contained a secret outline that he promised the reader would understand only retrospectively, once the novel's outcome became clear. The proof of this might be found in what Proust confided to Souday in 1919, after *A l'ombre des jeunes filles en fleurs* had received the Prix Goncourt: "The last chapter of the last volume was written immediately after the first chapter of the first volume. All of the 'in-between' material [*Tout l'"entre-deux"*] was written afterward."[2] This, of course, was not completely accurate, or rather it was both true and false.

It was false because Proust had written "Combray," the first part of *Du côté de chez Swann,* in 1909, but at the time he intended to end the novel with a conversation between the hero and his mother about Sainte-Beuve. *A la recherche du temps perdu,* as is well known, developed out of *Contre Sainte-Beuve:* more precisely, the novel has its origin in an introductory narrative that is supposed to have illustrated Proust's thesis before revealing it. Sensations and reminiscences were supposed to have preceded and prepared for the critique of intelligence and the refutation of Sainte-Beuve. Not until 1911 was the critical conversation about Sainte-Beuve replaced by the narration of the *matinée* at the Princesse de Guermantes', with its two complementary sections, "L'adoration perpétuelle" [Perpetual Adoration]—the revelation of an aesthetic that transcended time—and "Le bal de têtes" [Masked Ball], the pageant of aging characters and the discovery of the effects of time.

But Proust's statement to Souday was also true because in the 1909 version of "Combray," each impression or reminiscence—including the one inspired by the well-known madeleine—was followed by a commentary that immediately drew its philosophical and theoretical consequences. Thus *Le Temps retrouvé* simply defers the doctrine until the novel's climax, and this transforms the novel's earlier impressions and reminiscences into failures, or at least into half successes: for the reader they remain enigmas until the final apotheosis. Suspense is thus created at the risk of taking the readers beyond their depth. From 1909 to 1911, then, what would become *Le Temps retrouvé* was an integral part of "Combray"; in a sense the final chapter informed the first chapter.

When *Le Temps retrouvé* grouped together, at the end of the novel, the explanations that previously had been distributed throughout its pages, it changed the critique of intelligence into a search for the truth and changed the book's polemical intention into an *apologia.* At the same time the indictment of Sainte-Beuve, removed from the conclusion, was diffused throughout the novel, with Madame de Villeparisis becoming his most faithful supporter.

Most of the characters provide an illustration of the distinction between the social self and a deeper self; they reveal themselves to be quite different from what they had at first seemed to be: Charlus, for example, whose true nature is exposed in a dramatic turn of events, and the novel's artists—above all Vinteuil, the piano teacher from Combray who Swann cannot believe is none other than the composer of the sonata.

Granted that "Combray" and *Le Temps retrouvé* were in fact written together and before everything else, we must emphasize nonetheless that the two chapters then constituted a single one. The aesthetic doctrine was revealed little by little instead of being deferred until the climax. Proust was not lying to Paul Souday, but neither was he being completely sincere.

"Combray" and the "Matinée at the Princesse de Guermantes' " thus define the two extreme supports of a prodigious stretched bow. They are so powerfully grounded, so necessary to each other in their interdependence, that between them the novel was subsequently able to stretch out as much as it pleased and to take in numerous unexpected and often parasitical developments without losing its form or momentum. It is as if the beginning and the end held the cycle of novels so tightly together that nearly anything could fit into the middle. The most important graft was "The Novel of Albertine" or the "Episode of Albertine," as Proust also calls it, which was not planned for when *Du côté de chez Swann* was published in 1913. It is undoubtedly what Proust was thinking of in his letter to Paul Souday.

The symmetry within a symmetry created by the titles of the three volumes announced in 1913—the symmetry of *Le Temps perdu* and *Le Temps retrouvé* complemented by the symmetry of *Le Côté de chez Swann* and *Le Côté de Guermantes* within *Le Temps perdu*—was disturbed to make room for Albertine between *Le Côté de Guermantes* and *Le Temps retrouvé*. It is well known that the model for Albertine was Alfred Agostinelli, a chauffeur whom Proust met in Cabourg in 1907 and hired as a secretary in 1913 to type out the second part of the work. His presence—and to an even greater extent his absence—was in fact to disrupt the novel completely. He left Proust in December 1913 and died in May 1914 at a time when he was taking flying lessons under the name of Marcel Swann. Proust immediately wrote out a first draft of *Albertine disparue* and then moved backward to *La Prisonnière* and "preparations," as he called them, for the novel of Albertine, material that was to be inserted into the first stay in Balbec and *Le Côté de Guermantes.* Finally, he composed the second stay in Balbec and all of *Sodome et Gomorrhe.*

The middle of *A la recherche du temps perdu* is thus occupied by the novel of Albertine, buried between the two great slopes of the 1913 outline. But the "in-between" material is *Sodome et Gomorrhe,* which joins the novel as it was before 1914 to the novel as it was after that date. *Sodome et Gomorrhe* is an immense transition—as well as being a novel in its own right—between the novel of memory and the novel of Albertine, the latter also being the novel of homosexuality (for a long time Proust included *La Prisonnière* and *Albertine disparue* under the titles *Sodome et Gomorrhe III* and *IV*). The present *Sodome et Gomorrhe II* with its two parts, the Princesse de Guermantes' reception and the second stay in Balbec, is linked, on the one hand, to the high society element of the novel and, on the other, to the love story. In a strict sense, the true "in-between" material of the *Recherche,* its bending point, is *Sodome et Gomorrhe I.* The discovery of M. de Charlus' homosexuality and the section in which the author holds forth about the "race of fairies" clamorously herald in the end of the Guermantes component and the novel's new direction. It is for this reason that the episode of Charlus' and Jupien's meeting could be moved around for such a long time; its placement was not clear in the 1913 script, and Proust did not decide where to put it until quite late, probably not until 1916. When he made this episode into the keystone of the entire novel, that decision was his last major structural choice, a sign of completion. Until then, the hero's *alter ego* had been Swann, both in high society and in the realm of love. But from now on it was Charlus who would take over that role.

The notion of the "in-between" so dear to Pascal—he saw in it the place of truth—is essential to Proust's work. Proust sets forth symmetries only to slant them; he establishes poles and then brings them together. The use of the first person is the most important innovation Proust brought to *Jean Santeuil* in the 1909 *Contre Sainte-Beuve,* and the "I" was responsible for the success of *A la recherche du temps perdu.* But the function of the first person is not only to distinguish the hero from the narrator and the past from the present. Even in the opening section, from the very first page of "Combray," intervening between the past and the present—and between the hero and the narrator—we find a third "I," an "I" who floats between the past and the present, or rather between the distant past and the recent past, a go-between. This "waking sleeper" is an insomniac who, between "once" and "long ago," awakened in the dark of night and remembered his old rooms. The narrator sleeps by day and stays awake by night; he remembers a time when he used to sleep at night, a time when, if he couldn't sleep, he would remember the past; the narrator remembers the waking sleeper and the waking sleeper remembers the hero, in Combray and in Tansonville, by way of Paris, Balbec, Doncières, and so on.

The oxymoron of the "waking sleeper," a reminiscence of the "Tale of the Sleeper and the Waker" in the *Thousand and One Arabian Nights,* is a real find, one that forms the core of the narrative system of the *Recherche*: "When a man is asleep, he has in a circle round him the chain of the hours, the sequence of the years, the order of the heavenly host," we read at the beginning of "Combray."[3] Between the narrator's voluntary memory and the hero's involuntary memory, between watchfulness and sleep, a third kind of memory intervenes: the spontaneous memory of the sleeper as he is waking up. For an instant this memory is muddled: he believes he is in this room, or that one. The waking sleeper, at the center of the novel like a spider in its web, is the guarantor of the flexible chronological framework of the *Recherche,* which is halfway between a novel of linear progression and a collection of poetic prose.

The last room, at the end of *Albertine disparue,* is the room in Tansonville, at Gilberte Swann's house after she has become Madame de Saint-Loup; after that the insomniac passes the torch on to the narrator, who is contemporary with the events of *Le Temps retrouvé.* In Tansonville, the hero learns that a connecting path did indeed exist between Méséglise and Guermantes, those two walks in the vicinity of Combray that have become emblematic of two worlds long thought to be irreconcilable, Swann's way and the

Guermantes way. Gilberte, by moving from one "way" to the other, herself becomes an intermediate figure, and her daughter, who joins the two ways, even more so. Finally, the novel of Albertine opposes Sodom to Gomorrha, but Albertine herself—along with Morel, who turns out to be her double—affects the link between the two biblical cities, between the sexes.

A la recherche du temps perdu is a novel of the in-between: not of contradiction resolved, not of dialectical synthesis, but rather of limping, or defective symmetry, of imbalance and disproportion, of stumbling, as we see with the "two uneven stones" of the baptistry of Saint Mark's in Venice conjured up by the "uneven paving-stones" in the courtyard of the Guermantes' residence: "I continued, ignoring the evident amusement of the great crowd of chauffeurs, to stagger as I had staggered a few seconds ago, with one foot on the higher paving-stone and the other on the lower" (3:899; 4:445–46). Whether one emphasizes obstacles or transparency—the reality of the uneven cobblestones or the ideal and immaterial perfection of the revelation that follows—a better allegory of the novel, within this intermittency, is the hero's unsteady gait in the Guermantes' courtyard, like Charlie Chaplin dressed in black with hat and cane, or like Baudelaire "Tripping over his words as if over cobblestones" [*Trébuchant sur les mots comme sur les pavés*[4]] in the only passage from *Les Fleurs du mal* that, as Walter Benjamin puts it, "shows him hard at work on his poetry."[5] And the scene makes us laugh: we laugh a great deal with Proust, especially in the sections between "Combray" and *Le Temps retrouvé*.

In the interval between novel and criticism, between literature and philosophy, the whole novel—and the whole of what is in the novel—is a mixture, a hybrid, an intermediary. That is why Proust disconcerted his readers and continues to disconcert them today; paradoxically it is also why *A la recherche du temps perdu* quickly became a classic, if, that is, we agree that a classic may be not a stable work of art but rather a work that is off-balance, a work with gaps, lags, and flaws that endlessly invite us to read it. Now the structural "in-between" material of the *Recherche* also appears to be historically "in between." Perhaps we may understand it as the form taken by a crucial watershed, a watershed between the nineteenth and the twentieth centuries. *Sodome et Gomorrhe,* at the hinge between the novel of memory and the novel of Albertine, between the prewar novel and the postwar novel, right at the center of *A la recherche du temps perdu,* would appear to provide the finest vantage point from which to observe the entire novel.

But how are we to speak of someone who was simultaneously the last writer of the nineteenth century and the first writer of the twentieth, who both was intimately attached to the fin-de-siècle and miraculously escaped from it? The best way to perceive this formal and historical break is to combine historical approaches with formal analysis so that we may understand, for example, the distance to be found in Proust's work between the categories that determine how he conceives of the novel and the novel that he himself actually composes. In recent decades of literary criticism, historical approaches have come to be mistrusted, suspected of positivistic, deterministic, and psychological biases. The different areas of recent critical development have had one thing in common: they have all kept away from particular works in favor of general techniques and universal forms. In other words they have steered clear of the works themselves and focused on "literature," leaving aside the present or actual to go after the possible or potential. Perhaps the time has come once again to tackle this recently neglected question of the singularity of literary works.

It is now possible to imagine a form of criticism that would consider the literary work as both actual and possible, that would disregard neither history nor—as recent critical perspectives would have it—literature's openness to a meaning yet to be established. Between philology, which seeks to establish a literal meaning—or literary history in search of a universal meaning, or, failing that, the author's meaning—and criticism which takes literature as an open work and finds it has a multiplicity of meanings, there is a connecting path, yet another "in-between." Before speaking of Proust's "in-between," we must therefore establish a critical "in-between."

In *Critique et vérité,* Roland Barthes, defining the multiple meaning of literature, found it necessary to deny any contribution that history might make to the meaning of a work. He thus offered a challenge to the deterministic reduction of literature to historical event: "In our opinion the work has no contingency," he writes, it "is always in a position of prophecy"; "separated from any and all *positions,* by the same token [it] offers itself up for exploration."[6] The work thus appears, in its absolute status as an unidentifiable object, completely cut off from institutions, from literary functions, for example from reading, which according to Barthes should be studied by historians. Criticism, on the other hand, should content itself with forms: it is up to the science of literature to reveal "all the meanings which literature conceals, or—and this amounts to the same thing—the empty meaning which underlies all of the others."[7]

Would it not be more judicious to conceive of the relation between event and structure, or between the actual and the possible, in a less mysterious way? The meaning that lies in the inmost depths of the work—a meaning that is indeed irreducible, and the irreducibility of which is at the origin of the plurality of readings—cannot be absolutely empty, and its contents are not so very indifferent to the form. If the work is an open structure, this presupposes that it does not start out as nothing, and to this extent we can find a way of putting the purely literary into a historical context without necessarily reducing it to that context.

Proust's aesthetic theory belongs to the nineteenth century; in 1920, Proust was still reacting to the attacks leveled against the decadents—Huysmans, the impressionists, and Wagner—in 1880. But Proust's self-justifications go awry: they are contradictory and ultimately self-destructive, their strangeness manifest in their unsuitability to the novel they are purportedly defending. Stendhal, Proust claims in essence, was a great writer unbeknownst to himself; Proust was one as well! That is why his novel has a certain dissonance, why it is—fortunately—a failure, for it is precisely because it is a failure that it is a great novel, that is, open to the meaning we read into it, to the meaning future generations will attribute to it. It is, in the final analysis, a prophetic work, not because it is without contingency, but rather because it is ambiguous in its own time. The work opens itself up to future meanings in direct proportion to the unevenness of its historical meaning, by virtue of being in disagreement with itself historically. As Valéry puts it, "A work remains lasting as long as it is able to appear completely different from the way its author made it."[8] A work that is seamless in the present is an ephemeral work, a work condemned to move from the category of "modern" to that of "old-fashioned" without ever becoming a classic. A classic is not a work that transcends time; on the contrary it is a work that is disconcerting in any time, including its own. *Madame Bovary* became a classic because of the ambiguity that permeates the entire work, but the best-seller of the day on a similar topic, Ernest Feydeau's *Fanny,* is completely out-of-date. Thus Proust's novel is "out of sync" with its aesthetic doctrine; to borrow the terms of Gadamer's hermeneutics, it asks one question and answers another.[9] In the gap between the question it asks and the question that reading the novel allows us to reconstruct from the answer it provides resides the plurality of meanings we attribute to the work because they are already in the work. That is why we cannot spare ourselves the trouble of studying the work in its own time; our goal is not to take it back to a historical meaning as if that were a stable and uniquely true reference, but rather to appraise its lapses in the present, the dissonance between the part of the work that belongs to the past and the future that the work announces.

Flaubert's *Bouvard et Pécuchet,* for example, corresponds to the same ideological project as Taine's *Origins of Contemporary France,* or rather does not correspond to it, for the project is associated with the question that Flaubert poses but that his own book distorts: how could we have sunk as low as the 1870 defeat, Napoleon III's surrender at Sedan, and the Commune? And like Taine, Flaubert crusades against the French "disease": abstract reason in the manner of Rousseau, revolution, popular sovereignty, universal suffrage, and so on. But as a circumstantial political essay *Bouvard et Pécuchet* is a flop; literature resides in the disparity between the question the work asks and the answer it provides. And this slippage can be traced in the play of literary form and content.[10]

I have mentioned Proust and Flaubert, both highly conscious of their art, in whose work the poetic function and the critical function are inseparable, a characteristic of modernity since Baudelaire. But why not also chalk up to the same kind of historical flaw the greatness of the tragedies of Racine? Racine's tragedy, from its inception on, was attributed to the influences of Versailles or the Jansenists, but at the end of the nineteenth century its "cruelty" was discovered, so that eventually we find Brunetière—I have purposely chosen this bastion of the moral order—making Racine into a naturalist. Brunetière's goal may well have been to condemn Zola by extension and to assimilate true nineteenth-century naturalism to neoclassicism, but here again intentions are of no great importance. In his discovery of Racine's realism—indeed, his exaggeration of it—Brunetière recognized the "sin" in Racine's works, a sin that was in fact perceptible even in his day: a historical dissonance that was later to be called Racine's "Baroque" tendency and that placed *Phèdre* at the very height—as well as at the very end—of classicism in the theater (see chapter 3).

The idea of reinserting a literary event into its historical context and linking the plurality of a work's meanings to a dissonance perceptible in its own time is not an altogether original one. It is reminiscent of the Constance school of criticism and Hans Robert Jauss' aesthetics of reception, which finds a reconciliation between structural method and historical hermeneutics in the notion of a "horizon of expectations" allowing one to distinguish the reader's historical function.[11] The reader—rather than the author, who is generally favored by traditional literary history—becomes the mediator between literature and society. Reading, which may be thought of as contributing to yet another literary history, is present in the text in the form of a scheme that the work plays with, a kind of norm that it shifts, modifies, or strikes up against. I am in fact displacing the aesthetics of reception, which is essentially sociological, when I turn to it for an analysis of the strange discrepancy in Proust's work; from this discrepancy stems the misunderstanding—which Proust himself emphasized—"between those whose eyes are full of yesterday's paintings, albeit unwillingly, and authors whose works will be worthy of the past because they have already been situated in the future ahead of time."[12]

Similarly, Jean Starobinski points out that the structural approach is applicable to literature only when it is conceived of as a "regulated play in a regulated society."[13] But when a work challenges both the game and its rules and in fact opens itself up to history, it can no longer be described in terms of a synchronic structure. This is just what happens in great works; for these works, then, the critic's task consists of analyzing the difference that sets them apart, the difference between, on the one hand, the work as an event and, on the other hand, its context—present in the text in the form of a reading scheme—as a structure. In speaking of Proust, Flaubert, and Racine, I have suggested nothing less than an analysis of the play set up between a question and an answer, a content and a form; showing how the content tries to catch up with the form, indeed, how the form tries to catch up with the content. Rimbaud used to say of Baudelaire that he was the first *voyant,* but he added this reservation: "The form he uses, which has been so highly praised, is small-minded: inventing the unknown requires new forms."[14] Thus, putting the literary event back into history would mean demonstrating how the question tries to catch up with the answer; it would mean examining the discrepancy within this issue, within the work itself.

This difference or gap can perhaps also be conceived of using the notion of symptomatic reading that Louis Althusser set forth in his reading of Marx. This is a reading of a text's blindness in terms of the symptoms of problems the text can neither articulate nor resolve; a reading of the shifts produced by the text that show up as answers to badly formulated (or unformulated) questions, that is, answers to the wrong questions.[15] The methods of deconstruction may also come to mind—for deconstruction pores over the nodes of the text, its paradoxical places, as Derrida does with Rousseau[16]—and symptomatic or deconstructive reading may thus take a benevolent turn, as its goal in setting the text at odds with itself is not to put it on trial (as symptomatic or deconstructive reading would have it), but, on the contrary, to show that the historical rift in the hollow of the text gives it a prophetic meaning and opens it up to the infinite domain of meaning. Whereas symptomatic or deconstructive reading believes in an infallible text in whose name it reveals the text's flaws, I do not believe in any analyses of the defects of *A la recherche du temps perdu;* or perhaps only in what Baudelaire says in closing his praise of Delacroix in 1846: "We know that great geniuses never make half-mistakes, and that they have the privilege of enormity in all senses of the term" (*Salon de 1846,* OC 2:441).

Proust's work continues to provoke us and to defy reading precisely because it is dissonant and paradoxical; because it is a sign of history and of resistance to history; because a difference is hollowed out within it. A work without difference, a becalmed work, is an indifferent work. Or, as Reynaldo Hahn wrote in 1913, as early as the first publication of *Du côté de chez Swann,* "Proust's book is not a masterpiece if what you call a masterpiece is something *perfect* and *flawlessly organized.*"[17]

The following studies focus on the "in-between" in *A la recherche du temps perdu,* that is, on Proust at the watershed of two centuries. The connecting path I have followed is the path of genetic criticism, both because it is practical and because its legitimacy is incontestable: between history and the text, there is a history of the text. Perhaps this is fanciful; but how can we know the structure of *A la recherche du temps perdu,* and in particular its deficiencies, without understanding the movement from *Contre Sainte-Beuve* to the novel? We will emphasize a number of Proust's recurrent motifs, obsessions, or allegories that criss-cross the work. By bringing together two realms of observation, some relative to the history of the text, others relative to the history of representations, our goal is to become aware of Proust's place between decadence and modernity. Proust is not a philosopher, and *A la recherche du temps perdu* is not a work of applied philosophy. Philosophy produces concepts, literature truisms; as Baudelaire puts it in *Fusées,* "To create a truism is an act of genius."[18] Each chapter will try to make clear how writing upsets doctrine, for this tilting is what defines literature.

The first chapter situates Proust within a dispute that occupied the entire second half of the nineteenth century: between those who held that the literary work must be seen as a totality and those who supported fragmentation. "Unity, unity, that's all you need," Flaubert wrote to Louise Colet in 1846, and he went on to deplore the inadequacy of contemporary works: "A thousand lovely spots, but not a single work."[19] When Proust comes to Wagner's rescue against Nietzsche, what he is defending is his very own work. But along with Manet in the field of painting or Fauré in music, Proust is one of those ambivalent artists whose innovations come in spite of themselves, and his work goes beyond the debate to which he himself relates it. Chapter 2, dedicated to Fauré, in fact contrasts the kind of interim unity the composer gave to his most innovative works with the kind of unity Proust was after.

Proust's day saw a major revision in the interpretation of two of the author's literary "beacons": Baudelaire, a symbol of decadence for Bourget or Brunetière, becomes, according to Anatole France in particular, a classical poet, whereas the romantics' bland Racine becomes transformed into a figure of violence. Even though Brunetière, the principal promoter of Racine, remains Baudelaire's most heartless enemy, this back-and-forth critical revision makes the two poets into brothers, and Proust feels he is the youngest addition to the family. Chapter 3 analyzes the presence of a new, ambivalent Racine in *A la recherche du temps perdu,* using Proust's frequent "pederastic" allusions to the choruses of *Esther* and *Athalie.* In chapter 4 I compare Huysmans' and Proust's treatment of a somewhat dated theme: the perversion attributed to Italian painters. Because he adopts the commonplaces of decadent sexuality in the sketches for the *Recherche,* Proust doesn't really come into his own until he invents Albertine; from that moment on he rids the novel of its fin-de-siècle characters.

Chapter 5 is the only one that does not specifically provide a contrast between Proust and another artist; rather it is devoted to several cases where life and the novel intersect. Proust amalgamates mimetic fiction, which is based on models, and the experimental novel, in which reality is sectioned off into *tableaux vivants,* that is, into epiphanies or allegories.

Baudelaire is a tutelary figure for Proust, a virtual guardian angel present on every page of this book, but two chapters are more particularly devoted to him. Chapter 6 attempts to define evil in Proust's work. Two references are at play here: to Sade, or rather to the kind of "sadism" that was clinically catalogued by nineteenth-century medical science and that does not always have very much to do with Sade; and to Baudelaire, or rather to the satanism and depravity for which his name became a kind of shorthand as early as Gautier's prefatory note to the 1868 edition of *Les Fleurs du mal* and subsequent to the publication of Baudelaire's personal diaries in 1887. Chapter 7 is a stylistic study of Proust's use of the adjective: does it resemble Baudelaire's use or Sainte-Beuve's, or perhaps that of the surrealists?

Chapter 8 broaches one of the more peculiar aspects of the *Recherche:* Brichot's mania for etymologies. Proust's knowledge is old-fashioned by the time it gets into the novel, halfway between local erudition and the lexicology of the German school. Allegory in the sense that Walter Benjamin gives it allows us to appreciate these collages and to measure how—and how much—Proust takes his distance from turn-of-the-century idolatry. Chapter 9, harking back to chapter 1, examines another quarrel that divided the entire era, this one between proponents of revolution and proponents of evolution, of tradition and originality or of innovation and imitation. This time it is Barrès who acts as the foil, and Proust's doctrine of inversion provides a model for the conception of art as resurrection, as well as for a critique of the avant-garde. Finally, a brief conclusion suggests another possible meaning in Proust's duality, a meaning that will already have been hinted at several times. Is Proust's duality not also a form of duplicity? Do we in fact have to choose between the two? Like Melville's hero, Bartleby the Scrivener, I would rather not. Let us leave this final instance of the "in-between" or of intermittency intact, for this notion borrowed from Proust will have gradually shown itself to be of crucial importance.

Even my own experience of *A la recherche du temps perdu* is intermittent; it largely comes from working on the critical edition of *Sodome et Gomorrhe*. That is why these studies, which I worked on along with that more philological task, are grouped around that part of Proust's work as around a structural and historical hearth. My knowledge of the end of the nineteenth century is somewhat uneven, and I make no claim to a methodical treatment of Proust's relations with his time. But particular circumstances do not prevent an argument from being well founded if the instrument of genetics is a satisfying intermediary between philology and criticism, and if *Sodome et Gomorrhe* provides the best vantage point for looking at what we might call Proust *bifrons*, like Janus facing both the past and the future.

I

The Last Writer of the Nineteenth Century and the First Writer of the Twentieth

Is the very idea of pinning Proust down to a literary generation and reconnecting *A la recherche du temps perdu* to history and its onward movement not a contradiction? Proust is among the most vehement of writers in his denials of history. The very chronology of his novel is incoherent, and history is barely present in it, and then only indirectly, in bits and pieces: "I remember I slept with her on the day Mac-Mahon resigned" (1:455; 1:413), proclaims a stroller when he catches a glimpse of Madame Swann in the Bois de Boulogne. For this reason any "documentary" or sociological reading of the *Recherche* along the lines of Balzac's *Comédie humaine* is spurious. Most important, in Proust's eyes literature has nothing to do with historical determinism. The three elements that Taine used to define individuality—race, milieu, and moment, the factors that make up an event—always recur in one form or another as the basis for any historical sociology or sociological history of literature. Against this notion of "milieu," Proust took up the banner of genius, just as Flaubert before him attacked the historical criticism of his day already being espoused by Sainte-Beuve and Taine, and expressed his wish for a kind of criticism that might be more oriented toward the artist and take some interest in creation itself. In Proust's mind, as in Flaubert's, two points of view can be conceived, the point of view of Art and the point of view of History, and they are irreconcilable. Nowhere does Proust state this more clearly than in his preface to his friend Jacques-Emile Blanche's *Propos de peintre,* in which he scolds Blanche for reproducing Sainte-Beuve's mistake: "What shocks me about this point of view of history is that it makes Blanche (like Saint-Beuve) attribute too much importance to the epoch, to models" (CSB 580). In contrast Proust proposes his own, more idealistic doctrine—harking back to Schelling and Schopenhauer—that says the Beautiful can emanate only from the deepest and most unsuspected parts of ourselves.

But can we completely accept Proust's idea? Can we abstract out everything having to do with the work's era and its milieu, its school and its genre? Unless we are willing to reduce the work to the expression of a society or even an economic structure, as the old Marxist theory of reflection did, do we not need to recognize a series of mediations, historic and aesthetic, between the author and the work, between the reader and the book? It seems legitimate, in spite of Proust, to reflect on the relations between *A la recherche du temps perdu* and history. We must go beyond the need to choose between aesthetic approaches and historical approaches to the work if we wish to capture the historical and aesthetic ambiguity of Proust's novel. It would be possible to make "Un Amour de Swann" into a turn-of-the-century-style plot, a script worthy of Paul Bourget, René Boylesve, or Marcel Prévost—*L'Etape, Le Parfum des Iles Borromées,* or *Les Demi-Vierges*—as Volker Schlöndorff's film has shown. But one also cannot help but wonder about the film version Visconti was not able to make. The director of *Senso, The Leopard,* and *The Innocent* (taken from D'Annunzio's novel) would probably have been more eager to keep the ambiguity of Proust's work, straddling two centuries as it does.[1] The decision to organize the script around the character of Charlus would surely have preserved an essential aspect of the novel, conceived as a complex network of anticipations and aftershocks, echoes and reflections, a network of uncertain back-and-forth movements between the part and the whole.

This is an issue that is difficult for history, in particular for art history: the issue of thresholds and turning points, crises and revolutions. Are these even historical categories, given that history as a discipline favors the long run, that is, slow evolutions? Yet there is another reason we cannot spare ourselves the trouble of considering Proust's aesthetics in a historical light: an aesthetic threshold is supposed to have been crossed just before World War I, with Apollinaire, for example, or Marcel Duchamp, conversation-poems and the first "ready-mades." Now Proust's work is one-of-a-kind, extraordinary; it is so difficult to connect it to the issues of the time that one is actually tempted to lend credence to Proust's idée fixe, which was expressed in this way during the period of *Contre Sainte-Beuve:*

> The principle which is acting within us when we are in the process of writing and creating our work is so personal and so unique that in the same generations minds of the same kind, the same family, the same culture, the same inspiration, the same milieu and the same social position take up the pen to write almost the same thing in the same way, but each one embroiders on it in a way which is particular to him and which makes of the very same thing something completely new, in which all of the proportions of the others' qualities are shifted. (CSB 306)

Anatole France, Henri de Régnier, René Boylesve, and Francis Jammes are then cited as examples of "immortal but very different flowers" growing out of the same soil.

Who is Proust in this flower arrangement? He seems to shy away from any confrontation with his contemporaries, though he showers them with compliments, even on their most insubstantial offerings. The artistic "beacons" of *A la recherche du temps perdu* (to borrow an image from Baudelaire's "Les Phares")—Elstir, Bergotte, and Vinteuil—are also lacking in rivals, but each is a synthesis of many artists. Nevertheless Proust, in a letter to Reynaldo Hahn dated November 1911, playfully rhymes:

> I am writing a little book
> Which will leave Bourget flat and Boylesve in the muck.
> (*Corr.* 10:374)

This is a rare instance of rivalry and generations, at a time when Proust was about to let those close to him read his work, and

Bourget and Boylesve are indeed his chosen counterparts, just as in 1920, in his preface to Paul Morand's *Tendres Stocks,* Proust is still trying to measure up to the aged Anatole France and his decree that people have been writing badly in France since the end of the eighteenth century (CSB 607). On the other hand, the surrealists, whose pamphlet *Un cadavre* was soon to be inspired by Anatole France's death, would appear to have been unknown to Proust at this time. If art was at a turning point just before World War I, Proust took that turn in a rather peculiar way. Some people cross—or think they are crossing—a threshold facing forward; we call them, or they call themselves, the "avant-garde." Others cross a threshold facing backward, still others not at all. What about Proust? Perhaps he went through the prewar period in reverse, just as one backs up to get a running start. Or perhaps he even got rid of the idea of a threshold by refusing to believe, like Pascal before him, that the search for truth could be carried out by a single path: "It is not from reaching an extreme that we show our greatness," we are told in the *Pensées,* "but rather by touching both ends at the same time and filling up everything that is in between."[2]

When *A la recherche du temps perdu* was published after the war, the work gave the impression of being a monument from another era, a prehistoric monster that had been washed up on the beaches of the Roaring Twenties. Proust himself wonders, in *Le Temps retrouvé,* if the book, "like a druidic monument on a rocky isle," is going to remain "something for ever unfrequented" (3:1098; 4:618). The war shattered everything; it was a break in history. Perhaps in 1913 people still had one foot in the last century. The nineteenth century lasted until August 1914; the age of bourgeois classicism stretches from 1870 to 1914. And Proust's book is connected in many ways to an era that was rejected around 1912 by poetry and painting, and to a slightly lesser extent the novel. The war was certainly brought into *A la recherche du temps perdu* even as it was still going on, although it was seen from the rear, from houses of ill repute, and even if such places provide good vantage points from which to observe the latest upheavals, the *Recherche* was received like a monument of antiquity. Whence the controversy set off by the awarding of the Prix Goncourt to Proust for *A l'ombre des jeunes filles en fleurs* in 1919, rather than to Dorgelès for his war novel, *Les Croix de bois.* Proust was criticized for his age and called a reactionary, for his cause had been taken up by Léon Daudet. Aragon called him a "tiresome snob." Jacques Rivière, the director of *La Nouvelle Revue Française,* came to his defense. He stood up to the supporters of "revolutionary art" who were against Proust, and in his attempt to describe the originality of the *Recherche,* was one of the first to speak of a renewal of psychological literature.[3] Perhaps Rivière was walking down the same blind alley that many subsequent readers of Proust were to take, but his classification of the novel shows to what extent he—along with other Proust enthusiasts at *La Nouvelle Revue Française* and elsewhere—felt at a loss in the presence of something quite new that he was unable to put his finger on. Rivière, in responding to those militants who were calling Proust a reactionary, thus emphasized that in literature revolutions do not always go forward, that there can be backward-moving revolutions, revolutions that go against the current, so to speak. So that was the meaning of the Proustian "revolution": it was in the great classical tradition—a tradition going back to Racine—of the study of feelings and passions, over and against the novel that, since Flaubert's time, had been sacrificing intelligence to sensation. Soon Proust was reputed to belong to the "new literary school"; in the words of a piece that appeared in *Le Gaulois* in May 1922, shortly before his death, Proust was supposed to represent the "new psychology."[4]

The war, which elicited a great deal of literature with ideological goals, strengthened the contrast between the *roman à thèse*—the kind of novel that tries to make a fairly clear point—and the Proustian novel. Yet the earliest sketches for "L'Adoration perpétuelle," the programmatic and doctrine-imbued climax of *Le Temps retrouvé* that Proust had begun working on as early as 1910, contained pages highly critical of the sort of popular patriotic literature with a moral, social, or religious content that the Dreyfus affair in its time had inspired from both sides of the controversy.[5] From this point of view, the war actually changed nothing, and even had Proust's book been published in its entirety before 1914, it would have been found puzzling; readers would most likely have had trouble figuring out that its uniqueness was in fact related to its antediluvian element. The ambiguity of the *Recherche* is inherent in the text quite as much as it is a function of the conditions of its reception and the transformations that took place in public expectations around the time it was published.

Proust's place in literature is analogous to Manet's in painting: was he the last of the great classics or the first of the revolutionaries? Manet's work is linked to the art of the past through its sources and often through the subjects it treats, but it looks ahead to the most radical innovations of Monet and the impressionists, although Manet still resisted having his works exhibited alongside theirs in the Salons des Refusés. In fact Manet maintained to the last an ambiguous attitude toward official art and "academicism," even though he was rebuffed by the public and the press at the different salons that took place over the years. In Proust, as in Manet, continuity and discontinuity, tradition and revolution, make for a strange, unstable mixture in which meaningfulness and the purely "pictorial," the novelistic and the impressionistic, realism and blurred vision coexist.

Proust was keenly aware of the mediating role Manet had played. He often cited Manet's *Olympia* as an example of a work that was considered scandalous to begin with but gradually became a classic, or, to be more precise, as a work whose classicism, which had previously gone unnoticed, finally came to be recognized. The Duchesse de Guermantes, always on the cutting edge in questions of taste, observes that the public has finally caught up with her in adjusting its eyes—and itself—to *Olympia:* "Nowadays nobody is in the least surprised by it. It looks just like an Ingres! And yet, heaven knows how I had to take up the cudgels on behalf of that picture, which I don't altogether like but which is unquestionably the work of *somebody*" (2:542; 2:812). Her opinion is reminiscent of the narrator's when he is convinced that Elstir's paintings, presently considered to be monstrous, will soon be appreciated:

> The older among them might have reminded themselves that in the course of their lives they had gradually seen, as the years bore them away from it, the unbridgeable gulf between what they considered to be a masterpiece by Ingres and what they had supposed must for ever remain a "horror" (Manet's *Olympia,* for example) shrink until the two canvases looked like twins. (2:436; 2:713)

This is one of Proust's obsessions: true genius, which upsets artistic models, can never be understood immediately. This can be taken to be an idealistic theory of genius or a sociological judgment that adopts the point of view of an aesthetics of reception. The true modernist becomes a classic rather than becoming old-fashioned.

Proust repeated this idea after the war, once his work had been written: "All true art is classical, but the laws of the mind only rarely allow it to be recognized as such at the time it makes its first appearance" (CSB 617). Manet is still the single example—although Baudelaire starts to creep in as well—that holds the center of attention in all Proust's reflections about literature and history:

> Manet was wasting his breath when he insisted that his *Olympia* was classical and told those who looked at the painting: "This is exactly what you admire in the Old Masters"; all the public could see in it was a mockery. But nowadays when we look at *Olympia* we taste the same kind of pleasure given us by the older masterpieces which surround it, just as reading Baudelaire [gives us the same kind of pleasure] as reading Racine. (CSB 617)

The comparison with Racine, which was meant to show that Baudelaire's *Les Fleurs du mal* was a classic, became a leitmotiv of Proust's in the final years of his life, as we shall see. And he goes on: "These great innovators are the only true classics, and they form an almost continuous series." What Proust is implying here is that the series leads up to him, and he seems to be pleading his own case just as he is coming out with *Sodome et Gomorrhe,* for he is fearful of the kind of scandal that greeted *Les Fleurs du mal* and *Olympia.* Baudelaire and Manet, he recalls, have become classics, whereas the neoclassicists and the avant-garde movements of the time have gone out of fashion.

What is the meaning of classicism for Proust if not precisely the tradition of works that, in their own time, caused a scandal in spite of themselves? This is the "almost continuous series" to which we now realize Baudelaire and Manet belong; a threshold is equivocal, hindsight allowing us to see the sequence of things and continuity erasing all traces of a break. Thus classicism does not posit the intemporality of a work, but perhaps its dissonance in any present time, its own as well as ours, in contrast to the kind of work that goes out of fashion.

In his preface to Blanche's *Propos de peintre*, Proust mentions another characteristic that brings out the ambivalence common to Manet and Baudelaire: "Everything which . . . Jacques Blanche says about Manet—whom his friends found charming but did not take seriously, for they 'did not know he was so talented'—I've seen happen to Blanche as well" (CSB 570). While the middle-class public was dumbfounded at the vulgarity of Blanche's new works, a kind of symmetry was maintained by the opposite illusion held by the artist's friends, who noticed only the conventionality of the works. Only the aesthete—Proust's term—judges the work from the point of view of art, that is, tradition: time dissipates the misunderstanding that separates the public from works that are "worthy of the past because they have been placed ahead of time in the future." This dialectic was in fact too subtle not only for the general public, but even for those in Proust's immediate circle!

Lack of comprehension is thus aggravated in the case of Manet and Blanche—Proust is playing up to the latter with this comparison—by virtue of the fact that as high-society, elegant dandies, they do not look anything like artistic innovators to eyes trained by Sainte-Beuve's theories; they are perceived purely in terms of fashion—the modern and the old-fashioned—rather than in terms of tradition—the modern and the classical.

> Blanche very kindly says of Manet things which are also true of Blanche himself (and this goes a long way toward explaining why it has taken so long to get him out of the category of "eminent amateurs"): that he was modest, human, sensitive to criticism. We ought to be able to emphasize these familiar qualities which are generally associated with talent but which for the most part prevent it from being recognized. (CSB 573–74)

In a similar vein, Sainte-Beuve had considered Baudelaire to be too nice a fellow to be, conceivably, a great writer, and he discouraged him from trying to become a member of the Académie française. Elegant, witty, worldly, Manet and Blanche, Baudelaire—shall we add Proust to the list?—encountered a great deal of incomprehension, especially since the dandy himself always remains divided, hesitating between the wish to integrate himself and the desire to remain distinct, dreaming of being inside and outside at the same time, of being in between: it was said of Manet that he was a combination of Marat and Brummell. Proust understands full well that Manet is a paradox—Fauré stands in a comparable position in music (see chapter 2)—and that is why he emphasizes the difference between the man and the creator, the life and the work: "What a shock for Manet's admirers to learn that this revolutionary 'coveted decorations and medals,' that he wanted to prove to my great friend Madame Madeleine Lemaire that he could give Chaplin a run for his money, that he worked only with an eye toward exhibiting at 'Salons' and paid more attention to Roll than to Monet, Renoir, and Degas" (CSB 579). Manet's entire consciousness was tempted by academicism, by careerist tendencies, by traditionalism and conventionality, but something within him, something stronger and deeper, something irrepressible, carried him along, as a demon might have prodded him to blaspheme his sworn ideals.

Classicism and romanticism, tradition and revolution, the two impulses are always closely linked, like profanation and expiation, both of which fascinate Proust (see chapter 6). Rivière hit the nail on the head when he spoke of a backward revolution—not a reaction, but a revolution in spite of itself. There is in Proust a bit of Manet, dreaming of social success through literature—the kind of success that makes one's reputation, just like the career suggested by Monsieur de Norpois. He is proud of his Legion of Honor in 1920 and is starting to think about the Académie française at the very moment Breton and the surrealists are going after Barrès. After the war Proust, struggling to finish his book, is still trying to please his friends in the Faubourg Saint-Germain; perhaps he does not quite grasp the scope of his work.

There were people who fell into the trap of judging the *Recherche* by the man himself. Gide, for example, turned down *Du côté de chez Swann* in 1912 without even reading it, only to confess a year later in a letter to Proust: "For me, you were still the fellow who hung around with Madame X or Y, the one who wrote articles for *Le*

Figaro. I must confess I thought you were following *the Verdurin way!* A snob, an amateur social-climber—something most distressing for our magazine" (*Corr.* 13:53). Even if we cannot excuse Gide's blindness—and that of the *Nouvelle Revue Française*—we can at least explain it as the result of an association (courtesy of Sainte-Beuve) between the man and the work, between Proust and the kind of snobbery in fashion before the war, or even around the turn of the century. Proust could be nothing more than another Abel Hermant setting out to depict the world of the salons. He was close friends with the dandies of the day, Marcel Boulenger, Jean-Louis Vaudoyer, and especially Robert de Montesquiou, all great fans of the Russian Ballet around 1910, since they had exhausted the appeal of Wagnerianism in the 1890s. *A la recherche du temps perdu* has a whole fin-de-siècle aspect to it, a decadent baggage—Wagner, *Pelléas et Mélisande,* Botticelli and the pre-Raphaelites, the cathedral, the androgyne, the correspondences between the arts, hawthorns, the color mauve—a collection of commonplaces for young gentlemen.

Gide is perhaps not the only one to have been taken in by this, for it is not altogether certain that Proust himself saw through it. The pastiche of the Goncourt brothers, added to *Le Temps retrouvé* quite late, condemns "artistic style," from which it dissociates itself. But the hero was under the spell of Bergotte, whom Norpois judged to be a "flute player" full of mannerisms and affectations, "very precious, very thin, and altogether lacking in virility" (1:510; 1:464–65). From his own point of view, in a single speech Legrandin accuses the hero of having a weakness for high society and overrefined tastes. As he offers him his latest book to read, he exclaims: "But you will not care for it, it is not deliquescent enough, not fin de siècle enough for you. . . . What you want is Bergotte, you have confessed it, gamy stuff for the jaded palates of refined voluptuaries" (2:156; 2:452). But those condemning Bergotte and the hero's tastes in this way are none other than Norpois, another disciple of Sainte-Beuve, and Legrandin, that paragon of snobbery. It is difficult to draw any firm conclusion about how the narrator and Proust himself position themselves in terms of decadentism. And this poses a major problem for us in attempting to situate the *Recherche* in the in-between time of the centuries.

The Intermittencies of the Masterpiece

Proust's aesthetic is usually associated with a meditation about time lost and recaptured, about the law of involuntary memory that brings time back to life in all its fullness and continuity and brings back the immortality and intemporality of being. But there is in the *Recherche* yet another conception of art and its movement, one that emphasizes the fractured temporality of creation (see chapter 9). Artistic forms follow each other not in a kind of obstacle course in which barriers fall one after another, as avant-garde movements—which claim to go further and further, to reach higher and higher, and to get better and better—imagine. Nor do they follow each other in a sort of immobile, eternal realm, through fixed essences, for the classical is not at all a stationary thing in Proust's eyes; artistic rhythm, which is unforseeable and can be recognized only retrospectively, is scanned to the beats of tradition and modernity, the true modernity that will be tomorrow's tradition. The duration of the classical is intermittent.

In the *Recherche* "The Intermittencies of the Heart" constitute a back-and-forth movement both random and uncontrolled, a movement that *Le Temps retrouvé,* unlike the reminiscences, does not sublimate in the work. They are fractures that are the origins of the novel, fractures whose violence escapes any dogmatic schematization. On the evening of the second arrival in Balbec in *Sodome et Gomorrhe,* for example, the hero understands that his grandmother is dead when he bends over to take off his shoes; at the end of the same trip, he learns that Albertine knew Mademoiselle Vinteuil: the two events represent insurmountable eruptions of reality—death and sexual pleasure. They are dramatic turns of events in the plot, and the hero leaves Balbec with Albertine, bound for *La Prisonnière* and *Albertine disparue*. Artistic time, like the time of the heart, goes forward by intermittency; it makes for a wandering, erratic plot (see chapter 5).

Two moments in the *Recherche* function as limits or thresholds between which the work is supposed to be contained. First of all an endpoint: an anonymous "new writer" appears in *Le Côté de Guermantes II,* when Bergotte, old and unwell, has at last conquered the glory he deserved (2:337–40; 2:622–25). Once again we have the theme of art and time, and more specifically the time necessary for aesthetic reception: from this point on, Bergotte is comprehensible, everything in his books has become clear from force of habit. But Proust adds that "a new writer had recently begun to publish work in which the relations between things were so different from those that connected them for me that I could understand hardly anything of what he wrote" (2:337; 2:622). Bergotte seems to have gone out of fashion rather than becoming a classic. A similar development is featured in the preface to *Tendres Stocks,* written in the autumn of 1920: "Now and again, a new and original writer comes along (let us call him, if you will, Jean Giraudoux or Paul Morand . . .). This new writer is generally rather tiring to read and difficult to understand because he brings things together through new relations" (CSB 615). In these two passages, Proust associates newness with a novel view of things:

> The original painter or the original writer proceeds on the lines of the oculist. The course of treatment they give us by their painting or by their prose is not always pleasant. When it is at an end the practitioner says to us: "Now look!" And, lo and behold, the world around us . . . appears to us entirely different from the old world, but perfectly clear. (2:338; 2:623)

The original artist transforms the world. On the street, women are Renoirs—as are automobiles, water, sky—until a new painter or an original writer comes along. Originality has to do with a different kind of sentence, a different vision, a different style, concepts that are all synonymous in Proust's mind. After Proust there would be Giraudoux and Morand, but did they make the *Recherche* old-fashioned or, quite the contrary, did they make it into a classic? Are they not rather in the strain of Bourget and Boylesve, or Bergotte?

As for the starting point, Proust defines it more shrewdly, in *La Prisonnière,* by Wagner's music (3:155–59; 3:664–68). The narrator plays Vinteuil's sonata on the piano; he ponders over each artist's individuality and originality. Meanwhile a measure of the music reminds him of *Tristan and Isolde* and he reflects about art and life, and about Wagner's greatness. But a serious reservation stops him:

> I thought how markedly, all the same, these works partake of that quality of being—albeit marvellously—always incomplete, which is

> the characteristic of all the great works of the nineteenth century, that century whose greatest writers somehow botched their books, but, watching themselves work as though they were at once workman and judge, derived from this self-contemplation a new form of beauty, exterior and superior to the work itself, imposing on it a retroactive unity, a grandeur which it does not possess.
> (3:157; 3:666)[6]

The remark is stern.

In the prewar script of the *Recherche,* the remark came at a more decisive moment of the plot, but in the form of a digression that lessened its dramatic intensity: it was part of an addition to the description of a Wagner opera (3:948),[7] shortly before the hero in the course of the show came across Monsieur de Gurcy—who was to become Charlus—and discovered the woman in him (3:943ff.).[8] That was then the setting for the revelation of inversion and the lengthy rumination about the "race of fairies" that in the definitive text was to be introduced by the meeting of Charlus and Jupien. Wagner's music was called "a deafening and confused tumult" (3:944),[9] an amorphous mass, and the public, failing to see how the extracts on the program were related, fell asleep. This called for a clarification of the unity of Wagner's work, or rather of its lack of unity, its flawed conception that the musician was thought to have patched up retrospectively and hence artificially.

Proust seems to imply that the works of the nineteenth century made up for their lack of premeditation or critical awareness by a retrospective judgment, rather than the critical function being merged with the poetic function from the start. In *La Prisonnière,* Proust gives numerous examples of the sort of postponement and inadequacy he considers characteristic of the nineteenth century: *La Comédie humaine, La Légende des siècles, La Bible de l'humanité,* along with Wagner's *Ring,* were each put together into a cycle of works by a "retrospective illumination" needing to be highlighted by one final brushstroke, "the last and the most sublime" (3:158; 3:667).

"An ulterior unity," Proust continues in a somewhat baffling way, apparently back on his guard, "but not a factitious one, otherwise it would have crumbled into dust like all the other systematisations of mediocre writers who with copious titles and sub-titles give themselves the appearance of having pursued a single and transcendent design" (3:158; 3:667). The alternative is between truth and artifice, or, to borrow Proust's terms, between intuition and intelligence. The ulterior unity now seems to have been cleared of a momentary suspicion of artificiality. On the other hand, Proust says nothing about what a true anterior unity might be, the kind of unity he himself always claimed he gave to his book by purportedly conceiving and even writing the end almost at the same time as the beginning. What then is missing from a retrospective unity—as distinct from a previously established unity—if it, too, brings together all the qualities of truth?

> Not factitious, perhaps indeed all the more real for being ulterior, for being born of a moment of enthusiasm when it is discovered to exist among fragments which need only to be joined together; a unity that was unaware of itself, hence vital and not logical, that did not prohibit variety, dampen invention. (3:158; 3:667)

If this is so, what is unfinished or unsuccessful about these nineteenth-century works that recognized their unity only after the fact and that Proust started out condemning for that reason? The initial opposition appears to have been reversed, and a priori unity, unity of a premeditated plan, seems after all to be artificial and logical, a product of doctrine and dogma; in short, intellectual rather than vital.

How can we resist thinking about the cathedral-like structure Proust planned at one time to give to his book, with his wish to develop its various parts using titles and subtitles borrowed from the domain of architecture? The metaphor is undoubtedly reminiscent of Hugo and the well-known chapter of *The Hunchback of Notre-Dame,* "Ceci tuera cela"; or of Balzac, who described his *Comédie humaine* with a similar term, although retrospectively; at any rate, it most definitely has a turn-of-the-century flavor. This was a time when the fashion for the Middle Ages had begun to snowball: Ruskin, Huysmans, and Emile Mâle are but a few examples of it. The Comte de Montesquiou organized his 1896 collection, *Les Hortensias bleus,* like this: "Introït," "Chapelle blanche," "Chambre claire," "Chambre obscure." He would have been better off limiting himself to a simple diptych—like *Le Temps perdu* and

Le Temps retrouvé—that could then have been developed into a series of symmetries, as Proust was fond of doing: Swann's way and the Guermantes way, Sodom and Gomorrha, *La Prisonnière* and *La Fugitive,* and so forth.

The ideal unity of the *Recherche* is defined as an impasse by the end of *Le Temps retrouvé,* but even more so by the equivocal, perhaps even contradictory passages from *La Prisonnière* about the incompleteness or inadequacy of the great works of the nineteenth century, which Proust appears not to stick to even though he first condemns it; on the contrary, he ultimately seems to excuse it in the name of authenticity. Placing himself in the opposite camp to the nineteenth century as a whole, Proust becomes the standard-bearer of premeditated unity, but only if it can be as vital, real, and organic as retrospective unity, the kind projected after the fact by Balzac or Wagner onto their completed work. Whether or not this preconceived but unconscious unity is realizable, the fantasy results from a debate of capital importance to Proust, who conceives of a *Divine Comedy* that has been fully mapped out rather than a *Human Comedy* ruled by chance. Is this why he does not mention Baudelaire among the unfinished artists of the nineteenth century, the last classical artist and the first modern one, in the sense of having a critical awareness that is always his own and that gives *Les Fleurs du mal* the sort of unity Proust wishes for? "The only praise I ask for this book is that it be recognized as more than a simple album, as having a beginning and an end,"[10] Baudelaire wrote to Vigny in December 1861, and Barbey d'Aurevilly, in his 1857 review, had already pointed out the work's "secret architecture." But Proust's knowledge of Baudelaire's poems, as we shall see, comes mostly from song settings, that is, out of context, and nothing proves he had any awareness of the overall composition of *Les Fleurs du mal* (see chapter 7).

Critics almost universally reproached the first volumes of the *Recherche,* in particular *Du côté de chez Swann,* for its "overabundance of minute facts," as Paul Souday put it,[11] the novel's diversity and "pulverization," its absence of organization, form, and choices. Proust was especially disturbed by Henri Ghéon's article in *La Nouvelle Revue Française:*

> Monsieur Marcel Proust, instead of summing up or being concise about what he has to say, gives himself free rein. He does not even bother to be logical, still less to "compose." We get a certain organic satisfaction from works which are discernible, in all of their parts and their form, in a single glance, but he obstinately refuses us this satisfaction. . . . What he writes is "pieces." He stakes all his pride on the "piece," or if the truth be told, on the sentence. And calling them pieces or sentences is saying a great deal.[12]

Proust always reacted swiftly to these reproaches by emphasizing the importance of the entire project and its construction, which would indeed become apparent only "at the end of the book." To a letter from Jacques Rivière written in February 1914, he responded in these terms: "Finally I have found a reader who has *guessed* that my book is a dogmatic work, a constructed work!. . . It is only at the end of the book, once the lessons of life have been understood, that my thought will be unveiled" (*Corr.* 13:98–99). Thus *Du côté de chez Swann* ends with the narrator's eye-opening walk in the Bois de Boulogne, in the course of which he notes the effect of time and fails to bring the past back to life. But the lesson of the *Recherche* in its entirety will be different, even opposite, and the model here once again is Wagner, whose music lends itself to the same kind of misapprehension:

> If this led one to conclude that my thought is a form of disenchanted skepticism, it would be absolutely the same thing as if at the end of the first act of *Parsifal,* when that character understands nothing of the ceremony and is chased away by Gurnemantz, one thus assumed that Wagner meant to say that simplicity of heart leads to nothing. . . . The second volume will exacerbate this misunderstanding. I hope the last one will clear it up. (*Corr.* 13:99–100)

Proust's conclusion is of course dependent on his plan at the time to publish the *Recherche* in three volumes.

Unity or diversity, construction or confusion, convergence or explosion, organic totality or amalgamation of details: Proust can hardly be unaware of these alternatives, even if they are not, properly speaking, his own. But the repeated allusions to Wagner show that Proust fears being called a decadent. Indeed, to burden a work with the charge of dissipation amounts to the same thing as passing judgment on it as a work of decadence, and it is for this reason that Proust often reaffirms the architectural unity of his book, even if the whole is not at first perceptible. In his work on decadent Latin poetry, Désiré Nisard defined that poetry by the primacy of description over any other rhetorical form, by attention to detail, and by the substitution of erudition for inspiration. As early as 1834 he noted: "Our literature has also reached—or, if you prefer, fallen into—its descriptive period."[13] Huysmans systematically took a position diametrically opposed to Nisard's and at the end of the century transformed every blameworthy characteristic into a source of praise, even making Lucan into des Esseintes' favorite Latin poet: his "enamel-plated, gem-paved lines of poetry captivated him."[14]

Hyperbolic detail independent of any relation to the whole is the distinctive feature of an important study of Baudelaire by Paul Bourget—one of the most influential theoreticians of decadence—which opens Bourget's *Essais de psychologie contemporaine.*[15] Bourget attributes this feature socially to an excess of individualism that undermines and disintegrates social organization, as well as to universal suffrage, which, since 1848, has dissolved the mediating groups of the nation. Then comes the analogy with art: "A decadent style is a style in which the unity of the book decomposes to make way for the independence of the page; in which the page decomposes to make way for the independence of the sentence; and the sentence to make way for the independence of the word."[16] In addition to Baudelaire, whose prose poems Bourget takes as the epitome of decadence in literature, Bourget is thinking of the artistic style of the Goncourt brothers, who use substantives in place of adjectives to express sensations and thus speak of the "black of the hats" rather than the "black hats"; of impressionism, which substitutes spots for lines and blurs outlines; of Huysmans, of course; and especially of modern life, technology, the city seen from a streetcar roaring down the boulevards. Decadence—a decomposition or decay of forms and a concentration on detail—is the aesthetic of pessimism, nihilism, and idolatry, which Bourget defines as "the passionate surge by which man displaces onto some creature or some object the exalted fervor which has turned away from God."[17] In Bourget's opinion, music lovers—those who make a cult of Wagner or Donizetti, or later of *Pelléas et Mélisande* or Diaghilev—

offer the most widespread examples of this kind of idolatry. In the *Recherche,* Swann represents idolatry defined in this way: his love for Odette is inseparable from Botticelli's Zephora in the Sistine Chapel, inseparable from Vinteuil's little phrase. Nietzsche himself took inspiration from Bourget in the aphorisms that would be collected after his death in *The Will to Power*. In this work Nietzsche defines European nihilism as one last form of idealism, in the sense of a sort of nostalgia that takes note of the weakening of values but maintains the idea of values, a nostalgia that refuses any belief but is incapable of giving up all ideals: God is dead, but God's place is held in abeyance.[18] Bourget had already said that the nihilist "held on to the need to feel the same as when he was a believer."[19]

Conceived of as the explosion of the book, of the page, and of the sentence, decadence is diametrically opposed—point by point and word for word—to the organic ideal of the autonomy of the work of art seen as whole and total, an ideal set forth at the same time by people like Gabriel Séailles. His *Essai sur le génie dans l'art* spread Schelling's aesthetic theories throughout France, and these seem to have affected Proust quite strongly.[20] In fact the entire nineteenth century went back and forth on this point. Baudelaire, in the *Salon de 1846,* already used the same antithesis to criticize Hugo, "a decadent or transitional composer," so as to compare him to Delacroix: "[Hugo] starts out with detail, [Delacroix] with an intimate knowledge of the subject," and Delacroix sacrifices "details to the whole constantly."[21] Baudelaire also pointed out that Delacroix's attention to the whole resulted in the slowness, the very kind of premeditation, Proust judged absent from most nineteenth-century works, as well as a quickness of execution: "The slower, the more painstaking and the more conscientious the great artist's conception, the nimbler his execution" (Baudelaire, OC 2:433). Séailles also speaks of this characteristic, which has become a commonplace of holistic aesthetic theories; for him the work must be one—like the vision that inspires it—and painted with a single brushstroke. Proust was to carry this idea a step further. The true writer is the man with a single book; great artists have never created more than a single work.

Organicism, particularly of the kind that Séailles practiced, is a kind of structuralism before the letter:

> Each syllable has its own character and personality and exists only through the word of which it is a part; each word has its own value and is nothing by itself, it is inserted into the clause which is then inserted into the sentence. The sentence is a unit, but only to the extent that an organ in an animate body is a unit. Style is a living form in which living beings are enclosed *ad infinitum.*[22]

From the syllable to the book and to the work as a whole, everything must hold together, everything must be one, according to a philosophy of unity and hierarchical totality that recalls many principles scattered throughout the *Recherche*. Unfortunately, one is always on the decadent side of someone, as is illustrated by the turn-of-the-century's reading of Baudelaire long before the classicism of *Les Fleurs du mal* was praised; and before, in 1922, Valéry in his *Cahiers* borrowed the very distinction Baudelaire had made between Hugo and Delacroix and applied it to Hugo and, implicitly, to Baudelaire himself:

> Hugo—Admirable builder of a detail. Mediocre composition. The details are immense. (Details = isolated lines of poetry and their content.)
>
> The wholes are nothing but the sum of these details (and other equally boring ones).
>
> Baudelaire.[23]

The decadence condemned by Bourget and the vitalism or organicism exalted by Séailles: these are the two sides between which Proust struggles. Can we imagine there is a way to join them, as there is between Méséglise and Guermantes? Moreover, is the dilemma not out-of-date in the twentieth century, marked as it is by an aesthetics of collage? Nonetheless Proust appears completely caught up in this struggle at the time of publication of *Du côté de chez Swann,* which he skillfully tries to present in relation to the whole: "I want to make it seem (a little bit) like a whole, even though it is a part," he writes to André Beaunier,[24] or, more eloquently still, to René Blum:"It would be better not to call it the first volume, since I am pretending that all by itself it forms a small unity, like *L'Orme du mail* in *Histoire contemporaine* or *Les Déracinés* in *Le Roman de l'énergie nationale.*"[25] When Proust tries to think up an appropriate link between titles and subtitles—one that would bear witness to a real unity within the work—Anatole France and Maurice Barrès remain his models, or at least those models whom he judges accessible to his correspondent.

Part and whole, fragment and unity thus remain the terms in which Proust perceives literature in 1913. For example, he defends Francis Jammes against those who criticize him for his lack of order:

> It could well be that I would prefer all of these parcels of truth to form a wonderful unity which would be the revelation of the real world. But I prefer true signs to grand constructions in which ten thousand flops, dressed up by intelligence and rhetoric, give the impression (not to me) of being a success.[26]

This theme brings to mind the pages in *La Prisonnière* about the works of the nineteenth century; perhaps in this way one can assign a date to the conception of those pages. In thanking Anna de Noailles for sending him her book, *Les Vivants et les morts,* Proust similarly wonders about the relations between the poems and the collection. He simultaneously denies that the fragment is exemplary of the whole, "as a Monad reflects the universe," and that there is "a novelistic and dramatic link between the pieces," as there is in Lamartine or Vigny.[27] There is yet a third type of unity, neither metaphorical nor metonymic—or perhaps both at the same time—that would be linked to "the identity of the feelings one has when one is composing": a unity of inspiration or an intuitive unity of the kind that Baudelaire found in Delacroix and that one could call analogical or allegorical unity. Proust takes Wagner as its model, for selected pieces of his music never suggest the idea of the work as a whole: "He is the one whom the extraordinary burgeoning of your genius (and especially its increasingly organic interpenetration with your form) makes me think of." The adjective "organic" is remarkable, and the comparison to Wagner suggests that the letter to Anna de Noailles dates from the same time as Proust's piece on Wagner, which, before being incorporated into *La Prisonnière,* had been an addendum to the description of an evening at the opera.

When in February 1913 Proust presented his own book to René Blum and asked him to act as his intermediary with the publisher Bernard Grasset, he used the same terms he had used to describe the collections of Francis Jammes and Anna de Noailles: "As for this book, it is, on the contrary [rather than a group of articles from *Le Figaro* collected as an afterthought], very much a composed whole, although its composition is so complex that I fear no one will take notice and that it may appear to be a series of digressions. It is quite the opposite."[28] The "composed whole" is reminiscent of Diderot's "composed stage"; by that Diderot meant a theater that rose up against the ideal of unity upheld by rhetorical composition, a theater that entertained the notion of a plurality of divided meanings. The "composed" work is thus a work in which several things happen at the same time, not like the complex actions of classical tragedy whose threads form a single knot, but rather like colors and forms in the books and paintings preferred by Bergotte: the little stretch of yellow wall in the "View of Delft,"

> some scene that furnished the reader with an image, some picture [in a book] that had no rational meaning. "Ah, yes!" he would exclaim, "it's good! There's a little girl in an orange shawl. It's excellent!" or again, "Oh yes, there's a passage in which there's a regiment marching along the street; yes, it's good!" (1:598; 1:546)

But how to make a whole out of these details, for example out of the pieces of time and space piled together in *Jean Santeuil?* "You keep talking to me about my minute art of detail, of the imperceptible," Proust was still saying to Louis de Robert as late as 1913. "I don't know what it is that I'm doing, but I know what I want to do; in fact I omit . . . all details, all facts, the only thing I latch onto is what seems to me . . . to detect some general law."[29] Let us return to Wagner and to Nietzsche who, in his *The Case of Wagner* (1888), also takes inspiration from Bourget's analyses to turn against his former idol.

"Wagner's art is diseased," wrote Nietzsche, "*Wagner est une névrose.*"[30] And the symptom of this is indeed that his work does not hold together: "Life no longer animates the whole. Words become predominant and leap right out of the sentence to which they belong, the sentences themselves trespass beyond their bounds, and obscure the sense of the whole page, and the page in its turn gains in vigour at the cost of the whole—the whole is no longer a whole."[31] This is Bourget speaking. "The whole no longer lives at all: it is composed, reckoned up, artificial, a fictitious thing."[32]

Such is Wagner's music according to Nietzsche: "Wagner disguised his inability to create organic forms, under the cloak of a principle."[33]

In this context, the object of Proust's pages on the incompleteness of the great works of the nineteenth century becomes obvious: "He is the Victor Hugo of music,"[34] Nietzsche said in a further observation about Wagner. These pages of Proust take up Nietzsche's and Baudelaire's dispute about the lack of a unity of conception in Wagner or Hugo, but only to grant an immediate pardon: when unity is implemented without the creator's conscious knowledge, it is that much more authentic. In the preface to *Tendres Stocks,* Proust calls Stendhal—famous for his improvisations and his difficulty in coming up with endings—a "great writer without knowing he was one," because of the "great unconscious skeletal structure" that exists in his works, hidden even from his own eyes by the "conscious gathering of ideas" (CSB 611). In spite of Bergson and Verdun, Proust's terms remain those of the same quarrel that had been going on for well over forty years: the time lag is quite remarkable, for what is at issue here is still reconciling Wagner—or Stendhal, or Balzac—with the vitalism and the organicism that require the great work to have a structuring unity. Undoubtedly that unity is recognized only retrospectively by Wagner or Balzac, but it is "like such and such a fragment composed separately, born of an inspiration, not required by the artificial development of a thesis, which comes to be integrated with the rest" (3:158; 3:667).

Proust is not unaware of Nietzsche's change of heart about Wagner. In *Le Côté de Guermantes II,* he is amazed "that a man who carried honesty with himself to the point of cutting himself off from Wagner's music from scruples of conscience" (2:409; 2:688–89) could attach an intellectual value to friendship. The first French translation of *The Case of Wagner* was published as early as 1893;[35] it was the work of two of Proust's closest friends, Daniel Halévy and Robert Dreyfus. They were former school friends from the Lycée Condorcet and all were members of the editorial board of the review *Le Banquet,* which came out at exactly the same time, from March 1892 to March 1893. There can be no doubt that the pages about Wagner in *La Prisonnière* are colored by Nietzsche's *The Case of Wagner;* indeed, Proust's reflection begins with an allusion to philosophy. Finding an echo of *Tristan and Isolde* in Vinteuil's sonata, the narrator instantly climbs on his high horse:

> In admiring the Bayreuth master, I had none of the scruples of those who, like Nietzsche, are bidden by a sense of duty to shun in art as in life the beauty that tempts them, and who, tearing themselves from *Tristan* as they renounce *Parsifal,* and, in their spiritual asceticism, progressing from one mortification to another, succeed, by following the most painful of *viae Crucis,* in exalting themselves to the pure cognition and perfect adoration of *Le Postillon de Longjumeau.* (3:155–56; 3:665)[36]

In the prewar draft, Proust, who obviously wants to make fun of Nietzsche, added *Monsieur, Madame et Bébé, a comédie de boulevard* by Gustave Droz dating from 1866, for the comparison with *Tristan and Isolde* and *Parsifal.*[37]

In fact, *The Case of Wagner* began with enthusiastic praise for *Carmen:* "Yesterday—would you believe it?—I heard Bizet's masterpiece for the twentieth time."[38] Nietzsche presented *Carmen* as the exact antithesis and antidote to Wagner; what he meant was that he had freed himself from the charms of the German musician: "Bizet's music seems to me perfect. It comes forward lightly, gracefully, stylishly. It is lovable, it does not sweat."[39] Now the reference to Bizet could not leave Proust indifferent: another of his school friends at the Lycée Condorcet had been Jacques Bizet, the composer's son; and Madame Straus, Jacques' mother and Bizet's widow, was one of his best friends. Daniel Halévy, the cotranslator of *The Case of Wagner,* along with Robert Dreyfus, the future author of a work entitled *La Vie de Frédéric Nietzsche,*[40] were, respectively, Jacques Bizet's cousin and the nephew of Madame Straus, who was herself the daughter of the composer Fromental Halévy, the author of *La Juive.* Nietzsche's insinuations about Wagner's possibly Jewish background[41] must not have been lost on Proust either. So it comes as no surprise that Proust substituted *Le Postillon de Longjumeau* for *Carmen* as the height of musical frivolity. Proust's hypothesis is an immediate result of this confrontation with Adam's comic opera: "I was struck by how much reality there is in the work of Wagner." His themes are immediately judged to be "so internal, so organic, so visceral, that they seem like the reprise not so much of a musical motif as of an attack of neuralgia" (3:156; 3:665).[42] Neuralgia, an organic symptom, is opposed to neurosis, Nietzsche's accusation against Wagner.

The Miniaturist and the Carrier Pigeon

> Nietzsche also accused Wagner of nearsightedness: Wagner's art is calculated to appeal to short-sighted people—one has to get much too close up to it (Miniature): it also appeals to long-sighted people, but not to those with normal sight.[43]

In this he was also in agreement with the assessment of Bourget, who characterized decadence as a problem of vision: the vision of today's writers, he said with Huysmans in mind, "has undergone—what shall we call it? an improvement or a transformation? At any rate a change."[44] That is how he analyzed impressionism, with its sensitivity to light rather than shape, but in "Le Peintre de la vie moderne," Baudelaire had already linked attention to detail with a problem of vision: "The further the artist leans impartially toward detail, the greater the anarchy. Whether he is nearsighted or far-sighted, all hierarchy and subordination disappear" (OC 2:699). Nietzsche in turn says of Wagner: "The first thing his art places in our hands is a magnifying glass."[45] What stems from this is the paradox that for Nietzsche, Wagner is a miniaturist: "Wagner is really only worthy of admiration and love by virtue of his inventiveness in small things, in his elaboration of details—here one is quite justified in proclaiming him a master of the first rank, as our greatest musical *miniaturist,* who compresses an infinity of meaning and sweetness into the smallest space."[46] Proust had to fight against the same reproach. "He looks at people through a magnifying glass," Blanche wrote when *Du côté de chez Swann* came out.[47]

Fascination with detail is always interpreted as a symptom of decadence; it goes along with the disintegration of the work. In *Le Temps retrouvé* Proust responded after the fact to those who had accused him of nearsightedness, those who chided him for the absence of unity in his work:

> Before very long I was able to show a few sketches. No one understood anything of them. Even those who commended my perception

> of the truths which I wanted eventually to engrave within the temple, congratulated me on having discovered them "with a microscope," when on the contrary it was a telescope I had used to observe things which were indeed very small to the naked eye, but only because they were situated at a great distance, and which were each one of them in itself a world. Those passages in which I was trying to arrive at general laws were described as so much pedantic investigation of detail. (3:1098–99; 4:618)

Proust used the very same terms in the July 1913 letter to Louis de Robert quoted above. In this letter Proust took exception to his correspondent's reference to his "minute art of detail" and reaffirmed his interest in seeking out "some general law": "But since that is never revealed to us by intelligence, and since we must fish for it, so to speak, in the depths of our unconscious, it is indeed imperceptible because it is distant and difficult to perceive, but it is not in the slightest degree a minute detail" (*Corr.* 12:230–31). Proust then went on to give an example, the madeleine soaked in tea: "This is not in the slightest degree a minutely observed detail, it is an entire theory of memory and knowledge." It is by this kind of general law that Proust hopes to give consistency to the novel over and above the dissipation of its individual instants. But do we have to believe in this law?

Proust's defense is elementary, just as it was concerning the question of the incompleteness of the great works of the nineteenth century. He simply takes a position opposite that of his critics, substitutes the telescope for the microscope, and replaces the analysis of details with the search for laws. But he does not shift the issue itself or alter the question; he does not imagine that long before surrealism, the art of the early part of the century has already rejected this alternative. Whence the strangeness and inadequacy of defenses that are based particularly on the ambiguity proper to Proust's work, straddling two centuries as it might straddle two chairs, wobbly or limping, and drawing its energy from this split. What does Proust mean by "telescope"? What are these great laws he is claiming to discover? Is their greatness not such that they verge on truisms? Proust breaks off at this point and moves on to other things. In 1913, in 1920, he tries once again to justify himself in the eyes of the censors of his adolescence, Bourget, or Tolstoy, who, in *What is Art?*, called Wagner's work "a model work of counterfeit art."[48]

Proust cannot exhaust the problem of the unity of the work. He is not a philosopher. *A la recherche du temps perdu* is not a work of applied philosophy. But the contradictions that remain unresolved from the point of view of doctrine account for the very form of the novel. If the novels of the nineteenth century are incomplete because their unity is retrospective and in that sense fortuitous, and if a preconceived unity remains dogmatic and artificial, what will be the unity of the greatest work of the in-between time of the centuries, perhaps even of the twentieth century? It would have to be both prior and posterior, prospective and retroactive, conscious and unconscious, premeditated and nonetheless misunderstood: in this way the work would be both organic and formal, vital and at the same time logical. Is this a utopia, or perhaps an aporia? No, but that is why *A la recherche du temps perdu* ought to circle back onto itself. It should tell the story of a vocation, so that the retrospective discovery of the unity of the hero's life can be the principle that has already been implemented by the narrator throughout the entire book, unbeknownst to the reader.

A sleight of hand, perhaps, a trick just waiting to be discovered. But without this trick *A la recherche du temps perdu* would not exist; for lack of it *Jean Santeuil* was abandoned. *A la recherche du temps perdu* is between two centuries, the last great organic novel of the nineteenth century and the first great experimental novel of the twentieth century. It is the imbalance that caused Proust to move sideways, to balk, to call on the telescope as a protection against the microscope and the magnifying glass—the emblems of decadence—and to play with the casuistry of the retrospective or premeditated unity of the work in his defense of Balzac and Wagner—and himself—against the insinuations of Nietzsche, Tolstoy, and Bourget. Proust himself activated another aesthetics, one in which detail and whole, unity and diversity are no longer hard-and-fast terms; an aesthetics of infinite intermittencies, of inappreciable differences; an aesthetics that the law of reminiscence seeks to mask so as to make the book palatable to the supporters of idealism, vitalism, and organicism.

Proust speaks of the "general laws" he claims his novel would explore, but the novel itself has given up all idea of determinism; it describes a universe truly based on probability. The parallel often suggested between Proust and Einstein is not meaningless: Einstein conceived of the probability involved in the mechanics of relativity as a strategy used for lack of a better one, a strategy destined to give way if there should ever be a determinism more powerful than that of Newtonian mechanics. It is only subsequent generations that have accepted the fact that one cannot go beyond the physics of probability, that it is inherent to reality. By the same token Proust absolutely wants to reach certain laws, but his book nonetheless contradicts their very possibility. True intermittencies, those of the heart and those of art, do not fall under the authority of any law, unlike reminiscences that are in themselves reducible to a theory of memory. Thus any reading of the *Recherche* that seeks to pin the novel down to the references and theories Proust uses to justify it is deceptive: the novel heads off in a different direction, and the critical gap between what it says it does and what it actually does is much more important.[49] All great works—the future classical work in the sense Proust gives to that adjective—involve an overhang of this kind.

Nevertheless, the narrator of the *Recherche* sometimes manages almost to denounce the categories in which he conceives of the novel. He catches himself instantly, but that momentary doubt is enough to plant suspicion in the reader's mind. The passage in *La Prisonnière* about the great works of the nineteenth century ends with this remark about Wagner: "In him, however great the melancholy of the poet, it is consoled, transcended—that is to say, alas, to some extent destroyed—by the exhilaration of the fabricator" (3:158; 3:667). Once Wagner has been victoriously defended against Nietzsche and Bourget in the name of the unconscious truth of his work, we see the sudden appearance of a contradictory idea, the idea of an aesthetics of fabrication defining the work of art as a machine. Proust brings the idea up only to dismiss it immediately, refusing to confirm it and merely leaving the irony of the suggestion: "I was troubled by this Vulcan-like skill. Could it be this that gave to great artists the illusory aspect of a fundamental, irreducible originality, apparently the reflexion of a more than human reality, actually the result of industrious toil?" (3:158–59; 3:667). The idealistic doctrine of the genius and the transcendence of art over life, which seems to underpin the entire work, would be collapsed in a single blow by the perception of the artist's work in its reality. The narrator forgets himself in an astonishing daydream about machines and horse-power, and Wagner's airy phrase, rather than bringing the fabulous swan from *Lohengrin* to mind, is rather reminiscent of an airplane. The airplane, which we get back to after a long meditation, was precisely the incongruous metaphor that, in the prewar draft, in a passage that had the hero listening to extracts of Wagner at the Opera House, had led to the addendum about the works of the nineteenth century: "Soon I felt in seeing these marvelously constructed, well-balanced, and powerful phrases the same impression I had had one day as I looked up from my window in Querqueville in seeing an airplane flying above the sea and rising up higher and higher" (3:1003).[50] The digression is over: perhaps Wagner makes us confuse airplanes and swans, manufactured items and living organs.

> Perhaps . . . one of these frankly material vehicles was needed to explore the infinite, one of these 120–horsepower machines—brand-name Mystère—in which nevertheless, however high one flies, one is prevented to some extent from enjoying the silence of space by the overpowering roar of the engine! (3:159; 3:668)[51]

The irony of the punchline is such that one is forced to wonder whether Proust is really taken in by the ambiguity—which he prolongs for the pleasure of it—between the organic and the mechanical, between vitalism and mechanization. Is he making fun of his readers? In spite of all the theories of genius, of the sublime and transcendent unity of the work to which the narrator of the *Recherche* seems to subscribe, can we not understand this fellow, after all, as a trickster? Halfway between a swan and an airplane, between nature and artifice, what Proust compared himself to in 1913 in his search for general laws rather than minute details was a "carrier pigeon," that is, a machinelike animal.[52] Does this beautiful machine that is *A la recherche du temps perdu* not take on the appearance of the story of someone's life all the better to seduce us, to cast a spell over that double reader within us, the reader of two centuries?

2

Fauré and Unity Recaptured

Proust and Fauré crossed the threshold of 1900 in a similar way.[1] Their creations are connected to both the nineteenth and the twentieth centuries; these works are unclassifiable, belonging neither to the nineteenth nor to the twentieth century. Falling in the gap that separates Berlioz from Schoenberg and Flaubert from Joyce, they represent one last unlikely attempt to synthesize tradition and modernity without excluding any element of the reading public. The phrase *to be new* is so frequent as to become a kind of slogan in Fauré's writings, but his music keeps one eye on the past; it moves forward while looking backward. The old and the new—the tonal system and the modal system—come together in Fauré's music. Like Manet, Fauré's society connections were such that his contemporaries did not expect him to be a revolutionary of form. He was prominent under the Third Republic and directed the Conservatory from 1905 to 1920; in all likelihood, Proust integrates him into the cast of characters of the *Recherche* as an "eminent musician, a member of the *Institut,* occupying a high official position, . . . exclusively and passionately a lover of women," who nonetheless encourages Charlus' relationship with Morel (2:1081; 3:434). Fauré is exemplary of the Athenian Republic, a kind of between-the-centuries bourgeois. And Proust is not unaware of the ambivalence of his work.

Fauré's melodies are marvelous illustrations of salon music in the second half of the nineteenth century. Thus, in a draft of a conversation with the young Marquise de Cambremer in Balbec in *Sodome et Gomorrhe,* the hero alludes to Baudelaire's "Chant d'automne," and Fauré—*snobisme oblige*—is a kind of password: "You undoubtedly know the admirable melody which Fauré wrote for those lines" (3:1084).[2] To conceal her ignorance, Madame de Cambremer responds in kind, with another nod to the musician:

> "Do I know it!" Madame de Cambremer said to me. And from her voice, which was obviously unconnected to any memory and spoke in a vacuum, I could tell she did not know it. "What a marvelous musician! You must surely know *Les Berceaux,* which is quite simply a small masterpiece," and she hummed "And that day the great ships." "Say, great ships are certainly in season here," she pointed out laughing, enchanted by her own cleverness.[3]

She is unfamiliar with one of Proust's favorite melodies, based on a poem of Baudelaire, or perhaps she has forgotten it, but it goes without saying that she is crazy about *Les Berceaux,* based on a poem of Sully Prudhomme, a melody sometimes considered Fauré's most representative work; Fauré had better success with bad poetry, from Romain Bussine to Armand Silvestre.

Proust is not at all taken in by this salon-style Fauré. As early as 1894, he confides in his friend Pierre Lavallée: "*Au cimetière* is truly awful and *Après un rêve* worthless."[4] Proust met Fauré in 1895, and reports on their meeting to Reynaldo Hahn: "He told me that all of his music must really irritate you, since the very same poetry probably found its definitive expression in your work. And I told him that on the contrary, I have more often heard you sing his serenade-pleasers than your own, and that you do a fine rendition of *Chant d'automne.*"[5] Between Sully Prudhomme and Baudelaire, between Jean Richepin and Verlaine, Proust sees the difference, just as he does between Fauré's first melodies and his more recent ones, between those belonging to the first collection and those belonging to the third. Proust clearly zeroes in on Fauré's decadent or fin-de-siècle aspect.

Robert de Montesquiou was sorry that Fauré never set any of his poems to music. After the publication of an extract from *Du côté de chez Swann,* "Epines blanches, épines roses," in *Le Figaro* in March 1912, Montesquiou wrote Proust a letter of praise in which he made the following racy allusion: "I have gathered your pretty prickles; but you did not speak of the *sexual* odor . . . which would have allowed you to *chop the end off* the *noun,* while laying emphasis on the *adjectives.* But the 'month of Mary' would not have benefited from that" (*Corr.* 11:66). Montesquiou joked about the flower's smell, "a bittersweet smell of almonds." Proust replied with unwonted triviality, at Fauré's expense: "As for the cross between litanies and orgasms which you mention in your letter, the most delightful expression I know of that sort of thing is a piano piece by Fauré which has already been around for some time but is intoxicating, I think it's called *Romance sans paroles.* I imagine that's what a pederast might sing as he was ravishing a choirboy" (*Corr:* 11.79). The allusion is certainly to the last, far and away the most famous of Fauré's three *Romances sans paroles,* Opus 17 (1863), his most sedate piano work, in the style of Mendelssohn, a classic of the salons of the Second Empire.

But there is another Fauré, the Fauré of the new music whose setting is not the salon and to which Proust proves to be immeasurably more attuned. The Fauré music Proust knew was the music of his own youth, the music played in the 1890s—melodies, piano works, and chamber music—for Proust did not follow the musician's evolution past the beginning of the twentieth century. The same rule might be said to apply to Proust's entire cultural universe, which as late as 1920 had not only not gone beyond the start of the First World War, but essentially still belonged to the end of the nineteenth century. Fauré's three early masterpieces were undoubtedly what remained in Proust's memory as exemplary points of reference.

The first of these is the Sonata No. 1, Opus 13, for violin and piano, composed in 1875, ten years before Franck's sonata. Performed in 1877 at the Salle Pleyel, it became a representative example of new French chamber music. Proust mentions it in "Le salon de la princesse Edmond de Polignac," published in *Le Figaro* in 1903, as an example of the modern works heard by that society of music lovers: "sometimes original and heartfelt performances of all Fauré's latest tunes, or of Fauré's sonata" (CSB 468). The sonata was performed along with the well-known 1880 *Lullaby,* Opus 16, by the pianist Marguerite Hasselmans and the violinist Maurice Hayot on July 1, 1907, at the dinner Proust gave at the Ritz for Gaston Calmette, editor-in-chief of *Le Figaro,* and for various friends from the Faubourg Saint-Germain.[6] Fauré was supposed to attend the dinner party and play several suites with Marguerite Hasselmans, as well as some other pieces with Maurice Hayot, but he was indisposed. He was replaced by the pianist Edouard Risler.

Fauré's sonata is alluded to twice in the *Recherche,* both times in the context of Monsieur de Charlus' relationship with Morel. During the Verdurins' soirée in *La Prisonnière,* after Morel and some other musicians have played Vinteuil's septet, a guest dares to compare him to another musician:

> "Talking of that marvellous violinist, . . . do you happen to know one whom I heard the other day playing a Fauré sonata wonderfully well. He's called Frank— . . ."
>
> "Oh, he's ghastly," replied M. de Charlus. "As far as violinists are concerned, I advise you to confine yourself to mine."
>
> (3:270; 3:773)

This Frank does not reappear in the novel, but it is difficult to avoid the conclusion that his name is a variation on the name of the musician César Franck. The association of the names might well be motivated by the context of the other allusion to the Fauré sonata in the *Recherche,* which comes when Monsieur de Charlus plays the sonata with Morel after their first dinner with the Verdurins at the Raspelière, in *Sodome et Gomorrhe:* "To the general astonishment, M. de Charlus, who never spoke of his own considerable gifts, accompanied, in the purest style, the closing passage (uneasy, tormented, Schumannesque, but, for all that, earlier than Franck's sonata) of the sonata for piano and violin by Fauré" (2:985; 3:343). The passage serves to illustrate a theme dear to Proust's heart: the natural imbalance that makes Monsieur de Charlus into an invert by the same token makes him artistic. But just the same, the analysis of the "rapid, nervous, charming style with which M. de Charlus played the Schumannesque passage of Fauré's sonata" (2:986; 3:344) is quite accurate: the fourth and final movement, the *allegro* of Fauré's sonata, starts out with a broad and hearty theme with a lyrical style often compared to Schumann. Next a second theme, full of strength, is brought out by the piano. Then we find the development and the restatement leading up to the coda. Whereas the reference to the sonata in *La Prisonnière* was nothing more than a high-society in-joke of the same sort as the allusions to melodies in the draft of the conversation with Madame de Cambremer, the passage from *Sodome et Gomorrhe* assumes a real musical analysis of the sonata, albeit a conventional one.

The second early work of Fauré that Proust sizes up is the Quartet No. 1, Opus 15, for piano and string trio, begun in 1876 and performed in February 1880. Proust heard the piece on April 14, 1916, at the Gabriel Fauré Festival held at the Odéon, with the composer himself at the piano. He immediately had the idea of having it performed again at home by the Quatuor Poulet, after Franck's Quartet in D Major.[7] At the time he was probably working on a passage for *Le Temps retrouvé* about Vinteuil's quartet—in *La Prisonnière* it was to become a septet—or at least so we are led to believe by a note from Carnet 3: "Similarly, when I had heard Vinteuil's quartet for the first time (in fact I am thinking here of a violin piece from Fauré's Quartet No. 1 in C minor played by Capet) probably in the third part."[8] Lucien Capet played the piano part at the April 14 concert.

Fauré's Quartet No. 1 thus appears to have been one of the models for Vinteuil's septet. There is no doubt that Fauré is one of the components of Vinteuil. In Cahier 49, a draft for the middle section of the novel in the prewar script, the hero happens to be with Swann during the performance of an "orchestral suite" in the course of a soirée given by the Marengos in the milieu of Empire aristocracy. The "little phrase" is thus heard once again by Swann in the hero's presence in a setting that will disappear from the definitive text. Now Proust notes, for his own use and parenthetically, "Make sure that this is related to the happiness described in the analysis of Fauré's cantique" (3:991)."[9] This is usually seen as a reference to the *Cantique de Jean Racine*, Opus 11, for which Fauré was awarded the first prize in composition on leaving the Ecole Niedermeyer in 1865, but the explanation is not absolutely convincing. Fauré's *Ballade,* Opus 19, is a more likely model for Vinteuil's sonata.

In a 1918 dedication of *Du côté de chez Swann* to Jacques de Lacretelle, Proust lists a long series of models: Saint-Saëns' Sonata No. 1 for Piano and Violin, Opus 75 (1885); Wagner's Good Friday Spell from *Parsifal;* Franck's Sonata for Piano and Violin (1886), performed by Enesco; the prelude from *Lohengrin;* a piece by Schubert; and finally "a delightful piano piece by Fauré" (CSB 565). According to a letter to Antoine Bibesco dating from the autumn of 1915, the Fauré piece in question was the *Ballade:*

> Vinteuil's Sonata is not Franck's. If you're at all interested (which I doubt!) I can tell you with copies in hand all of the works (some of them quite mediocre) which "modeled" [for] my Sonata. For example the "little phrase" is a phrase from a sonata [for] piano and violin by Saint-Saëns that I'll sing for you (get ready!), the turbulence of the tremolos above it is in a Wagner prelude, its wailing, shifting opening comes from the Franck Sonata, its broad movements the Fauré Ballad, etc. etc. etc. (*Corr.* 14:234–36)

Perhaps Proust has the ballad in mind when Swann, hearing the Vinteuil sonata at the Verdurins' in *Un Amour de Swann,* recalls the first time he heard it a year earlier:

> With a slow and rhythmical movement it led him first this way, then that, towards a state of happiness that was noble, unintelligibile, and yet precise. And then suddenly, having reached a certain point from which he was preparing to follow it, after a momentary pause, abruptly it changed direction, and in a fresh movement, more rapid, fragile, melancholy, incessant, sweet, it bore him off with it towards new vistas. Then it vanished. He hoped, with a passionate longing, that he might find it again, a third time. And reappear it did.
> (1:228–29; 1:207)

The analysis seems faithful to the slow rhythm of the beginning of the *Ballade:* the first theme with its unforeseeable meandering is stated three times, the third time being a simple reminiscence after the statement of the second theme. Moreover, this parallel explains why in the *Recherche* Vinteuil's sonata is usually played on the piano, unaccompanied. Indeed, before the 1881 version of the

Ballade for piano and orchestra, Fauré had in 1879 composed a version for solo piano.

Now the *Ballade* is without a doubt Fauré's most original early work. Most likely Proust's interest in it shows that he was struck by its formal structure. Here is how Fauré described the piece to his friend Madame Clerc during a trip to Munich in September 1879 to hear Wagner's *Ring*:

> The piano pieces no. 2 and no. 3 have taken on a much greater importance because of no. 5, which is a kind of hyphen linking no. 2 and no. 3. What I mean is that using new *processes*—which are at the same time *old*—I have found a way to develop, in a sort of intermezzo, phrases taken from no. 2 and to use the beginning of no. 3, so that the three pieces are really one. What resulted was a Fantasy which is somewhat out of the ordinary, or at least so I would like to believe.[10]

This kind of equivocation between old and new is of the sort that Proust often draws attention to, for example in Baudelaire. But what is most important here is the concern for unity shown by the musician, in terms quite close to those used by Proust when he defines the unity of his novel. Fauré accounts for the elaborate construction of the *Ballade*: first a series of fragments, or separate pieces, which then find their unity. The three unconnected pieces he alludes to correspond to the three themes, with a pause remaining in the work between the first two.

The first movement, *andante cantabile,* slowly introduces the A theme: supple, graceful, ingenuous, accompanied by chords, this is probably the theme Proust is describing when at the Verdurins' Swann recalls the first time he heard the Vinteuil sonata. The B theme, *allegro moderato,* appears after a pause. "It is a descending motif, a kind of scale which suddenly takes on a complicated, typically fin-de-siècle shape," writes Jean-Michel Nectoux.[11] Then the A and B themes are developed. Next comes a brief transition, *andante,* with an anticipatory C theme; this passage introduces the second movement, the main *allegro* of the piece. The C′ theme of the *allegro* is a rhythmic variation and an expressive transformation of the anticipatory C theme of the first movement; in the second movement this C theme is developed along with the B theme. This is the "sort of intermezzo" mentioned by Fauré in his letter. Then a short *andante* brings the C theme back in, and this receives its true development in the third and final movement, the *allegro moderato,* with bursts of trills that, although they are in no way realistic or descriptive, are suggestive of birdsongs and fluttering leaves. Because of this woodsy feeling the piece was linked to the aesthetics of impressionism. Proust is not unaware of this, and the first description of the Vinteuil sonata, or rather of its effect on Swann, is obviously reminiscent of impressionism, particularly in the colorist comparison between the piano part and "the blue tumult of the sea, silvered and charmed into a minor key by the moonlight" (1:227; 1:205). But Swann goes beyond this fin-de-siècle mood of the piece and gets through to its elaborate composition: "He could picture to himself its extent, its symmetrical arrangement, its notation, its expressive value; he had before him something that was no longer pure music, but rather design, architecture, thought, and which allowed the actual music to be recalled" (1:228; 1:206). We are moving here from impressionism to formalism: in his knowing appraisal of Fauré's early masterpiece, which dates from 1879, Proust in fact looks forward to the tastes of the period between the two wars; and as Jean-Michel Nectoux points out, the innovative conception of Fauré's *Ballade* was misunderstood until that later period.[12] Belonging to the nineteenth century, modestly, perhaps timidly, and certainly ambiguously presented by Fauré himself as the result of "new processes—which are at the same time old," the *Ballade* is nonetheless one of the earliest works to look forward to the twentieth century. It invents its own form without any preconceived plan and adopts a convergent structure, A-B-C′-B′-C, in which the middle movement develops themes stated in the two extreme movements. Thus, the statement of the C theme in the finale comes after its development in the *allegro* of the second movement. Fauré's *Ballade* resolutely escapes the criticisms about the lack of conception and unity of nineteenth-century works to which Proust gives voice in *La Prisonnière* (see chapter 1).

But was Proust aware of the remarkably innovative nature of the *Ballade?* Did he understand how original a response it gave to the aesthetic challenge of the late nineteenth century, the challenge of the unity and the totality of the work of art? Fauré's letters show that he was haunted by the same concern that must have preoccupied Proust. Both men give up the idea of rhetorical or rhapsodic composition, all the while refusing to give up the idea of some principle of composition. Obviously, both of them have to deal with Wagner, and neither is fully satisfied with Wagner's solution to the problem of aesthetic unity. The formal unity of the *Ballade* is one of the novel, unpublicized responses given by the late nineteenth century. As such, it is discreet; it has none of the trappings of a proclamation or an avant-garde manifesto. And there is no doubt whatsoever that it did not escape Proust's notice. Evidence for this is Proust's interest in Fauré's second-most innovative work before the turn of the century (next to the *Ballade*), *La Bonne Chanson,* Opus 61, a cycle of melodies composed between 1892 and 1894 that are settings of Verlaine poems. Here, Fauré is after a kind of unity that is neither descriptive nor impressionistic nor literary, but properly musical. For Fauré, writes Vladimir Jankélévich, "the cycle is no longer a collection, but a small lyrical symphony in which the poems, when put together, themselves compose a poem. . . . When this song-writer composes a song cycle, we see the architectonic instinct taking its revenge."[13] In *La Bonne Chanson,* Fauré keeps nine of the twenty-one Verlaine poems and rearranges them so as to compose a true cycle rather than a simple series of juxtaposed pieces, like most song collections, even including those of Schubert and Schumann. In 1891 Fauré had already attacked the problem of the musical cycle in the *Cinq Mélodies,* Opus 58, known as the "Venice" melodies, all of which have a common motif.

When we get to *La Bonne Chanson,* we find six principal themes, which are musical motifs and not Wagnerian themes. The work becomes more and more complex as it goes along, all the way up to the final song, *L'hiver a cessé,* in which all the themes are brought together. The piece took the listening public aback and was misunderstood when first performed on April 20, 1895. Saint-Saëns, for example, reckoned that Fauré had lost his mind. Proust, who even before the work's first public performance appears to have heard it at Madame Lemaire's on March 26, 1895, wrote to Pierre Lavallée as early as autumn 1894:

> Did you know that young musicians are practically unanimous in their dislike of Fauré's *La Bonne Chanson?* It has the reputation of being unnecessarily complicated, etc., quite inferior to the other works. That is what Bréville and Debussy (who is reputed to be a great genius, greater still than Fauré) believe. Personally I don't care, I still love that sketchbook [*cahier*], and on the contrary what I don't like are the earlier pieces that the others purportedly prefer.
>
> (*Corr.* 1:340)

While he gives some idea of what people hold against *La Bonne Chanson,* Proust does not explain his own preference. But he does speak of a "cahier," as if the piece formed a whole. Is this evidence enough to suggest that even at an age when he was very much caught up in society life, Proust was already affected by Fauré's solution to the quest for a new aesthetic unity? How can a book be made from the pieces of *Jean Santeuil?* How can the novel between two centuries be conceived?

It would appear that Proust was unfamiliar with Fauré's music dating from after the turn of the century, in particular his Sonata No. 2 for Violin and Piano, Opus 108 (1916). But the Sonata No. 1 and the Quartet No. 1, the *Ballade* and *La Bonne Chanson* were probably enough to define the unity of *A la recherche du temps perdu.* A draft from Cahier 57, for the performance of the Vinteuil quartet and its comparison to the sonata, describes the quartet as a work that is "completely different, as original as the sonata, so that the sonata, which had seemed to me to form a totality, was now nothing more than a unity, and I could now go beyond the notion of the one and understand multiplicity."[14] What is being "gone beyond" here is Wagner and thematic unity, in the name of a formal unity, a complex unity, a kind of unity I would call, once again, allegorical. It is not unlikely that Fauré's works, in particular his early masterpieces, allowed Proust to "go beyond" the choice between composition and decomposition, the dilemma of organicism and decadentism, that the fin-de-siècle seemed to thrust upon him. Along the path that leads to *A la recherche du temps perdu,* the *Ballade* and *La Bonne Chanson* provide the finest example of a multiple, complex work that holds on to a sense of unity and totality, that is, that reaches the unity of a form.

3

"Racine is more immoral!"

Every reader is, while he is reading, the reader of his own self," Proust asserts in *Le Temps retrouvé* (3:949; 4:489). This very subjective, partial, and introspective idea of the encounter between book and reader was foreshadowed from the time of Proust's preface to his translation of Ruskin's *Sesame and Lilies,* which was first published in 1905 and was a sort of prelude to the *Recherche* ("Journées de lecture," CSB 160–94). But in *Le Temps retrouvé* the maxim is used to generalize, and hence justify, a more remarkable and perhaps unseemly assertion: "The writer must not be indignant if the invert who reads his book gives to his heroines a masculine countenance." The pronouncement moreover recalls this description of the young homosexual, as yet unaware of himself, right at the start of *Sodome et Gomorrhe I:*

> How should he suppose that he is not like everybody else when he recognizes the substance of what he feels in reading Mme de La Fayette, Racine, Baudelaire, Walter Scott, at a time when he is still too little capable of observing himself to take into account what he has added from his own store to the picture, and to realize that if the sentiment be the same the object differs, that what he desires is Rob Roy and not Diana Vernon? (2:646–47; 3:25)

To the list of authors open to misunderstanding, the sketches added Montaigne, Stendhal, and Nerval.[1] All literature is equivocal.

Inversion and reading are associated several times in the *Recherche*. The situation of the homosexual reader, or rather of the reading homosexual, confirms the fact that reading is never intellectual, objective, and pure, but, on the contrary, always affective and imaginary, fanciful in its essence; contextual and not textual, so to speak. On the other hand, this does not prohibit it from achieving a certain universality and truth: through the detour of inverting the sex of heroines, the homosexual gets back to the common sense of love. In this, according to *Le Temps retrouvé,* reading is no different from writing: "Racine himself was obliged, as a first step towards giving her a universal validity, for a moment to turn the antique figure of Phèdre into a Jansenist" (3:949; 4:489).

The image of Phèdre as a Christian and a Jansenist was a nineteenth-century commonplace from the time of Chateaubriand, and Proust seems to adopt it. In fact he gives it an original twist. Far from reducing Racine's work to the morality of Port-Royal, the example helps him to open up Racine's work to the infinite field of interpretation. After the Christian and Jansenist Racine, scorned by the romantics, came a hysterical fin-de-siècle Phèdre and a perverse Racine. After 1900, Péguy, in his famous commentary on Corneille and Racine, will basically combine the two critical clichés. From one to the other, between the two, what is Proust's Racine—just as Proust speaks of "Monsieur de Guermantes' Balzac"? Because, in *Le Temps retrouvé,* the way Racine wrote *Phèdre* is strangely used to suggest how the invert reads, the peculiar affinity of Racine's tragedy for disguise and transvestism seems a good point to start.

The Homosexual Leitmotiv of the Choruses from *Esther* and *Athalie* in *Sodome et Gomorrhe*

Let us then look at a striking case of Proustian reading, the reading of Racine, and more specifically that of *Esther* and *Athalie* in *Sodome et Gomorrhe*. The interest of this reading—beyond the reference to classical literature as an authority or an emblem of bourgeois culture—is that the quotations and allusions to Racine's last two plays, his biblical tragedies, come to represent a veritable motif, indeed a Wagnerian leitmotiv, in Proust's novel. How is this theme composed? What might its meaning be? Will it allow us access to Proust's Racine, this writer of whom Charlus, in conformity with the reevaluation of the 1880s, says in *A l'ombre des jeunes filles en fleurs*, "There is more truth in a single tragedy of Racine than in all the dramatic works of Monsieur Victor Hugo" (1:819; 2:122)?

The appearances of the leitmotiv are four in number:

1. (2:689–90; 3:64–66)

At the soirée given by the Princesse de Guermantes, Monsieur de Vaugoubert learns from Monsieur de Charlus that the secretaries of the embassy of X belong to the accursed race. Vaugoubert is then compared by the narrator to Athalie and Abner learning that "Joas is of the House of David, that Esther 'enthroned in the purple' [*dans la pourpre assise*] has 'Yid' parents." Whence the assimilation of the Guermantes residence to the Temple of Jerusalem and the throne room at Susa. Three lines from *Esther* identify Vaugoubert's joy with that of Elise discovering that Esther is surrounded by Israelite maidens:

> Ciel! quel nombreux essaim d'innocentes beautés
> S'offre à mes yeux en foule et sort de tous côtés!
> Quelle aimable pudeur sur leur visage est peinte!
> (*Esther* 1.2.122–24)

> Heavens! what a numerous swarm of innocent beauties
> Gathers before my eyes, and comes out from everywhere!
> What lovely modesty is painted on their faces!

Then come six other lines, in which Elise and Esther comment on Mardochée's decision to surround the queen only with girls taken from among her own people:

> Accustomed from childhood to apply, even to what is voiceless, the language of the classics, I read into M. de Vaugoubert's eyes the lines . . .
>
> Cependant son amour pour notre nation
> A peuplé ce palais de filles de Sion.
> Jeunes et tendres fleurs par le sort agitées,

Sous un ciel étranger comme moi transplantées.
Dans un lieu séparé de profanes témoins,
Il (*the excellent ambassador*) met à les former son étude et ses soins.
(*Esther* 1.1.101–6; modified quotation)

Meanwhile his love for our nation
Has filled this palace with girls of Zion.
Young and tender flowers shaken by fate,
Transplanted, like me, under a foreign sky.
In a place isolated from profane witnesses,
He takes care and thought in training them.

Finally, two lines from *Esther* compare the secret of Monsieur de Vaugoubert, King Theodosius' ambassador, to the one Esther is keeping from Assuérus:

Le Roi jusqu'à ce jour ignore qui je suis,
Et ce secret toujours tient ma langue enchaînée.
(*Esther* 1.1.90, 92; modified quotation)

The King up to this day does not know who I am,
And this secret always holds my tongue prisoner.

2. (2:801–2; 3:171)
At the Grand Hotel in Balbec, the squads of idle page boys remind Marcel of a "Judeo-Christian tragedy given bodily form and perpetually in performance." Four lines of *Athalie* are quoted, taken from the scene in which Athalie goes to the Temple and questions Joas.

Quel est donc votre emploi?
. . . .
Mais tout ce peuple enfermé dans ce lieu,
A quoi s'occupe-t-il?
. . . .
Je vois l'ordre pompeux de ces cérémonies.
(*Athalie* 2.7.661, 669–70, 676,
modified quotation)

What then is your function?
. . . .

> But this whole people locked up in this place,
> What do they do?
> . . . .
> I see the pompous order of these ceremonies.

Then two lines from different places are inserted into the text—"loin du monde élevés" [raised far from the world] (772) and "troupe jeune et fidèle" [young and faithful troupe] (299)—and they confirm the resemblance of the hotel in Balbec and Solomon's Temple.

3. (2:872–73; 3:237–38)

This is the great escapade of Monsieur Nissim Bernard, Bloch's uncle, who is supporting a young waiter from the Grand Hotel. Whence another allusion to Racine's choruses, followed by a page-long commentary made up of a montage of quotations taken from many different places in *Athalie* (788–91, 772, 1279, 253–54, 794 [modified quotation], 821–22, 824–25, 1201–04 [modified quotation]), which allows the narrator to tell the story of Nissim Bernard and the waiter:

> Mon Dieu, qu'une vertu naissante
> Parmi tant de périls marche à pas incertains!
> Qu'une âme qui te cherche et veut être innocente
> Trouve d'obstacle à ses desseins!
> (*Athalie* 2.9.788–91)

> My God, how a budding virtue
> Walks with uncertain steps amidst so many perils!
> How many obstacles to its intentions are met by a soul
> Who seeks you out and wants to be innocent!

Even though the young waiter had been "raised far from the world" ("loin du monde élevé," *Athalie* 2.9.772), in the Palace-Temple of Balbec, he had not followed Joad's advice not to put too much emphasis on gold and riches ("Sur la richesse et l'or ne mets point ton appui," *Athalie* 4.2.1279). Perhaps he had justified his behavior by telling himself that sinners cover the entire world ("Les pécheurs couvrent la terre," *Athalie* 2.9.794). At any rate, Monsieur Nissim Bernard, who dared not hope anything of the kind would happen so quickly, was pleasantly surprised to find that he felt his innocent arms press against him, whether from fear or in order to caress him ("Et soit frayeur encore ou pour le caresser, / De ses bras innocents il se sentit presser," *Athalie* 1.2.253–54; modified quotation). And from the second day on, as Monsieur Nissim Bernard took a stroll with the waiter, his contagious presence compromised his innocence ("l'abord contagieux altérait son innocence," *Athalie* 2.9.784–85). Starting with that moment, the boy's life had changed. Even though he followed his boss's orders to bring out the bread and the salt, his entire face sang out:

> De fleurs en fleurs, de plaisirs en plaisirs
> Promenons nos désirs. (2.9.821–22)
>
> De nos ans passagers le nombre est incertain.
> Hâtons-nous aujourd'hui de jouir de la vie.
> (2.9.824–25)
>
> L'honneur et les emplois
> Sont le prix d'une aveugle et douce obéissance,
> Pour la triste innocence
> Qui viendrait élever la voix.
> (3.8.1201–4; modified quotation)
>
> From flower to flower, from pleasure to pleasure
> Let us stroll with our desires.
> The number of our short-lived years is unclear.
> Let us hasten today to taste the joy of life.
> Honor and occupations
> Are the price of a blind and submissive obedience,
> For the sad innocence
> Which might come to raise its voice.

About twenty lines are quoted in this unusual montage, put together by the narrator but attributed to Nissim Bernard.

4. (2:1019; 3:376)

Monsieur de Charlus has dinner at the Grand Hotel in the company of the footman of a cousin of the Cambremer family. The young page boys are there, quickly compared, with no further elaboration, to the Levites on the Temple stairs. As he crosses the lobby Charlus himself, rather than the narrator, murmurs one of

Elise's lines from the beginning of *Esther*: "Prospérez, cher espoir d'une nation sainte" (1.2.125) [Prosper, dear hope of a holy nation]. He continues with a line spoken by Esther, but strangely enough the two lines are wrongly attributed to Josabeth in *Athalie*: "But, having continued to quote the speech of Josabeth: 'Venez, venez, mes filles' [Come, come, my girls], he felt a revulsion and did not, like her, add: 'il faut les appeler' " [they must be called] (*Esther* 1.1.112).[2]

These four appearances of the theme form a unity:

- In the first three occurrences, it is the narrator who associates young men or boys (embassy secretaries, page boys) with the girls in Racine's choruses. In the fourth one it is Monsieur de Charlus: we know he shares the hero's literary tastes—and his mother's and grandmother's—for Racine and Madame de Sévigné.
- In three cases we are dealing with caricatured depictions of homosexuals: the hero sees through the eyes of Vaugoubert, Nissim Bernard, or Charlus. Like a voyeur, he watches them watching, he observes their desire. But in the second occurrence he is the only one to observe the page boys' ploys, and this gives a sort of objectivity to the comparison that goes beyond Sodom.
- The four passages allude to each other, like an extended metaphor or an allegory. Nissim Bernard's waiter is "of much the same type as the pages of whom we have spoken, and who made us think of the young Israelites in *Esther* and *Athalie*" (2:871–72; 3:236–37). The fourth time the narrator is careful to distinguish himself from Charlus, who quotes *Esther*, "recalling a passage from Racine, and applying to it a wholly different meaning" (2:1019; 3:376).[3] The theme's repetitiveness is quite obvious, perhaps even a bit ponderous to some readers, and the narrator tries to own up to it: "And so I could not help reciting to myself, when I saw them, not indeed the lines of Racine that had come into my head at the Princesse de Guermantes's . . . , but other lines of Racine, taken this time not from *Esther* but from *Athalie*" (2:802; 3:171).

- In spite of this last distinction, which is in a late marginal addition to the corrected typescript, Racine's last two plays are really one and the same from the point of view of the leitmotiv: witness the confusion between the two in the fourth appearance.

The Birth and Development of the Leitmotiv

The genesis of the Racinian motif in *Sodome et Gormorrhe* is complex, its stratification delicate; its occurrences changed a great deal through a number of shifts and transformations.

1. The Vaugoubert episode appears on four manuscript pages (the first two not handwritten by Proust, the last two in his handwriting) added to the typescript—widely amended and filled with handwritten pages—which was used for the printing of *Jalousie*, the advance publication of the beginning of *Sodome et Gomorrhe II* which appeared in extracts in *Les Oeuvres libres* in November 1921.[4] Instead of these pages, the manuscript contained a long insert that gave a very different dimension to the comparison of the Guermantes residence to Assuérus' palace:

> Meanwhile, at the moment Monsieur de Charlus, having seen Countess Molé out, was crossing the threshold and reentering this classical palace—as the Duchesse de Guermantes called her cousin's house, which overlooked "the superb gardens of Esther" [*d'Esther les superbes jardins*]—exactly at that moment Esther's exclamation at seeing Elise left his lips as he found himself face to face with his former friend Monsieur de Vaugoubert. As the latter had continued to occupy increasingly important diplomatic posts, Monsieur de Charlus had not seen him for a long time. Not only did Monsieur de Vaugoubert share the same tastes as the Baron, but he was the only one of Monsieur de Charlus' friends with whom he had long ago exchanged confidences. At the time when Monsieur de Charlus had a bachelor apartment where he and two of his friends, the Duke of X and the Duke of XX, brought women, Monsieur de Vaugoubert had come over one day and propositioned Monsieur de Charlus. Monsieur de Charlus thought he had no choice but to throw the young Vaugoubert naked and whipped out into the street in order to impress his three friends. Vaugoubert was charming at that age.

> Monsieur de Charlus could not keep from admiring him as he stripped him, and even while he struck him he was also touching him. But they went a long time without seeing each other again, such a long time that Vaugoubert had changed, was no longer attractive to Monsieur de Charlus, and could no longer be anything more than his confidant. Little by little as Monsieur de Charlus' two friends learned of the Baron's tastes, which they had never suspected, it was revealed to Monsieur de Charlus that they (without knowing it about each other) had the same tastes. And at last all three finally understood that each one, believing himself to be an exception in the universe, had had mistresses and made public display of a violent taste for women—so as to be admired by two friends who were taking the same trouble—but did not like them. Later still, while chatting with Vaugoubert, Monsieur de Charlus discovered that he had been the most innocent of the three. For no later than the day after Vaugoubert's drubbing, each of the two others, unbeknownst to Monsieur de Charlus and to the third friend, had arranged a secret rendez-vous with Vaugoubert, had made him swear that he would say nothing, and had asked him for the pleasures that Monsieur de Charlus had not dared to take. Monsieur de Vaugoubert had violated this oath as often as he could, along with many others. For many people confided in him because of the assurances that he gave, often with the simple phrase: "It's my job to keep quiet and never to say anything." He was alluding, of course, to his career. But what power did the diplomat's discretion have against the far deeper need of confidences, revelations, and gossip which was that of the invert?
> (3:1346 [3:34, var. b])[5]

Thus the manuscript insert began with a quick parallel between Esther's gardens and the princess', thanks to a quotation of the first line of act 3 of *Esther,* spoken by Zarès: "C'est donc ici d'Esther le superbe jardin" (3.1.826) [This then is Esther's superb garden]. This first allusion then evoked a reference to the first line of the play—"Est-ce toi, chère Elise?" [Is it you, dear Elise?]—in the form of a simple transition to the description of Charlus and Vaugoubert. In other words, when the theme—or at least the insert—first began, the evocation of *Esther* and Racine was not linked to sexual inversion, but to the princess' palace.

This allusion is moreover prepared in *Le Côté de Guermantes II,* when Charlus concludes his glowing description of the Princesse de

Guermantes in this way: "And the Esther gardens alone!" (2:587; 2:853). This remains mysterious in the definitive text, in which this passage is no longer about Esther of Mecklenburg, a great friend of Wagner's and the Princesse de Guermantes' mother-in-law. But in the manuscript of *Sodome et Gomorrhe,* the confirmation was given. The Duchesse de Guermantes said to the hero: "When Hubert's mother, the Prince de Bade's sister, lived here, since her name was Esther, Swann during his visits never missed an opportunity to say: 'So here are the superb gardens of Esther.' I was grateful to the duchess for reminding me of this tragedy, on which I was literally raised" (3:1323 [3:34, var. b]).[6] On another page of the manuscript, the name Esther is used in a word play, almost a spoonerism, spoken by Charlus, who praises his cousin's palace to the hero: "You seem to be unaware that you are in the most beautiful place in the world, and you have not exclaimed like Elise: 'What, here then are the superb gardens of Esther!' Unfortunately you're missing the best part of the whole thing, which was Aunt Esther herself. We cannot bring her back to life for you" (3:1318 [3:34, var. b]).[7] Charlus, who is quoting from memory, makes a mistake: the line belongs to Zarès, not to Elise. But the response is found in a marginal addition, elicited by the following: "Just imagine that my cousin Marie prefers not to use the name Thérèse which the Gotha Almanac also gives her. Because then it becomes the 'Fête chez Thérèse' and by the way that's exactly what it's like" (3:1318 [3:34, var. b]).[8] "Thérèse" called forth "Esther"; the allusion is to "La Fête chez Thérèse," a ballet by Catulle Mendès with music by Reynaldo Hahn, which reuses the title of a poem from Victor Hugo's *Les Contemplations.* The ballet was performed at the Opéra in 1910.[9] The echoes of a Racine quotation seem infinite, and from Esther to Thérèse, in the inversion of the two syllables of the name, it is not without interest, as we delve into the homosexual theme borrowed from Racine, to discover a form of language that united Proust to Reynaldo Hahn, one of those affectionate inversions of the syllables of their names that Proust, the Bibescos and Fénelon—"Nonelef" by the terms of the game—indulged in.

Thus the long narration of Charlus' and Vaugoubert's earlier escapades was introduced on the manuscript insert by a quick allusion to Esther's gardens, but the narration did not then make use of the comparison, which remained tangential, unconnected to the theme of homosexuality. The only purpose it seems to serve here is to fill in one of the gaps left earlier by the *Recherche*: here we chance to learn the name of the man who, "now one of the brightest luminaries of the Faubourg Saint-Germain," was said by Saint-Loup—speaking of his Uncle Charlus to the hero before the latter has met him—to have propositioned Charlus and to have been found, naked and whipped, "in ten degrees of frost" (1:805; 2:109): Vaugoubert.

It was only then, after this narration was over, that Proust came back to Racine, as if he had just found a second motivating factor for the analogy in addition to the comparison of the gardens, a factor that was to be the only one left in the definitive text. Charlus' revelations to Vaugoubert, "visibly changing the aspect of the Quai d'Orsay or the Wilhelmstrasse, made these palaces retrospectively mysterious, like Racinian palaces": "If Monsieur de Charlus had learned *Esther* by heart from childhood, it is probable that he applied to the ambassador he was discussing with Monsieur de Vaugoubert the lines in which the queen explains to Elise that Mardochée has put together for her an exclusively but secretly Israelite staff" (3:1347 [3:34, var. b]). The lines the definitive text was to quote are all there in the form of successive additions to the first insert.[10]

2. The description of the Grand Hotel in Balbec that the narrator gives the first time he goes out similarly belongs to a manuscript insert, including the comparison to a theater: "It was set up like a theater, and many walk-on actors enlivened it to the plinths [sic]." The allusion to Racine's choruses appears in an interlinear addition, and the narrator is careful to attribute it to Charlus: "But since the masculine element was dominant, undoubtedly thinking of Monsieur de Charlus, as Racinian as my grandmother and myself . . . "; in this way the hotel was reminiscent of "the embodiment of a sort of tragedy, not ancient, but Christian" (3:1439 [3:171, var. a]).[11] But this disclaimer was skipped in the typescript, and when he was correcting it Proust, rather than bringing the disclaimer back in, substituted an echo of the first appearance of the theme, that is, Vaugoubert; this was another way of taking his distance.[12] Then

came the same lines from *Athalie* as in the definitive text, but the quotation was drawn out by a return to Charlus, crossed out on the typescript:

> Certainly Monsieur de Charlus, I said to myself, might have had a better time there than the year when I had known him, but in that I was mistaken. I imagined him lingering in all those little corners corresponding to the "interior courtyards" of the Jewish Temple, and in some little shrine where it is easy to avoid being seen.
>
> (3:1439 [3:171, var. c])

Thus, the only time the leitmotiv appears when the narrator is alone looking at boys (without Vaugoubert, Nissim Bernard, or Charlus), Proust made clear twice in the manuscript—in two interlinear additions—that he was watching through Charlus' eyes, and most certainly not through his own.

3. The escapades of Nissim Bernard take up five pages, three handwritten and two typed, inserted into the typescript.[13] At this point in the manuscript, at the end of a notebook, where anecdotes pile up without considerations of composition and Proust often makes his most copious revisions on the typescript, came the scenes that suggested to the hero that Albertine might be attracted to women: the scene of Albertine watching Bloch's sister and cousin in a mirror, the strange woman from the casino, the friend of Albertine's aunt to whom Albertine is impolite.[14] Proust scattered them. But if the Nissim Bernard episode consists of an addition that is in part already typed out, that is because it makes use of a passage that had been placed elsewhere in the manuscript: in fact, it belonged to the next appearance of the theme. Proust moved it and brought it forward in the typescript.

4. The allusions to *Esther*—wrongly attributed to *Athalie*—during Charlus' dinner with the footman at the Grand Hotel, is an addition written by hand in the margin of the typescript.[15] But in the manuscript, this episode was already present on an immense insert,[16] which includes not only Charlus' dinner with the footman and the story of his passion for Aimé—the *maître d'hôtel* of the Grand Hotel—which comes afterward in the definitive text (2:1019–26; 3:378–82), but also the escapades of Nissim Bernard and his

waiter, inserted between the other two burlesque narratives about Charlus. In this case it is at the beginning of a notebook—just as earlier it was at the end of one—that complications abound, and they are then redistributed on the typescript.

On the manuscript insert, the Baron lowered his eyes as he went past the page boys:

> He looked if he were separating them to clear the way for himself and his companion, and he murmured:
>
> Ciel! quel nombreux essaim d'innocentes beautés
> S'offre à mes yeux en foule, et sort de tous côtés?
> Quelle aimable pudeur sur leur visage est peinte!
>
> The footman, who did not know this passage from *Esther,* said to the Baron: "I beg your pardon?" But Monsieur de Charlus took a certain pride in never answering questions. He continued as if he had not heard.
>
> Prospérez, chez espoir d'une nation sainte!
>
> (3:1560 [3:375, var. d])

The meaning is more or less the same in the definitive text, but Proust gets rid of the first three lines quoted by Charlus, since the narrator has already applied them to Vaugoubert.

The rest of the insert is crossed out, but it was not at all redundant, and it was only very briefly summed up in the margins of the typescript:

> But he does not say:
> Il faut les appeler. Venez, venez mes filles.
> That was precisely because these children were not yet of a completely determinate sex and had not yet reached the age that Monsieur de Charlus liked. To his eyes they still looked too much like girls. Nevertheless, if one lowered one's sights, there were among those waiting on the tables—or rather clearing them—some who were already grown-up young men. One, slender and tall, lifting above his black uniform a face tinted with the same modesty as Hippolyte's, looked like a pink bush. He might even, perhaps, have been attractive to Monsieur de Charlus. At first there seemed nothing astonishing about the extremely refined apparel of this officiating priest whose task it was to arrange the hors-d'oeuvres and the salt

> on the tables and whose linen was as white as a surplis. But as soon as he was asked a question, the exquisite sweetness of his answer, the shy smile of his dark eyes, the coyness of his high starched collar all made clear that he was not a man. Had Monsieur de Charlus spoken to this magnificient elder brother of Eliacin, he would have seen immediately that his role was being played by a young lady from Saint-Cyr. This was not what Monsieur de Charlus desired, but rather men, full-grown men. He thought that his companion could get him some, especially since his likes and dislikes were not shared by everyone.

This additional allusion—eliminated from the definitive text—to *Phèdre,* to the chaste and pure Hippolyte, shows that for Proust, all of Racine's theater—and not only the plays commissioned by Madame de Maintenon for Saint-Cyr—is about disguise and transvestism.

Moreover, what came next, without transition, was the story of Nissim Bernard's escapades with the waiter, which was not yet in the form of a montage of quotations from *Athalie,* but in which another reference to Racine was present, also omitted by Proust when he corrected the typescript. Nissim Bernard's penchant for the labyrinth of the Grand Hotel is explained in the definitive text by means of heredity: "With a strain of Oriental atavism he loved a seraglio, and when he went out at night might be seen furtively exploring its purlieus" (2:874; 3:239). Here the allusion to *Bajazet* is barely recognizable, whereas the manuscript explicitly mentioned Racine's single profane Oriental tragedy as a new model for the palace:

> What made Monsieur Nissim Bernard enjoy the hotel in Balbec was I think partly that Monsieur Nissim Bernard had an Oriental taste for multiple entries, hidden exits, intrigues, complications, and nighttime. If *Esther* and *Athalie* were being publicly performed on the ground floor of the Hotel in Balbec, the corridors of the main floor and especially the upper stories looked more like a setting from *Bajazet,* a magnificent setting, since the Hotel had added on annexes (the director thought on a big scale, and had perfected his own comfort without changing anything about the admirable simplicity of the rooms, which made each one look like a sort of swimming pool), and hired a staff belonging in part to the same ancient race as

> that of the Guermantes residence; all of elegant society, all those who might have preferred to spend their vacations in some resort town like Dinard, had set their hearts on this establishment in Balbec, with its almost Persian name.

Proust even did a pastiche of Acomat's famous line, "Nourri dans le sérail, j'en connais les détours" (*Bajazet* 4.7.1423) [Raised in the seraglio, I know all its ins and outs], with the words "Nourri dans le sérail, il ne faisait pas ici qu'en retrouver, il en aimait les détours" (3:1476 [3:239, var. d]) [Raised in the seraglio, here he was doing more than rediscovering its ins and outs, he loved them]. But all that remains of *Bajazet* in the definitive text is the "sérail" along with its "détours."

After Nissim Bernard's escapades, the manuscript insert returned to Charlus and the footman, whose dinner at the Grand Hotel had been its starting point; evidence that Nissim Bernard's liaison with the waiter was initially an addition to the narrative of Charlus' dinner with the servant, a digression from the portrait of the Baron's homosexuality.[17]

Thus, on this manuscript insert, homosexual narratives proliferated at the same time as references to Racine, bringing in *Phèdre* and *Bajazet* as well as *Esther* and *Athalie*. From the point of view of its genesis, one might say that the homosexual theme and the Racine allegory developed concurrently, calling each other forth, finding mutual justification. But the definitive text is more economical and alludes only to the sacred tragedies. Moreover, the parallels with *Phèdre* and *Bajazet* belonged to the narrator himself and, as we have seen, Proust subsequently went out of his way to distance the narrator from the homosexual theme.

What can we make of this complicated genesis? The Racinian leitmotiv of *Sodome et Gomorrhe* is especially elaborated by hand and redistributed on the typescript, this being the case with the most recent layers of the manuscript, especially the inserts that accumulated at the beginnings and ends of notebooks. The leitmotiv is a latecomer: the manuscript's allusions to Racine occur only in the inserts, and nothing in the first drafts of *Sodome* sets the stage for them. Probably these manuscript additions were made at the same time as the ones that mention an improvement in the standard of service at the Grand Hotel, during the first stay at Balbec in *A l'ombre des jeunes filles en fleurs;* as the manager announces, "The pages left something to be desired. You will see, next year, what a phalanx I shall collect" (1:1014; 2:303).[18] The additions surely date from the end of the war and are meant to help legitimize *post facto* the title of this part of the work, which was much less justified in the manuscript than in the definitive text. The portrait of Sodom, with the comic, Balzacian, and fantastical details that the reader remembers more than anything else, depends on anecdotal additions. And they are more and more forced: the Duc de Châtellerault's misadventures with the usher, Nissim Bernard and the tomato-head brothers, or the Prince de Guermantes and Morel, all three of which appeared on the typescript. This development goes so far that at the last minute, in 1921 and 1922, Proust sometimes went in the opposite direction and toned down the most comical or caricatured elements in the escapades of Vaugoubert, Charlus, or Nissim Bernard.

The long handwritten insert from the beginning of Cahier 6, in which Nissim Bernard's liaison with the waiter interrupted the narration of Charlus' dinner with the footman, contained the lines from the beginning of act 1, scene 2 of *Esther,* which also serve as the starting point for the Racinian leitmotiv connected to Vaugoubert. Proust distributed the verses among the different appearances of the theme on the typescript in such a way that the same ones are never quoted twice.[19] This suggests that the immense insert with its phenomenal twists of plot (Charlus and the footman, Nissim Bernard and his waiter, Charlus and Aimé) was the real germ of the theme, which could thus trace its origins to Elise's exclamation in act 1, scene 2 of *Esther*: "Ciel! quel nombreux essaim!"

The development of the theme implies that Proust returned to the Racine text with which his own text is playing, and this is especially clear in two cases. In the Vaugoubert episode, the manuscript shows that the quotations are added, that Proust looks for new ones in addition to Elise's four lines and develops an initial conjunction that is not illustrated by Racine's text. In the case of Nissim Bernard, the montage of lines from *Athalie,* which Proust seems to know less well than *Esther,* is perfectly true to Racine's text. As for the error of attributing the fourth occurrence to *Athalie* instead of *Esther,* it is not significant; it is written in the margins of the typescript, as a final touch, once the Nissim Bernard episode has been moved and the immense insert divided up, and, most important, it concerns precisely the most famous lines, from the beginning of *Esther,* which are the kernel of the entire theme. But this error marks a paradox: in the place where the theme was for the most part initially inserted, there is almost nothing left of it in the definitive text; the theme has been practically used up by its redistribution into earlier passages. Here is yet another example of the regressive nature of Proustian writing, constantly in search of "preparations" to such a degree that sometimes, at the moment of revelation, the final explosion fizzles: this is perhaps one way to explain the confusion between Racine's last two tragedies. What is quite striking in any case is the way in which, in the free movement of the text and the intertext, the Racine quotations contribute to some of the funniest—or, in the readers' eyes, perhaps the most tedious—episodes of *Sodome et Gomorrhe.*

Budding Young Men

In spite of its obvious comic aspects, the homosexual leitmotiv of Racine choruses has often been taken as a masochistic profanation on Proust's part, an insult to his mother, who was a great admirer of Racine and the seventeenth century: "Once again he deliberately tortures himself by profaning what he loves and using his mother's favorite quotations to depict the sexual inversion which she detested."[20] If this is true, Proust's use of Racine depends on the theme of blasphemy that runs through the entire *Recherche,* starting from the scene at Montjouvain in which Mademoiselle Vinteuil and her friend defile the musician's photograph. This impious motivation is in fact suggested in the passage about the pleasure Nissim Bernard takes in the Racinian ceremony at the Grand Hotel: "Whether from Hebraic atavism or in profanation of its Christian feeling, he took a singular pleasure in the Racinian ceremony, were it Jewish or Catholic" (2:873; 3:238). Judaism and sadism are thus linked, as in Monsieur de Charlus' long anti-Semitic speech in *Sodome et Gomorrhe,* which is brought on by his desire for Bloch, and emphasizes the "curious instinct for sacrilege, peculiar to that race" (2:1141; 3:490). The homosexual motif borrowed from Racine reinforces the analogy between Jews and homosexuals that is so often repeated in the *Recherche* and is particularly developed in *Sodome et Gomorrhe I*; the words *like the Jews* are a kind of refrain in the passage about the "accursed race."

However attractive this interpretation may be, it still does not seem quite adequate; the leitmotiv is a belated one and is not tragic in nature. It belongs to the burlesque touch Proust brought to the Sodomite fresco at the end of the war, a fresco that is often exaggerated, as in the bad wordplays on "en être" [being one]—a Jew, an artist, a homosexual, it's all the same—that Proust rehashes again and again in *Sodome et Gomorrhe*. Neither masochism nor sadism are especially apparent here, and we must therefore try to bring together several clues, both internal and external to the novel, that will make it possible for us to get an idea of Proust's Racine, and also to propose a different meaning for the allegory; for quotations *within* a text are the privileged locus of the revelation of its truth.

Here, then, is the point toward which I am heading: Racine's theater is in Proust's eyes a model of disguise and transvestism, and thus an excellent image—even the image *par excellence*—of sexual inversion. For Proust, even if this seems crude for the moment, Racine is a woman, a woman-man, in the same way that the hero, in the 1910 version, exclaims on seeing Charlus asleep in a box at the opera, "C'en était une!" [He was a woman!] (3:946).[21] And suddenly the veil is lifted from the series of enigmas that the Baron's behavior previously held in store. Charlus' life is a high point in that subjective exercise called love, which necessarily travesties the other. And disguise and transvestism always appear to use Racine as a paradigm, as we find in this fragment from Carnet 3 about Maria (who will turn into Albertine): "I loved the mistress in Maria, the girl whom one sees again and again, etc. But as for him, it is a kind of double transsubstantiation, for in a girl I saw a Racinian heroine, but in a young man I saw him."[22] The term *transsubstantiation,* which inevitably evokes the sacrament of the Eucharist, once again suggests that the context of love for Proust is profanation. But Proust's Racine, the Racine of the homosexual leitmotiv, is nonetheless almost exactly the Racine of the turn of the century.

As early as the beginning of *Du côté de chez Swann,* the narrator relates that on the day of leaving Combray at the end of the summer holidays:

> My mother. . . found me standing in tears on the steep little path near Tansonville, bidding farewell to my hawthorns, clasping their sharp branches in my arms and, like a princess in a tragedy oppressed by the weight of these vain ornaments [*à qui pèseraient ces vains ornements*], with no gratitude towards the importunate hand which, in curling all those ringlets, had been at pains to arrange my hair upon my forehead [*l'importune main qui en formant tous ces noeuds avait pris soin sur mon front d'assembler mes cheveux*], trampling underfoot the curl-papers which I had torn from my head, and my new hat with them. (1:158; 1:143)

The description alludes to the famous words Phèdre speaks as she arrives onstage:

> Que ces vains ornements, que ces voiles me pèsent!
> Quelle importune main, en formant tous ces noeuds,
> A pris soin sur mon front d'assembler mes cheveux?
> Tout m'afflige et me nuit, et conspire à me nuire.
> (*Phèdre* 1.3)

> How these vain ornaments, how these veils weigh on me!
> What importunate hand formed all these curls
> And took pains to arrange my hair upon my forehead?
> Everything afflicts and harms me, and conspires to harm me.

The hero, hugging his dear pink hawthorns, is thus compared to Phèdre, a woman.

Let us recall that in a passage from the manuscript, eliminated in the typescript, Charlus, dining at the Grand Hotel with the footman, paid little attention to a waiter whose face was "tinted with the same modesty as Hippolyte's," and who "looked like a pink bush." That was the other side of this same image, its complement: Hippolyte is the pink bush that Charlus will not embrace.

The assimilation of the servant to a pink bush recalls the "vegetable immobility" of the "arborescent page" who, in *A l'ombre des jeunes filles en fleurs,* most specifically looks ahead to the homosexual leitmotiv that will be developed in the second stay at Balbec: "Beside the row of carriages, in front of the porch in which I stood waiting, was planted, like some shrub of a rare species, a young page who attracted the eye no less by the unusual and harmonious colouring of his hair than by his plant-like epidermis" (1:758–59; 2:66). After this comes a passage that elaborates on the idleness of the bellboys, "like chorus members who, even when they serve no purpose, remain onstage to round out the cast"; they fill "the lulls in the action, like those pupils of Mme de Maintenon who, dressed as young Israelites, provide an interlude whenever Esther or Joad leave the stage." Along the way, the motif of *Sodome et Gomorrhe* has been prepared, according to Proust's usual technique: "The general manager, the one who scared me so much, was planning to swell their ranks considerably the following year, for he 'thought on a big scale.' "

The vegetable metaphor and the Racine allegory are thus covers for a sexual metamorphosis or ambiguity, just as the meeting of the orchid and the bee in *Sodome et Gomorrhe I* unveils these same things in Charlus and Jupien. Whereas the hero hugging the hawthorns is assimilated to Phèdre, symmetrically the plantlike page boy is taken for Hippolyte, but an Hippolyte of a peculiar type and gender, a transvestized Hippolyte, since, as we have seen, "he was not a man," and if Monsieur de Charlus had approached "this magnificent elder brother of Eliacin, he would have seen immediately that his role was being played by a young lady from Saint-Cyr." This link between *Phèdre* and *Athalie,* which gradually generalizes transvestism to all of Racine's theater, is essential. But the image of Hippolyte as Eliacin's elder brother is yet another commonplace of Racine criticism, for the virility of the Amazon's son has often been questioned. It is a well-known fact that Racine invented Aricie partly to make Hippolyte guilty, but also to counter the insinuations of the dandies who found that a chaste hero strained the limits of belief. He was a woman! A princess, a "queen." Princess Marcel and Queen Hippolyte: a double inversion around the pink hawthorn or bush that may be taken as one wishes but, as we shall see, in Proust's eyes hugging it is the Racinian gesture *par excellence,* the gesture that confuses Baudelaire and Racine. Proust actually saw this scene onstage; what the novel is transposing is a *tableau vivant.* How did the Proustian allegory detach itself from the cliché of decadentism?

"Ses bras vaincus, jetés comme de vaines armes"

Esther and *Athalie* were often performed in the early part of this century. Sarah Bernhardt put on *Athalie* in 1920, but her 1905 production of *Esther*, revived in 1912, is much more germane to Proust's Racine.[23] In this production Sarah herself played with Racine's duplicity, his ambiguous position in between purity and impurity.

Reynaldo Hahn did the music for this production, as is recalled by a page from *Contre Sainte-Beuve*. The hero's mother has just quoted and applied to her son the lines Esther speaks in opposition to Mardochée's plan when she informs him that Assuérus' chambers are closed to him:

> Peut-il donc ignorer quelle sévère loi
> Aux timides mortels cache ici notre roi,
> Que la mort est le prix de tout audacieux
> Qui sans être appelé se présente à ses yeux?
> (*Esther* 1.2.191–92, 195–96, modified quotation)

> Can he then be unaware of the severe law
> Which here hides our king to timorous mortals,
> That death is the price for any bold person
> Who appears before his eyes without first being called?

> And Mama, thinking of *Esther*, her favorite play, timidly, as if fearing to chase people away, hums in a voice too loud and bold the divine melody that she feels to be close to her: "Il s'apaise, il pardonne," those divine choruses that Reynaldo Hahn wrote for *Esther*. He sang them for the first time at the little piano near the fireplace, while I was in bed; Papa had come in noiselessly and sat down on the easy chair and Mama remained standing and listening to the enchanting voice. Mama timidly tried a tune from the chorus, like one of the girls from Saint-Cyr trying out for Racine. And the beautiful lines of her Jewish face, imprinted with Christian gentleness and Jansenist courage, made her into Esther herself in this little family—almost convent—performance. . . . And Reynaldo's voice took up the words again, which were so applicable to my life with my parents:
>
> O douce paix
> Beauté toujours nouvelle,

Heureux le coeur épris de tes attraits!
O douce paix
O lumière éternelle,
Heureux le coeur qui ne te perd jamais!
(*Esther* 2.8.802–8)[24]

O gentle peace,
Beauty always new,
Happy the heart enamored of your charms!
O gentle peace,
O eternal light,
Happy the heart that never loses you!

The family scene is laden with emotion. *Esther* awakens the sympathy of the parents and the friend and reconciles Judaism and Christianity. *Esther* is like the soothing of divisions, the sublimation of heartbreak. But in spite of the intimacy of the tone, the reference to the history of theater is precise and alludes to a memorable production of the play.

Sarah Bernhardt chose to put on *Esther* in a stage facsimile of Louis XIV's court theater: a little stage was built above the big one, and here the king, Madame de Maintenon, and the audience of young girls take their seats during a prologue before the beginning of the play-within-a-play, with actors dressed up as Versailles courtiers.[25] This height of disguise perfectly illustrates the problems raised by productions of Racine at the turn of the century, divided as they were between purism and "authenticity." Sarah Bernhardt's *Esther* is all the more exemplary in its use of *mise en abyme* in that the production was put on at the same time as another *Esther,* not Racine's, which was being performed at the Odéon Theater: *Esther, princesse d'Israël,* by Dumas, subprefect of Mantes, and Leconte, a Judeo-Persian tragedy with Russian music and archaeological settings authenticated by Madame Dieulafoy.[26] To "the great accompaniment of Russian music, with settings from Monaco, archaeological costumes and dances which leave nothing to the imagination," the stage is reminiscent of the Grand Hotel of Balbec that Proust will associate with Assuérus' palace. "Assuérus' palace," Henry Bordeaux adds, "looks rather like the Palais-Royal during the Regency period, when commissioner of police Renaut did his best to have it classified as a place of ill repute."[27]

Between the Versailles Racine of Sarah Bernhardt and the Odéon's Oriental parody, here are the alternatives—as well as the dilemmas—of interpreting Racine's biblical plays which Emile Deschanel summed up in 1884:

> When *Esther* was put on at Saint-Cyr using minimal settings appropriate for Versailles, that was certainly better than performing the play, as is now done, using an architecture from the Persian—or perhaps Ninivite—museum. Indeed, it still remains to be seen if the affectation involved is at least redeemed by authenticity; for I believe that there is a great deal of arbitrariness in all this archaeological clutter. I am afraid we are being offered up Assyrian in the place of Persian.[28]

This dispute over the production of *Esther* is undoubtedly related to the debate among critics of the time about Racine's classicism or romanticism. The "authentic" *Esther,* Oriental or Judeo-Persian, against which Deschanel cautions his readers is the *Esther* of Paul de Saint-Victor, the *Esther* whose merits were excessively praised by Rustinlor, Jean Santeuil's teacher: " 'To *Esther,*' he said, 'I prefer two pages about *Esther* by Paul de Saint-Victor which are a pure masterpiece.' "[29] Moreover, Rustinlor upholds the same paradox about Racine's pure poetry as Bloch does in "Combray" but he attributes the paradox to Gautier: "His tragedies are certainly boring, but there are several beautiful lines in *Phèdre,* like "La fille de Minos et de Pasiphaé," which Gautier claimed was the only beautiful line he ever found in Racine" (JS 239).[30] Probably Jean no more concurs with Rustinlor's puzzling judgment than Marcel will be convinced by Bloch's, but he is still disturbed by his master's opinion of Saint-Victor, who was one of the first to have emphasized the Oriental side of *Esther* and even went so far as to see Assuérus as a caliph from the *Thousand and One Arabian Nights.*[31] Jules Lemaitre was to remember this comparison in his *Racine* of 1908, and the chapter about *Esther* seems to have provided inspiration for the Odéon tragedians in 1912: "It is a fairy tale, a voluptuous and bloody fairy tale, and a poem of Jewish fanaticism," warned Lemaitre in his efforts to lay to rest Taine's Cartesian image of Racine.[32] All of *Esther's* Orientalism is summed up by the association of Racine and the *Thousand and One Arabian Nights,* of which Proust was also very fond. Proust's hero in fact rereads the *Arabian Nights* in Balbec and compares Galland's and Mardrus' translations, several pages before the pleasure that Nissim Bernard takes in the corridors of the Grand Hotel provides an implicit allusion to the harem in *Bajazet* (2:864–66; 3:230).

Even though Paul de Saint-Victor helped bring Oriental productions of *Esther* into fashion, he still had high praise for the drama's pious gracefulness. The coexistence of cruelty and piety, which suggests that chastity always has its hidden underside, that impurity is a part of purity, was to remain an essential characteristic of the turn-of-the-century view of Racine. "*Esther* is, above all, a virginal tragedy. . . . Racine himself chose and trained the chaste actresses. All of them were fifteen years old, the age when childhood is at the height of its flower but youth has not yet bloomed."[33] This is the very same ambivalence—even down to the plant imagery—in the page boys at the Grand Hotel.

The critics of 1912 quite naturally compared the Oriental *Esther* at the Odéon with Sarah Bernhardt's Versailles-style *Esther;* both of them were considered a bit unsavory, but in different ways. Bernhardt carried purism so far that all the roles were played by women, as if transvestism were inevitable whatever one's approach to Racine, and she herself played Assuérus. As Henry Bidou writes in his review: "The first outburst of her anger was veiled, slowed down and charmed away by Monsieur Reynaldo Hahn's stage music, which it is difficult not to find inappropriate here. What a voice of tender reproach she has when she leans her head weakly back and says, 'C'est vous, Esther? Quoi! sans être attendue?' [It is you, Esther? What? You did not wait to be called?] How carefully she held the princess in her arms!"[34] Now by a remarkable coincidence, these lines spoken in a way so appealing to the audience by Assuérus—"the blond, delicate adolescent played by Sarah Bernhardt"[35]—before he goes on to assuage Esther's fears are the very lines that, in "Conversation avec Maman" from *Contre Sainte-Beuve,* the mother says as she enters her son's room, on the page following the allusion to Reynaldo Hahn's choruses for *Esther:*

"Let me tell you, I was afraid that I might have made a mistake, and that my little wolf might say to me: 'It is you Esther without being expected . . . / Without my orders someone is entering here. / What insolent mortal is looking for death?' "

"Why no, dear Mommy: 'What do you fear, am I not your brother? / Was it for you that such a stern decree was made?' "[36]

And these same lines will be echoed again when Albertine, made prisoner, dares enter Marcel's room: "I was afraid you'd say to me: 'What insolent mortal is looking for death?' " . . . "I replied in the same jesting vein: 'Was it for you that such a stern decree was made?' " (3:115; 3:120). Onstage, two women kissed, one of them disguised as a man, a blond delicate adolescent like the plantlike Hippolyte of Balbec or the arborescent page boy: a man who was a woman.

Transvestism is an endless theme in Proust, ranging from Elstir's painting of Odette dressed up as Miss Sacripant, to Sarah Bernhardt herself in the well-known role of *L'Aiglon,* who Charlus exclaimed—yet another blasphemy—was "trash" (2:1105; 3:456). Even as early as November 1888, in the "Impressions de théâtre"—a parody of Lemaitre and Sarcey—published in the *Revue lilas* at the Lycée Condorcet, Proust reviewed a production of *Athalie* at the Odéon in which "Mademoiselle Weber is admirable as Zacharie. . . . If I have time, I'll tell you more about this astonishing Weber in the next issue" (CSB 334–35). And behind this transvestism, which still goes back to the model of the young ladies of Saint-Cyr, all of Gomorrha comes into view, in the scene of a woman holding another woman in her arms and pressing her against herself, against her breasts, like the passage in which Albertine and Andrée dance together in the casino at Incarville (2:822–24; 3:190–91).

> Ses bras vaincus, jetés comme de vaines armes,
> Tout servait, tout parait sa fragile beauté.
>
> Her defeated arms, cast down like useless weapons,
> Everything heightened and ornamented her fragile beauty.

Proust quotes these two lines from the third stanza of Baudelaire's "Femmes damnées" several times, and he does so to compare Baudelaire to Racine. "Moreover Baudelaire is a great classical poet, and the strange thing is that his classicism of form grows in direct proportion to the licentiousness of his images," Proust states in the preface to Paul Morand's *Tendres Stocks,* a preface that was first published in the *Revue de Paris* in November 1920. And he finds the lines quoted above "like something out of *Britannicus*" (CSB 609).

Several months later, in an article on Baudelaire written in April 1921 and published in *La Nouvelle Revue Française* in June 1921, while the final proofs of *Le Côté de Guermantes II* and *Sodome et Gomorrhe I* were being corrected, Proust comes back to this idea of Baudelaire's classicism, thus reversing the terms of the idea voiced in 1823 by Stendhal in *Racine et Shakespeare:* "I shall state wholeheartedly that Racine was a romantic."[37] According to Stendhal, all classical works were also romantic in their own time: "Sophocles and Euripides were eminently romantic."[38] Romanticism and classicism no longer define two antithetical aesthetics, but simply distinguish the present from the past, a present destined to become past.[39] Emile Deschanel systematized this historical point of view in *Le Romantisme des classiques,* which did a great deal to modify interpretations of Racine in the final decades of the nineteenth century.[40] If Racine is a romantic, by the same token Baudelaire is a classicist. But Proust does not give a historical meaning to this statement; the romanticism of the classics and the classicism of the romantics are not indicative—or not simply indicative—of an evolution of tastes, but rather of an essential duality. Racine is still a romantic and Baudelaire has always been a classicist; Racine and Baudelaire are brothers. In Proust's view the preface to *Phèdre,* in which Racine claims he never wrote a more virtuous tragedy, is in reality more underhanded and secretive than Baudelaire's words at the beginning of *Les Fleurs du mal,* "Hypocrite lecteur, mon semblable, mon frère." The kinship between Racine and Baudelaire is so self-evident that when Rivière encourages Proust about his article he writes, in the same sentence, "I am prepared to have you sent the Grands Ecrivains edition of Racine and the most scientific Baudelaire I can find (I will find out about editions)."[41] Even though he is impatiently correcting his novel, Proust takes a few days to polish off what he calls "a huge and boring article on Baudelaire" and sees to it that the article will not come out before *Sodome et Gomorrhe I,* for a reason that will soon become clear.[42]

"And once one has accounted for their different time periods, nothing is as Baudelairean as *Phèdre,* nothing so worthy of Racine, or even of Malherbe, as *Les Fleurs du mal*" (CSB 627). Baudelaire and Racine are brothers, like Eliacin and Hippolyte; Baudelaire wrote like a classicist. Indeed, Proust makes the following comment about the two lines from "Femmes damnées" quoted above: "We know that these last lines refer to a woman being smothered by another woman's caresses. But if this were a description of Junie standing before Néron, would Racine speak any differently?" Junie standing before Néron is another sadistic scene, the most obvious of all of them in Racine's theater.[43] The downcast arms, like a *tableau vivant,* are emblematic of a princess of tragedy; Ovid's Phaedra declared her love to Hippolytus in this way: "Toward your knees I stretch out my queenly arms."[44] Baudelaire's most Racinian lines inevitably belong to the most depraved poems, the condemned pieces, like the "Femmes damnées: Delphine et Hippolyte." Delphine is also the name of one of Paul Morand's heroines, and Hippolyte, an ambivalent name in itself, is not Theseus' son here but rather the queen of the Amazons:

> A la pâle clarté des lampes languissantes,
> Sur de profonds coussins tout imprégnés d'odeur,
> Hippolyte rêvait aux caresses puissantes
> Qui levaient le rideau de sa jeune candeur.
>
> Elle cherchait. . .
>
> In the pale light of the languid lamps,
> On plush cushions permeated with scent,
> Hippolyta was dreaming of powerful caresses
> Which raised the curtain of her young innocence.
>
> She was searching. . .

He was a woman!

Gisèle's Essay

Gisèle's amusing essay in *A l'ombre des jeunes filles en fleurs* is another sign of the importance of *Esther* and its choruses in the world of Proust's imagination. Gisèle has sent Albertine the composition from her graduation examinations in which she had two subjects to choose from: "Sophocles, from the Shades, writes to

Racine to console him for the failure of *Athalie*," and "Suppose that, after the first performance of *Esther*, Mme de Sévigné is writing to Mme de La Fayette to tell her how much she regretted her absence" (1:972; 2:264–65). Gisèle has chosen the first topic and Albertine reads her essay, after which Andrée conducts a correction session.

In a letter of January 31, 1916, Proust thanks Marcelle Larivière, a niece of his housekeeper Céleste Albaret, for giving him two outlines for Gisèle's essay, and he concludes with this compliment: "There are few male students who could do anything nearly as good" (*Corr.* 15:43). Even if we attribute this touch of misogyny to the still rudimentary state of female education around the time of the First World War, there remains much to be said about these four pages of Gisèle's essay, the two subjects, the composition itself, Andrée's correction session, and finally Proust's pastiche. The learned allusions suggested by Andrée would also have to be gone into—Garnier's *Les Juives* and Montchrestien's *Aman*, both of which made use of choruses before *Esther* and *Athalie*—as would the critics that Andrée recommends, Merlet and Sainte-Beuve, and especially Deltour and Gasc-Desfossés. Suffice it to say that Gisèle's essay, with its precise references, is one of those rare examples of academic culture (to which Baudelaire did not yet belong at the end of the nineteenth century) in a writer who was indifferent to it and in a novel that generally seems far more affected by the bourgeois culture of the family and of the *Revue des Deux Mondes*. But Racine, classical art, and the theater in general provide a valuable point of contact between the two cultures at the end of the nineteenth century, one that is not free of conflict, since Proust went to school, as we have seen, during a transitional period in Racine criticism.

In his composition class Proust wrote a paper on the traditional comparison of Corneille and Racine: "He who is passionately in love with Corneille may not be averse to a certain amount of conceit. To be passionately in love with Racine is to run the risk of having too much of what we in France call taste, and which sometimes causes so much distaste" (CSB 329). This judgment, borrowed from Sainte-Beuve, smacks of the romantics' prejudice against the narrowness of Racine's Versailles-style "bienséance." We should point out that already at this early stage, Proust defends Racine by emphasizing that Racinian tragedy is an art of dissimulation in which the veil of elegance and refined manners hides an intense "horror." After first concurring with the old criticism of Racine's weakness for elegance and "complicated niceties," Proust uses the following transition to get to his argument about the horror of Racine's theater: "If these days critics claim to have discovered the fierce realism behind Racine's tragedies, can they turn us against it?" (CSB 331). Between the old and the new critical school, Proust's position is still unclear; perhaps it is blurred by the mechanical dialectics of the essay. But what is this new critical school that has just transformed the perception of Racine's tragedy and discovered the horror and passion hiding underneath the perfection of its form?

It is made up of critics like the above-mentioned Emile Deschanel, in his series entitled *Le Romantisme des classiques,* two volumes of which, published in 1884, were devoted to Racine; or Victor Stapfer, who in the same year shook the pompous commonplaces about the Versailles Racine or the Cartesian Racine out of their complacency with his *Racine et Victor Hugo.*[45] But above all Ferdinand Brunetière is the one who overthrew the reigning image of Racine, and he did this with only two articles: his review of Deschanel's work in the *Revue des Deux Mondes,*[46] and an earlier review of a new edition of *Les Ennemis de Racine au dix-septième siècle* by the same Deltour that Andrée wanted Albertine to mention in her examination essays.[47] Deltour was also a school inspector, and it so happens that he was the last one to observe the classes of Proust's composition teacher, Gaucher, in 1886, and was prevented from visiting Gaucher's classes a second time only by the teacher's death during the school year 1887–88, the year Proust, in his paper on Corneille and Racine, alluded to this new critical school that was making a fierce realist out of Racine.[48]

It was in speaking of Deltour's work that Brunetière for the first time formulated his theory—which was to have a bright future—of Racine's modernity as a painter of sensuous jealousy:

> I will tell you what may appear to be a monstrous thing, but a true one nonetheless if one thinks about it: those four great poets (Molière, Racine, Boileau, La Fontaine), and along with them the prose writers Bossuet and La Bruyère, are the naturalists of the seventeenth century.[49]

Brunetière seizes the opportunity to attack Zola and nineteenth-century naturalism on the pretext that true modernity is found in the neoclassicism inherited from Racine. But as tendentious as this idea may appear, it is still quite remarkable:

> Change the names, it is a vulgar story, it is the story of all of us. Yesterday some Roxane murdered the Bajazet that was cheating on her, opened the gas jets and died of asphyxiation on top of his dead body. Tomorrow Phèdre will jump into the Seine, and every day, in every part of the world, there is some Titus who is breaking the heart of some Bérénice.[50]

Racine's realism, Brunetière will later explain, does not come from any similarity of his theater to court morality, but rather in its depiction of women, in its immorality.[51]

A second school essay, or rather an outline for one, provides further evidence for the slippage that takes place during the years of Proust's adolescence between a gallant and courtly Racine and a passionate Racine who by the same token himself becomes feminine. The topic was: "Can one truthfully say that in Racine's tragedies the masculine roles have always been background roles?"[52] Proust planned to list a number of fashionable ideas: "The dominant quality in Racine is sensitivity."[53] He is therefore the "premier and infinitely varied painter of female love."[54] But in a second part that would have taken the other side of the question, Proust planned to develop this argument: "Racine's female sensitivity was a positive hindrance to his depiction of masculine energies." His men are "charming," "sensitive," "tender": they are not men.[55]

Although we should not take these old school compositions too seriously, there is no way around the fact that the "female sensitivity" the young Proust perceived in Racine, thanks to Brunetière and Lemaitre, remains a recurrent theme of the *Recherche*. Albertine and Andrée comment on Gisèle's essay, scholarly rhetoric is parodied, but Racine is still Racine: Albertine "was sweating profusely," but Andrée "preserved the unruffled calm of a female dandy" (1:976; 2:268). A *female dandy!* This is the Racinian creature *par excellence* and at the same time the androgyne of the turn of the century: Sarah Bernhardt playing Assuérus, the arborescent Hippolyte of Balbec. Hippolyte was literally a "chasseur," a hunter, but also, like the *garçons* of the Grand Hotel, figuratively a "chasseur," a page boy. In a famous comment Jules Lemaitre made of Hippolyte a "young hunter-monk" [*moine chasseur*] who is an habitué of "catechisms of perseverance,"[56] a choirboy, like the *garçons* of Balbec in the leitmotiv of *Sodome*. But Hippolyte, disdainful of power and women, handsome and fierce, proud and impervious, "traînait tous les coeurs après soi" [dragged all hearts after him]; he is also a lion, a dandy. Saint-Loup has the ambiguity of the lion when the hero meets him for the first time in *A l'ombre des jeunes filles en fleurs:* "Because of his 'tone,' because he had the insolent manner of a young 'blood' [lion], above all because of his extraordinary good looks, some even thought him effeminate-looking, though without holding it against him since they knew how virile he was and how passionately fond of women" (1:783; 2:88–89). But is this not the first veiled allusion to Saint-Loup's true nature?

A female dandy is a contradiction in terms, a creature against nature that once again refers us back to Baudelaire, never very far from Racine:

> Woman is the opposite of Dandy. . . . Woman is *natural,* that is, abominable. By the same token she is vulgar, that is, the opposite of the Dandy.[57]

An alternate title Baudelaire had thought of giving to *Les Fleurs du mal* was *Les Lesbiennes.* The *Jeunes filles en fleurs,* the gang or chorus of adolescent girls at Balbec, will go on to become *Gomorrhe:* transvestism overflows from all sides.

"He's a woman!"

Thus, after Brunetière, Racine became a deranged and even an immoral naturalist, but the critic for the *Revue des Deux Mondes* was not quite the inventor of this cliché. By his emphasis on the passions at work in *Britannicus,* Louis Veuillot had already cast doubt on the idea that Racine's plays are peopled by courtisans whose ways are as refined as their language is polished.[58] And even before the romantic onslaught, Joseph Joubert was already saying catty things about Racine: "Certainly to be admired for making the most bourgeois feelings and the most mediocre passions poetic."[59] Brunetière basically did nothing more than develop this aphorism. Joubert also hinted at Racine's femininity: "Effeminate charms. Perhaps they are in Racine. There are in many speeches women's voices rather than men's voices." And he goes on: "The voice of wisdom holds to the middle, like a heavenly voice of indeterminate sex."[60] But the single name most often associated with the revival of Racine criticism at the turn of the century is that of Lemaitre, whose work was known to Proust as early as 1888, when Proust did pastiches of him in composition class.

Twenty years later, in his notes about Nerval in *Contre Sainte-Beuve,* Proust opposes Lemaitre's idea that the beginning of *Sylvie* is "traditional, very French" (CSB 235).[61] Lemaitre's judgment is given on the last page of his *Racine* of 1908, when he compares Nerval and Racine. Here is Proust's comment: "What could be less Racinian than this [Nerval's poetry]?. . . and when I say that it does not in the least affect my deep admiration for him [Lemaitre], it takes nothing away from his marvelous, incomparable book on Racine" (CSB 236). In his final lecture, Lemaitre draws his conclusions about Racine's theater: a theater of passions, of "elementary forces" and "primitive instincts," a theater as "brutal" as its author. Since women are "greater slaves to instinct and passion than men," " 'Racine's theater will be feminine, as Corneille's was virile' (Lanson). 'Women are placed in the foreground. From Racine on,' and all the way up to the present time, 'woman reigns in literature' (Lanson)."[62] Lemaitre reveals his sources. Indeed there is nothing very original in this grand conclusion, which comes only several pages before the section on Nerval that Proust will take issue with. Lemaitre makes a broad summary of the chapter in Gustave Lanson's *Histoire de la littérature française* that deals with Racine and his "passionate and true tragedy." In fact Lanson discusses nothing other than the topic given in Proust's composition class: "Racine was a remarkable painter of the female soul. . . . His men are weaker."[63]

But these borrowed phrases reproduced by Lemaitre do not actually belong to Lanson either. Lanson is himself copying, almost word for word, Brunetière's original article about Deschanel's *Le Romantisme des classiques.* Both the book and the article broke ground for the theory that was to allow Proust to match Racine and Baudelaire: "Today's *classics* are yesterday's *romantics* and today's *romantics* are tomorrow's *classics,*" which in Bruntière's spicy style turned into "the boldest *romantics* make the most illustrious *classics,* just as the worst cads, or so the saying goes, make the best family men."[64] Brunetière resolutely maintained Racine's modernity: he found energy and ferocity "underneath the superficial elegance of the tragedies."[65] And he clearly linked realism and feminization in tragedy: tragedy "is humanized, or, if you wish, feminized, and its feminization marks an era not only in the history of French theater, but also in the history of European literature."[66] According to Brunetière "since Racine's tragedy woman has reigned" in modern literature,[67] a phrase appropriated, as we have seen, by Lanson; Racine is the initiator of an entire "literature of passion and love."[68] Brunetière, it would appear, is doing nothing more than plagiarizing his own 1879 article on Deltour.

How did this image of Racine as a realist and a portrayer of feminine violence develop up until Proust's time? Quite simply, the inventor of woman in literature himself came to be suspected of femininity. If he wrote so perfectly about women, there must have been something of woman within him. "Racine, the only woman in the arts who ever had genius,"[69] André Suarès was to assert, lighting into Racine in the same spirit as the romantics. In another vein, Péguy's *Victor-Marie, comte Hugo* includes a series of remarkable notes on Corneille and Racine, on the "cruelty of tenderness" in that "master of cruelty," Racine, and on the "innocent cruelty," the "girlish but grown-up cruelty" of heroines like Iphigénie.[70] "Corneille's most hardened old criminals have a purer heart than Racine's youngest adolescents (especially the girls)."[71] No one has ever managed to describe the hidden stores of maliciousness in the most chaste of Racine's young heroines as well as Péguy, and he even goes so far as to make this statement, consistent with Freud's psychology and the emergence of the concept of adolescence as an intermediate and ambiguous age: "There is perhaps no other place where we can see the touching but cruel problem of the innocence—or purported innocence—of childhood better than in Racine."[72] Of course Péguy had to come to terms with the commonplace of Racine's femininity, and here he is as biting as ever: "And his women are naturally crueller than his men, which is saying a great deal. Or rather to go to the heart of the matter, his men are women, they have all suffered from female contamination of one kind or another. They are all emasculated, and what we find in them is precisely feminine cruelty."[73] Péguy made no bones about his preference for Corneille's generosity and virility as opposed to Racine's effeminate "sadism," but if he spoke so convincingly about Racine—just as he never forgave Racine for speaking so convincingly about women—must there not have been in him as well an element of femininity ready to come to the surface?

In Proust the same idea takes shape, albeit without the masculine protest; Proust goes so far as to call Racine a "hysterical woman of genius" in the preface to *Tendres Stocks:* "And certainly a hysterical woman of genius thrashed around inside Racine, kept under control by a superior intelligence, and in his tragedies she undoubtedly simulated for him the ebbs and flows of passion, and managed to capture its endless tossings with a completeness and a perfection that have never been equaled" (CSB 614).[74] According to Edmond de Goncourt, Phèdre was "the great hysterical woman of legend."[75] Proust takes the plunge and puts the hysterical woman inside of Racine himself, like a demon, an inspiring muse.

The real originality of Proust's Racine, otherwise close to Brunetière's or Péguy's, stems from the repeated association of Racine and Baudelaire; this obviously could not come from Brunetière, who was quite unsympathetic toward the author of *Les Fleurs du mal.* Proust compares the two poets with growing frequency from the autumn of 1920 on, but even as early as 1905, speaking about an "unfair" article on Baudelaire by Lemaitre, he wrote: "Has it been said that [Baudelaire] is a decadent? Nothing is further from the truth. Baudelaire is not even a romantic. He writes like Racine. I could quote you twenty examples." Proust works backward from decadent to romantic to classic, and incorporates Baudelaire in his inversion of Deschanel's thesis on the romanticism of the classics. And the allusion to Racine immediately leads him to add: "Moreover he is a Christian poet and that's why he speaks constantly about sin, just like Bossuet and Massillon. Let's put it this way: like all Christians who are also hysterical . . . he was familiar with the sadism of blasphemy."[76] Sin and hysteria, blasphemy and sadism: the entire complex of *Sodome et Gomorrhe* is prefigured here. Racine and Baudelaire are one and the same.

In fact in his defense of Baudelaire against Lemaitre, Proust comes up with all the arguments—and even the precise terms—of an old article by Anatole France.[77] In 1889 France had come to the poet's rescue when Brunetière called him a "flophouse Satan" and a "boarding-house Beelzebub" after the first publication of Baudelaire's diaries in 1887.[78] Although he admitted that Baudelaire was "rather perverse and unhealthy," France still thought he was a "very Christian poet": "Baudelaire is not the poet of vice; he is the poet of sin, which is altogether different."[79] In support of his hypothesis France already quotes the third stanza of "Femmes damnées," "ses bras jetés comme de vaines armes": "What in contemporary poetry . . . is more beautiful than this stanza, a finely wrought portrait of voluptuous weariness?. . . Is there anything in Alfred de Vigny himself that is more magnificient than this curse full of piety which the poet casts over the 'damned women'?"[80] Proust remembers this in his 1921 article about Baudelaire, and he even shows a slight reserve: "I must say that I do not absolutely concur with the judgment which I once heard given by Monsieur Anatole France, that this is the most beautiful thing Baudelaire ever wrote" (CSB 630).

Like Proust, France made of Baudelaire a poet of the people, using "Le Vin des chiffonniers" as evidence. Last but not least, France found Baudelaire to be basically a classical poet: "And take note, in passing, of how classical and traditional Baudelaire's poetry is, how full it is."[81] The coincidence is striking, and allows us to date the beginning of the reevaluation of Baudelaire, who had been identified with decadentism since Gautier's remarks in the first posthumous edition of *Les Fleurs du mal* (1868). By an exaggeration in the other direction, Baudelaire's classicism was to become a commonplace by the turn of the century. But as far as France—and ultimately Proust—is concerned, the most obvious result of the parallel reevaluations of Racine and Baudelaire is that they meet each other halfway.

After the war Proust, who is not free of ulterior motives, constantly used Baudelaire's similarity to Racine to identify Baudelaire as a classical poet. Thus, in his response to a 1920 questionnaire concerning classicism and romanticism, he reiterates Deschanel's earlier argument for bringing the two terms closer together: "These days we take [the same pleasure] in reading Baudelaire as in reading Racine," which brings us to this extremely paradoxical statement:

"But the style of the condemned poems, which is exactly the style of the tragedies, perhaps even goes beyond it in its nobility" (CSB 617). This argument, developed in the 1921 article on Baudelaire, is repeated in a questionnaire about literary "schools" early in 1922—"Baudelaire, once his conviction has been reviewed, is in good company with Racine"—and brought to its culmination with the comment: "Last slight difference [between Baudelaire and Racine]: Racine is more immoral" (CSB 641).

If we now look at the events of late 1920 and 1921, *Le Côte de Guermantes I* came out in October 1920, and Paul Souday's review of it in *Le Temps* described Proust as "feminine," which hurt his feelings and moved him to make this reply:

> Just as I am about to publish *Sodome et Gomorrhe* and no one will dare take up my defense because I will be talking about Sodom, before the fact (and with no unkind intentions, I feel sure) you are paving the way for all kinds of cruel remarks by calling me "feminine." From feminine to effeminate there is but a short step to take. Those who have seconded me in my duels will tell you if I have the spinelessness of an effeminate man.[82]

Proust tackles the theme of homosexuality: *Sodome et Gomorrhe I,* with its revelation of Charlus' and Jupien's homosexuality in the rather theatrical scene of their first meeting, is sent to Gallimard in January 1921 and put on sale alongside *Le Côté de Guermantes II* in May 1921. *Sodome et Gomorrhe II* is being revised in the typescript, and Proust is refining and redistributing the leitmotiv of Racine's choruses. It is in these circumstances that he emphasizes the kinship between Baudelaire and Racine, and he gives the impression of trying to lighten the burden of the vice-laden Baudelaire by placing it on the pious Racine. It is as if Proust himself, about to publish pages as daring as anything in *Les Fleurs du mal,* were thinking of a possible precedent he could use in his own defense.

Let us recall Proust's theory about Baudelaire, reported by André Gide in a diary entry of May 14, 1921 (shortly after *Sodome I* went on sale): "He told me of his conviction that Baudelaire was a homosexual: 'the way he speaks of Lesbos, and even the need to speak of it, would already be enough to convince me of it.' "[83] Baudelaire, too, was a woman-man. In the Baudelaire article from the same period, Proust raises the question more subtly: "How could [Baudelaire] have been so especially interested in lesbians that he even wanted to use their name for the title of his splendid work?" (CSB 632). Proust is perhaps wrong about the effect this title produced on its first readers, as the earlier meaning of "Lesbiennes" (capitalized), female inhabitants of Lesbos, was still frequent—at least if we put our faith in the dictionaries of the time—as opposed to the modern sense of the word. But dictionaries are always some time behind current usage, and it is doubtful Baudelaire would have thought of using this title if it had had only a geographical meaning. The title would probably have been less provocative than Proust or the modern reader might believe,[84] but still obviously ambiguous. At any rate Proust suggests an explanation for Baudelaire's interest in lesbians by means of a comparison with Vigny. Anatole France considered Vigny "the most Racinian of the romantics," whereas Proust declared at the beginning of his article: "I take Baudelaire—along with Alfred de Vigny—to be the greatest poet of the nineteenth century" (CSB 618). The comparison between the two poets was therefore to be expected.

In Proust's eyes, Vigny's attitude is more understandable than Baudelaire's, and simpler as well. Believing he has been betrayed by Marie Dorval, he separates the two sexes for all eternity:

> It is understandable that in the disappointment and jealousy of his love, he wrote: "La Femme aura Sodome et l'Homme aura Gomorrhe" [Woman will have Sodom and Man will have Gomorrha]. But at least it is as irreconcilable enemies that he sets them far apart from each other: "Et se jetant de loin un regard irrité, / Les deux sexes mourront chacun de son côté" [And looking at each other with irritation from afar, / The sexes will die apart from each other]. For Baudelaire it is not at all the same thing. (CSB 632–33)

Proust, strangely enough, used the first line as the epigraph to *Sodome et Gomorrhe I* and put the second one into the body of the text (2:638; 3:17), whereas in fact the two lines state the exact opposite of the love-hate relationships that fascinate him and become a major theme in the latter part of the *Recherche*. Even if Vigny provides the epigraph, it is rather in Baudelaire that Proust recognizes his own curiosity about Sodom and Gomorrha: the confusion of the sexes, the creature who is at the same time man and woman, like Albertine or Morel, Baudelaire or Racine.

> In the later sections of my work (and not in *Sodome I* which has just come out), I have entrusted this "link" between Sodom and Gomorrha to a brute, Charles Morel (moreover this role is usually given out to brutes), and it would appear that Baudelaire "allotted" this very role to himself in a very special way. How interesting it would be to know why Baudelaire chose this role and how he carried it out. What is understandable in Charles Morel remains a deep mystery about the author of *Les Fleurs du mal.* (CSB 633)[85]

There is a mystery behind Baudelaire, a mystery behind Racine. How could they turn themselves into women to such a degree that they could write *Phèdre* and *Les Fleurs du mal?* Still, in early 1921, Proust phrases a compliment to a poet in this way: "How have you managed to revive Racine's miracle of becoming a woman, as he did in his tragedies?"[86]

The dream of being a woman, a woman-man, to write like Baudelaire or Racine: beyond Proust's profanation of a text that was sacred to his mother, beyond his invocation—during the very time he was readying *Sodome et Gomorrhe* for publication—of a man who was a shrewd innovator in disguise and who figured out a way to dress up vice so well in the ideal of pure poetry that he usually didn't get caught, this is perhaps the enigma, the dream that goes to the heart of Proust's Racine and lends weight to the burlesque leitmotiv of *Esther* and *Athalie* in *Sodome et Gomorrhe*. But is this not simply another turn-of-the-century commonplace? Once again, the answer is both yes and no.

In a 1907 review of Anna de Noailles' *Les Eblouissements,* Proust already wonders about the enigma of the writer's gender. He alludes to the paintings of Gustave Moreau, who often "tried to paint that abstraction, the Poet"; "one wonders, upon closer inspection, if this poet is not a woman" (CSB 534). "Perhaps the painter was trying to say that the poet contains all of humanity within himself, and thus must possess the tenderness of a woman." At this point Proust takes off from Moreau's hesitation over the poet's gender and muses: "I don't know if Gustave Moreau understood to what extent this lovely conception of a woman Poet could have the indirect result of one day renewing the economy of the poetic work itself" (CSB 535). Unlike man, who does not himself belong to the universe of poetry, who is not himself poetic, unlike the "man poet who is ashamed of his body," who is condemned to "invent a character," to "make a woman speak" if he is to gain access to the realm of poetry, the woman poet—in particular Madame de Noailles, to whom the compliment is addressed, but the observation goes far beyond its immediate context–has the unique privilege of being "at the same time poet and heroine," of being able to express "directly what she has felt, without the artifice of any fiction, and with a more touching truth" (CSB 536). The female body is present on every page of a woman poet's book, this body of woman that has been ruling over literature since Racine, but this time it appears, as Mallarmé might have said, such as eternity has changed it into itself, without mediation, without interpretation: "Both the author and the subject of her poetry, she can then be, in a single person, Racine and his princess, Chénier and his young captive."

When Flaubert said, "Madame Bovary is myself," he summed up this entire debate without making such an issue of it, and the indulgence Proust shows the Comtesse de Noailles is probably slightly ridiculous. Is there anything less controversial than the decadents' fine phrases about androgyny and the allusions to Gustave Moreau? Yet how can we fail to take Proust seriously when the familiar rhetoric finds its resolution in this ideal that man cannot reach: *to be, in a single person, Racine and his princess?* The condition of authentic writing—being simultaneously one and the other, man and woman, hero and author, to be in between the two—would appear to be nothing more than a flight of fancy.

Nevertheless, when Proust comes back to Racine and Baudelaire after 1920, once his own book is done, the impasse is unblocked, or rather eliminated. Baudelaire was, in a single person, Racine and his princess, Chénier and his captive. Racine himself was also the princess, both poet and heroine, man and woman, like Hippolyte or the female dandy: "The Dandy must constantly aspire to the sublime; he must live and sleep in front of a mirror," Baudelaire said.[87] Paradoxically the fascination for Lesbos or Gomorrha is evidence of a will to give man back to literature; like a mirror man holds up to himself, Gomorrha opens up his body to poetry. We are no longer dealing with the decadents' wild speculations about hermaphrodites, or with the transposition of young men into budding young women, or with Albertine as a cover for Agostinelli, but rather with the fleeting metamorphoses and endless fluctuations that make every body both a masculine body and a feminine body, and that make the body's duality present in writing as early as the opening pages of "Combray":

> Sometimes, too, as Eve was created from a rib of Adam, a woman would be born during my sleep from some strain in the position of my thighs. Conceived from the pleasure I was on the point of consummating, she it was, I imagined, who offered me that pleasure. My body, conscious that its own warmth was permeating hers, would strive to become one with her, and I would awake.
>
> (1:4–5; 1:4–5)

A la recherche du temps perdu is entirely under the sign of this experience. Proust's originality is in the image of Racine's inventiveness, or, to parody Brunetière, it is since Proust's novel—through the discovery of the fraternity between Baudelaire and Racine, through the simultaneous understanding of their shared duality—that man and his body have reigned, or at least been present, in literature.

4

Huysmans; or, Reading the Italian Renaissance Perversely

There is no dearth of shared motifs linking Proust and Huysmans, one of the writers who best represent the spirit of the fin-de-siècle. First of all Robert de Montesquiou, who was one of the models for des Esseintes in Huysmans' *A rebours*, was also to become a source of inspiration for Proust's Baron de Charlus. Both writers thought highly of Gothic art, and more specifically cathedrals, although this interest of Proust's owes more to Ruskin and Emile Mâle than to Huysmans. Still, Proust is not unfamiliar with *La Cathédrale*, which is in fact the only work of Huysmans he quotes, and perhaps even the only one he knew. Then there is the Abbé Mugnier, whom both men saw socially; aesthetic idolatry and the taste for profanation that mark their works; and any number of other points of intersection.

Unfortunately, none of this takes us very far. Did Proust even ever read *A rebours?* We cannot say for sure. It is for this reason that I will focus on a particular point of intersection—and also of separation—between the two writers: the perverse way they have of reading Italian painters before Raphael. Probably this was not specific to them but rather belongs to the decadent mode, the sensibility of the fin-de-siècle: Swinburne and Walter Pater propagated it in England, the Goncourt brothers and Péladan were to do the same in France. Botticelli's "Primavera" is the archetypal painting that at the time formed the object of a cult worship.[1] But our aim here will be to emphasize how Huysmans and Proust give a personal flavor to this artistic commonplace.

In *Certains,* Huysmans spends some time interpreting a painting that hangs in the Louvre and that he attributes to Bianchi; from it he feels "the gentle breath of delicious emanations, sorrowful solicitations; insidious sacrileges, disturbing prayers."[2] The panel—Huysmans calls it a canvas—is now attributed to Marmitta.[3] Huysmans first offers a description of the painting suitable for a catalogue: the Virgin, seated on her throne, holds the Infant Jesus on her lap, flanked by St. Benoît and St. Quentin, an old man and a young man. Two angels at the foot of the throne are holding musical instruments. What interests Huysmans most is the young man, "clad in armor, like a soldier" (*Certains,* 221): "How can we define the troubling figure of St. Quentin, an ephebe of indeterminate sex, a hybrid of mysterious beauty, with long, dark-brown hair parted in the middle of the forehead and flowing down onto his iron-clad throat. . . . You might think it was the traditional costume of Bradamante or St. George" (*Certains,* 222–23). This is a cross between Bradamante, the Amazon from Ariosto's *Orlando furioso,* one of the boldest warriors in Charlemagne's camp, and St. George, the Christian Perseus with the face of a lad; just as when the hero of *A la recherche du temps perdu* sees the portrait of Odette dressed up as Miss Sacripant and hesitates between "a somewhat boyish girl" and an "effeminate, vicious and pensive youth" (1:908; 2:205).

In his interpretation Huysmans immediately gets carried away in the direction of androgyny or hermaphroditism, a commonplace of the decadent movement with its fondness for ambiguous bodies:

> And the saint's entire look is dreamlike. Those tomboy shapes, with a faint development of the hips; that girlish neck, its flesh as white as the pith of an elder tree; that mouth, with the lips of a despoiler; that slender waist; those inquisitive fingers carelessly resting on a weapon; that swelling of the breast-plate, which bulges out where the breasts would be and protects the disclosed sweep of the chest; that piece of underclothing which is just visible under the armpit,

> peeking out from between the shoulder-plate and the neck-plate; even that bit of girlish blue ribbon tied under the chin: how not to be obsessed by all of these things? This androgyne with his ingratiating beauty seems to have consented to all of the wild goings-on of Sodom. (*Certains*, 223–24)

This rambling, we must admit, is in no way novel. It is reminiscent of the hackneyed interpretation of Signorelli's angels, or of Leonardo da Vinci's St. John, in the Louvre. What gives it beauty is the way Huysmans draws attention to the armor and its chinks, to the contrast between the different materials, the hardness of the armor as opposed to the downiness of the flesh. And what makes the passage exemplary is that Huysmans does not stop there, with the cliché of the feminine ephebe—"a hermaphrodite with an iron breast-plate" (*Certains*, 225)—but rather joins to it the other commonplace of the decadent movement, incest, which he suspects because of the likeness of the two figures. This is what he imagines:

> From St. Benoît, the father, from Mary and St. Quentin, the sister and the brother, and from the little angel dressed in pink playing the viola d'amore, the child born from the diabolical coupling of these Saints. . . . The son and the daughter have given in to the temptations of incest and judge life to be too short to expiate the terrifying delights of their crime. (*Certains*, 226)

But why would the fruit of the incestuous union of the Virgin and the saint be only the angel and not the newborn, the Infant Jesus himself? Perhaps because of the sterility often associated with incest, or the inevitable ambiguity about the angel's gender; or possibly Huysmans retains a modicum of respect in spite of his profanity. At any rate, the evocation of lust leads to a feeling of sin, to a form of grief in which desire and pleasure are never fully separable.

This guided tour of perversion is complete once we have mentioned the smug anticipation of the young martyr's torments, which will destroy the beauty of his body, along with the stress placed on the gaze of the saint and the Virgin, which in both cases is laden with vice and sin: "light eyes, but of a dull blue color which covers over an underlayer of mire," "eyes burnt by the temptations to which they have succumbed" (*Certains*, 223), "limpid on the surface and cloudy underneath" (*Certains*, 226). These are the eyes of perverse adolescence, of a form of beauty that bears corruption and death within it, a mesmerizing beauty since Baudelaire; the decadents can conceive of no other kind of beauty than this, with its contradictory union of tenderness and impurity, virginity and lechery, chastity and vice. Sadism and Catholicism are intertwined here in a way that is quite recognizable, in the sensual enjoyment of blasphemy.

To Huysmans' eyes Bianchi's painting, like Marmitta's, is typical of a state of transition between the Middle Ages and the Renaissance: it represents pre-Raphaelism. "The sullen mediocrities of Raphael" (*Certains*, 220), exclaims Huysmans, are about to denature Christian art. Later on, the writer was to make open condemnations of "hateful Raphael," whose "sickly-sweet Madonas" have led to the "horrible idiocies of the vendors of sacred objects on the Rue Saint-Sulpice and the Rue Madame."[4] In Bianchi's work, "the auburn, flexuous perversity of a Renaissance is already beginning to spring forth from the rigid whiteness of the Middle Ages" (*Certains*, 227). Huysmans was to put it differently after his conversion, but the idea is the same: "the paganism of the Renaissance infected religious painting with its virus of eroticism and soiled—at the same time as Catholicism—its way of expressing itself in art."[5] In Perugino, Raphael's master, Huysmans perceived the dawning "of Madonas and Saints who are not Madonas and Saints" but rather "Apollos and Aphrodites,"[6] and he burnt the idols he had adored: "What is there in almost all of these Primitives, except for Fra Angelico? Sodomy. Everywhere you look you see ephebes with long golden hair, dull complexions and droopy eyes, enigmatic androgynes, mawkish and unsexed beings!"[7] Huysmans preferred Flemish painters, who were truly mystical, and when he came back to the subject of Bianchi, he was utterly discreet on the subject of St. Quentin: "In Bianchi's panel, so strange, so captivating, with its two standing figures looking at you with their light eyes, forever sorrowful, the figure of Jesus is faint: he is a ball of fat with joints, a doll with a lifeless smile, a kid just like any other kid, caught in the split-second he is not screaming."[8]

Androgyny and incest—read sterility and expiation—are the two secrets, indeed the only secrets involved in reading the pre-Raphaelites perversely, and they are brought together in Huysmans' explanation of the St. Quentin of Marmitta.

There is one painter among many who is indistinguishable from these two major themes of the decadent movement: Gustave Moreau, whose men and women, like his virgins and youths, are indistinct, like adolescent brothers and sisters. Proust, as we have seen, praised Gustave Moreau precisely for his indecisive representation of the Poet, who is at the same time a man and a woman (see chapter 3),[9] and Huysmans' pages about Moreau in *A rebours, L'Art moderne,* and *Certains* already sketched out this idea.

Salomé, whom Moreau endlessly reproduced—des Esseintes was said to own a version—represents the contradictory union of chastity and vice better than any other heroine: her very name has come to stand for the lecherous virgin. In fact Huysmans reads Bianchi's painting *like* a Gustave Moreau painting from which, as he puts it in *Certains,* there emanates "a feeling of spiritual and habitual onanism in a chaste flesh; the feeling of a virgin housed in a body of solemn grace; of a soul worn out by lonely ideas and secret thoughts" (*Certains,* 19). Félicien Rops, according to Huysmans, is fascinated by the same conjunction of contraries, his art being nothing but one long development of this single paradox: "the only thing that is really obscene is chaste people" (*Certains,* 78). Sadism and Catholicism come together once again in the cult of strange, mystical love and sexual deficiency. Gustave Moreau—this is not a coincidence—made a copy of the Bianchi panel, in pencil and watercolor. The copy was never completed, but the most fully fleshed-out figure—this is really not a coincidence—is St. Quentin, the Antinous with the breastplate and with Mary's blue ribbon.[10]

Albertine's Mackintosh

The passage from Proust that I will be putting in tandem with Huysmans' discussion is not taken from *A la recherche du temps perdu;* it belongs to a sketchbook for *Sodome et Gomorrhe* dating from the beginning of the First World War, Cahier 46. After the invention of Albertine, this sketchbook outlines the second visit to Balbec. The hero is off searching for Albertine in a nearby resort, but he cannot find her.

> After a moment she arrived. On her way back from a bicycle ride, she was wearing a long mackintosh, in which I had often seen her go by as if dressed in armor, for it was as tight around the legs as a molded thigh-plate and covered her breast with an impenetrable shield. Now loosened and half undone, it made her look like a young warrior who lays down her arms and whose cheeks, jutting out from the mackintosh, sweet, fresh, and pink, would be all the sweeter for me to kiss as the mackintosh, reminding me of the long hikes she took in the rain the first year I was in Balbec, was still, in my mind, a kind of symbol of the journey.[11] (3:1089)

The comparison of the mackintosh to a suit of armor, which calls forth the related image of the shield and makes of Albertine a kind of Bradamante at rest, motivates a further development on an insert glued onto the page: the series of metaphors leads to an allusion to St. George, to painting, and an explicit reference to Mantegna.

> Riding at breakneck speed through the streets of Balbec, her shoulders hunched over the handlebars, when, in spite of the bad weather, she went off for a long ride. That mackintosh—a substance which, although flexible, looked hardened wherever it had formed large cracks—dressed her knees in noble leggings which looked to be made out of metal, as in Mantegna's *St. George;* on her head it put a hat with long horns; and it made a kind of saddle-strap ripple around her chest, which was deeply hidden as if under a suit of armor, inside an impenetrable shelter. People leaped out of her way in terror and said they would lodge a complaint with the mayor about speeding like that. But for me just seeing that mackintosh made me imagine, project and share the long rides of this traveling girl, far beyond Balbec, we would stop, the two of us alone, taking shelter in the Chantepie Forest when the rain got too hard, and beneath such a sterile substance Albertine's smooth cheeks would have seemed smoother still to kiss, and her breast a greater secret to uncover if she had agreed to put down her arms for me and undo her shield.[12] (3:1089–90)

The insert itself covers up a marginal addition, which was an earlier form of the allusion to St. George and painting:

> Riding at breakneck speed through the streets of Balbec, her shoulders hunched over the handlebars, wrapped up in a mackintosh as

> in Medusa's tunic, under which her breasts seemed hidden as one takes shelter from the rain in the cover of a forest. Instantly I felt I was with her, on the roads, in the woods, seeing this mackintosh I traveled miles with her, a whole journey, unconstrained. And at the place where the mackintosh was pulled tight around the knees by the bicycle wheel what lovely humps it made, like the iron thigh-plates of a young warrior, a St. George in one of the old paintings.[13] (3:1090)

Valéry hesitated to use the word *caoutchouc* ("rubber" or "mackintosh") in a poem. Here, however, it is used to designate the poetic object *par excellence*. A substance halfway between flesh and iron that takes on the characteristics of both, neither hard nor soft, both supple and rigid, cold and hot, protective and inviting, the rubber of Albertine's mackintosh transmits qualities; it is the very substance of metaphor, or at least of Proustian metaphor which, as Gérard Genette has shown, retains a link to metonymy through the relation of container to contained.[14] It is moreover a sterile substance, as Proust reminds us, and in this sense it is emblematic of androgyny and incest; it is tantamount to desire. All of this was clearer still in the first outline for this scene, written as early as the summer of 1914 in Cahier 71:

> Among the many Albertines: On days when it looked [like] rain I liked to watch her go by on her bicycle, with her mackintosh which came all the way down to her legs and stuck to them as if in fact instead of being designed to keep out water it had already been flooded and was meant to take on the imprint of the forms of the lovely young girl whom [it] covered with a cloak as terrible as Medusa's [tunic] and with kneepads as tight and yet at the same time as broad and soft as Mantegna thigh-plates.[15] (3:1069)

A marginal addition gave more detail:

> It was not so much an item of clothing as a tunic similar to the one worn by Nessus, a kind of attribute representing her strength and the pleasure of the journey, covering her lovely breast with a vast, almost solid expanse, furrowed only by a few folds, under which it seemed one would have instantly found her bare breasts, an expanse which molded itself to her knees and topped them with bas-relief hats.

Medusa-Nessus and Mantegna first appear on this emblem of desire, among the most precise found in all of Proust's writings. Nothing prevents us from seeing in it a reminiscence of Alfred Agostinelli, whom Proust described driving his automobile on their trips around Cabourg in 1907 in this way: "My mechanic had put on a vast rubber cloak and put on a sort of hood which, hugging the fullness of his young beardless face, made him, as we went deeper and deeper on into the night, look like some speeding pilgrim or nun" (CSB 66–67). The mackintosh, which made Agostinelli into a woman—and not just any woman, a nun—causes Albertine's mutation into an ephebe. The substance of metaphor and an object of desire, the mackintosh allows for all kinds of cross-dressings and the endless mobility they bring about.

Mantegna's St. George, which makes an appearance at the center of all the descriptions of Albertine in her mackintosh, and which Proust would have had the opportunity to see in the gallery of the Academy in Venice in 1900, is, along with Botticelli's "Primavera," one of the paradigms of reading the beginnings of the Italian Renaissance perversely. That is also why Huysmans marveled at his discovery of another incarnation of St. George in a new setting on the Bianchi panel. In the chapter of *A rebours* devoted to Gustave Moreau—a painter considered to be lacking in precursors—des Esseintes still finds in his work "vague reminiscences of Mantegna,"[16] and Péladan, who among all the decadents is the most obsessed by the ideal of hermaphroditism, took pleasure in linking it to Mantegna. When the heroes of *Curieuse* and *A coeur perdu,* Princess Riazan and the painter Nebo, both perfect androgynes, are compared to Mantegna paintings, what suggests the association is their legs and calves: they are shaped exactly like those of Mantegna's St. George in the Academy.

In *Curieuse,* the second volume of *La Décadence latine,* Princess Riazan, a "page-boy disguised as a girl," is "built like someone in a Mantegna painting, fleshy but slim,"[17] with "hard legs, firm calves, every kind of manliness compatible with gracefulness."[18] Again in the fourth volume, *A coeur perdu,* we hear about her knees worthy of a painting by Mazzola or Primaticcio. The painter Nebo looks like her, he has a "certain kinship" with her.[19] Nebo's sketches, like those of Gustave Moreau, are reminiscent of Mantegna, and the first time she goes to visit him, the Princess is struck by "the frail and sinuous Mantegna-style legs," which he reproduces "with such androgynous preoccupation that the Princess blushes."[20] On this visit the princess also notices a stained-glass window depicting St. George slaying the dragon, with this striking detail: "The head of a virgin sat on the body of a dragon with a figure of St. George." This association of the virgin with the dragon—like man and horse joined together in the centaur—suggests the interpretation that what the decadents adored in St. George had to do with a victory over woman and sexuality. Thus the stained-glass window becomes a symbol in *A coeur perdu:* the princess smothers the painter with her attentions and the painter, like a kind of St. George slaying the "Beast with the head of a woman,"[21] or like Raphael's St. George "stomping on his Beast," initiates her into the doubtful joys of chastity.

In Cahier 46 Proust does not name Mantegna until the third version of the passage, on the insert; in the marginal addition he only alluded to "a St. George in one of the old paintings." The other famous versions of St. George—Carpaccio's, also in Venice, or Raphael's, in the Louvre—are on horseback, and indeed Albertine appears to the hero riding her bicycle. But even if, as we have just seen, Péladan in *A coeur perdu* also refers to Raphael's St. George, Mantegna's St. George corresponds more closely to the associations present in the Proust passage. Moreover, Mantegna, and even "Mantegna thigh-plates," were mentioned as early as the first sketch in Cahier 71: as in the case of Péladan, the Mantegna-style leg seems the source of the vision—or the *tableau vivant*—of Albertine as St. George.

Mantegna is mentioned several times in the *Recherche*. During Madame de Saint-Euverte's evening party in "Un Amour de Swann," a "strapping great fellow in livery," "motionless, statuesque, useless," is compared to a warrior leaning on his shield in a Mantegna painting (1:352–53; 1:318). One is reminded of a warrior deep in thought, in the fresco of "St. James Led to Martyrdom" at the Church of the Eremitani in Padua: no relation at all to androgyny. But elsewhere, in "Place-Names: The Name," perched on top of

Madame Swann's victoria as she rides through the Bois de Boulogne we see "a groom no bigger than [the coachman's] fist and as infantile as St. George in the picture" (1:459; 1:417). The comparison is rich in allusions. The "groom no bigger than [the coachman's] fist" harkens back to the "tiger" that is described by Balzac in *La Maison Nucingen*—"a tiger no bigger than a fist, fresh and pink like Toby, Joby, Passy"[22]—and that reappears in *Les Secrets de la princesse de Cadignan*. A few pages earlier, Proust explicitly compares Madame Swann's groom to " 'the late Beaudenord's tiger' "; here the motif of androgyny is obvious. Balzac's hero is actually called "Beaudenord," but Proust writes "Baudenord" in the very sentence in which the "tiger" is sighted next to the coachman on Madame Swann's victoria, pulled by horses "as one sees them in the drawings of Constantin Guys," (1:453; 1:411), or as Baudelaire faithfully described them in the chapter entitled "Les voitures" in his essay on Guys, *Le Peintre de la vie moderne*. After all "Baudenord," as if by contamination, or perhaps to avoid the common mistake in spelling the poet's name, refers not only to Balzac, but once again to Baudelaire, as Proust's special model for the in-between time of the two centuries.

In any case, Balzac's "tiger" worked for an English lord who was forced to get rid of him because of some nasty insinuations: he had "hair as blond as a Rubens virgin, pink cheeks"; "an English journalist came up with a delightful description of the little angel, he found him too good-looking to be a tiger and said he was willing to bet that Paddy was a tamed tigress."[23] When Godefroid de Beaudenord hired him, the tiger contributed to his reputation as "the finest flower of the Parisian dandies." But Beaudenord, ruined when Nucingen went bankrupt, was forced to let Paddy go. A few years later, the tiger was working for Georges de Maufrigneuse, the Princesse de Cadignan's son: "At that time the duke's tiger had a rather harsh task. Toby, the late Beaudenord's former tiger—or so the story ran in high society about this ruined man of fashion, this young man who, at twenty-five, was still supposed to be only fourteen . . . "[24] The parallel between the "groom no bigger than [the coachman's] fist" and St. George is thus overflowing with allusions to transvestism and androgyny, and the St. George in question is undoubtedly Mantegna's at the Venice Academy, an unmistakable sign of the fin-de-siècle. If that sign reappears, this time openly, in the insert that describes Albertine in her rubber mackintosh, is that not because from the very beginning Mantegna was involved with the birth of desire for the "rubberized" Albertine, as the first sketch for this page suggests?

From the very first words of the comparison in Cahier 46 we find a momentous term that was to undergo a curious fate in the subsequent drafts, the term *shield:* the "impenetrable shield" that defends Albertine's breast and makes her still more desirable. What is fascinating about Bradamante are the breasts underneath the armor, like the statues of the hermaphrodite in antiquity; a virgin's breasts on the chest of a beautiful young man. On the other hand Swinburne drew attention to the metal straps emphasizing the nakedness of the breasts in the studies of women from the school of Michelangelo.[25] Proust seems to use the words *armor* and *shield* indistinguishably, as synonymous terms referring to something that, by making the bosom a prohibited zone, makes it into an object of desire. The first addition to Cahier 46, which develops the image in the margins, ricochets off in a peculiar direction: Albertine is "wrapped up in a mackintosh as in Medusa's tunic." Two phrases are confused here and need to be untangled: Nessus' tunic and the shield with Medusa's head. Proust persists in his oversight, since "Medusa's tunic" was already mentioned in the first sketch from Cahier 71, along with the "Mantegna thigh-plates."

That page was destined to be eliminated from the definitive text, which incorporates only the end of the episode. After the hero has been reunited with Albertine, they take the train back to Balbec:

> And, looking at Albertine's mackintosh . . . which, close-fitting, malleable and grey, seemed at that moment not so much intended to protect her clothes from the rain as to have been soaked by it and to be clinging to her body as though to take the imprint of her form for a sculptor, I tore off that tunic which jealously enwrapped a longed-for breast. (2:894; 3:258–59)

The dynamics of the metaphor—clothing that masks yet reveals, that is both ductile and statuesque, that freezes the body like a piece of sculpture—have not changed. The armor and the shield are gone, as are St. George and Mantegna, but in the manuscript "Nessus' tunic" rather than simply "tunic" is still legible, but the typist could not make it out and Proust neglected to put it back in. It is true the phrase was hardly appropriate: the centaur Nessus, who wanted to carry off Dejanira, was struck by the arrows of her husband Heracles; before expiring, he gave Dejanira the tunic that was supposed to guarantee Heracles' fidelity to her, but when he put it on it consumed him with burning. What is the link with Albertine's mackintosh? In spite of the adverb "jealously," which makes the tunic "jealously enwrapp[ing] a longed-for breast" into the hero's rival for Albertine's affections, the relation to Nessus remains a mystery. "Medusa's tunic," which appeared in the first writings of Cahier 71, was more eloquent: "a cloak as fearful as Medusa's [tunic]." Medusa is the Gorgon whose hair was changed into snakes by Athena and whose look turned people to stone; her head was cut off by Perseus, the ancient equivalent of St. George, who kept it—the Medusa of the shields—to paralyze his enemies. Medusa is the epitome of the petrifying and petrified woman; it is her tunic that the hero admits—contradicting himself later on in *Albertine disparue*—he has not torn off: "Never had I caressed the waterproofed Albertine of the rainy days; I wanted to ask her to take off that armour, in order to experience with her the love of the tented field, the fraternity of travel" (3:498; 4:70–71). Medusa is turned to stone by her own armor.

Now Medusa, the *femme fatale* who turns men to stone, is the other side of the coin in the romantic and decadent myth of a kind of woman opposite and complementary to Salomé: not the perverse adolescent—the sinful chastity, the impure tenderness, "the rotted graces of childhood" that des Esseintes himself tires of (*A rebours,* 216)—but the withered, neglected woman of spoiled beauty, the decaying body. Medusa and Salomé are the two sides of woman, perhaps Helen and Galatea, as in the two Gustave Moreau paintings described by Huysmans in his "Salon de 1880."[26] In *Sodome et Gomorrhe I,* this is what Proust calls the woman secretly hiding inside the young invert without his knowing it yet: "the Galatea barely awakened to life in the unconscious mass of this male body in which she is imprisoned" (2:643–44; 3:22).[27] In reading the Italian Renaissance perversely, one finds another example of the two sides of woman, or of sexuality: Leonardo's St. John and the Mona Lisa, opposed to each other like physical androgyny and moral androgyny, the effeminate ephebe and the virile woman, which was what the second half of the nineteenth century, following the lead of Walter Pater, saw in the Mona Lisa's smile. Péladan, as always, exaggerates: "In the Mona Lisa, the cerebral authority of the man of genius merges with the voluptuousness of the gentlewoman; it's a case of moral androgyny."[28] In similar terms Huysmans, in an article on Bianchi, purposely opposed the two sides of perversion: "Connaisseurs praise the Mona Lisa's faltering smile; but . . . how empty, how devoid of the unexpected are da Vinci's steady eyes, if they are compared to those eyes as clear as the water of a spring or a brook which, lightning-struck, is purified by the storm!" (*Certains,* 227). The incestuous eyes of the Virgin and St. Quentin, or of Salomé and St. George, seem evil by comparison. In *A Rebours,* Miss Urania seems to des Esseintes the incarnation of the man-woman: "After first being a woman, then, after a period of hesitation, after flirting with androgyny, she seemed to make up her mind, to define herself, to become a man completely" (*A rebours,* 210–11). In return des Esseintes "himself became feminized"; there was "an exchange of sexes between Miss Urania and him." This episode is followed by the episode of the female ventriloquist whose hair was "combed with a boy's part," and the pederastic fling on the Rue de Babylone. Sexual uncertainty becomes widespread. The in-between of the sexes is a major figure of the fin-de-siècle. Albertine with the tunic of Medusa is thus the other woman, the androgyne's other, or rather an other androgyne, the man-woman in place of the woman-man.

We still have to explain the elimination of St. George and Medusa, the two aspects of decadent sexuality, between the draft and the manuscript of *Sodome et Gomorrhe.* Were these leftovers of the fin-de-siècle spirit in the mind of the writer who is always in between? Were they references that Proust subsequently decided were obsolete? Probably, but that is not the whole story. In the script of the *Recherche* that Proust wrote before the war postponed publication of the novel and before the invention of Albertine, what we find between *Le Côté de Guermantes* and *Le Temps retrouvé,* instead of *Sodome et Gomorrhe,* is the hero in search of a sexual initiation, in lengthy pursuit of two women who exactly correspond to the two women of the decadent movement, or to the two sides of woman (and the two ages as well): a young girl with red roses, and the chambermaid of the Baronne de Putbus (or Picpus). The definitive text keeps only enigmatic traces of these two characters. The girl with the red roses brushed up against the hero at a ball, egged him on, and leaned up against him with her breasts: she was the perverse adolescent. As for the chambermaid, Montargis, who was to become Saint-Loup, had met her in a bordello: "buxom and blond" (3:975),[29] "a wonderful Giorgione painting," "a large body, wavy and blond," "a female doge" (3:1004).[30] A Giorgione, a Gorgon, a doge, the hero finally met her in Venice, or rather in Padua, damaged, her face burnt in a fire, spoiled, her body mistreated. Is there any doubt that she is Medusa, her beauty withered, Baudelaire's debased courtisan, the burns on her face like a kind of smallpox? As Baudelaire has it: "Everyone knows that Trenk, *Burnt-Mug*, was adored by women" ("Choix de maximes consolantes sur l'amour," OC 1:548).

Once Albertine is invented, the girl with the red roses and Madame de Putbus' chambermaid fade away, as do Medusa and Salomé, Helen and Galatea. The decadent couple leaves the stage, and another couple makes its entry into this novel full of symmetries: Albertine and Morel, that is, Sodom and Gomorrha. The parallelism is spelled out in the notebooks for the second stay in Balbec written at the beginning of the war. During the train journey in which Albertine's mackintosh sets off the hero's desires, the two young people notice Monsieur de Charlus accosting a musician, who was to become Morel but is nameless here, on the platform of the Doncières train station. The musician, who was described as womanish in the 1911 version of the meeting, a St. George, a "little queer disguised as a soldier" (3:1022),[31] becomes very different this time: "make this young man look so downright masculine that it puts him beyond suspicion" (3:1091),[32] adds Proust in the margins. Albertine and Morel, in place of St. George and the Gorgon, the two sides of the decadent androgyne that are in strong contrast, will remain unfathomable. And that is how Proust both attaches himself to the nineteenth century and detaches himself from it, how he shifts the perverse reading—of which Huysmans is the finest example—of the Italian Renaissance.

5

Tableaux Vivants in the Novel

Among the seventy-five notebooks of drafts in the Bibliothèque Nationale's Fonds Marcel Proust, we find, on the back of page 52 of Cahier 62—a notebook of postwar additions for the end of the *Recherche* and particularly *Sodome et Gomorrhe II*—the following: "June 13 20 minutes to 7 Céleste states it is impossible to prepare a dinner for 8:45." This is life—a name, a date, a time; life intruding into fiction. What can one do with this life, except perhaps use it as a springboard for reflecting on life and the novel, the living and the fictional in Proust and their interpenetration? Life provides models, as it does in the realist or naturalist novel, but that is undoubtedly much less important than the feeling of a fragmentation of reality that seeps into the novel, like the allegories one finds in the experimental novel. In the end, what constitutes a Proustian epiphany?

So here we are, on June 13, 1921. Let me point out in passing that Proust's remark allows us to date the middle of Cahier 62, which is no small matter and which, from a certain point of view, that of the history of the text, is in fact the only important matter; but this is not the point of view I shall be taking. It is shortly after half past six, and I imagine that Marcel Proust has just asked Céleste

Albaret, his housekeeper, to prepare a small dinner party for this evening, two hours from now, and that she has refused. Proust, dumbfounded or perhaps furious—even though he is surely used to the whims of his cantankerous Céleste—makes note of the incident in a perfectly noncommital and objective way in the notebook that lies open on his bed and in which he is composing an addition to *Sodome et Gomorrhe.* Why? So that it will be written down, so that it cannot be denied, so that he remembers it, so that people will know about it. Does one not always write for someone? On the right-hand page of the notebook, "extenders," as Montaigne called them: additions for the soirée at the princess' house, for the second stay in Balbec. On the left-hand page, this memorable incident: Céleste will not make a dinner for a friend who will be coming over in a little while. Yet there is certainly no dearth of grocery stores in the neighborhood: Félix Potin on the corner of the Place Saint-Augustin, Prunier on the Rue Vignon, near the Place de la Madeleine. But the scene turns out otherwise. Céleste always makes a fuss but she winds up giving in. She rushes over to Prunier and buys two filets of sole. Too late, Proust writes.

Proust's notebooks sometimes include, although quite rarely (reading them is disappointing for anyone on the lookout for intimate details), this kind of note that brings us into his life in one fell swoop. Usually there is no story involved: names, addresses, telephone numbers. How can we read the coexistence of personal notes and drafts or sketches for the novel? The relation between them is one of exclusion, as well as one of inclusion; it is a relation of contiguity. On the right-hand page, the novel; on the left-hand page, life; two disjointed areas. Proust writes not only from left to right like everyone else, but also from right to left. He leaves the left-hand pages blank, and they subsequently get filled up with extras, almost by themselves; it is life that takes care of filling up these blank undersides with additions and inserts, like the margins of the book of life comprised by Montaigne's *Essais.* This is writing of the present and of presence, writing of the instant, writing distinct from the work of memory that constructs the guardian text, but writing that can perhaps be seen to proceed in a similar way. We may say that between the novel and life there is a break, the in-between space of the pages, that the novel and life are separate. But we may also say that life is an addition to the novel, that it comes after the novel, like something extra. And the additions, especially those of the final period, from Cahiers 59 through 62, are often heavy with lived—or rather living—experience.

A bit further, in Cahier 62, on pages 57 and 58, front and back—for once life and the novel are intermingled and continuous—we find the narration of the death of Bergotte (3:180–86; 3:687–693), struck down as he stands in front of the "little patch of yellow wall" (3:185; 3:692) by Vermeer; we know that Proust visited the exhibition of Dutch paintings at the Jeu de Paume Museum in May 1921. Life fits itself into the composed novel; the left-hand pages move over into the right-hand ones and expand them with what might be called elements worthy of a novel. The novelistic in the *Recherche* is often the trace of life, of the present that happens after the fact.

But in this case, if the front of the page corresponds to the novel and the back of the page to life, if the death of Bergotte, a well-known and rare intersection of life and the novel in *A la recherche du temps perdu,* actually takes place on the left-hand pages without any possibility of continuity, what shall we make of the following notation on the front of page 51, which comes before the planned dinner party that sets off Céleste's revolt?

> An author who writes about homosexuals with fairness owes it to himself never to share their pleasures, even if he considers them blameless. He is like a defrocked priest who, once he has convinced people how absurd it is to impose celibacy upon the clergy, must remain chaste, so that he is not suspected of having been led into an indulgent moral position by personal interest rather than by love of the truth.

This statement is not incorporated into the novel. Nevertheless, does it not have the sense of an existential resolution?

Here is yet another misfortune, or perhaps simply another complication: Céleste does not only belong to life. She rebels against her boss while he is putting the finishing touches on *Sodome et Gomorrhe II,* in which she appears in all her glory, in a favorable light. For Céleste is also a character in the novel, one of the few—along with her sister Marie Gineste, the other maid from Balbec, and the Larivières, her cousins—who are actually given their own names in the book (2:875–79 and 3:875–77; 3:239–44 and 4:424–25). And the character Céleste—if we can call her that—is also present on the right-hand pages of the notebooks of additions, as, for example, on page 80 of Cahier 59, where Proust writes: "Céleste's words to be added." The border between life and the novel is breached, and it is breached more and more often in the latest notebooks, as when Proust puts in the margins of a meditation on sleep in Cahier 59 (page 51): "Think about putting that dictated section into my will." The right side and the left side intermingle; the novel, which is still continuing to be written, accommodates life—what is left of it—with no longer a thought for the reservations that kept them apart at the outset. Tragically, in the face of death, the separation between life and the novel succumbs. Writing—for it is never a question of anything else—moves without mediation from the novel to life, and from life to the novel, until death occurs. It will not be long in coming.

But here is a counterexample to this growing tendency of the novel to merge with life: the Duc de Guermantes changes his mind and becomes a supporter of Dreyfus as a result of meeting three charming ladies while recuperating at a spa. This is also a late addition, dating from the period of the page proofs of *Le Côté de Guermantes I,* sketched out in Cahier 60 and included in a handwritten insert glued to the typescript of *Sodome et Gomorrhe II* (2:766–67; 3:137–38).[1] Basin's new pro-Dreyfus position is indicated by this reply, which is attributed to him: "Did you ever see anyone so gaga as Froberville? An officer leading the French people to the slaughter (meaning war)!" (2:766; 3:137). Proust is here alluding to something actually said by General de Pellieux in his eloquent defense of the army during Zola's 1898 law trial:

> What would you like to see become of this army on the day of reckoning, which may well be closer than you believe? What would you have these wretched soldiers do when they are led into fire by leaders whom they have been encouraged to distrust? What would happen is that your sons would be led to the slaughter, gentlemen of the jury! But if that day ever comes, Monsieur Zola will have won a new victory, he will have rewritten *La Débâcle,* he will have spread

> the French language throughout the entire universe, throughout Europe; but France will have ceased to exist.[2]

Proust attended Zola's trial, and he speaks of it in *Jean Santeuil*. He probably heard General de Pellieux's famous harangue. But on the insert to the typescript he crosses out the allusion; the professional soldier is replaced by a literary soldier, although not without a slip of the pen: after crossing out "de Pellieux," Proust writes in "Forcheville"—Odette's former lover and Swann's rival—instead of "Froberville," the colonel, who is General Froberville's nephew. Yet Proust leaves in the duke's exclamation, "An officer threatening the French people with slaughter, meaning war," which no longer makes any sense once the historical reference is omitted. Froberville "threatening" the French people with slaughter is completely meaningless, Forcheville even more so. Above the word *threatening*, another hand has added *leading*, although the preposition has not been changed, and the definitive text will be: "leading the French people to the slaughter." The transformation has taken place in several steps, as we see the gradual passage from the real world to the world of the novel.

Even this small example shows how the novel, once it has become a world of its own, takes over history. It also suggests that toward the end of its composition the novel is less and less concerned with what Roland Barthes calls "the reality effect" [*l'effet de réel*], since writing no longer has to be involved with establishing its verisimilitude. Indeed, on the same page we have been discussing, whereas in the published version the duke simply goes to "a spa," Proust had originally sent him more specifically "to Barèges." Actual proper names are found in greater number in the drafts and the manuscripts than in the definitive text. It often happens that the typist cannot decipher them, so they are left blank on the typescript and Proust does not bother to put them back in as he is reading it over. To take another example having to do with the Dreyfus Affair, the Prince de Guermantes confesses his pro-Dreyfus position to Swann without embarrassment because he knows that Swann condemned "the insults to the Army and the fact that the Dreyfusists agreed to ally themselves with those who insulted it" (2:737; 3:109), but the manuscript mentioned the name of the pro-Dreyfus journalist Monsieur Gohier. The typist could only make out "Monsieur Go . . .," and Proust did not fill in the rest of the name (3:1384 [3:109, var. d]).[3]

We may use Céleste's refusal to serve Proust dinner on June 13, 1921 (without making too much of this particular anecdote) to support the conclusion that there is, theoretically, continuity between life and the work in the drafts of the *Recherche*—since life is allowed only the left-hand pages—but at the same time to suggest that life becomes a kind of novelistic extra, added on after the fact, which finds it easier and easier—and ultimately effortless—to fit into the novel that has taken shape and become a world of its own. The two maids in Balbec, the Norwegian philosopher, and Bergotte's death are like so many booster shots of life into the book. Conversely, once the novel has taken shape it becomes less and less burdened by history, which originally helped to ground its verisimilitude.

Nevertheless, none of this suggests anything more than a point of view about the retrospective openness of writing to life, to what is left of life. If we consider the relations of writing to life to constitute not a presence, through what Montaigne would call "extenders" of the instant—what has already been written and is rewritten by writing—but rather an absence, precisely a "lost time," those relations would be of a different order, unless, perhaps, the same procedure is at work, as, once again, in Montaigne's *Essais,* in which the additions allow us to see the commentary on the text being written, and this is already the writing of the text.

Of Letters and Sounds

It is generally assumed that Brichot, the academic in *A la recherche du temps perdu,* was modeled after Victor Brochard, a professor of ancient philosophy at the Sorbonne and an habitué of Madame Aubernon's salon in Paris and Louveciennes.[4] *Brochard, Brichot:* living and writing are connected by *Br* and *ch.* Before solidifying in the form *Brichot,* the name of the Verdurins' pompous friend went through a number of variations: *Cruchot* in Cahier 24, dating from 1909, in a draft of a conversation between the hero and the professor about Monsieur de Charlus, placed in the definitive text in *La Prisonnière* (3:332–336; 3:830–33),[5] *Crochard* for a part of Cahier 47 from 1911, in a version of the chapter "Monsieur de Charlus and the Verdurins" (3:1021–30).[6] *Cruchot, Crochard, Brichot: Brochard* undeniably fits in here. This is a case of transposition of life into the novel, confirmed by the near-anagram that gives rise to the name. Actually this transposition obeys the laws of phonetic evolution, and it illustrates the fact that vowels have less of a tendency to remain the same than consonants, and that Romance liquid consonants (in this case *r*) within a word, between a consonant and a vowel, tend to persist across time. We start out with *Cruchot* in the fragmentary sketch of Cahier 24, "a professor of classical literature at the Sorbonne": this is the name furthest away from *Brochard,* with only the sounds *r* and *ch* in common. It was also the name of a character in a book by Abel Hermant.[7]

When in Cahier 47 Proust revises and amplifies this fragment, the character is first called *Brichot* (3:1019–21),[8] a name that has *Br* and *ch* in common with *Brochard,* that is, the consonant framework. But later, in the little train that takes the Verdurins' faithful guests to visit them in Ville d'Avray, starting with the description of the meeting between Monsieur de Gurcy and the musician in the waiting room of the Saint-Lazare train station—a sketch for the meeting between Charlus and Morel on the platform of the Doncières train station—the character is suddenly given the name *Crochard,* which is identical to *Brochard* except for the initial consonant. On the page where this name appears a peculiar confusion arises with the name *Cottard,* the doctor's name that has been established since 1909 and the Sainte-Beuve sketchbooks: for several lines the doctor and the professor have the same name, *Crochard,* which was the name of a character in Stendhal's *Lucien Leuwen.*

Those who believe in onomastics will point out that Proust could not force himself to give up the *Br* of *Brochard* and *Brichot,* for *br* (or *ber,* or *b, e, r*) forms the root of many of Proust's names: *Gilberte, Bergotte, Berma, Albertine,* and so forth. The only way Proust would have been able to resist *Br* would have been even worse, that is, to sacrifice the first letter and keep the rest of the name: *Crochard.* The character will be given back the name *Brichot* after this brief attempt to break out of the pattern in the course of Cahier 47.

Through this example, our focus moves from the model to his name, which arouses our interest not because of its relation to the real world but because of its sounds and letters, which form an integral part of it. In the novel the truth of life is not the same as being historically or biographically accurate, and Victor Brochard does not have a great deal to do with it, except for the *Br* of his name, and the *ch,* which is also worthy of some comment, the *ch* of *Charlus, Rachel, Charlie,* and so on. The framework of the name was so intimately Proustian that it started to become indispensable. Jupien was first called *Brichot,* in Carnet 1 (3:1031), and *Borniche,* in Cahier 51 (3:936–38).[9] This, then, is what life is made up of: letters and sounds, something that is in fact already writing, with the deeply rooted reflex of thought that makes writing ricochet into the novel.

A great deal has already been written about the relation between biography and fiction in the *Recherche,* and about the novel's biographical (or autobiographical) status: there are models, and Painter's book figures them out more or less convincingly. Some of them are beyond all doubt, but that does not matter very much: *Br* and *ch* are much more necessary than Victor Brochard. By the same token, however, the conventional wisdom that consists of reversing the terms of the problem and claiming that the only life is the life of writing, the only biography that of the work, is also somewhat tiresome. Writing is not all of life, even in Proust's case after his retreat into solitude in 1908. Once we have dismissed the biographical illusion, as well as the textual illusion, the recurrences of life in the work—for example between Proust's letters and his novel—are all the more disturbing.

The Voice Is Enough

Between the sketches of *A la recherche du temps perdu* written before the war and the definitive text, the character of Morel, who did not even have a name to begin with, benefited from considerable development and underwent a complete transformation. In 1911 the musician was, as we have seen, a turn-of-the-century-style St. George, "a made-up Pierrot, covered with face-powder and greasepaint," a "little queer disguised as a soldier" (3:1022)[10] (see chapter 4). By allowing Monsieur de Charlus—who at the time was called Monsieur de Gurcy—to see in him the man that he was not, his feminine bearing served as an illustration of the power of the imagination. During the war years we see a reversal in the conception of the pianist, who in the meantime has become a violin player so as to be more distinct from his model, Léon Delafosse, Montesquiou's favorite from 1894 to 1897. In the margins of the passage describing his appearance on the platform of the Doncières train station, Proust makes a note to himself, as we pointed out earlier, to "make this young man look so downright masculine that it puts him beyond suspicion," and he further adds, in what would appear to be a reference to one of his models, "sort of like young Hermant" (3:1876–77 [3:1091, var. a])[11] (see chapter 4). Let us approach this from the point of view of an editor: a note would appear in order to illuminate the allusion.

My idea—although let us not make it into a "general hypothesis," as the Duc de Guermantes might put it—is that there are no *hapax legomena* or one-time occurrences in Proust's writing, that everything in it—in particular material from letters that become part of the novel—repeats itself. Proust's correspondence allows us to raise almost all of the text's veils of mystery: references and allusions, quotations and proper names, and so on. It is as if the only thing that came—or rather came back—to the writer's pen and his memory were words already set down on paper; if not in the left-hand pages of the notebooks, then at least in a letter.

It would appear that Proust met Abel Hermant's adopted son in 1908—I shall return to this fateful year, which in itself is practically enough to record the entire novel, a year spent in a kind of coalescence or confusion between life and writing, as if life were written down ahead of time, even before being lived. In March 1908 he confides to Madame de Noailles:

> I told the Princesse de Chimay that I would tell her—and you—about a conversation with Hermant. And about how nice I found his son to be. For I refuse to believe that awful hypothesis. Even though the pomp and circumstance of a legal form like adoption does nothing more than add a bit of flavor to the banality of dubious situations, I simply cannot believe that he wanted to dress up a banal homosexual fling in the infinitely respectable trappings of incest. I

> am convinced and certain that those are not at all his preferences. And undoubtedly the young man, like him, likes only women. Otherwise they would not treat women so well. Adoption! But not marriage. It is true that homosexuality shows more discretion, for it is still attached to its pure origin, friendship, and retains some of its virtues. (*Corr.* 8:72–73)

Apparently high-society gossip had it that Abel Hermant had formed a liaison with his adopted son, who nonetheless appeared beyond suspicion. Proust encourages Madame de Noailles to disbelieve the rumor, although his final remarks comparing marriage to inversion come down on the side of inversion. In 1914, six years later, as he is about to transform the character of the young piano player, Proust remembers. The life that surfaces in writing depends on a form of memory that has nothing involuntary about it, but rather is related to a kind of mnemonic device. Proust's immense memory is surrounded by his stockpile of sketchbooks teeming with allusions and cross-references; for years on end it recalls where such and such a development is stored in its treasury, to be taken out, to be put back again as it moves flawlessly between writing and life. But the question remains: in what form does memory record life?

The answer comes in a note that allows us to establish a link between the 1908 letter to Anna de Noailles and the marginal addition from Cahier 46. It is found in Cahier 57, and as the names involved are Charlus and Bobby, it must come from the period of the First World War: "Someone asks for an explanation from this masculine young man (Hermant's son). Then, in the vocal register of his long and rather heartfelt response, I suddenly noticed several revealing notes, and I said to myself, 'What, him too?' "[12] In this way Hermant's son becomes associated with that all-important scene, the *tableau vivant* often described in the drafts and the definitive text: the invert being betrayed by his own voice. Voice is even the sign that most clearly links homosexuality and Judaism as congenital traits, as in this decisive addition—written during the war years in Cahier 49—to the passage that reveals the truth about Monsieur de Gurcy:

> About Monsieur de Charlus' voice. All in all his intonation of certain words, so characteristic of homosexuals, should perhaps not have

> been interpreted in that way, since Madame de Marsantes gave the same modulation to the word "honneur." Unless she had inherited it herself from a father endowed with the same vice. For how can one find one's way when one is interpreting physical signs? I have said it is wrong to take a Jewish nose for a sign of Judaism, since one can turn up in the most Catholic of families. But who knows if it has not been brought there by some Jewish ancestor?[13] (3:954)

The image comes back most strikingly in the definitive text of *Sodome et Gomorrhe,* in the episode of the "strawberry-juice" at the Verdurins' summer place at La Raspelière; in choosing it, Monsieur de Charlus manifests "a love of the kind called unnatural":

> On hearing M. de Charlus say, in that shrill voice and with that smile and those gestures, "No, I preferred its neighbour, the strawberry-juice," one could say: "Ah, he likes the stronger sex," with the same certainty as enables a judge to sentence a criminal who has not confessed, or a doctor a patient suffering from general paralysis who himself is perhaps unaware of his malady. (2:999; 3:356)

This fantasy that "the voice is enough," which is so omnipresent that the novel almost seems to be harping on it, has already appeared in this same volume, in the course of the conversation between Charlus and Vaugoubert, at the soirée given by the Princesse de Guermantes (2:688; 3:63). It is evidence of a recurrent curiosity about the homosexual's voice, and it shows how much Proust makes homosexuality into a medical issue: he even compares his hero's ability to recognize it to that of a doctor giving a diagnosis without making use of a stethoscope (see chapter 9).

Now what is of greatest interest here is not, as in the case of Brichot and Brochard, the model; it is rather life as a *tableau vivant,* as a scene that creates an image: "Hermant's son" is the name of the fantasy of the virile homosexual who betrays himself by an inflection of his voice. Fantasies have proper names; proper names are names of fantasies. Interest shifts from the model considered as "what has been" to the model taken as lived experience: an image, a surprising scene, already written, lived as if written, "some scene that furnished the reader with an image, some picture that had no rational meaning" (1:598; 1:546), the sort of thing Bergotte appreciates in books.

The Butterfly and the Flower

Let us look at the botanical metaphor used to develop "The race of fairies": the hero chances on the meeting between Jupien and Charlus while he is watching for the meeting between the orchid and the bumblebee. Two lines of this passage are emblematic, two mediocre lines that appear in the manuscript but that Proust dropped after the first of the two typescripts of *Sodome et Gomorrhe I;* two lines that are no less important for being deleted from the definitive text: "Certainly, I could never forget Jupien's ridiculous pose, his mincing about and his ploys when he had noticed Monsieur de Charlus and, standing in front of his shop, had appeared to be saying to him (like 'the poor flower speaking to the heavenly butterfly,' and forgetting the fact that they were 'both flowers'): 'Don't fly away' " (3:1288 [3:31, var. a]).[14] This simile, the first hint of the anthropomorphic reading of the sexuality of flowers, was placed near the end of the section; an explicit allusion to Darwin replaced it in the second typescript.

For the time being, let us pretend we are unfamiliar with the poet quoted by Proust, the author of "the poor flower speaking to the heavenly butterfly." The very same lines are mentioned, also without the poet's name, by Professor Amédée Coutance, in the outpourings that conclude his preface to the French translation of Darwin's work, *Des différentes formes de fleurs dans une même espèce.*[15] All of Proust's knowledge about the fertilization of orchids by insects comes from this preface; in it Coutance sums up another of Darwin's works that had appeared in French translation the year before with the same publisher under the title, *Des effets de la fécondation croisée et de la fécondation directe dans le règne végétal.* In the preface we find the following:

> Who has not read that plaintive elegy of the flower and the butterfly which begins with these words:
>
> > Said the poor flower speaking to the heavenly butterfly:
> > Don't fly away;
> > See how different are our fates: I stay still,
> > You go away.[16]

Thus when Proust quotes these lines, he is following the lead of Amédée Coutance. In fact, he is quoting them a second time, for he has already used them in a letter of June 1902 to Antoine Bibesco in which he apologizes for the "antisocial advice" he gave to the prince, and that "was perhaps nothing more than an unconscious, didactic and pejorative form of the sublime lines, 'Said the poor flower speaking to the heavenly butterfly: / Don't fly away . . . I stay still, you go away' " (*Corr*. 3:61).

While working on *Sodome et Gomorrhe I* in 1915, Proust thus rediscovered, in Professor Coutance's preface, lines that as early as 1902 had been symbolic of his own existence as an immobilized invalid, isolated like the poor flower. The association is strengthened in that the letter to Bibesco also contains another image that Proust frequently applies to himself and that he again makes use of in *Sodome et Gomorrhe I* to describe the solitary invert. In presenting his apologies to Bibesco in June 1902, Proust claimed his improper advice reflected his "subjective and jealous tendencies, like those of a masculine Andromeda always chained to his rock and suffering when he sees Antoine Bibesco going off in a thousand directions but cannot follow him." In a July 1905 letter to Montesquiou, he also describes the "torture of being like Andromeda chained to the rock" and prevented from visiting the count. Now in *Sodome et Gomorrhe I*, Proust, confusing Perseus and the Argonauts, was to say that the solitary invert, "Griselda-like, in his tower, loiters upon the beach, a strange Andromeda whom no Argonaut will come to free" (2:649; 3:27–28). The sketch for "The race of fairies" was less precise at the time of *Contre Sainte-Beuve:* "Several of them, silent and of a marvelous beauty, wonderful Andromedas chained to a sex which will condemn them to solitude . . ." (3:933).[17] Andromeda and "The butterfly and the flower" are images, already present in the letters, that are rediscovered and taken over wholesale for the novel after many long years. They, too, are names of fantasies: solitude, illness, abandonment.

"I stay still, you go away . . .": these lines come from *Les Chants du crépuscule* (XXVII); they were written by Victor Hugo, the author of many of the mediocre lines quoted by Proust. Probably Proust knew these particular lines thanks to Gabriel Fauré, whose first melody (Opus 1, No. 1, 1862), a setting of the lines, was often sung in the salons. Reynaldo Hahn also composed his first tune to the words of a rather paltry Victor Hugo poem, also cited in *Sodome et Gomorrhe I:*

> Since every creature here below
> Imparts to some other
> His music or his flame
> Or his fragrance[18]

The raw materials taken from the correspondence are the building blocks of the novel: Andromeda, the butterfly and the flower, Hermant's son. From life to the novel, the letter is a taking of form, or rather a taking of memory. It turns life into lived experience: images and tableaux. And these are the very tableaux the novel rediscovers, puts on, and stages. This is where the break takes place. For a novel is not simply an unfolding of images and vignettes. Hermant's son, the butterfly and the flower disappear from the novel; they belong to its prehistory.

The Girl with the Red Roses

Now it sometimes happens that life provides not only images, but even a primitive framework, a script for the novel; the correspondence gives evidence of this as well. According to the prewar script, before the creation of Albertine, the middle section of the *Recherche* was devoted, as we have seen (see chapter 4), to the hero's quest for sexual initiation and his pursuit of two women, including a girl with red roses whom he sees briefly at the soirée given by the Princesse de Guermantes (3:979–81 and 3:983ff.).[19]

The hero's attempts to catch up with this girl—which lead him, among other places, to the Opéra where he catches sight of Gurcy dozing off and discovers the woman in him—provide many correspondences with Proust's occupations and preoccupations in the first months of 1908; we can see this in his letters. Perhaps Proust's correspondence reveals only a particular side of his life, whereas Carnet 1, for example, which begins in early 1908 during the very period when Proust's novel was first germinating, gives another whole aspect of his life—his reading material, among other things—

that is not apparent in his letters, except for a few stray references. But the points of contact between the plot as it takes shape in the notebooks from 1910 to 1911 and in Proust's social calendar in the first half of 1908 (even though they often have to do with details) are so numerous, and they form such a tight network, that the relation between life and the novel seems reversed. The question is no longer, how does the plot of 1910 to 1911 transpose the life Proust led in 1908, but rather, did Proust's outings in the spring of that year not serve the purpose of enriching the novel's framework as it was being worked out?

From March to June 1908, Proust mentions a girl in many of his letters. He asks for information about her from Madame Léon Fould, from Louis d'Albufera; he tries to get a photograph of her (*Corr.* 8:63, 93, 112), and to wrangle invitations to balls where he might meet her. At the beginning of June, he confides in Madame de Caraman-Chimay: "Because of something I am writing, and also for sentimental reasons, I would like to go to a ball" (*Corr.* 8:135). Indeed, he catches a glimpse of this girl on June 12, at a ball given by the Princesse de Polignac, but he is not introduced to "the loveliest girl I have ever seen" (*Corr.* 8:138), as he calls her in a letter to François de Pâris. At last, on June 22, at a reception given by the Princesse Murat, André de Fouquières introduces them. Proust immediately writes to Albufera:

> It was extremely emotional for me—I thought I was going to collapse—but it was also a great disappointment, because from close up she was not so good looking, and as soon as she opened her mouth she sounded a bit irritating, more flirtatious than appealing. Now I can spend some time thinking about her more at my leisure, all of my ideas are somewhat mixed up. (*Corr.* 8:147–48)

Then, almost without any transition, he adds: "I have enough ideas for work to last me for months." His infatuation peters out quite rapidly, starting with his next letter to Albufera: "The fact that I found her much less good looking than I thought I would has done me a world of good and calmed me down a great deal" (*Corr.* 8:175). She will never come up again, in conformance with the cycle of enthusiastic fantasy followed by fatal disappointment, a mechanism endlessly repeated in the prewar script.

The girl was called Mademoiselle de Goyon, her first name Oriane. Born in 1887, she was twenty years old and just beginning to frequent high society. How can we believe for a single instant that Proust—busy working at the very same time on Carnet 1, which gives ample evidence of how many other ideas he was ruminating—thought about Oriane de Goyon in any realistic way? She has less to do with the author's biography than with the history of the book. Not only did she leave her first name to the Duchesse de Guermantes—whose name changes from Rosemonde to Oriane in Cahier 43, in the course of the princess' soirée—but she is also the inspiration for the provocative girl whom the hero meets at the same reception (like the seductive Mademoiselle de Goyon at the Princesse de Polignac's); he follows her to the Marengos' in Cahier 49 (just as Proust goes to the Murats'), and she disappears from his life without a trace when he quickly loses interest and sets off in pursuit of the chambermaid.

Once Albertine has replaced her, all that remains is the occasional reference in the *Recherche* to the girl with the red roses, like the passage in *Le Temps retrouvé* that lists the women the narrator has loved, all those whose images he has briefly cherished, including those he has never seen. In this passage, he gives three examples grouped together in a significant way: "Mme Putbus' maid or Mlle d'Orgeville or some young woman or other whose name had caught my eye on the society page of a newspaper, amongst 'the swarm of charming waltzers' " (3:1038; 4:567). A hasty plot summary of Cahiers 43 and 49 is provided by this allusion to the three women introduced at the reception given by the Princesse de Guermantes, the first two in Montargis' narration about brothels, and the girl with the red roses, who had pressed her bosom against the hero's chest: the three women in the novel before the creation of Albertine.

As for the long, wonderful description of the Empire aristocracy at the reception given by the Marengos, it is not included in the definitive text, but the Iénas have inherited their furniture, which is so pointedly admired by the Duchesse de Guermantes in *Le Côté de Guermantes II* (2:537–42; 2:807–11). But in "Un Amour de Swann," we are told that the Prince des Laumes, the future Duc de Guermantes, goes to the Iénas' without his wife (1:369; 1:332), as does the Prince de Guermantes in Cahier 49 (3:986).[20]

In the definitive text, the prewar script has become dispersed into barely recognizable pieces. Life first nourished the novel, providing it not only with images but also with a framework. Then that framework, with its resemblance to a kind of chronicle, came apart. But in the spring of 1908, did Proust not stage his life like a novel? Was his life not lived as if it had already been written?

The Intermittencies of the Heart

In early 1908, a crucial year for the genesis of *A la recherche du temps perdu,* Proust seems to have had the strange experience of assimilating existence and writing to each other, as if the novel had been immediately lived, in the hyperlucidity of a kind of dream. This particular moment prefigures the objective chance of the surrealists, and the state of mania experienced and written about by André Breton in *Nadja,* at the young woman's request: "You will write a novel about me." There are several turning points of this kind in the history of *A la recherche du temps perdu,* and these are its key time periods: 1908; 1914, at which time Alfred Agostinelli's death sends the novel off on a new tack with the developments surrounding the character of Albertine; and 1921, when Proust's visit to the Jeu de paume museum inspires the death of Bergotte. These intense moments, these Proustian epiphanies, always have to do with death. For example, Proust copied out into the novel virtually word for word the letter he had written to Agostinelli on the day of his former secretary's fatal accident, a letter destined never to be received (3:462–65; 4:37–39; Cf. *Corr.* 13:217–21).

One of the novel's most moving and least dogmatic episodes, and one intimately connected with Proust's experiences of the year 1908, is "The Intermittencies of the Heart" in *Sodome et Gomorrhe.* "The Retroactive Loss of My Grandmother," as Proust also calls this section,[21] counterbalances the grandmother's death scene in *Le Côté de Guermantes II.* The idea of "The Intermittencies of the Heart"—that is, the discontinuity of our powers of sensitivity, the unruly succession of the many selves that make up our subjectivity—is fundamental; let us not forget that at one time Proust thought of calling the entire novel *Les Intermittences du coeur.* It is an idea even more important than the scene with the madeleine and the concept of involuntary memory that, raised to the stature of an aesthetic law, was to provide a structure for the novel's creation. If involuntary memory is the aesthetic foundation of the novel, perhaps intermittency corresponds to its origins in lived experience. Indeed, reminiscence is a kind of transcended or domesticated intermittency, but pure intermittency—as we find at the beginning and end of the second stay in Balbec, when the hero dreams about his grandmother, and when he learns of Albertine's intimate relation with Mademoiselle Vinteuil—is too absolute an event to undergo the kind of theoretical taming applied to the madeleine, the paving stones, the spoon or the napkin. Moreover, reminiscence is a form of happiness; it fills one with joy. By contrast intermittency is a catastrophe, a form of mourning and sorrow.

In Carnet 1 the theory of involuntary memory is prefigured by its very absence, that is, as something needed but not yet developed, and Proust, still lacking the theory, interrupts the so-called 1908 novel in this way:[22] "We believe that the past is mediocre because we try to *conceive* of it but that is not it, rather it is a particular unevenness in the paving stones of the baptistry of Saint Mark."[23] And on the following page: "Must we make a novel of it, a philosophical study, am I a novelist?."[24] And two pages further, yet another reminiscence: "Perhaps in houses of the past a piece of green percaline used to plug a windowpane in the sunlight so that I might have that impression."[25] This is the piece of green luster, a reminiscence developed in the manuscript of *Sodome et Gomorrhe* at the time of the narrator's visit with the Verdurins at La Raspelière and briefly alluded to in the definitive text, which cuts out all the dogmatic passages foreshadowing the dénouement of *Le Temps retrouvé* (2:976, 981; 3:335, 339).

Several reminiscences are thus mentioned in Carnet 1, but the novel does not take hold at this point. Proust drops it and moves on to readings for his essay on Sainte-Beuve, which was to bring him back to the novel in 1909. In the very first pages of Carnet 1, before the novel of 1908 was abandoned for lack of the theory of memory, we find several autobiographical notations—including three short dream narratives—that seem to be at the origin of the notebook if not of the novel itself: "Mother's dream, her breathing, turns over, moans. 'You love me, please don't let them operate on me again, I think I am going to die, and there's no point in prolonging the agony' " (3:1031).[26] In the prewar script, "The Intermittencies of the Heart" takes place during the hero's trip to Italy, and this dream, with the grandmother replacing the mother, is the subject of a marginal addition, in the course of a train journey between Padua and Venice, after the hero has met Baronne Putbus' chambermaid and at last quenched his desires: the dream is what initiates the entire memory (3:1032–33).[27] But in the definitive text, the narrator sets off "The Intermittencies of the Heart" by taking off his shoes, and here the dream has disappeared.

The second dream is on page 3 of Carnet 1: "Dream. Father near us. Robert is speaking to him, making him smile, making him give a precise answer to each thing. Absolute illusion of life. So you see that dead one is almost alive. Perhaps he might be wrong in his responses, but at least a facsimile of life. Perhaps he is not dead" (3:1031).[28] This dream is kept in the 1911 draft (3:1048),[29] as well as in the definitive text (2:806–7; 3:175–76); there the father gives over the role of the dead person to the grandmother and becomes the mediator in the place of Proust's brother, Robert. An important sentence, however, from the narration of Carnet 1 and also from the 1911 draft, "Perhaps he might be wrong in his responses," is omitted from the definitive text, as a mark of authenticity.

The third dream is found on page 4:

> Dream, quickly following some people along a cliff, at sunset, we go past them, we do not recognize them perfectly, there is Mother, but she does not care about my life, she says hello, I feel that I will not see her again for months. Would she understand my book? No. And yet the power of the spirit does not depend on the body. Robert tells me that I ought to find out her address, just in case they called me about her death, I don't know what neighborhood she lives in, or the name of the person who is looking after her.[30] (3:1031)

Certain elements recall Swann's dream at the end of "Un Amour de Swann," "along a path which followed the line of the coast, and overhung the sea" (1:411; 1:372). Others, after being shifted into the 1911 draft,[31] are kept in the definitive text (2:788–89; 3:157–59). In particular, the crucial reference to the book remains, although its meaning is reversed: "She was told you were going to write a book. She seemed pleased. She wiped away a tear" (2:788; 3:158).

Thus "The Intermittencies of the Heart," a kind of vestige in the novel, corresponds to a subject matter that predates the novel. Three pages later in Carnet 1, yet another clearly autobiographical notation establishes the setting of "The Intermittencies of the Heart" in the prewar script as well as in the definitive text, a hotel room, whether in Milan or in Balbec: "Met Mother on her trip, after her arrival in Cabourg, same kind of room as in Evian, square mirror."[32] On his arrival in Cabourg in July 1908, Proust probably stayed in a room that reminded him of the hotel in Evian where he had gone with his mother in September 1905, and where she had fallen ill; she was taken back to Paris by Robert Proust and died a few days later. On the very day he arrived in Cabourg in July 1908, Proust, feeling unwell, wrote to Albufera: "I have gone to bed with a rather high fever and probably will stay there for several days, so I have not been able to think about seeing anybody" (*Corr.* 8:183). The hero's isolation when he arrives in Balbec is identical, at least until he agrees to see Albertine. Thus, after a detour through Milan and Venice in the prewar script, "The Intermittencies of the Heart" was placed in a framework that was truer to life: it went from Cabourg to Balbec. And life—the life that continues to reappear, virtually unchanged, from Carnet 1 in 1908 all the way through 1922 and Proust's final work on the novel—is the stuff of dreams. It is always the same material that moves from left to right: sounds and letters, fantasies, dreams; in short, *tableaux vivants.*

Toward the end of Carnet 1 we find two later fragments, dating from 1910 or 1911, that also look ahead to "The Intermittencies of the Heart," but the transition to the novel proper has clearly taken place since the beginning of the notebook. In the first of the two, set in Querqueville (which was to become Balbec), the grandmother asks the hero to recommend a florist by the name of Brichot to his friend Montargis (who was to become Saint-Loup). After his grandmother's death, one day the hero sees her sorrowful face, and he feels suffering at his inability to erase the suffering and disappointment he reads on her face. This time we are dealing with characters in a novel, and from now on the theme of the "intermittencies of the heart" is set: "Probably this same idea often came back to me later and left me cold, but that is because it was separated from that superior aspect, that high position which ideas have for me only on certain days, the only days in life that count, the only days when ideas are complete, rather than being ineffectual fragments of ideas (3:1032)."[33] The extraordinary days of "The Intermittencies of the Heart" are those very days when life and the novel suddenly merge, when life is a novel. A book not built around these kinds of meeting points is not a book that demands to be written.

The last fragment from Carnet 1 that is related to "The Intermittencies of the Heart" is another dream narrative. In this one it is Françoise who plays the role of mediator:

> My Grandmother
>
> Every time I dreamed about her I thought she had gone to bed without telling me I was so sad I saw Françoise go by furtively. She was in bed but not sleeping yet, but she sent me away quickly, impatiently, as if I had missed my chance at wanting to see her by giving preference to everyone else besides her during the daytime and now she did not want to see me. She put out her light and pretended to be asleep.[34] (3:1032)

Here the grandmother takes revenge for the sufferings caused her by the hero: this image, which is still present in the prewar script (3:1042),[35] is eliminated from the definitive text.

"The Intermittencies of the Heart" dominates Carnet 1 from beginning to end: first in the domain of life, then in the realm of fiction, it is of primordial importance to the conception of the 1908 novel, the novel that is interrupted, for lack of the theory of involuntary memory, so that Proust could work on the essay about Sainte-Beuve. "The Intermittencies of the Heart" allows us to witness clearly the evolution from autobiographical notation (Father, Mother, Robert, Cabourg) to novelistic sketching out (Grandmother, Françoise, Montargis, Querqueville).

"Met [*retrouvée*] Mother on her trip," Carnet 1 read, and Cahier 50 will take up this point in 1911: "in that room in Milan where I had first lost [*perdu*] my grandmother—and found her again [*retrouvé*] (3:1038)."[36] *Retrouvé, perdu, retrouvé:* the opposition is already set in motion long before Proust thinks up the title that will sublimate it. The history of the novel begins with "Met Mother" [*Maman retrouvée*]. Time recaptured was time lived, and writing is joined onto it as a necessary antecedent. Beginning meant writing the end.

"Would she understand my book? No," read the autobiographical narrative of 1908. "She was told you were going to write a book. She seemed pleased," we find in the definitive text, as well as in the 1911 draft. In the heart of the dreams of 1908 and the visions of the mother and reunions with her, the question of the book is found. Between 1908 and 1922, between the autobiography and the novel, the grandmother's attitude toward the book contradicts the mother's: the mother in the dream did not understand, the grandmother in the novel will. As for the book project, the fresh start for the novel—which had been abandoned since *Jean Santeuil*—the new beginning mentioned in several letters dating from early 1908, is it not this that brings forth the dreams about Mother and Father? If so, then the work precedes life.

The same can be said of these words in the only dream about the grandmother that does not appear in germ in Carnet 1, a dream that Cahier 48 in 1911 gives in a fuller form than does the definitive text: "Deer, deer, Francis Jammes, fork," according to the definitive text, and a little later, "Francis Jammes, deer, deer" (2:789; 3:159). But in Cahier 48 we find: "Deer, deer, succinctly, Francis Jammes, deer, forks, to recompose yourself, deer, deer, succinctly Francis Jammes, fork." And then, as an echo, "Succinctly, Francis Jammes, fork, deer, to recompose yourself" (3:1046).[37] Two terms have disappeared between 1911 and 1922: *succinctly* and *to recompose yourself*. Proust can hardly have been held responsible for the first omission, because the typist, who could not make out the adverb in the manuscript, left it blank.[38] But Proust himself did eliminate "to recompose yourself," which is no longer in the manuscript dating from the war years.[39] If all the other dreams went through an autobiographical stage in the notes from Carnet 1, was this dream also an actual dream to begin with?

Several critics have attempted to interpret this dream. The deer would appear to harken back to Flaubert's story from the *Trois contes*, "La Légende de Saint Julien l'Hospitalier," in which a stag, mortally wounded by Julien, predicts that the latter will kill his father and his mother. Around November 1908, Proust noted in Carnet 1, "*Saint Julien l'Hospitalier* quote it in Van Blarenberghe. Always remember it."[40] This is an allusion to the article "Sentiments filiaux d'un parricide" [Filial love of a parent-killer], published in

Le Figaro on February 1, 1907, that Proust planned to reprint in a collection. The piece was included in *Pastiches et Mélanges* in 1919, without the Flaubert quotation. Its theme appears to be the sadism a son fatally practices on his mother; perhaps it is related to the guilt Proust felt at the death of his own mother. This seems to be confirmed by the last word of the dream, *Aias*—which is said to mean "Take care you don't catch cold"—since *Aias* is the Greek spelling of Ajax, used by Leconte de Lisle in his new translation of Sophocles' plays;[41] in fact Proust, quoting Sophocles' tragedy, compared Henri Van Blarenberghe's crime in "Sentiments filiaux d'un parricide" to the madness of Ajax, when he mistook shepherds and their flocks for the Greeks and massacred them. The name "Jammes" goes back to the fact that Francis Jammes was so shocked by the scene of sadism at Montjouvain in *Du côté de chez Swann* that he asked Proust to delete it from the next edition,[42] whereas "fork" probably represents an alternative: the choice between "deer" and "Jammes," that is, between killing the father and obeying.[43] Let us also recall that in one of the earliest drafts for the "two ways," the striking of a fork against a plate is what set off the memory of arriving in Combray by train on a day when the workers had been hammering on the rails; this led to an expository section on Proust's aesthetics.[44] The fork, of course, became a spoon in *Le Temps retrouvé*. As there are no fixed limits on the interpretation of dreams, the adverb *succinctly* [*succinctement*] might be a condensation of several terms involving milking—*sein* [breast], *succion* [sucking], *suintement* [oozing]—which would confirm the omnipresence of breasts in *A la recherche du temps perdu*.[45]

Gérard Genette points out that this dream offers the single obvious exception to the absence of internal monologue in the *Recherche;* he is of the opinion that the dream is mainly important for its symbolic value, and that all that matters about it is the "witnessing of awakening, with the break it brings between [the language of dreams] and vigilant consciousness."[46] There is never any dearth of associations, but that is not a good enough reason to reject the need for interpretation out of hand. The words *to recompose yourself,* which Proust omitted between the 1911 draft and the wartime manuscript, are not without importance: in the middle of the first sequence in Cahier 48, the only segment not to be repeated at the end of the second sequence, the words appear to form the central motif of the dream. And is this not also the only nonenigmatic term in the entire series? Perhaps this is why Proust took it out. To recapture lived experience, the dear departed one, "to recompose yourself": this, then, would be the seminal mission of the book.

> Real books should be the offspring not of daylight and casual talk but of darkness and silence. And as art exactly reconstitutes life, around the truths to which we have attained inside ourselves there will always float an atmosphere of poetry, the soft charm of a mystery which is merely a vestige of the shadow which we have had to traverse, the indication, as precise as the markings of an altimeter, of the depth of a work. (3:934; 4:476)

Darkness, shadow, depth: the ideal of *Le Temps retrouvé* is rooted in the world of sleep and dreaming which "The Intermittencies of the Heart" journeys through, "upon the dark current of our own blood as upon an inward Lethe meandering sixfold" (2:787; 3:157).

6

"This shuddering of a heart being hurt"

No one would deny the power of evil in *A la recherche du temps perdu*. The scene in Montjouvain immediately comes to mind: here the hero happens upon Mademoiselle Vinteuil and her friend desecrating the photograph of the musician—"the ugly old monkey" (1:177; 1:160)—during the course of their erotic games. Then there are the tortures Odette puts Swann through, as well as those Swann puts Odette through, for example when he extracts her confession about her relations with women. As we saw at the end of chapter 5, all this shocked the first readers of the novel. Let us not dwell on the author's life, and the all-too-well-known story of how he supposedly stuck rats with hatpins to reach orgasm. Maurice Sachs, perhaps not the most trustworthy source, claimed to have heard the story from Albert Le Cuziat, the owner of the hotel on the Rue de l'Arcade that Proust often went to from 1917 on and that was the model of Jupien's hotel in *Le Temps retrouvé*,[1] a sort of peculiar clearing house reminiscent of Mirbeau and other decadents dazzled by depravity, or Alfred Binet and his *Fétichisme dans l'amour*.[2] Proust happily piles up perverse scenes until he reaches the apotheosis of Charlus' visit to Jupien's hotel.

Nevertheless, a sofa moved into a brothel, a father's memory desecrated, or a mother's, a stabbed rodent, a baron being whipped: none of this is sufficient evidence to prove that Proust is taken in by the fin-de-siècle fashion for evil. Indeed, in speaking of the scene at Montjouvain, he talks about the "appearance of evil" (1:178; 1:161). Aside from its melodramatic and exhibitionistic aspect, evil is depicted by Proust in all of its raw, almost photographic reality, such as the twentieth century—for example Bataille—would reveal it, even if this banalization of evil is never fully recognized. Evil is inseparable from desire, as hatred is from love, yet Proustian eroticism, even if it always has an element of guilt, does not appear to be particularly charged with religion or metaphysics. Somewhere between Mirbeau and Bataille—yet another example of an "in-between"—Proustian evil is again reminiscent of Baudelaire; it is as ambiguous as the hero of corruption who turns out to be Racine's brother under the skin and an emblem of classicism. In 1930 Mario Praz pointed out that "what was holiest and most universal in Baudelaire's poetry was tending to be set apart," and that Baudelaire was "on his way to becoming canonized as a saint once and for all," whereas the "Baudelaire of his own time," the nineteenth century, had been the "satanic Baudelaire" who sent shivers up and down the spines of his contemporaries and then became the paragon of French decadence.[3] "Proust's sadism" owes something to both Baudelaires, the martyr and the monster, and yet is something else again; it cannot be reduced either to the sadism of Sade or to the clinical definition of sadism given by nineteenth-century medecine. What was it then? Our intention in this chapter is to gain an understanding of it, for evil is one of the criteria of being between two centuries.

The characters in *A la recherche du temps perdu* hurt each other, but to hurt someone [*faire mal*] is not necessarily the same thing as to do evil [*faire le mal*]. In fact Proust avoids the word *mal*, along with the term *méchanceté* [unkindness]; he prefers the adjective and its opposite: *méchant* [unkind] and *gentil* [nice]. *Moschant, genstil* is the refrain in Proust's letters to Reynaldo Hahn. "What an old spoilsport [*méchant*] you are!" Albertine says to the hero when, after an argument, he refuses to open his lips in response to her attempts to kiss him (2:863; 3:229). And Saint-Loup, at the end of his rope over his mistress' whims, gives her this advice: "Come on, don't be nasty [*méchante*] . . . I promised you the necklace if you behaved nicely to me [*si tu étais gentille*], but since you treat me like this . . . " (2:182; 2:476). The opposition of "nice" and "mean" is constantly at work in the novel. "You know, . . . your poor grandmother used to say: It's curious, there's nobody who can be as unbearable or as nice as that child" (3:670; 4:1129 [4:234, var. a]), the hero's mother reminds him in *Albertine disparue,* when he jumps onto her train just as it is about to pull out of the station in Venice. Probably people truly worthy of being called evil are few and far between. Most people are mediocre, "nice" or "mean": Meursault, the hero of Camus' *L'Etranger,* also perceives humans in these terms. Let us not be too hasty to jump from adjectives, qualities, and value judgments to substantives and worked-out ideas: Proust himself does not do so.[4]

"Little Old Ladies"

In the prewar script of the novel, "The Intermittencies of the Heart," as we have seen, took place in Italy (see chapter 5). Several different conceits run together in the drafts of Cahiers 48 and 50, but in what appears to be the earliest version, the hero and his mother are on their way back to Paris, in the train leaving Venice. The hero dozes off, and the motion of the train makes him have the following dream:

> My grandmother appeared to me. She was going along a path that led to a train station, walking as quickly as she could. Whistling trains could be heard as they were leaving and she was practically running. She had gotten dirt on her dress, practically lost one of her shoes, her hat was quite crooked and she had a splash of mud going all the way up to her veil. She was red-faced and flushed and she looked so poorly that the bags under her eyes went almost down to her mouth. Her eyes were indescribably sad, but also full of anger and spitefulness. (3:1033)[5]

The grandmother as a little old lady, trotting along and covered with dirt, soiled and missing a shoe, damaged, disgusting, her hair in disarray, but at the same time mean and spiteful: this sinister, hideous image is what led to the most moving pages in the novel, a remarkable illustration of how close the horrible can be to the emotional. This unattractive grandmother was both unwell and mean, mean because she was unwell, because "the only thing apparent to her was the selfishness that had killed her." She takes revenge on her grandson, who has mistreated her for so long: "She climbed the steps to one of the railway cars, stumbled, fell back, an employee brutally perhaps wounding her—oh! if I could only have been sure he had not hurt her—pushed her like a sack into the car and closed the door" (3:1034, Esquisse XIII). In the definitive text, this frightful image has disappeared as the source of the emotion. It was omitted quite late, as if out of a concern for propriety, since it was still in the manuscript of *Sodome et Gomorrhe,* although not at the beginning of "The Intermittencies of the Heart" but rather on the hero's return to Balbec, after the first dinner at the Verdurins' in La Raspelière. When the typescript was corrected, an abstract meditation about sleep and dreams inspired by Bergson took the place of this vision of horror worthy of Athalie's dream in Racine's play.

The grandmother humiliated and described as a little old lady is a dream image separated from the conscious thought that would make it palatable, an unnatural vision with all the cruelty of dreams that refuse to respect the conventions of decency. The image belongs to Baudelaire, particularly the eyes, enormous, with bags under them, full of pain and also a sense of justice. They are the eyes of anger, the eyes of Baudelaire's poem "Les Petites Vieilles":

> eyes as piercing as drills,
> Shining like holes where water nightly slumbers . . .
>
> These eyes are wells made of a million tears
>
> (17–18, 33)

They are also like the eyes of the poor: "I cannot bear those people, with their eyes open wide as carriage entrances! Couldn't you please ask the head waiter to make them leave the café?" (Baudelaire, "Les Yeux des Pauvres," OC 1:319).

The dream of the sullied grandmother has all the trappings of a short Baudelaire prose poem, including the same sort of insensitivity that gave the mother in *Contre Sainte-Beuve* mixed emotions about Baudelaire. She both likes him and hates him, as the protagonist of "Les Yeux des pauvres" feels about his friend: "Ah! you want to know why I hate you today" (OC 1:317). The mother's affection for Baudelaire goes only halfway because of the "cruel things about his family" that are found in his letters (CSB 250). "And as for his cruelty, it shows in his poetry, cruelty with an infinite amount of sensitivity," the son adds, attempting to justify Baudelaire to his mother and to make her understand and accept his sublime savagery, all the more astonishing "in that one feels sure he has felt to the depths of his being the sufferings that he mocks and presents with so little emotion." The poem Proust is commenting on in this passage is, precisely, "Les Petites Vieilles": "not a single one of their sufferings escapes his notice." This is why there is such raw truth in the poem's details:

> whipped by hostile north winds,
> Shivering at the buses' rolling roar . . .
> [They] Drag themselves along like wounded animals
> (9–10, 14)

This is the paradox that the mother in *Contre Sainte-Beuve* cannot understand. Baudelaire was not himself inhuman; according to Proust, it is Baudelaire's readers who run the risk of being inhuman. "Loving Baudelaire . . . is not necessarily a sign of great sensitivity," and "truly hardhearted people can thoroughly enjoy him," because his portrayal of the visions that "hurt" him are "utterly lacking in expressions of sensitivity" (CSB 251).

Evil shows up as an absence of pity or compassion; it is thus a form of cruelty. Mother and son are in agreement about this, but not about Baudelaire's unkindness: "To feel all manner of pain but to be enough in control of oneself to be able to examine it without displeasure, to be able to stand the pain that an unkind act artificially causes . . . : perhaps this subordination of sensitivity to truth, to expression, is essentially a mark of genius, of strength, of an art superior to individual pity" (CSB 251–52). Proust finds Baudelaire innocent by finding his readers guilty. The distance and irony of the good poet are what bad readers and pitiless audiences mistake for unkindness. Baudelaire was not an evil creature, unlike his readers, who thoroughly enjoy *Les Fleurs du mal* without an inkling of the poet's veiled feelings, and unlike the scoundrels blinded by the seeming insensitivity and the sublime impassiveness of the line "The violin shudders like an afflicted heart" ("Harmonie du soir," line 9). This image, as Proust emphasizes, presupposes that Baudelaire felt pain to the depths of his heart. It is because he has known this pain, because it has also been his pain, that he expresses it in a description that is ironic but not indifferent. The witty woman—does she not almost have the Duchesse de Guermantes' voice?—who whispers into an old lady's ear as she goes by "Debris of humanity ripe for eternity!" is not only cruel [*mauvaise*], but her reading is also wrong [*mauvaise*].

Readers who are *mauvais* in these two senses, "cruel" and "wrong," are unaware of the fact that art is a sublimation of life, and as they do not share Proust's emotion in reading "such pitiful and human" lines of Baudelaire's poetry, they misunderstand the truth of *Les Fleurs du mal:* "Oh! this shuddering of a heart being hurt" (CSB 251). And yet is Proust himself convinced by this argument? He keeps coming back to the same paradox in many different forms: "But there is something stranger still in the case of Baudelaire. In the most sublime expressions he has given of certain feelings, he seems to have created an external painting of their form, without sympathizing with them" (CSB 252). Indeed, the mother does not allow her judgment of Baudelaire to be swayed:

> The other one, stabbed by her Madonna-like daughter,
> They could have all made a river with their tears!
> ("Les Petites Vieilles," lines 47–48, CSB 253)

Here, so she claims, Baudelaire does not seem to have shown the slightest sympathy for the mother. Proust himself asks, "But does he appear to feel 'compassion,' to be inside of these people's hearts?" And he leaves the question unanswered. The mother cannot bear the stunning indifference of a dream devoid of tenderness and oblivious to humanity; she sides with the poet's mother with her virtuous revenge:

> It is she, in the depths of Gehenna, who prepares
> The stakes at which maternal crimes are burnt away.
> ("Bénédiction," lines 19–20, CSB 254)

Maternal crimes: are they crimes of mothers, or crimes against mothers? At any rate there is an absence of pity here. That is what is wrong according to the mother in *Contre Sainte-Beuve*—as well as Brunetière, Bourget, and Baudelaire's many critics—and she refuses to forget it: this is the quintessential vision of the mother as little old lady. Baudelaire wrote to his mother, Madame Aupick, "Do you really think that if I wanted to, I couldn't cost you a fortune and make you spend your old age in complete poverty? . . . But I have been holding myself back, and with each new crisis I tell myself, 'No, my mother is old and poor, I must leave her in peace.' "[6] It is letters like this that bothered the mother in *Contre Sainte-Beuve*. Taken out of context, the quotation is unbearable, but in fact its true meaning is that of a declaration of love.

If this is evil, it does indeed make frequent appearances in Proust's novel, in the form of a seemingly pitiless vision, for example at the end of *Sodome et Gomorrhe,* with the "Désolation au lever du soleil" [Sorrow at sunrise]. The hero has just learned that Albertine knows Mademoiselle Vinteuil, and he has spent a night of insomnia, suffering, and tears. "But at that moment, to my astonishment, the door opened and, with a throbbing heart, I seemed to see my grandmother standing before me, as in one of those apparitions that had already visited me, but only in my sleep. Was it all only a dream, then?" (2:1166; 3:513). This is a vision of the mother playing the role of the grandmother, of the mother as a little old lady. The dream world is alluded to, the one that up to this point has been the sole repository of the cruel Baudelairean vision of the damaged woman: "Her dishevelled hair, whose grey tresses were not hidden and strayed about her troubled eyes, her ageing cheeks, my grandmother's own dressing-gown which she was wearing, all these had for a moment prevented me from recognising her and had made me uncertain whether I was still asleep or my grandmother had come back to life" (2:1166–67; 3:513). Her hair is in disorder, as is the grandmother's in the dream, her tresses serpentine, like those of the woman who turns men to stone, Medusa. Her cheeks—the very cheeks that are the site of eroticism in Proust, like Odette's cheeks devoured by Swann ("with eyes starting from his head and jaws tensed as though to devour her, he would fling himself upon this Botticelli maiden and kiss and bite her cheeks"

[1:260; 1:234–35])—are withered, henceforth devoid of desirability, her robe the very one worn by the grandmother on that first evening in Balbec, when she helped the hero off with his shoes.

Desecrated Mothers

As is shown by an analysis of *Contre Sainte-Beuve,* Proust interprets the cruelty of *Les Fleurs du mal* as love seen from the outside, coldly, by a third party observing with feigned indifference; it is a marriage of pity and irony.[7] There is something filtered and prepackaged, something distant in the vision of the mother as a little old lady, crystallized by Saint-Loup's snapshot of the grandmother in Balbec. Yet the most famous examples of evil in Proust's work, particularly the "desecrated mothers," also—or perhaps still—have an element of pathos, that is, theatricality and sentimentality. Between the 1896 publication of the story "La Confession d'une jeune fille" in *Les Plaisirs et les Jours* and the 1907 article in *Le Figaro,* "Sentiments filiaux d'un parricide" (reprinted in *Pastiches et Mélanges*), cruelty has certainly taken on a purer form, but it still retains a melodramatic dimension, almost like a black mass.

The heroine of "La Confession d'une jeune fille" gives up pleasure and vice for a time, but when the man who originally corrupted her comes to dinner at her parents' house, she once again goes astray. Pleasure and pain, sexual enjoyment and evil are inextricably linked: "So while pleasure held me tighter and tighter in its grip, I felt, in the depths of my heart, the stirrings of a boundless sadness and sorrow; it seemed to me that I was making my mother's soul weep, the soul of my guardian angel, the soul of God" (JS 95). There is a Baudelairean element here, reminiscent of Baudelaire's "Fusées": "And man and woman know from birth that all sexual enjoyment is found in evil" (OC 1:652). The inseparability of sexual enjoyment and evil gives pleasure a sense of blasphemy, seen in the girl's recourse to Christian vocabulary ("soul," "guardian angel," "God"); only this vocabulary can express sexual pleasure in terms of a coinciding or an overlapping of ecstasy and horror:

> I had never been able to read without a shudder stories of scoundrels torturing animals, or their own wives and children; now I had the

> confused impression that every guilty act of sexual enjoyment has just as much savagery for the body experiencing pleasure, and that just as many good intentions, just as many blameless angels inside of us meet their martyrdom and weep. (JS 95)

The wording of this passage makes it read like a popularized version of Baudelaire; this is dime-store satanism. It is almost like reading one of those masterpieces of banality produced around the turn of the century by the likes of Péladan or Rachilde, complete with sensationalized ending: the girl catches a glimpse of herself in the mirror, "changed into an animal" by pleasure; at that very moment she thinks of her mother, whom she happens to notice just then on the balcony; she watches her mother watching her and witnessing her daughter's climax: "I saw my mother looking at me in a daze."[8] The mother, stunned, immediately falls dead from shock, "her head caught between two railings of the balcony." The last gasp of this melodrama so horrible it affects even God is mysticism: "God, who knows everything, would not have wished it" (JS 96). Or if there is evil, if the climax of the daughter turns into the murder of the mother, if the daughter's pleasure—or the son's—assumes the desecration of the mother, God is the one responsible; evil is in God.

In "Sentiments filiaux d'un parricide," the liturgical setting has more or less disappeared in the description of Henri Van Blarenberghe's "maternal crime." At first, Proust even appears to affect the playful tone of an Edgar Allan Poe tale, or one of Baudelaire's prose poems like "Le Mauvais Vitrier." He is familiar with the gratuitous and charming perversity of Lucretius' *suave mari magno*—the pleasure one feels, if one is safely in the port, in gazing on the great sea's troubled waves putting others at risk—or rather the ambiguous pleasure of the "blend of *suave mari magno* and *memento quia pulvis*" (2:715; 3:89) with which the Princesse de Guermantes' guests observe Swann's terminal illness. This combination of selfishness and piousness—a phrase the narrator attributes to Saint-Loup (as "Robert would have said")—quite accurately defines the sadistic, Christian Baudelaire of the turn of the century. Now the writer has these ill-defined feelings while reading the newspaper, just as in *Le Temps retrouvé* Madame Verdurin was to find out about the wreck of the Lusitania with its 1,200 victims:

> As she dipped it [her croissant] in her coffee and gave a series of little flicks to her newspaper with one hand so as to make it stay open without her having to remove her other hand from the cup, "How horrible!" she said. "This is something more horrible than the most terrible stage tragedy." (3:797; 4:352)

But the tragedy of others makes her croissant taste even more delicious and brings to her face a look of deep satisfaction. Baudelaire as well, borrowing the thought from Emerson, had spoken of this divided, disturbing element: "When a man gets into bed, almost every one of his friends has a secret desire to see him die," he wrote in "Fusées" (OC 1:652).

Proust's article about Van Blarenberghe's matricide thus begins with "that abominable and voluptuous act that is called *reading the newspaper*" (CSB 154). Abominable and voluptuous: this joining together of voluptuousness and evil, the quintessential Baudelairean oxymoron, goes along with Proust's belief that all the world's misfortunes reported in the newspaper are turned into a "morning feast" and "become wonderfully associated in a particularly stimulating and exciting way, with the sipping of a few prescribed sips of *café au lait*," the drink Proust lived on during the last few years of his life.

But this playful, gracefully jubilant style, like Poe's or Baudelaire's, cannot fend off the news of the "maternal crime." This time, Greek mythology rather than Christian ritual is called on to speak of madness, and a refrain borrowed from Tolstoy is attributed to the mother in the throes of death: "Henri, what have you done to me! What have you done to me!" (CSB 156). In spite of the allusions to Ajax and Oedipus, what really fascinates Proust is the ordinariness of hatred mixed with love, the everyday aspect of crime, its true banality. "I have tried to show the pure, religious atmosphere of moral beauty presiding over the explosion of madness and blood that splashes it but does not succeed in soiling it" (CSB 157). Oedipus of course—but we are all Oedipus, as Freud also believed. This refined man, who sent Proust such sensitive condolences on the death of his mother, was the same man who the very next day would take his own mother's life. Love of the mother includes hatred of the mother, not only the love of the son for the mother but also, in a far more disturbing way, as in the opening poem of *Les Fleurs du mal,* "Bénédiction," the love of the mother for the son, which does not stop her from hating and cursing the poet within him.

Proust had already alluded to this hatred of the mother for the son in *Jean Santeuil.* The presence of this feeling mitigates, and even modifies, the image of the all-loving, all-suffering mother of *A la recherche du temps perdu.* The *mater dolorosa* is also the resentful Madona of "Bénédiction," a harpy: the mother, too, contributes to the son's wounds. In the son's memory, the wound made by the mother is still bleeding. Proust writes: "For sometimes hatred snakes its way into the heart of the most limitless love, and seems almost lost there" (JS 689). Sometimes? Would it not be more accurate to say "always"? It is not so much that hatred accidentally blunders into the greatest of loves, but rather that it belongs there, as a requisite accompaniment to love: on the very same page, Proust opines that words of tenderness we have failed to speak to those we love will always remain "the cruel underside of the wrongs against us that their own tenderness indulged in." Thus, in the *Recherche,* the hero will eternally regret the consolation he withheld from his grandmother after hurting her. Love and hatred, tenderness and wrongs once again prove inseparable in the only form of reciprocity imaginable: "I hate you as much as I love you!" wrote Baudelaire in "A celle qui est trop gaie" (line 16). And what Proust began with the reading of a newspaper, like something out of a Poe story, he ends like a Freud essay, his casual tone completely lost: " 'What have you done to me? What have you done to me?' If we took the time to think about it, perhaps we wouldn't find a single truly loving mother unable, on her dying day, and often long before, to make this reproach to her son" (CSB 158).

In *Jean Santeuil,* Proust reached the same painful conclusion in his description of the old age of Jean's parents: "Little by little, this son whose intelligence, morals, and way of life she had tried to shape had managed to inculcate his own intelligence, morals, and way of life in her and had modified those of his mother" (JS 871). The mother is denatured by the son's vices. "Love," Proust writes, "is our great initiator, our great corrupter. It assimilates us to itself and alienates us from ourselves. She has become like her son" (JS 874)—that is, evil.

It is written that because the mother loved the son, the son shall kill the mother—or perhaps the mother shall kill the son. All sons are mother killers, and "Sentiments filiaux d'un parricide" ends with the same image as *Sodome et Gomorrhe,* the mother as a little old lady: "we kill everything that loves us with the worries we cause" (CSB 158). "If we could see, in the body we hold dear, the slow work of destruction carried out by the painful tenderness that gives it life, if we could see the faded eyes, the hair so long defiantly black but finally beaten as well and touched with white, the hardening of the arteries, the failing kidneys" (CSB 159), then unlike Henri Van Blarenberghe, we would kill ourselves without waiting an instant longer, instead of—that is, before—killing our mothers. When Henri stabbed himself, his eyeball hung out over the pillow while he was dying, as Proust mentions on another melodramatic note.

Love of the mother includes hatred of the mother, in both senses of the word *of.* Love always includes hatred and culminates in murder, or at least that is the message of *Les Plaisirs et les Jours* and *Jean Santeuil.* But what about *A la recherche du temps perdu?* It is true that in *Albertine disparue* we read: "juxtaposing the deaths of my grandmother and of Albertine, I felt that my life was defiled by a double murder" (3:506; 4:78), but the chapter of the "desecrated mothers" is not included in the novel. It is subtly avoided in *Sodome et Gomorrhe,* that is, mentioned as something that should be gone into elsewhere: "But let us not consider here a subject that deserves a chapter to itself: the Profanation of the Mother" (2:939; 3:300). This earlier theme has already been recalled by Monsieur de Charlus' "ladylike" aspect, his resemblance to a woman, his mother: sons "consummate upon their faces the profanation of their mothers" (2:938–39; 3:300). Whether they are inverts or not, their quest for pleasure is necessarily a desecration, given their resemblance to their mothers.

Every mother is desecrated; every son is a desecrater. Sexual enjoyment is once again inextricably linked to pain, at least pain inflicted on the mother if not on one's partner, and the presence of pain is revealed to one if one abstracts oneself from desire: in a mirror, in a dream. All sensual pleasure does harm to the mother, a connection more clearly suggested in the sketches for *Contre Sainte-Beuve:* "The face of a living son, a kind of monstrance displaying all the hopes of a sublime mother who has died, is a sort of desecration of this sacred memory," for, in the same spirit, "it is by flashing his mother's smile that he goads girls on to debauchery."[9] By making the monstrance into an emblem of memory, like the last line of Baudelaire's "Harmonie du soir" ("Your memory in me lights up like a monstrance"), Proust's sentence confirms how inseparable Baudelaire is from the theme of desecrated mothers. But in *Contre Sainte-Beuve,* Proust discerned in the work of Baudelaire himself "great blazing lines of poetry 'like monstrances' " (CSB 254), and the examples he gave were "Bénédiction" and the "maternal crimes" of Baudelaire's Racinian poetry. Proust will end up leaving this flamboyant-style Baudelaire behind. Is that why *A la recherche du temps perdu* does not continue down the path of the "desecrated mothers"?

Baudelairean Devotion

It is peculiar that Proust never mentions Baudelaire's diaries—published for the first time in 1887 and reprinted in 1908—which strengthened the poet's assimilation to the decadent movement. Nonetheless, there is little doubt that he sees in Baudelaire the model of the "disease of will" to which he chalks up his protagonist's character traits, even as early as "La Confession d'une jeune fille," as well as his hero's deficiencies. Evil, as Proust portrays it—at least up until *Contre Sainte-Beuve,* especially in the form of "little old ladies" and "desecrated mothers"—seems close to Baudelairean evil as it was perceived at the end of the nineteenth century: confusing sexual enjoyment with evil, feeling torn between horror and ecstasy, and knowing hatred to coexist with love. "In every man, at every moment," Baudelaire wrote in "Mon coeur mis à nu," "there are to be found two simultaneous postulates, one toward God, the other toward Satan" (OC 1:682). "Even as a child, I felt in my heart two contradictory feelings, the horror of life and the ecstasy of life. That's just the way it is with someone who is lazy and high-strung" (OC 1:703). There is no dearth of arguments establishing a kinship between Baudelaire and Proust in the realm of fin-de-siècle evil. But as we shall see, there is no certainty that quite apart from the manifestations of evil, its origins are the same in the two writers.

Here is the plot outline of a melodrama that Proust thought of writing in 1906, as it is given in a letter to Reynaldo Hahn in September of that year:

> A married couple love each other, the husband feels a boundless, saintly, pure (but naturally not chaste) affection for his wife. But the man is a sadist, and outside of his love for his wife he has relations with whores in which he finds pleasure in sullying his own feelings of tenderness. And in the end the sadist's needs escalate, and he even goes so far as to speak degradingly of his wife to these whores and to have them say bad things about her (he is disgusted five minutes later). On one occasion while he is speaking in this way, his wife enters the room without his noticing; she cannot believe her eyes and ears, and collapses. Then she leaves her husband. He begs her not to, but nothing can change her mind. The whores want to continue, but sadism would be too painful now, and after trying one last time to win back his wife's heart without her even responding, he kills himself. (*Corr*. 6:216)

A mixture of desecration and mawkishness, this plot cannot fail to call to mind the equally horrible ones Baudelaire sketched out—and similarly abandoned—for "L'Ivrogne" and "La Pente du mal." Baudelaire's dream was to make "a gratuitous atrocity" (OC 1:632) comprehensible. A man loves his wife and kills her in spite of his love: "he particularly resents his wife's resignation, her gentleness, her patience and her virtue." And as a demonstration of the executioner's love for his victim, her death makes him cry out: "Poor angel, how she must have suffered!" (OC 1:633).

Proust's plot outline, like Baudelaire's, recognizes the reflexive nature of cruelty, culminating in the pleasure Baudelaire's killer takes in confessing his crime, or, to a somewhat lesser extent, in the suicide of Proust's hero. According to the model of "L'Héautontimorouménos":

> I am the wound and the knife!
> I am the slap and the cheek!

I am the limbs and the rack!
And the victim and the executioner.
(21–24)

The executioner of the loved woman is also the executioner of himself, both murderer and victim, "homicidal and suicidal."

In a letter to Louis de Robert dating from the summer of 1913, seven years later, Proust suggests for the Montjouvain scene a model that was obviously already the same one as the melodrama:

> The idea for this scene was suggested to me by various things, but especially this: an eminently worthy, well-known man was the lover of a prostitute, even though he was married and had children. Now in order to have complete pleasure, he had to say to this prostitute, "the little monster," referring to his own son. And yet once he was back home, he was a very good father. (*Corr.* 12:238)

Here, too, ambivalence is the moral of the story, as the father debases the son he loves, but Baudelaire's project, although it is strongly influenced by Poe—to analyze "a gratuitous act of atrocity"—has been turned in the direction of a clinical description; this is fiction taken from the card catalog of criminal anthropology.

Perhaps the similarity of these two melodramatic fantasies belongs in the annals of literary anecdotes. But what is more important is that Proust seems to share one of the most conspicuous features of Baudelairean evil: hatred of sexual reproduction. As Georges Blin has demonstrated, associating the act of love with torture or surgery implies a depiction of love as something incomplete; that is, love is perceived outside the domain of procreation.[10] For Baudelaire—and for Maupassant and Céline after him—no middle course exists between the Scyllas and Charybdises of reproduction and disease; no love remains untouched by evil and suffering. As early as "La Fanfarlo," Samuel Cramer, the poet's double, "thought of reproduction as a vice of love, and of pregnancy as an illness proper to a spider. Somewhere he wrote: 'Angels are hermaphroditic and sterile' " (Baudelaire, OC 1:577). Pregnancy itself appears to be nothing more than a disease maliciously weighing love down. Later on, Baudelaire jubilantly described his prose poems as "horrors and monstrosities that would make your pregnant readers lose their babies."[11] That was his way of expressing his desire to make his prose poems repulsive.

Although we would be at pains to find anything quite so overt in Proust, reproduction, pregnancy, and pregnant women are still regularly objects of sarcasm in the *Recherche,* most prominently perhaps in the Duchesse de Guermantes' joke about Général de Montserfeuil, who consoles himself over his electoral defeat by getting his wife pregnant again: "It's the one *arrondissement* where the poor General has never failed" (2:532; 2:802). Even more direct is Françoise's cruelty toward the kitchen maid who in "Combray" is compared by Swann to Giotto's "Charity," "a poor sickly creature, some way 'gone' in pregnancy" (1:86; 1:79). Reproduction and disease become associated in "the poor girl, whose pregnancy had swelled and stoutened every part of her, even including her face and her squarish, elongated cheeks" (1:87; 1:80); her very cheeks have become corrupted. Through the kitchen maid, Charity itself—that is, love of one's neighbor through love of God—is undermined, and Françoise's cruelty has the impact of blasphemy.

Several of the narrator's remarks about reproduction also have a Baudelairean flavor, including two peculiar comparisons in the space of a few pages during the passage in *Sodome et Gomorrhe I* that reveals Charlus' homosexuality, or rather, according to the doctrine defended by Proust, his feminine nature.

The first comparison is brought on by the savage noises heard by the hero once Charlus and Jupien have withdrawn into the shop. The racket they make at the moment of orgasm leads him to interpret the sexual act—in conformance with a remark by Freud—as a kind of attack: "I might have thought that one person was slitting another's throat within a few feet of me" (2:631; 3:11). Now the narrator's comment, reminiscent of the scene at Montjouvain, was to determine his subsequent conception of sadism, and it contains a lesson for the future: "I concluded from this later on that there is another thing as vociferous as pain, namely pleasure" (2:631; 3:11). This is the same association of suffering and pleasure that has become habitual, but here it is related only to noise. The observer is no longer in the position of a voyeur, which suggests an element of complicity, but rather is in the position of a pure listener, separate, foreign, as in Baudelairean surgery and its extraction from desire: "There is another thing as vociferous as pain, namely pleasure," Proust goes on, "especially when there is added to it—in the absence of the fear of an eventual parturition, which could not be the case here, despite the hardly convincing example in the *Golden Legend*—an immediate concern about cleanliness" (2:631; 3:11). Noise seems to bring pleasure and pain even closer together insofar as the partners are preoccupied with the fear of conceiving a child or with some aspect of hygiene: reproduction or disease are still in the neighborhood of love, even if there is in fact no pregnant man in *La Légende dorée.*[12] The fear of conceiving a child, that is, the premeditated attempt to separate the sexual act and reproduction—which is also the refusal of the genetic goal of the sexual act—facilitates its assimilation to torture. Another way of looking at it is that homosexuals' concern with hygiene, as well as heterosexuals' preoccupation with contraception, makes the brutality of love obvious. The sexual act is conceived of as a medical relation with the body of the other: surgery or butchery. Even without disease, sexual pleasure implies a reification of the body.

A few pages later, after the cruel and almost supernatural revelation of the woman in Charlus, the narrator comes back to the subject of his lengthy obtuseness, and here again he reverts to a comparison between pregnancy and sexual inversion:

> Until that moment, in the presence of M. de Charlus I had been in the position of an unobservant man who, standing before a pregnant woman whose distended outline he has failed to remark, persists, while she smilingly reiterates "Yes, I'm a little tired just now," in asking her tactlessly: "Why, what's the matter with you?" But let someone say to him: "She is expecting a child," and suddenly he catches sight of her stomach and ceases to see anything else.
>
> (2:636; 3:15)

This is a strange image: the woman in Charlus, that is, *vice*—Proust condemns the term but uses it again and again—is assimilated to the woman's pregnancy, to the child she is carrying. Because Proust regularly conceives of sexual inversion as a congenital, nervous disorder, the equating of pregnancy and illness—which finds its linguistic analogue in the French phrases *tomber enceinte* and *tomber malade* [to "fall" pregnant and to fall ill]—is reinforced once again.

One final allusion to reproduction closes the circle. All of *Sodome et Gomorrhe,* or at least the entire second stay in Balbec that makes up the majority of the novel, is built around the strife-ridden interplay between desire and mourning, between sexual enjoyment and death; the hero is split between his grandmother and Albertine as he is split between the two "Intermittencies of the Heart" which open and close his time in Balbec. The passage in which these two sides—mourning and desire, or the horror of life and the ecstasy of life—become intertwined and reveal the volume's principal theme comes after the dreams about the grandmother. The hero struggles against the resurgence of his desires while observing that his sadness is fading: "even in the midst of a grief that is still acute, physical desire will revive" (2:811; 3:179). Mourning and desire, like pain and sexual pleasure, inevitably meld. Proust gives this example: "Do we not see, in the very room in which they have lost a child, its parents soon come together again to give the little angel a baby brother?" (2:811; 3:179). Love could not be closer to grief, or reproduction to morbidity, or in fact life to death: after David killed Bathsheba's first husband, she bore him the child Solomon. But outside of its reproductive goals, when it is concerned with hygiene or contraception, love is a torment. With the exception of angels and hermaphrodites, sterility is identified with savagery. In Proust's eyes, as in Baudelaire's, when love is not a means of reproduction, it is a form of cruelty: it is doomed to suffering and evil.

Sadism as the Aesthetics of Melodrama

During the summer of 1913, when he has found a publisher for *Du côté de chez Swann,* Proust defends the Montjouvain scene to Louis de Robert, who has been working as his agent in trying to get the novel published; he emphasizes that sadists will not like this episode any more than homosexuals will like the homosexual scenes, and he puts forth this argument: "As for people who seek out cruelty"—this, then, is how Proust defines sadists—"they would find nothing more displeasing than to be told: 'You are sensitive, but perverted' " (*Corr.* 12:238). Just as Proust diagnoses homosexuality as an illness having to do with defective nerves, he understands sadism to be a form of perverted sensitivity, quite the opposite of the sublimated sensitivity or the sublime impassivity he used to defend Baudelaire in *Contre Sainte-Beuve*. This time Proust limits himself to the categories of medicine that had been used to discuss the case of Baudelaire as early as Cesare Lombroso's book, which appeared in French in 1889 under the title *L'Homme de génie*.[13] It is true that Proust was so good at adapting his letters to the expectations of his correspondents that the letters sometimes give the impression that they were written by the people to whom they were addressed, like Robert de Montesquiou or Madame Straus. Nevertheless, a note Proust made in Carnet 1 in 1908 confirms the theory that he tends to see sadism as a symptom: "What the sadist is, pleasure is pain, more a result than a cause of sadism."[14]

Even so, Charlus' tirade in *Sodome et Gomorrhe* against Jews who live on the Rue des Blancs-Manteaux or enjoy listening to Wagner's Good Friday Spell (2:1141–43; 3:490–91) is liberally sprinkled with the terms *sadism*, *perfidy*, and *profanation*, and here the manuscript has been corrected to avoid repeating what was originally the single term "*perversité*": if sadism is always Christian and pathological, Jews would appear to be the true perverts of *A la recherche du temps perdu*, the only ones of any consequence, free of all sentimentality, like the "strange Jew" from the Rue des Blancs-Manteaux "who boiled the Host, after which"—or so Charlus joyfully imagines—"I think they boiled him" (2:1143; 3:492). But aside from the Jews—or rather the Jews as Charlus perceives them—Proust does not believe in sadism as unmitigated and heartless perversity. Moreover, the assimilation of homosexuals to Jews in *Sodome et Gomorrhe I* suggests that because homosexuals are themselves "sensitive, but perverted," Proust does not believe in gratuitous acts of perversion, even on the part of Jews, in the "gratuitous atrocity" of "Le Mauvais Vitrier."

As the narrator points out, the scene he observes in Montjouvain was later to determine "the notion I was to form of sadism" (1:173; 1:157). This is how Proust looks ahead to the events of *La Prisonnière*, after Vinteuil's septet is played at the Verdurins'. Now this idea of sadism projected into the future is tantamount to a denial of the very existence of sadism. Just as homosexuality is the homosexual's illusion, sadism is an illusion created when one observes cruelty; it corresponds to the point of view of a third party—who is, in fact, the voyeur—whereas cruelty itself always remains blinded to its own truth. Evil as such, or rather wickedness, is never anything more than a theatrical illusion in *A la recherche du temps perdu*.

It is true that Mademoiselle Vinteuil tortured her father, but she did so by pretending to have a streak of meanness that was not her true nature, that is, by playing a role that in a sense went against nature, at the very least against her own nature: "She reached out as far as she could across the limitations of her true nature to find the language appropriate to the vicious young woman she longed to be thought" (1:176; 1:159). She puts on an act, but it is unconvincing, as she speaks "in a strained tone, in which her ingrained timidity paralysed her impulse towards audacity" (1:176; 1:159). Mademoiselle Vinteuil and her friend have desecrated the musician's memory, but their confused feelings give no evidence whatsoever of any true wickedness on their part, so that the narrator concludes that "if M. Vinteuil had been able to be present at this scene, he might still, in spite of everything, have continued to believe in his daughter's goodness of heart, and perhaps in so doing he would not have been altogether wrong" (1:178; 1:161).

It is actually because of its clumsiness that Proust describes the Montjouvain scene as sadistic, for it is the product of a halfhearted attempt at theatricality: as Proust puts it, "when we find in real life the creation of an aesthetics of melodrama, it is generally sadism that is responsible for it" (1:178–79; 1:161; modified translation). Above all, desecration is proof of a belief in ritually violated values, and that is what gives it its element of pathos:

> A sadist of her kind is an artist in evil, which a wholly wicked person could not be, for in that case the evil would not have been external. . . . Sadists of Mlle Vinteuil's sort are creatures so purely sentimental, so naturally virtuous, that even sensual pleasure appears to them as something bad, the prerogative of the wicked. (1:179; 1:162)

This passage is ambiguous. Twice Proust appears to distinguish between Mademoiselle Vinteuil's sadism and sadism of another sort, an authentic kind of sadism that she fails to imitate: "[sadists like her] endeavour to impersonate, to identify with, the wicked, . . . in order to gain the momentary illusion of having escaped beyond the control of their own gentle and scrupulous nature. . . . And I could understand how she must have longed for such an escape when I saw how impossible it was for her to effect it" (1:179; 1:162). The way Mademoiselle Vinteuil has of associating sexual enjoyment and wickedness is less reminiscent of Sade than of Baudelaire; the difference between them—between true wickedness and the "appearance of evil" or the "aesthetics of melodrama"—is that the perspective is reversed, going from insensitive perversion to perverted sensitivity, from materialism to satanism. In a reversal reminiscent of the note from Carnet 1 quoted above, "It was not evil that gave her the idea of pleasure, that seemed to her attractive; it was pleasure, rather, that seemed evil" (1:180; 1:163).

Mademoiselle Vinteuil is also similar to the heroine of "La Confession d'une jeune fille" because of her Christian sense of guilt and sin: "She came at length to see in pleasure itself something diabolical, to identify it with Evil" (1:180; 1:162). It is unusual to find Evil capitalized in the *Recherche,* as if it were some sort of idol or mythological creature. Mademoiselle Vinteuil is "an ordinarily kind, suffering person" playacting at being "cruel and wanton" (1:180; 1:163). She believes in evil but she is mistaken, for evil is not to be found where she believes, in the liturgy of blasphemy and the rituals of desecration, but rather in everyday life:

> Perhaps she would not have thought of evil as a state so rare, so abnormal, so exotic, one in which it was so refreshing to sojourn, had she been able to discern in herself, as in everyone else, that indifference to the sufferings one causes which, whatever other names one gives it, is the most terrible and lasting form of cruelty.
> (1:180; 1:163)

We play act at being sadists precisely in order to block out the endless, ordinary bruises we inflict on those we love. Like Henri Van Blarenberghe, we kill our loved ones quickly to avoid recognizing that we are killing them slowly. Even before the description of the scene of sadism, the hero's mother provides us with the key to its meaning when she speaks of Mademoiselle Vinteuil's "remorse at having virtually killed her father" (1:175; 1:158). And Mademoiselle Vinteuil brings us back once again to Baudelaire and the "desecrated mothers," the paradigm of true cruelty, of common cruelty: readers who see in Vinteuil a transposition of Proust's mother are probably not completely in error.

In *La Prisonnière,* the narrator works out his adult conception of sadism. He explains the Montjouvain scene retrospectively as a perversion of love, and more specifically a love so excessive that it reverses into its opposite: "Her adoration of her father was the very condition of his daughter's sacrilege" (3:263; 3:765), he concludes, after judging that it was precisely because of their cult to Vinteuil, "in those moments in which people run counter to their true inclinations," that "the two girls had been able to take an insane pleasure in the profanations which have already been narrated" (3:263; 3:765). The debasement of the love object is essentially nothing more than another form of love, the sign or the proof of love, a gesture that is perhaps sadistic but not worthy of Sade, for let us not confuse the Marquis with the term derived from his name in psychiatric treatises. In this way Proust finally reaches the conclusion that sadism can be reduced to a shadow of itself:

> Mlle Vinteuil had acted only out of sadism, which did not excuse her, though it gave me a certain consolation to think so later on. No doubt she must have realised, I told myself, at the moment when she and her friend had profaned her father's photograph, that what they were doing was merely morbidity, silliness, and not the true and joyous wickedness which she would have liked to feel.
>
> (3:264; 3:766)

As in "Combray," instead of distinguishing between Mademoiselle Vinteuil's brand of sadism and the successfully staged sadism of Sade, Proust opposes her sadism to "true wickedness," "fundamental wickedness," by which he means an evil nature, an identity blinded to evil. But the latter is not worthy of Sade, because the awareness of evil, and hence the pleasure of evil, are lacking. If this is the case, who are the true, joyfully wicked characters in *A la recherche du temps perdu?* What heroes prove to be worthy of Sade?

With Rachel, who is an actress—albeit a mediocre one—the misunderstanding is different, but just as complete. In *Le Côté de Guermantes I,* she is described as being possessed by "a momentary impulse of sadistic cruelty," but Proust immediately adds that this impulse is "totally out of keeping with her genuine feelings of affection for Saint-Loup" (2:183; 2:477). Although she does not set out merely to imitate wickedness as does Mademoiselle Vinteuil, this does not mean she is inherently wicked; rather, when she harms someone, she believes the other has deserved it and she is merely taking her revenge. For her, cruelty is no more joyful than it is for Mademoiselle Vinteuil. Is there not a suggestion that neither woman is quite equal to the task of sadism? The narrator, on the other hand, who understands them, who judges them and reveals their lack of true sadism, is the only one who, if he so desired, if he felt like it . . . Now it is true that after Rachel—still unconsciously, of course—has wounded a rival of hers by starting up a feud with her, the narrator concludes: "I did my utmost to pay no more heed to the incident than I had paid to my grandmother's sufferings when my great-uncle, to tease her, used to give my grandfather brandy, the idea of deliberate unkindness being too painful for me to bear" (2:177; 2:471). But if the idea of unkindness makes him suffer, this still proves that unkindness does exist, and that it is possible to act out of unkindness. Actually, no one in the novel appears to do so. Mademoiselle Vinteuil hurts people out of love, Rachel out of stupidity. Only the hero has a conception of true, joyful unkindness, his great-uncle's and his own, but the narrator covers it up.

Evil is one of those domains that requires a distinction between the hero and the narrator of the novel, for the narrator, usually so prolific, never provides an analysis of the hero's potential for unkindness. Indeed, after recognizing that the hero willfully closes his eyes to the problem of cruelty, the narrator does the same thing. Confession and forgetfulness: this is the very definition of denial. Moreover, the narrator somewhat overstates his case: he first admits the existence of cruelty and then refutes it by again reducing evil to a theatrical illusion:

> And yet, . . . unkindness has probably not in the minds of the unkind that pure and voluptuous cruelty which we find it so painful to imagine. Hatred inspires them, anger prompts them to an ardour and an activity in which there is no great joy; sadism is needed to extract any pleasure from it; whereas unkind people suppose themselves to be punishing someone equally unkind.
>
> (2:177; 2:471–72)

This passage is not quite compatible with the section about Mademoiselle Vinteuil. In that section we found an opposition between Mademoiselle Vinteuil's veneer of sadism and joyful cruelty; in this passage joyful sadism is opposed to Rachel's blind cruelty. The narrator undoubtedly keeps open the possibility of a pleasure-filled sadism unlike either Mademoiselle Vinteuil's obsessive blasphemy or Rachel's empty-headed meanness, but this potential cruelty worthy of Sade remains hypothetical and conditional: Rachel does not find it any more than does Mademoiselle Vinteuil, or anyone else in the novel.

Just as love observed externally can be seen as a surgical operation or an act of torture, it is only through the eyes of a stranger that evil can be taken to be the product of sadism, the object of a cold and distant voluptuousness rather than that of a self-deluding sensitivity. Only the narrator might have had the power to make Rachel into a sadist by showing her that her victim was innocent and her unkindness gratuitous, that she was fooling herself if she imagined her own wickedness was nothing more than a response to the wickedness of her victim. Under those circumstances Rachel might have been able to relish evil. But, as the narrator says, "it would have been too painful for me, by speaking well of their victim, to assimilate the sentiments which animated the tormentors of the novice singer to the gratifications of cruelty" (2:177; 2:472). True sadism does not act, rather it takes its pleasure from a show of cruelty committed by those who are sensitive but perverted, and the hero of the *Recherche* would appear to be alone in understanding this lesson.

What about Charlus? Like Rachel, he has moments of "sadistic pleasure," for example, when he compares Morel to a choirboy (2:998; 3:355); or when Morel gives voice to his fantasy of deflowering Jupien's daughter and then ditching her (2:1042; 3:398); or when he visits the gigolos in Jupien's hotel (3:854; 4:404). But he does not find the joyful cruelty opposed to Mademoiselle Vinteuil's sadism any more than he finds the joyful sadism opposed to Rachel's unkindness. He has himself whipped by phony murderers who are not even good actors; the melodrama is still not up to snuff. That elusive third term, joy in evil, is never present:

> And M. de Charlus was driven at once to despair and to exasperation by this factitious attempt at perversity, the result of which was only to reveal such depths both of stupidity and of innocence. Yet even the most determined thief or murderer would not have satisfied him, for that sort of man does not talk about his crimes; and besides there exists in the sadist—however kind he may be, in fact all the more the kinder he is—a thirst for evil which wicked men, doing what they do not because it is wicked but from other motives, are unable to assuage. (3:856; 4:406)

If, as we have seen, the abstract existence of a "thirst for evil" is not ruled out, Proust neither meets nor even imagines a single example of it. In short, where evil resides is not in the scenes described as sadistic, but rather in "that indifference to the sufferings one causes," that universal cruelty—ever-present, banal, and petty—symbolized by "Les Petites Vieilles."

Thus, not a single character in the *Recherche* is given access to the realm of gratuitous perversity. But with the possible exception of the Montjouvain scene, with its ritualistic atmosphere reminiscent of *Les Plaisirs et les jours,* this is not because the characters are tormented by a sense of fault or original sin. The narrator himself, who is well equipped to judge other people's shortcomings in the domain of evil—their faintheartedness as well as their blindness—is no longer the hero of *Jean Santeuil,* the perverter of his own mother.

Neither God Nor Devil

"I imagine that's what a pederast might sing as he was ravishing a choirboy" (*Corr.* 11:79), Proust wrote to Montesquiou in March 1912 about one of the three *Romances sans paroles* of Gabriel Fauré. The fantasy is an interesting one, but, as we have seen, it was elicited by a racy letter from the Count (see chapter 2). In his reply, Proust was doing nothing more than rising to the challenge: "As for the cross between litanies and orgasms that you mention in your letter, the most delightful expression I know of that sort of thing," he said, was to be found in Fauré's music.

The "cross between litanies and orgasms," the mixture of sexuality and religion, does not belong to Proust. A choirboy ravished by a fan of Fauré's music: this is a scene made up for the benefit of the receiver of the letter, and the receiver of one of Proust's letters is, as we have already pointed out, to a great extent its author. In *Sodome et Gomorrhe,* Proust uses Brichot's "inept and motley tirade" to poke fun at the mishmash of sadism and Catholicism that characterized French decadence. Once again we find the choirboy used as a symbol:

> I have no wish to be damned as a heretic and renegade in the Mallarméan chapel in which our new friend, like all the young men of his age, must have served the esoteric mass, at least as an acolyte, and have shown himself deliquescent or Rosicrucian. But really, we have seen more than enough of these intellectuals worshipping art with a capital A, who, when they can no longer intoxicate themselves upon Zola, inject themselves with Verlaine. Having become etheromaniacs out of Baudelairean devotion, they would no longer be capable of the virile effort which the country may one day or another demand of them, anaesthetised as they are by the great literary neurosis in the heated, enervating atmosphere, heavy with unwholesome vapours, of a symbolism of the opium-den. (2:988; 3:346)

All of Byzantium is brought together: Baudelaire, Péladan, Verlaine, Zola, Mallarmé and Adoré Floupette, along with the mass, alcohol, ether and opium, neurosis, symbolism, and effeminacy. Brunetière said more or less the same thing after the publication of Baudelaire's diaries:

> Baudelaire is one of the idols of this period—a sort of Oriental idol, monstrous and deformed, with a natural deformity heightened by strange colors—and his chapel is among the most frequently visited. The independent and the decadent, the symbolist and the deliquescent, the literary dandy and the Wagneromaniac, even the naturalist, this is where they all go to sacrifice, this is the sanctuary where their trade in high praise takes place, this is where they get drunk on the smells of scientific corruption and transcendental perversity which they say issue forth from their *Fleurs du mal.*[15]

The mixture of liturgy and psychopathology characterizes the depiction of evil and sexual pleasure from *Les Plaisirs et les jours* and *Jean Santeuil* to the melodrama conceived by Proust in 1906 and "Sentiments filiaux d'un parricide"; indeed Proust, in a 1912 letter to Montesquiou, or even in *A la recherche du temps perdu,* still makes use of all the trappings of decadence. Yet it would appear that all of this was only superficial, a parody, something he does not believe in; Brichot's inept tirade is more than enough proof of that. Proust is aware of the misunderstanding underlying the "Baudelairean devotion" of the fin-de-siècle. But this does not mean—let us say it at last—that his own understanding does Baudelaire justice.

There is no sense of the sacred in Proust's thought, which is strictly atheistic. But Baudelairean evil, the evil of *Les Fleurs du mal,* stems from a metaphysical conception of nature that has less to do with a moral evil or a Sade-like wickedness than with a sharing in evil, taken in a quasi-theological sense. Baudelairean evil depends on original sin, which makes nature into something essentially bad. Georges Blin has shown how this natural foundation of evil in Baudelaire, this human impulse toward evil, is indebted to Sade, Maistre, and Poe. "That primitive, irresistible force is our natural Perversity, which makes man permanently and simultaneously homicidal and suicidal, murderer and executioner," Baudelaire writes in his "Notes nouvelles sur Edgar Poe." "Each of us was born a marquis in the domain of evil!" (OC 2:323). Speaking more overtly about Sade, Baudelaire says, "One always has to come back to De Sade, that is, to the *Natural Man,*" ("Titres et canevas," OC 1:595). In "Eloge du maquillage," Baudelaire succinctly sums up his view of evil: "Crime, which the human animal gets a taste for in his mother's womb, is natural in origin" ("Le Peintre de la vie moderne," OC 2:715). Evil and nature, woman and reproduction are thus intertwined to the point of being identified with each other.

In *A la recherche du temps perdu,* there is no suggestion that the root cause of cruelty and suffering is nature. It is true that although the hypothesis of sadism is dismissed several times in the case of Mademoiselle Vinteuil and Rachel, on the other hand Proust does not openly refute the role Baudelaire attributed to nature as the origin of cruelty. Yet cruelty is never a function of nature in the novel. When Proust uses a phrase like *demon of perversity,* clearly inspired by Poe, he does so in an attempt to describe the ups and downs of Madame de Surgis' life in high society: "A demon of perversity had driven her, scorning the position ready-made for her, to flee from the conjugal roof and live a life of open scandal" (2:732; 3:105). The joy of lowering oneself, which from Poe's or Baudelaire's point of view is what defines human nature, is observed by Proust in Madame de Surgis' struggles with the social—or simply high-society—ladder, and Proust draws a universal moral from the adventures of this lady who first goes to some lengths to get back her social position and then takes fresh pleasure in her decline, "a return journey that is not uncommon," as the narrator comments. In Proust, that is the extent—or rather all that remains—of the "two simultaneous postulates, one striving toward God, the other toward Satan," that Baudelaire perceived in all human beings, determining their "desire for promotion" as well as their "joy in descent" ("Mon coeur mis à nu," OC 1:682–83).

In Proust we find neither God nor the devil: nature is rarely alluded to except in discussions of the individual nature of a character, and when it is mentioned, it is identified with the plant kingdom. In *Sodome et Gomorrhe I,* the nature that presides over the meeting between Charlus and Jupien and the doctrine of the "cursed race" is botanical, having to do with flowers and their intelligence, following the work of Darwin and Maeterlinck. This would not appear to be a malevolent nature; in fact, it is neither good nor bad. Consequently, it would be erroneous to read the botanical metaphor of homosexuality as a naturalization—that is to say, a justification—of homosexual love: for that to be true, nature would have to be conceived of in terms of good and evil, but Proust does not place nature under the sway of original sin. Proust writes of the "miracle of nature" that allows a homosexual like Monsieur de Vaugoubert to root out, and marry, a woman who is in reality a man with the outward appearance of a woman: "nature, by a fiendish and beneficent ruse, bestows on the girl the deceptive aspect of a man" (2:670; 3:46). In this particular case the opposite would appear to be true—nature has made a man look like a woman—but what is especially noteworthy is the interpolated phrase, *by a fiendish and beneficent ruse.* To make nature into a power that is simultaneously and interchangeably benevolent and malevolent, now kind, now cruel, implies that one has rid oneself of the question of good and evil, of satanism and angelism. Is this not generally the case for anyone who places little emphasis on metaphysics? We are dealing once again with an incidental remark, but as the oversight of substituting woman-man for man-woman suggests, homosexuality itself is being described, and the question becomes an important one.

Nature in Proust is not evil. That in itself is enough to make the cruelty of *A la recherche du temps perdu* profoundly distinct from the cruelty of *Les Fleurs du mal,* in spite of a great deal of affinity between the two works. On a theological and metaphysical level, Proust never justifies cruelty by making nature into something guilty, or by making it dependent on the evil of original sin. He finds nature neither innocent nor guilty, and to say it is not guilty—in particular not guilty of homosexuality—is not to say it makes homosexuality innocent. Nature medicalizes homosexuality, as it medicalizes love and the body.

An Erotics of Tragedy

The puzzle remains unsolved: where is the cruelty that is undoubtedly present in *A la recherche du temps perdu* but is not based on natural evil? It is neither sadistic, in the decadent or medical sense, nor true to Sade, nor authentically Baudelairean: even if its manifestations of pity and irony are reminiscent of *Les Fleurs du mal,* they are lacking any metaphysical element. Nor is it the kind of cruelty that Georges Bataille thought he saw in Proust: "Just as horror is a measure of love, the thirst for Evil is a measure of Good," he writes in *La Littérature et le mal.*[16] The second half of the sentence does not fit Proust's world, which is not inhabited by the Good and Evil that Bataille sees there.

Cruelty in Proust is neither metaphysical nor theological, nor is it even moral. It always remains uncertain and ambiguous: sometimes sadistic, sometimes worthy of Sade himself, and sometimes worthy of Baudelaire, but above all erotic. It retains the eroticism of Baudelaire's evil—that is, the equation of love and cruelty, the savagery of love—but it is free of any musings about origins and transcendence. Baudelaire writes in "Fusées," "one of the two [lovers] will always be calmer and less possessed than the other. That one—man or woman—is the operator or the executioner; the other is the subject or the victim" (OC 1:651). Proust inherits this conception of love, minus the conclusion, which is what gave it its entire meaning for Baudelaire: "I say that the only, the supreme pleasure of love resides in the certainty of *hurting* someone" (OC 1:652).

But what would a system of eroticism be without metaphysics? Is such a thing even conceivable? Proust chose some lines from Baudelaire's "Femmes damnées: Delphine et Hippolyte" as the epigraph for one of the chapters of "La Confession d'une jeune fille" (JS 90). These lines come from the end of the poem, when the two women's sexual climax tinged with sadism leads to a feeling of guilt undeniably laced with a dose of Christianity:

> And the raging wind of lust
> Sets your flesh to flapping like an old flag.
> (99–100)

The epigraph to the entire story, taken from the *Imitation de Jésus-Christ,* predisposes the reader to interpret Baudelaire's lines unambiguously:

> The desires of the senses lead us here and there, but once the moment has passed, what have you gained? Remorse of conscience and a dissipation of the spirit. One leaves home joyfully but often one comes back in sadness, and the pleasures of the evening sadden the morning. So it is that the joys of the senses are pleasing at first, but in the end they are harmful and murderous. (JS 85)

At this point, desecration and expiation were inextricably joined in pleasure.

Later, in the 1920s, and particularly in his 1921 article about Baudelaire, Proust quotes lines from the beginning of "Femmes damnées" so as to emphasize Baudelaire's classicism, his kinship with Racine:

> Her defeated arms, cast down like useless weapons,
> Everything heightened and ornamented her fragile beauty.[17]

Proust's cruelty is Racine's, the cruelty recently discovered in Racine, for example in the marvelous pages of Péguy about the lethal innocence of adolescent girls (see chapter 3). Albertine, who was invented in 1914 and, as we have seen, rids the novel of its last fin-de-siècle vestiges, is a Racinian heroine, one of those unconsciously cruel girls who torture Agamemnon or Assuérus; she is substituted for the two Baudelairean women who caused the hero to hesitate in his desires in the prewar novel, the pure woman whom the man desires so that he might defile her, and the impure woman whom he desires so as to be himself defiled, as Georges Blin points out.[18]

The justification for this erotic cruelty associated with love in Proust and in Baudelaire is not natural evil, but rather simply the idea that love is always based on hatred or horror. Not only does love include an element of hatred—"I hate you as much as I love you," writes Baudelaire, or "horror is a measure of love," as Bataille says of Proust, using an equation more appropriate to Baudelaire—but disgust and hatred define love in Proust. Swann's love already illustrates this, starting with the aversion he first feels for Odette, who has "a kind of beauty which left him indifferent, which aroused in him no desire, which gave him, indeed, a sort of physical repulsion" (1:213; 1:193), and going all the way up to his final assessment of the affair, in which he does not so much reverse his terms as he marvels at how far disgust can lead one: "To think that I've wasted years of my life, that I've longed to die, that I've experienced my greatest love, for a woman who didn't appeal to me, who wasn't even my type!" (1:415; 1:375). This is the very definition of eroticism, repulsion being the starting point for desire. This pitiful exclamation—a combination of regret and astonishment mixed in with a feeling of satisfaction, in spite of everything, of having gone through the experience—could be attributed to almost all of Racine's heroes at the end of his tragedies if only they survived.

Even more meaningful is Proust's analysis of homosexuality, which is portrayed as a trial emblematic of the human condition. According to the theory of homosexuality sketched out in *Sodome et Gomorrhe I,* what homosexuals feel for other homosexuals is repulsion, a basic disgust, a kind of hatred and bitterness that are the building blocks of love. Apparently, this repulsion or hatred does not stem from a sense of guilt but rather from the very definition of love. It is in the nature of desire to manifest itself in the form of an object that, by definition, cannot give satisfaction—Monsieur de Charlus' "real man"—and that, were it ever to do so, would by the same token lose its attraction and lead to resentment. Disgust and pain are thus the two inextricable elements of desire, given that one desires what is destined never to correspond to one's desires. Homosexuality articulates the truth of love, spinning between horror and grief. In *Sodome et Gomorrhe,* the accumulation of a vocabulary of disgust serves to qualify the homosexual's relation to the being he desires, the principle being that the homosexual sees in other homosexuals "an unpleasing image of himself" (2:951; 3:311).

The novel of Albertine bears out this rule of a love torn between horror and grief, suffering and cruelty. In *Sodome et Gomorrhe,* the hero remains indifferent to Albertine until he happens upon her at the casino, in the company of Dr. Cottard, dancing with Andrée in a tight embrace: desire is once again kindled in the voyeur's eyes, as in the Montjouvain scene, and immediately medicalized by the doctor's presence. In the manuscript, this is how the hero reacted to the scene:

> From that day forward, seeing Albertine never ceased causing me anger; it was not simply that I had caught sight of a new Albertine, whom I found hateful, . . . but that she had only to make the slightest adolescent joke about having ambiguous feelings toward Andrée for me to feel profoundly disgusted. Not only had I caught sight of a new Albertine, but I myself had become someone else. I had stopped wishing her well. (3:1455–56 [3:198, var. c])

This is love: to stop wishing the other well, to hurt the other, inflicting a series of wounds starting with a moment when one feels "profoundly disgusted," and despite the fact that, as they both say again and again, Albertine and Andrée dislike nothing more than the ways of Gomorrha (2:830 and 862; 3:197 and 227). But the cycle of love and hatred has been set into motion, and just when the hero begins once again to feel indifferent toward Albertine, hearing the news that she knows Mademoiselle Vinteuil casts him back into the horror and love of *La Prisonnière* and *Albertine disparue.* It is only when love disappears that hatred does so as well, or, as Proust says with no little banality when the hero no longer loves Gilberte, "as soon as one is no longer in love, one stops hating" (3:1385 [3:111, var. d]). A similar lesson can be drawn from all love in *A la recherche du temps perdu,* for the very condition of love is that it is based on hatred, disgust, and horror: love is without charity in a world without God.

One final consequence illustrates how far "Proust's sadism"—which, in the *Recherche,* has distanced itself from the unutterability of lust in the early texts, with all the confessional trappings of a diary—is from recreating the transcendental origins of "Baudelaire's sadism." Whereas a metaphysics of evil always leads to the preservation of an elite struggling against the stupidity of the world, and favors a kind of writing characterized by a desire for solitude and by a wish to be displeasing—to make pregnant readers lose their babies, as Baudelaire hoped to do—nothing at all like that is present in Proust. Cruelty and hatred have no social capacity, nor does fraternity, which in certain of Baudelaire's prose poems is presented as their opposite. Evil in Proust is ordinary. It is desire; desire and horror.

7

"The sun radiating out over the sea"; or, the Uneven Epithet

Proust compares the epithets used by old Madame de Cambremer with those of Sainte-Beuve. The passage is quite well known: the marquise respects the rule of the three adjectives, but instead of arranging them according to some principle of ordering, as is proper, she jumbles them together willy-nilly. What's more, she obtains an effect of "descent" or "reverse ordering." The narrator's conclusion is this:

> [She failed] always to observe the sequence that the recipient of her letter would naturally have expected, and with such unerring dexterity that I finally changed my mind as to the nature of these diminuendos, decided that they were deliberate, and found in them the same depravity of taste—transposed into the social key—that drove Sainte-Beuve to upset all the alliances between words [toutes les alliances de mots], to alter any expression that was at all habitual.
> (2:1123; 3:473; modified translation)

This passage echoes an earlier one from *Sodome et Gomorrhe*:

> It was the time when well-bred people observed the rule of affability and what was called the rule of the three adjectives. Mme de Cambremer combined both rules. One laudatory adjective was not enough

> for her, she followed it (after a little dash) with a second, then (after another dash) with a third. But, what was peculiar to her was that, in defiance of the literary and social aim which she set herself, the sequence of the three epithets assumed in Mme de Cambremer's letters the aspect not of a progression but of a diminuendo.
>
> (2:977; 3:336)

The only thing added is the allusion to Sainte-Beuve, and the basic repetition of the central idea of the two passages demonstrates its importance. In his arrangements of epithets, Sainte-Beuve indulged in redundancies, combined with unexpected juxtapositions, and he topped it all off, where possible, with either an archaicism or a neologism, as we find in this description of Madame de Couaën: "a chaste, forbidden, and unexpectable creature."[1] Madame de Cambremer's style, according to the narrator's hypothesis, is the product of two incompatible teachings: "Two methods, taught probably by different masters, were juxtaposed in this epistolary style, the second making Mme de Cambremer redeem the monotony of her multiple adjectives by employing them in a descending scale, and avoiding an ending on the common chord" (2:1123; 3:473). What are these two methods that get in each other's way? One calls for the multiplication of the adjective, the other for its uniqueness, principles irreconcilable by definition.

The drama Proust reveals through the character of Madame de Cambremer—also known as "Aunt Zélia"—is the drama of the adjective, the epithet, or the ready-made formula, the cliché. Nothing could be harder to find than a beautiful adjective. The marquise feels herself divided between a principle of banality and a principle of uniqueness, between the inventiveness of the multiple and the quest for the single right word. By the same token, she breaks the pattern of clichés as a way of escaping this dilemma rather than resolving the conflict. In her case, it is a process, unlike what happens with her nieces, who are no more responsible for using this figure of speech than they are for their moustaches, yet another hereditary attribute:

> For throughout the family, to quite a remote degree of kinship and in admiring imitation of Aunt Zélia, the rule of the three adjectives was held in great favour, as was a certain enthusiastic way of catching your breath when talking. An imitation that had passed into the blood, moreover; and whenever, in the family, a little girl from her

> earliest childhood took to stopping short while she was talking to swallow her saliva, her parents would say: "She takes after Aunt Zélia," would sense that as she grew older her upper lip would soon tend to be shadowed by a faint moustache.
>
> (2:1123–24; 3:473–74)

In the very sentence that associates the marquise's linguistic alterations with the ravings of Sainte-Beuve and denounces them in the name of normalcy of taste or linguistic good health, Proust commits a curious impropriety. When he describes Sainte-Beuve's vice with the phrases *to upset all the alliances between words* or *to alter any expression that was at all habitual,* he seems to be assigning to the phrase *alliance between words* exactly the opposite of its actual meaning, which is "a bold juxtaposition"; he appears to be identifying the alliance between words with the habitual or ready-made expression, whereas in fact the alliance is precisely what breaks apart ready-made expressions. In short, when the marquise and Sainte-Beuve alter habitual expressions, they are not, as Proust suggests, breaking alliances of words, but rather forming alliances of words. The peculiar confusion about this term is perhaps also indicative of the uncertainty of its status in Proust's poetics, "between" artistic writing and the surrealistic image.

The fact is Sainte-Beuve became famous for using a kind of language that fought with conventions, cultivated impropriety, and frequently resorted to archaicisms and neologisms. In a note to his own translation of Ruskin's *Sesame and Lilies,* we find Proust already comparing the English writer's learned archaicisms with those of Sainte-Beuve, who was not yet but was soon to become the object of his wrath:

> A peculiar writer, by the very fact of his peculiarity, stops being a great writer. In a writer like Sainte-Beuve, the endless deviation of expression—the way it has of constantly "jumping the rails" to avoid saying anything directly or reverting to common usage—is charming, but it instantly marks the limitations of a talent which, however extensive it might be, is nevertheless second-rate.[2]

This idiosyncracy of Sainte-Beuve's is like the moustache shadowing the marquise's upper lip, his linguistic "deviation" a moustache drawn on the smiling face of the Mona Lisa of language. In *Contre Sainte-Beuve,* Proust was to note, in similar terms, that the critic always writes "with a taste for deviating from the meaning of words" (CSB 248). For example, Sainte-Beuve said to the director of a journal in which Baudelaire had published an unsigned article about him, "I respect and raise my hat to my anonymous benefactor." In this kind of formulaic expression of politeness, the dowager's affected blunderings are as frequent as Sainte-Beuve's blundering affectations: "Perhaps it was because her desire to be amiable outran the fertility of her imagination and the riches of her vocabulary that the lady, while determined to utter three exclamations, was incapable of making the second and third anything more than feeble echoes of the first" (2:978; 3:336).

Proust does not like deviations in language, that is, the alliance of words, properly speaking. He is unremitting in his repeated use of them in his pastiches of Sainte-Beuve, "that cunning patcher-up of phrases," as he calls him (CSB 610). He has Sainte-Beuve say that Flaubert is "estimable . . . in his yearnings and his fondnesses."[3] On the other hand, Proust is also dead set against clichés. While the Marquise de Cambremer is the incarnation of deviations in expression in the *Recherche,* her daughter-in-law speaks only in clichés: "Do you really think she's 'talentuous'?" (2:852; 3:218), she asks the hero in speaking of Madame de Sévigné, using an adjective that the Goncourt brothers made fashionable and that almost immediately became a cliché. When Albertine draws the hero's attention to the seagulls in Balbec, Madame de Cambremer's daughter-in-law adapts a line from Baudelaire's "L'Albatros," with an extra syllable: "Their giant wings from walking hinder them" (2:842; 3:209). Is this sufficient evidence to indicate that Proust judges this line to be unremarkable, or the image to be flat? Probably it is, since in one of the versions, the young Madame de Cambremer quoted a line of Sully Prudhomme immediately before, as if it had the same value: "And that day the great ships" (3:1084).[4] Proust himself quotes much bad poetry, by the likes of Paul Desjardins and Armand Silvestre, Sully Prudhomme, Hugo, Musset, even Baudelaire:

> Now are the woods all black, but still the sky is blue.
> (1:130; 1:118)

> You will make them weep, darling, lovely girl.
> (3:611; 4:177)

> Here below the lilacs die.
> (2:878, 1163; 3:243, 509)

> Since every creature here below
> Imparts to some other
> His music or his fragrance
> Or his flame. (2:650; 3:28)

> What matters the bottle so long as one gets drunk?
> (2:235; 2:526)

Caught between the unusual and the banal, between devious alliances of words and limp clichés, what can one do besides throw up one's hands? Whereas Ruskin, with a certain degree of boldness, advises young writers to be economical in their means of expression—"A few words, well chosen and distinguished, will do work that a thousand cannot"[5]—Proust relishes his dreams of a sublime sparseness similar to the painter Eugène Fromentin's, a sparseness reminiscent of Albertine's suit in matching tones—unusual because of its combination of shades of gray—which in *Sodome et Gomorrhe* Monsieur de Charlus compares to the Princesse de Cadignan's gown (2:1089–90; 3:441–42). Fromentin writes, "I was delighted when, following the example of certain painters whose pallets are quite limited and yet whose works are richly expressive, I fancied I had infused a certain amount of color or depth into a word simple in itself, often the most ordinary, worn-out term that was positively drab when taken in isolation." From this he concludes: "Our language . . . , even in its everyday store of words and within its ordinary limits, seemed to me to have inexhaustible resources."[6] But this noble stylistic ideal, which is sublime in the proper sense of the term, is reached by very few. Thus it is with a certain irony that Proust draws his conclusions about Fromentin: "And probably this is the case. But it is certainly not the faded language of this eminently distinguished gentleman, a language that has not been properly 'aged,' that is dry and paltry and not very 'artistic,' so to speak, that will serve as an illustration of this wise principle." Sainte-Beuve is excessively devious, but Fromentin is excessively distinguished, or not sufficiently artistic. What can be done? The dilemma has to do with choosing a kind of writing in between two centuries. And once again, Baudelaire will point the way to a solution.

September Poetry

If a single line of Baudelaire had to be associated with Proust, it would be "le soleil rayonnant sur la mer" [the sun radiating out over the sea]. It is not even a complete line, but rather the last part of line 20 of "Chant d'automne," the very end of the poem's fifth stanza:

> And I value nothing, neither your love, nor the
> boudoir, nor the hearth,
> As much as the sun radiating out over the sea.

Moreover, Proust borrows this bit of a line, which verges on banality in its simplicity—but the sublime is not always separable from the very banal—not from *Les Fleurs du mal,* in the 1861 edition of which the poem appeared, but rather from the melody that Fauré composed to the words of "Chant d'automne":[7]

> I
>
> Soon we shall plunge into the cold darkness;
> Farewell, living light of our too short summers!
> I already hear, as it falls with mournful impact,
> The resonant wood on the courtyard paving-stones.
>
> The whole winter is entering my being: anger,
> Hatred, shivers, horror, hard forced labor,
> And like the sun in its arctic hell,
> My heart will be nothing but a red and icy block.
>
> I listen trembling to each branch that falls;
> The echo of a scaffold being built is not more muted.
> My mind is like a tower that collapses
> At the blows of a battering-ram, tireless and heavy.
>
> I seem to hear, cradled by this monotonous impact,
> A coffin being nailed shut somewhere in great haste.
> Whose is it?—Yesterday was summer; and autumn is here!
> That mysterious noise rings out like a departure.
>
> II
>
> I love the greenish light of your long eyes,
> Gentle beauty, but everything is bitter to me today,
> And I value nothing, neither your love, nor the
> boudoir, nor the hearth,
> As much as the sun radiating out over the sea.

Love me nonetheless, tender heart! be a mother
Even to one ungrateful, even to one unkind;
Lover or sister, be the ephemeral gentleness
Of a glorious autumn or a setting sun.

Quick work! The tomb is waiting; it is ravenous!
Oh! let me lay my head upon your lap,
And while I miss the white and torrid summer,
Taste the gentle yellow ray of autumn's end!

Fauré set only four of the seven stanzas of the poem to music: stanzas 1, 3, and 4 of the first part, which are linked together in the melody without any instrumental interlude, and then, after a long piano piece which brings out a very marked contrast that is in itself an interpretation, just the first stanza of the second part. Whereas the melody's unity is assured by the key (C) and the rhythmical balance (compound time), the opposition between the first three stanzas and the last one affects both the modal system and the rhythmical system. The mode goes from minor to major, the rhythm goes from quadruple time to triple time, and the tempo becomes twice as slow at the end. In addition, the few recognizable melodic elements—the piano theme, quite perceptible in the brief introduction, and the "Soon we shall plunge" theme, which is also used for "I listen trembling"—are not repeated at the end. On the contrary, the end develops around a new theme, made of only three notes, which appears several times. The first of these three notes, F, seems like a kind of ceiling that is being struck against:

J'aime de vos longs *yeux* . . .
[I love the greenish light . . .]
Et rien, ni votre *amour* . . .
[And I value nothing, neither your love . . .]
Ne me vaut *le so*leil *ray* . . .
[As much as the sun shin . . .]

And here, on the phrase *(ray)on-nant,* the ceiling is broken through. It is the climax not only of the final verse, but of the entire song. In addition to being the highest note (G), it also carries the greatest intensity after a *crescendo molto* (coming off of a *pianissimo* "J'aime de vos longs yeux") on an affirmative—indeed, almost flashy—chord (fourth and sixth in C major).[8]

"The sun radiating out over the sea," the line that becomes a fetish for Proust, is thus the sun from Baudelaire's poem filtered through Fauré's eyes. Here, the poet and the musician are not fully separable—any more than they are in Hugo's "Le Papillon et la Fleur,"[9] or in Sully Prudhomme's "Ici-bas tous les lilas meurent,"[10] to which Proust was similarly attached and which, as we have seen, he became familiar with through their musical settings. And the line comes back again and again in his writings, the line set to music.

In a letter to Reynaldo Hahn that probably dates from 1895, Proust gives the following account of a conversation he had with Fauré who, with a rather touching modesty, had expressed doubts about Reynaldo's appreciation of his melodies compared to the ones he himself had composed or could have composed: "And I said that on the contrary, I had more often heard you singing his serenades[11] than your own,[12] and that you sang 'Chant d'automne' very well" (*Corr.* 1:375). "Chant d'automne" was one of the tunes Reynaldo sang in his baritone voice, accompanying himself on the piano in salons.

In fact, Proust was familiar with the Baudelaire-Fauré "Chant d'automne" even before Reynaldo sang it. Fernand Gregh recollects having heard Proust humming the line "J'aime de vos longs yeux la lumière verdâtre" [I love the greenish light of your long eyes] "with an ecstatic look on his face, off-key, his eyes half-closed and his head thrown back." It would appear he dedicated this line to the green-eyed Marie Finaly during a stay with the Finalys in Trouville during the summer of 1892.[13]

On returning from Trouville in the autumn of the following year, it is not this line, but rather the end of the very same fifth stanza of the poem that Proust quotes in a letter to his father: "The pleasure of being back in the house keeps me from missing Normandy too much and consoles me about not being able to see (as Baudelaire puts it in a line which I hope you find as powerful as I do) *the sun radiating out over the sea*" (*Corr.* 1:238).[14] Was Dr. Proust as taken by the "power" of the line as his son was himself and wanted his father to be? Poetry of summers ending, poetry of returns to Paris: many years later, in a letter dedicating a copy of Ruskin's *The Bible of Amiens* to Marcel Plantevignes, in September 1908, on his return from Cabourg where he met the young man, Proust assembles all the melancholic poetry of his repertory, ranging from Sully Prudhomme's "Ici-bas" to Verlaine—"Ah! quand refleuriront les roses de septembre!"—to d'Aubigné—"Une rose d'automne est plus qu'une autre exquise"—and all the way up to Baudelaire once again:

> And those lines of Baudelaire, often in the evenings, fifteen years ago, when I, like my dear Marcel, still had marvelous parents, a mother who was intelligent and kind like his, a father who was intelligent and kind like his, and when I, too, was a little Marcel less wise and less strong and less intelligent and less kind than the person into whose friendly hands I entrust this book and other, more precious things, those lines that I often recited at sunset with a feeling that was less bitter and less completely autumnal than today:
>
> But everything is bitter to me today
> And I value nothing, neither the sun, nor
> your words, nor the hearth,
> As much as the sun radiating out over the sea
> Quick work! The tomb is waiting; it is
> ravenous!
> Oh! let me . . . .
> While I miss the white and torrid summer,
> Taste the gentle yellow ray of autumn's end!
> (*Corr.* 8:221–22)

The modifications Proust makes to the poem do not require extensive comments: "neither the sun, nor your words" instead of "neither your love, nor the boudoir," and the omission of "lay my head upon your lap." All the nostalgia concentrated in the "gentle yellow ray" which closes the poem was to be recalled by Proust several days later, in a letter to Reynaldo, and applied to Sarah Bernhardt: "May she live to a ripe old age, and keep on giving off, from her glory and her autumn's end, the 'gentle yellow ray' that you love to taste" (*Corr.* 8:229).[15]

In contrast with the "sun radiating out [rayonnant] over the sea," this "gentle yellow ray" [rayon] forms the other pole of the poem—as old age is opposed to being in one's prime—or at least the other pole of the second part of the poem, more present in Proust's mind than the other part, which is purely descriptive.

A letter dating from September 1912 to Madame Scheikévitch, once again written just as Proust is about to leave Cabourg, brings together the line of Verlaine ("Ah! quand refleuriront les roses de septembre!") and the fifth stanza of "Chant d'automne," quoted with more or less the same parts missing as in the letter to Marcel Plantevignes (*Corr.* 11:210).[16]

The "sun radiating out over the sea" and the "gentle yellow ray" both undoubtedly are a part of Proust's imaginary universe, if the sign of the imaginary is recurrence. Alluding to the poem's winter sun "in its arctic hell" like "a red and icy block," the hero of *Contre Sainte-Beuve* tells his mother that he has left out "autumn, since you know all its poetry by heart, as I do" (CSB 256–57). And the most implicit and intimate allusion is found in a letter, also dating from early autumn, to Reynaldo Hahn, the very person who sang the Fauré melody, in a reminiscence of Beg-Meil, where the two friends stayed in 1895. In October 1898, Proust writes from Trouville to Reynaldo, who is in Dieppe, "Reversing Baudelaire's lovely lines, I will say to you that I value nothing today, neither the boudoir, nor the sun radiating out over the sea, as much as the hearth" (*Corr.* 3:473). This is the final word of the letter, but perhaps the postscript gives us the key: "Wouldn't you like to be back in Beg-Meil?"

Baudelairean Pastiches

Throughout Proust's work, the "sun radiating out over the sea" will reappear again and again, starting with a prose poem about the moon from "Les Regrets, rêveries couleur du temps" in *Les Plaisirs et les jours*: "Night had fallen, I went to my room, anxious at the thought of remaining in darkness now and no longer seeing the sky, the fields, and the sea radiating out under the sun" ("Comme à la lumière de la lune," JS 138). In a letter written to Reynaldo Hahn from Trouville in September 1894, a few weeks after he met the musician, Proust may be alluding to these short lines: "The weather is charming, with moonlit nights; I'll have a description of them read to you which will be to your liking" (*Corr.* 1:326). September, Trouville, Beg-Meil or Cabourg, and Reynaldo Hahn: it is the combination of nostalgic elements that brings the line of Baudelaire to mind.

In "Mélancolique villégiature de Mme de Breyves," also from *Les Plaisirs et les jours*, "the sun setting over the sea" is already used as a term of comparison with the "inexpressible feeling of the mystery of things, when our mind founders on an outpouring [rayonnement] of beauty," and leads to a quotation of the poet of "Chant d'automne," "for (as Baudelaire said, speaking about late afternoons in autumn) sometimes vagueness of feeling does not exclude intensity of feeling, and there is no sharper point than that of infinity" (JS 75). The "sun radiating out over the sea," which at the time of *Les Plaisirs et les jours* Proust seems to associate with the shining of the autumn sun, is an instrument of exquisite pain. "How penetrating is day's end in autumn! Oh! how painfully penetrating!" (Baudelaire, OC 1:278). That was the beginning of "Le *confiteor* de l'artiste" from "Spleen de Paris" before Proust's somewhat rough quotation.

"La Mer," another prose poem from "Les Regrets, Rêveries couleur du temps," takes up the refrain: "It shines forth under the sun and seems every evening to die with it" (JS 143). Here is yet another clue: Proust associates this radiating out [rayonnement] with the sun setting over the sea, at dusk if not in late autumn. And we still find the same dreamy sadness: "The moment of its melancholic, gentle reflections makes one feel one's heart melting as one watches them." The Baudelairean tone of these prose poems is striking; we even find the same adjective, "doux," that Baudelaire uses to describe the "yellow ray," an adjective Proust overuses as much as Baudelaire does. The atmosphere is that of "Le Voyage," with its nostalgic description of the sun:

> The glory of the sun on the violet sea,
> The glory of the cities in the setting sun.

Finally, in "Marine," the proximity and also the thematic contrast of two phrases seem to suggest that "Chant d'automne" is their common source: the choice is between the sea that is "under a brilliant sun, reflecting the sea-blue sky," and the sea that is "restless, yellow under the sun like a great field of mud" (JS 144). In the end, the entire experience of the sea can be summed up by a variation on Baudelaire's line heightened by Fauré's music. *Les Plaisirs et les jours* goes back to the "sun radiating out over the sea" as soon as the sea is mentioned, and it would not be going too far to assume that without that line of Baudelaire, Proust's first collection would not include any seascapes. But Proust avoids using the phrase itself, with its "strength," as he called it in the letter to his father. "To see . . . the sea radiating out under the sun," "the sun setting over the sea," or "it shines forth under the sun"; it is as if he were turning around an idée fixe, an obsessive refrain, a word that is taboo. All of Proust's variations inevitably lack the "strength" of Baudelaire's line, and, insofar as they are poor seconds, make this irreplaceable "strength" something even more mysterious.

"The loathsome wares of scented letter-paper"

Is it not for this reason that the "sun radiating out over the sea" will make no further appearance in *Jean Santeuil,* in spite of Beg-Meil, in spite of the autumn, in spite of October? This time a "ray of sun" literally kindles Jean's soul (JS 390), or more metaphorically: "Jean felt his heart, swelled to the dimensions of the horizon, radiating out when the light touched it" (JS 364). There is no doubt that the heart, or the soul, and the ray are linked, the ray kindling the heart and the kindled heart radiating out like a ray. A nostalgic remark inspired by the sight of Lake Geneva confirms the connection: "His heart swells at the thought of those returns from long holiday celebrations, when the sun was going down and one could look straight out at the sea" (JS 398–99). This page from *Jean Santeuil,* "Souvenirs de la mer devant le lac de Genève," is crucial: in the sketches for the novel, it closely anticipates the theory of involuntary memory that was to give structure to the *Recherche,* but does not quite manage to give it a complete formulation. "When the sun was going down and one could look straight out at the sea": this was to be the original reminiscence that made *Jean Santeuil* stumble, unable to transform it into an aesthetic doctrine. This is a supremely Baudelairean moment.

It is not surprising that the variations on the theme of the "sun radiating out over the sea" stop in *Jean Santeuil,* because the imitation of poets is condemned several times in the novel. Now imitation is particularly associated with images: in his school days, Jean sprinkled his essays, "to draw attention to the vast array of his reading, with images borrowed from the poets he was reading" (JS 230). Imitation is the vice belonging to a time before one has "awakened to poetry," for the latter entails opening oneself up not to books but rather, beyond the realm of books, to the "greatest and simplest things, summer, the wind, sunset, the sound of bells, the sea" (JS 247). Greatness and simplicity are brought together here in an ideal of pure poetry, the emblem of which was the "sun radiating out over the sea." Awakening to poetry marks the end of the fetishism of words and coincides with being present to the world and sensitive to the elements; it goes along with an "awareness of the happy or sad beauty" of things. When Jean grows up and awakens to poetry, he will be moved simply by "poetry about the sun and the wind," the sublime echoing of an essential feeling. Once one has realized that the beauty of poetry comes from its faithfulness to the greatness and simplicity of the thing—the thing itself, the sea mixing with the sun—the point is no longer to imitate poets, to be inventive, or to make up images.

Such is the lesson given by Jean's public humiliation by Monsieur Beulier, his philosophy teacher: "You must take care to get rid of all these metaphors, all these images," he tells Jean as he gives him back a composition in which Jean had hoped he would be recognized as a future "great poet":

> Don't puff up your voice just to spout banalities. "The red conflagration of sunset": how dare you write that? That kind of purple prose is worthy of some little newspaper out in the middle of nowhere, in the provinces, not even that good, out in the colonies. Maybe the editor of the *Fanal de Mozambique* or some paper like that decorates his articles with these kinds of doodads, and the local ladies think it sounds like Chateaubriand. . . . Along the same lines you are constantly talking about exquisite perfumes and fragrant odors. What does that evoke in the imagination? These are the loathsome wares of scented letter-paper. (JS 263)

This is a lesson of simplicity and grandeur, a lesson that encourages sobriety and the elimination of all the ornaments and flourishes in which *Les Plaisirs et les jours* indulges, the "banalities of the day, all the bad writing habits you've picked up in newspapers and journals" (JS 262).

Indeed, the descriptions in *Jean Santeuil* are literal, the colors basic:

> In the distance, the fields were pink and the woods were blue. Then, above the line of the hills, of the same purple but lighter, vast clouds

> of an almost pink color stretched out mixed in with gray clouds, and soon, when the sun had gone in, the vastness before Jean's eyes lost these lovely colors and stayed blue on the edge of the woods and on the hillsides. (JS 363)

But once the affectations have been eliminated, what remains is awkward, and the passage is quite flat, its starkness giving the effect not of grandeur but rather of a zero degree of coloring, exactly what Proust was to criticize in Fromentin's work. The same might be said of a seascape in which Baudelaire is no longer perceptible in spite of a feeble attempt at synesthesia: "The sea was pink far off, yellow closer up, red in the distance, with the glossiness and velvetiness of oil" (JS 383). As if he were resisting images, the "banalities of the day" scorned by the austere Monsieur Beulier, Proust appears to be terrified of the epithet.

Another symptom of this is that Jean is disturbed by the poet Rustinlor's idea of dissociating the beauty of poetry from depth of meaning; following Gautier, the only line of Racine he finds beautiful is: "La fille de Minos et de Pasiphaé" (JS 240). Monsieur Beulier and Monsieur Rustinlor, the philosophy teacher and the *maître d'études*, embody the two irreconciliable aspects of style, the sublime and the affected; later, Fromentin and Sainte-Beuve, one dignified, the other raving, will replace them in the notes for *Sesame and Lilies*. Jean—and Proust with him—has taken sides. Tempted by Rustinlor but dominated by the philosophy teacher, the writing of *Jean Santeuil* resists poetry. The adjective is too risky. Only on rare occasions does it reach the unique harmony of simplicity and grandeur, or make itself felt with the necessity of the sublime. More often than not, it falls flat or becomes garbled. As Proust was to write much later, in the preface to *Tendres Stocks:*

> The only criticism I might be tempted to make to Morand is that he sometimes uses images that are not inevitable. Now approximation does not work with images. Water (under certain conditions) boils at 100 degrees Centigrade. At 98 or 99, it simply does not happen. It would be better not to have images at all. (CSB 616)

Jean Santeuil slips away from Baudelaire: it would be bold to measure oneself against him, as *Les Plaisirs et les jours* did so naïvely, before the true awakening to the poetry of the world that is pure poetry.

For this reason the formidable poet of *Les Fleurs du mal,* who is omnipresent in Proust's first book, is absent from *Jean Santeuil.* Whereas Hugo is mentioned often, Baudelaire is quoted only once, as we might expect in a passage about an irresistible adjective, an alliance of words that reaches the boiling point. The passage in question speaks of Jean's taste for society life: it results from a harmful laziness and prevents him from working and creating. In this context we find the following: "Laziness, on the other hand, when it gives itself over to the charming rhythm of the moment, the kind of laziness worthy of the qualification 'fertile' which Baudelaire gives to it, fit into the category of the good, of what should be sought after" (JS 703). Jean's idleness is base, Baudelaire's noble: one might well be confused by the contrast. To fail to mention Baudelaire here would have been tantamount to a confession: the phrase *O fertile laziness,* from "La Chevelure," is an unerring alliance of sound and sense, verging on oxymoron. The admirable Monsieur Beulier would have had nothing to complain about: the epithet is strong in its conception, with nothing flabby or rhetorical about it. But if images do not have the necessity and unity of Baudelaire's epithets, one might just as well give them up.

"Noon, King of the Summer"

In *A la recherche du temps perdu* we will find a different attitude toward Baudelaire: the "sun radiating out over the sea" is no longer imitated or pastiched as it was in *Les Plaisirs et les Jours,* nor is it prohibited or swept under the carpet as it is in *Jean Santeuil.* Rather, it is openly accepted as an inimitable and perfect line of poetry. Baudelaire remains the model of the legitimate epithet, and the "sun radiating out" will henceforth appear in quotations, replacing any other description of the sea, in *A l'ombre des jeunes filles en fleurs.* For example, during the narrator's rides with Madame de Villeparisis, "Before getting into the carriage, I had composed the seascape which I was going to look out for, which I hoped to see with the 'sun radiating out' upon it, and which at Balbec I could distinguish only in too fragmentary a form" (1:760; 2:67; modified translation). The "sun radiating out" retains the value of a password, an "open sesame" that condenses all the poetic visions of the sea because it is the origin of all of them. Back in Balbec, it is as if the hero were in search of "the effects described by Baudelaire" (1:746; 2:54). To get back to the feeling transposed in *Les Fleurs du mal* will be the goal of the journey: to find it once again, rather than to copy it or fear it.

Yet the enigma contained within the line, its power in Proust's eyes, still remains intact. What is the reason behind the effect it produces? How can it be that this line, which is not far removed from the realm of cliché, so entices him? The explanation is undoubtedly something clear and simple, the line's beauty related to that something. But what is it?

The prose poems of *Les Plaisirs et les Jours* connected the image to dusk, and associated the "sun radiating out" with the "rays of the setting sun," the September sun low in the sky. The "sun radiating out over the sea" thus became identified with the "sun setting in the sea."

By contrast, in *A l'ombre des jeunes filles en fleurs,* from the first morning in Balbec on, the image is expressly displaced and given quite a different interpretation. The hero observes the sea from the dining room of the Grand-Hôtel:

> Imagining that I was "sitting on the mole" or at rest in the "boudoir" of which Baudelaire speaks, I wondered whether his "sun's rays upon the sea" were not—a very different thing from the evening ray, simple and superficial as a tremulous golden shaft—just what at that moment was scorching the sea topaz-yellow, fermenting it, turning it pale and milky like beer, frothy like milk. (1:724–25; 2:34)

Proust is revising his reading of "Chant d'automne"; he is hesitating. To be sure, the last two stanzas of the poem evoke dusk:

> . . . be the ephemeral sweetness
> Of a glorious autumn or a setting sun.

But to build a contrast and to set the scene for nostalgia, the "sun radiating out" must be the summer sun:

> Oh! let me lay my head upon your lap,
> And while I miss the white and torrid summer,
> Taste the gentle yellow ray of autumn's end!

The "sun radiating out over the sea" is nothing but the star at its zenith—"Noon, King of the Summer"—and the hero of *A l'ombre des jeunes filles en fleurs* corrects the contradiction in *Les Plaisirs et les jours*. Since the time that work was written, the Proustian poetic moment has drifted from moonlight to midday, but the very same line—such is its "strength"—remains its emblem.

In fact the phrase *sitting on the mole,* which Proust juxtaposes with the "boudoir" from "Chant d'automne," is not found in any poem from *Les Fleurs du mal,* but is reminiscent of the phrase *reclining in the belvedere or leaning on the mole* in "Le Port," from *Spleen de Paris* (Baudelaire, OC 1:344). Nevertheless, a certain amount of static persists in the fine tuning. It is no longer from the "boudoir" that the "sun radiating out" is observed in "Chant d'automne," as Proust, never a particularly careful reader, already assumed in a draft written for the beginning of the stay in Balbec, in which Proust still understood the "sun radiating out" as a sun "scattered" over the sea:

> Is it not in this way, from a chilly, unfamiliar autumn room, that Baudelaire—since the previous line shows him the boudoir, the woman he loves, and the hearth—watches the sun radiating out over the sea? Is he not doing what I am, as he stands on the balcony of an autumn room and relishes the pleasure of the sight?[17] (3:906)

But if a kind of uncertainty about the reading of the poem remains in this draft, in the definitive text there is a clarification of the distinction between the ray—the uniqueness of a final, fragile shaft of light—and the radiating out seen as a conflagration of the sea's entire surface: the "sun radiating out" is nothing but "the winding path of its rays" (1:724; 2:34), to quote a phrase found on the same page of *A l'ombre des jeunes filles en fleurs*. At any rate, even if we grant that the "sun radiating out over the sea" is the incandescence of noon rather than a last final ray at sunset, is it not the beauty of the present participle, as we shall see, to allow one, because of the ambiguity it alone possesses, to slip between the adjective and the verb?

A draft for the second stay in Balbec, in *Sodome et Gomorrhe,* confirms this idea of a displacement. The passage is found in a section about the visit of old Madame de Cambremer and her daughter-in-law (née Legrandin) at the Grand Hotel: the old lady deforms language like Sainte-Beuve, and the young woman piles up cliché after cliché. "As the sun was beginning to set, the seagulls were now yellow" (2:839; 3:206). Yellow again! When he speaks to the younger Madame de Cambremer, the hero imitates her brother's flowery speech, saturated with adjectives and epithets. The pretentious Monsieur Legrandin is presented in *Du côté de chez Swann* as someone who "can listen to no music save what the moonlight breathes through the flue of silence" (1:138; 1:125). He quoted Desjardins, who "used to have the most charming water-colour touch": " 'Now are the woods all black, but still the sky is blue.' Isn't that a fine rendering of a moment like this?" (1:130; 1:118–19). Now the hero, aping the brother for the benefit of the sister, quotes Baudelaire. And what else does he choose to quote but the "sun radiating out"?

> Pointing to a trembling, golden shaft sent by the sun onto the surface of the sea: "I often wonder whether this is the 'radiating out' Baudelaire meant when he said, 'And I value nothing as much as the sun radiating out over the sea. . . .' It seems to me he must be thinking about something not quite so linear and not just on the surface, but rather the heating up of the entire sea at noon when the sea is strong, strewn with light and as frothy as milk."[18] (3:1084)

The passage is quite similar to the one in *A l'ombre des jeunes filles en fleurs* about the first lunch in Balbec, but here the logic is more devious, perhaps because it is the logic of a pastiche: a shaft of the setting sun recalls the line from Baudelaire, but then there is an immediate doubt cast on the appropriateness of the allusion. In *A l'ombre,* the association was clean, with no element of fetishism: the brilliance of the noontime sun led to a sanitory rereading of Baudelaire. The difference in the two styles is connected to the difference between the hero and Legrandin: one innocent, the other jaded, one giving himself up to his feelings, the other cramped by intellectualizing. Opposed to the linear ray that reaches only the surface, the sun of pretentiousness, we find the deep and powerful heating up of the sun of maturity. The aesthetic is completely different.

The hero continues: "You know that I am speaking of poetry: 'Chant d'automne.' Probably you are acquainted with the lovely melody Fauré wrote as a setting to those lines." This allusion, which we have already analyzed (see chapter 2), confirms the fact that

Baudelaire's poem is inseparable from the version written by the musician, and that poetry in the *Recherche* more generally is filtered through music. But the younger Madame de Cambremer, who is not familiar with "Chant d'automne," quotes instead a Fauré melody that is a setting of a poem by Sully Prudhomme. In the definitive text, all that remains of the episode is the younger Madame de Cambremer's confusion about seagulls—they make her think of a line from Baudelaire's "L'Albatros" (2:842; 3:209). In the earlier draft this misunderstanding came just after the allusion to Baudelaire and Sully Prudhomme, joined by their common link to Fauré.

From Failed Reminiscence to Successful Reminiscence

To be sensitive to Baudelaire's poetry—as opposed to the Legrandin family—means being sensitive to the greatest and the simplest of things, to the starkest of poetry, the kind that "comes close to prose," like Racine's: for example, the "azur du ciel immense et rond" that Proust quotes at the time of the aesthetic revelations of *Le Temps retrouvé* as an example of a "transposed sensation" (3:959; 4:498–99). In this line of poetry, transposition has accomplished its task, and involuntary memory has transcended the feelings of the moment, as the beginning of the line suggests: "You bring me back the azure of the vast, rounded sky." Something similar happens in "Parfum exotique," which is alluded to immediately after "La Chevelure": "I see a port filled with sails and masts." "Chant d'automne," on the contrary, emphasizes the failure of reminiscence: "And I value nothing, neither your love, nor the boudoir, nor the hearth, / As much as the sun radiating out over the sea." The path one follows to get from "Chant d'automne" to "La Chevelure" and "Parfum exotique" is thus similar to the path leading from *Le Temps perdu* to *Le Temps retrouvé*, or from the madeleine to the uneven paving stones, the spoon, and the starched napkin: from abortive reminiscence to "perpetual adoration."

Thus, at the very beginning of Carnet 1, in 1908, the "sun radiating out" is faintly perceptible in a fragment that is extremely important for the definition of reminiscence, as a prefiguration of the discoveries of *Le Temps retrouvé*:

> We believe the past to be mediocre because we do our best to *conceive* of it, but that is not what the past is, it is rather some uneven paving stones in the baptistry of St. Mark's . . . which we no longer give a thought to but which bring us back [nous rendant] the blinding sun over the canal [le soleil aveuglant sur le canal].[19]

"Nous rendant" is the verb used in "La Chevelure," whereas "le soleil aveuglant sur le canal" is undoubtedly a variation on "le soleil rayonnant sur la mer." Indeed, in *Le Temps retrouvé,* when the narrator's memory is jogged by the rough-hewn paving stones of the Guermantes courtyard, the same words are used again. A "profound azure," a "dazzling light" invade the hero: "It was Venice . . . which the sensation I had once experienced as I stood upon two uneven stones in the baptistery of St Mark's had, recurring a moment ago, restored to me [m'avait rendue]" (3:899–900; 4:445–46).

This is perhaps the reason for yet another motif, Proust's fascination for lines of poetry that stand for the entire series of failures of reminiscence, all the way from the "Souvenir de la mer devant le lac de Genève" in *Jean Santeuil* to the final revelation during the Princesse de Guermantes' matinée. Yet in the novel Proust never mentions the beginning of the Baudelaire quotation that indicates failure: "And I value nothing, neither your love, nor the boudoir, nor the hearth . . ." But he does quote it in the draft for the beginning of the first stay in Balbec—"Could I not say to Andrée: 'But I value nothing, neither your love, nor the boudoir, nor the hearth, as much as the sun radiating out over the sea'?" (2:906, Esquisse XXXIV)—as well as in the draft for the dialogue with the younger Madame de Cambremer, in an abridged form. Here we almost have the impression that "Rien ne me vaut le soleil rayonnant sur la mer" is an alexandrine made up of thirteen syllables. At sunset, unable to restore the fullness of noon, or of summer, to the autumn, "Chant d'automne" is an allegory of inaccessible reminiscence, and hence of the movement from *Le Temps perdu* to *Le Temps retrouvé.* The "sun radiating out over the sea" is not conjured up by the "gentle yellow ray"; it cannot be brought back or given back again.

Rayonnement: the word is perfectly suited to a meditation about reminiscence. It designates a principle of diffusion or effusion—in this sense it belongs to a neo-Platonic world in which being spreads out in a kind of procession—as well as a principle akin to displacement, the metonymic moving force behind Proust's poetics, as in the case of "a radiant smile, "a radiant face," or "radiant with happiness"; or even this line from "Une charogne," which parodies the "sun radiating out over the sea": "The sun was radiating out over that piece of rot." *Rayonner* means not only to be arranged in rays, but also to give off rays, to propagate by means of radiance, to radiate. *Rayonnant* adds an idea of action or contagion to the word *radieux* [radiant]. Thus, in *A l'ombre des jeunes filles en fleurs,* the young hero of the novel dreams that "that strange substance which was housed in Gilberte, and which radiated [rayonnait] from her parents and her home" (1:622–23; 1:568), also radiates in him. The substance emanating from Gilberte makes him fall in love with her, and his love prevents him from believing that that substance "could be liberated, could migrate into another person" (1:623; 1:568); in other words, that he could ever fall in love with another woman. Here the radiating of love is conceived in terms of a transmissible illness:

> Unquestionably the same substance, and yet one that would have a wholly different effect on me. For the same sickness evolves; and a delicious poison can no longer be taken with the same impunity when, with the passing of the years, the heart's resistance has diminished. (1:623; 1:568)

What we find in this "radiating out"—in the physical sense as well as the geometrical sense, an action related to heat as well as optics—is the very basis of the Proustian image. Thus, the "sun radiating out over the sea" is an emblem of the metaphor that "reaches the boiling-point," of the necessary epithet; it is the metaphor of metaphor, so to speak, the metaphor that transcends its function as an adjective and, like the present participle, is transformed into a verb, an action.

Thus, *Les Fleurs du mal,* and particularly "Chant d'automne," allow Proust to form a certain conception of the adjective, to discover an epithet that goes beyond the "banalities of the day" and the "bad writing habits" of *Les Plaisirs et les jours,* the ones Jean Santeuil was chided about by his philosophy teacher. The phrase *fertile laziness* was used to illustrate the well-wrought epithet in *Jean Santeuil.* Starting as a fetish-object in *Les Plaisirs et les jours,* the epithet becomes taboo in *Jean Santeuil.* In the *Recherche,* the hero does not fail to make ironic comments about the epithets used by poets, as when he takes a moonlit stroll in Paris with Albertine: "I recited to her some lines of verse or passages of prose about moonlight, pointing out to her how from 'silvery' which it had been at one time, it had turned 'blue' in Chateaubriand, and in the Victor Hugo of *Eviradnus* and *La Fête chez Thérèse,* to become in turn yellow and metallic in Baudelaire and Leconte de Lisle" (3:414; 3:909–10). There are generations of adjectives as well as generations of color-fashions, as when Saint-Loup qualifies the milieu of the Verdurins as "clerical" as a concession to "fashions in words" (2:1055; 3:410). But even if Baudelaire is named alongside Leconte de Lisle, he escapes all this by his use of unusual epithets that form strange "alliances" of words: the finest example of this in Proust's opinion is "the epithet 'delicious' " used to describe the sound of the trumpet. Proust alludes to this line from "L'Imprévu" in speaking of the "solemn sweetness"—yet another "alliance" of words—of the red carpets lighted up by the intermittent, hot sun, "bursting out again from behind a threatening cloud and darting the full force of its rays"—the sun "radiating out," surrounded by a flurry of adjectives—on the day the Duchesse de Guermantes appears in the church at Combray:

> [The sun] covered [the carpet's] woollen texture with a nap of rosy velvet, a bloom of luminosity, the sort of tenderness, of solemn sweetness in the pomp of a joyful celebration, which characterise certain pages of *Lohengrin,* certain paintings by Carpaccio, and make us understand how Baudelaire was able to apply to the sound of the trumpet the epithet "delicious." (1:194; 1:175–76)

The simple grandeur of the sun radiating out onto the red carpet allows us access to the mysteries of the most extravagant of Baudelairean epithets: that simple grandeur establishes the fact that the juxtaposition is not artificial, not cooked up for effect, but rather imposed by the sensation of the moment and the difficult quest to transpose it.

In his 1921 article, "A propos de Baudelaire," Proust twice quotes the first line of the last stanza of "L'Imprévu," "Le son de la trompette est si délicieux," as an example of a "sudden change in tone"; he wishes to demonstrate that "no poet had a [better] sense of renewal in the very midst of a work of poetry" (CSB 624). After alluding to "the sublime lines about public concerts" in "Les Petites vieilles," he goes on: "It would seem impossible to outdo this. And yet, Baudelaire finds a way to heighten this impression a step further, to give it a mystical significance in the unexpected finale, where the strange happiness of the chosen concludes a sinister piece about "Les Damnés" (CSB 623). Just as in "Combray" Proust associated the impression produced by the epithet with the impression given by a page from *Lohengrin,* here he suggests a motivating force behind the line: it might be taken as a "reminder" that Baudelaire was a "passionate admirer of Wagner." The ultimate adjective is concomitant with a break in tonality. What it would transpose, finally, would be not so much natural perception—the "greatest and simplest things" associated with Jean Santeuil's awakening to poetry—as an emotion that is already artistic, felt at a concert or in a museum, listening to *Lohengrin* or gazing at a painting by Carpaccio.

When Proust brings up yet again the marvelous feeling of transcendence brought to the poem by the epithet "délicieux," he continues:

> An even more striking example (one which Fauré translated wonderfully in one of his songs) is the poem that begins "Soon we shall plunge into the cold darkness" and then suddenly continues, with no transition, in a different tone, with these lines which, even in the book, are sung quite naturally: "I love the greenish light of your long eyes." (CSB 625)

Let us recall that "Chant d'automne" is divided into two parts—set off in the book by a roman numeral—of three and four stanzas, respectively,[20] and the line quoted by Proust—probably sung naturally—opens the second part: the effort of reminiscence comes after the mournful scene.

But the break, as we have seen, is highlighted in a different way by Fauré, in a manner rather more exaggerated than admirable. The melody is built around this opposition; the poem's balance has been completely upset, and in fact only now closely corresponds to Proust's comment about a "sudden change in tone." The contrast between the gloomy tonality of the "cold darkness" and the mysterious tonality of the "greenish light" has become extreme. And the song's last line, the ecstatically emphasized conclusion, is no longer "the gentle yellow ray of autumn's end," but rather—what a surprise!—the "sun radiating out over the sea" at noon on a summer's day. The allegory of Proustian metaphor becomes nothing less than the closing phrase of Fauré's song. What greater support could we find for the idea that Proust's relation to Baudelaire goes through the intermediary of Fauré and music, that "Proust's Baudelaire" is sung, naturally, and radiating out in all directions?[21]

"Long eyes," "greenish light"—if someone points out that Marie Daubrun and Marie Finaly actually had green eyes, we might still wonder whether their eyes were "long"—"uncertain fables," "ironic, cruelly blue sky," "charming and mournful" voices (*Corr.* 4:79, 138 and 404): all of these are Baudelairean alliances of words, epithets Proust praises here and there. And in the places where he finds none, Proust judges Baudelaire to be external, a purveyor of rhetoric, even in the conclusion of "that sublime 'Le Voyage' that begins so promisingly": "In the depths of the Unknown [*l'Inconnu*] to find the new [*le nouveau*]"; here, says Proust, Baudelaire "takes too much of a shortcut, and nearly falls flat on his face" (CSB 624). But let us not overlook the importance of the word *nearly*, for Proust does not seem utterly convinced of his own evaluation. "Perhaps there is something intentional in these very simple endings. Nevertheless there seems to be something foreshortened here, something that runs out of steam." Why in this case does the prosaic simplicity of the line not reach the sublime? I believe Proust has reservations about the way the adjective is turned into a noun by the use of the neuter—"l'Inconnu," "le nouveau"—to designate an abstract concept; it is as if there were an overemphasis on thought at the expense of images, a canceling out of the image by thought that ultimately leads to an abstract and dogmatic kind of poetry. Because he values the verbal adjective, it is no surprise that Proust disapproves of the nominal adjective, which is as listless as the natural epithet. Between the nominal adjective and the verbal adjective, between the natural epithet and the rare epithet, the path is not easy. What can be done other than to give up the epithet altogether—to follow Baudelaire except when thought makes him stray from the path of poetry?

Between Sainte-Beuve's Epithet and Baudelaire's

Proust's article, "A propos de Baudelaire," which was published in the June 1921 issue of *La Nouvelle Revue Française* in the form of a letter to Jacques Rivière, ends with a postscript that directly addresses the question of the epithet. In it, Proust is responding to Daniel Halévy's observation in his February 1920 article commemorating the fiftieth anniversary of the death of Sainte-Beuve in 1919.[22] Halévy had come to the critic's defense with respect to something Proust had insinuated in his remarks on Flaubert's style, published in the January 1920 issue of *La Nouvelle Revue Française*. "He speaks of the Goncourt brothers only as personal friends," Proust had observed ("A propos du 'style' de Flaubert," CSB 596). Halévy recalls that Sainte-Beuve was indeed hard on the theory of the unusual epithet that the Goncourt brothers used as a criterion to distinguish true writers.[23]

In fact, in an 1866 article about the Goncourt brothers' *Idées et Sensations,* Sainte-Beuve had started out by supplementing the idea of color added from the outside with the idea of a reflection emanating from within: "The moral and metaphysical epithet," he said, "often has its own magic, of a kind that would not be produced by thousands of sparkling adjectives."[24] Here Sainte-Beuve is pleading his own cause: had he not been reproached for his unharmonious adjectives, characteristic of his "improper" style, which was said to be as much a result of clumsy phrases intentionally chosen and faulty constructions as it was of "mistakes in French," as Balzac's judgment had it?[25] Sainte-Beuve's most original adjectives were discovered by a technique he used systematically in *Volupté* in 1834, the unusual alliance of words by transposition: a physical epithet was used to qualify a sentiment or vice versa, for example, a "poor gray Jansenist roof."[26] In a September 1834 letter to Sainte-Beuve, George Sand also chided him for "an excess of improper words . . . and of images that all ring false," and she had particularly harsh words for the technique of transposition: "I cannot abide by the technique of applying a word appropriate only to the idea itself to an object being compared to the idea: an *obscure sea lion,* an *absurd rock*—these seem to me to be purely grotesque images."[27] Sainte-Beuve defended his aesthetics in a note added to the 1840 edition of *Volupté*: "*An absurd rock,* a rock of absurdity, as it were, an oblivious rock. Similarly one speaks of *the demented spray* of the sea. When Homer speaks of the punishment of Sisyphus, he goes so far as to say *the impudent stone,* which Marmontel criticized. I am not claiming to justify Amaury's phrase, I am simply explaining it."[28]

Set against the unusual epithet of the Goncourt brothers—or rather beside it—Sainte-Beuve thus emphasized his own transposed epithet which, by allowing communication between the outside and the inside, the everyday and the intimate, phenomenon and impression, played a considerable role in Baudelaire's elaboration of his theory of correspondences. Baudelaire noted in "Fusées": "*Tragic sky*. An epithet of an abstract order applied to a material being." Even in the *Recherche* we find countless images—"holiday sky," "idle cloud" (1:186; 1:168); a path "throbbing with the fragrance of hawthorn-blossoms" (1:150; 1:136); a salamander with a "tapering allegorical body" (1:77; 1:71); "an infinitesimal gaze that swarmed with affability" (1:356; 1:321)—that are closer to Sainte-Beuve's novel juxtapositions than to Baudelaire's alliances of words that reach the boiling point. Even Monsieur de Cambremer's eyes, which "retained between their eyelids a trace of the sky of the Cotentin, so soft upon sunny days" (2:943; 3:304), are reminiscent of Monsieur de Couaën and the "azure field of his eye."[29] The "rare, almost archaic expressions" (1:101; 1:93), undoubtedly inspired by Anatole France and Leconte de Lisle, can also be traced back to a style inherited from Sainte-Beuve. Indeed, the transposition of the epithet goes all the way back to the language of classicism, Racine in particular: it is an extension of hypallage. When Proust sees in Baudelaire a classicist, a close kin to Racine, he is especially thinking of this characteristic, as in the third stanza of "Femmes damnées," which he always refers to in this context.[30]

As early as 1908, in Carnet 1, Proust took exception to Sainte-Beuve's adjectives, comparing them to Anatole France's: "In France's works unusual epithet is not like in Sainte-Beuve's, helps to express the superlative (never sleeps)."[31] France's adjective stands for a superlative, as in the example referred to by Proust, "That imperishable widow," whereas Sainte-Beuve's epithet always operates on a "difference of level." Ridiculous examples abound in Carnet 1: "Chamfort that distinguished and debatable man"; "Benign face, beloved and preferred habit. A regrettable society. Iroquois Homer"; "unqualifiable (I think *Athalie* in *Port-Royal*),"[32] and so on. Proust is in fact so attuned to the question of the epithet that the only addition to Carnet 1 after 1910 records a phrase used by André Suarès in 1912, *stormy aroma of meat in a museum,* and draws an analogy to Balzac, who "expresses the object itself by the use of his adjectives,"as in the case of "sleeping cannonballs that awake" or "a lamp lit up inside."[33] This is, of course, quite the opposite of Sainte-Beuve.

When Daniel Halévy came to Sainte-Beuve's defense, he took Proust to task over a single short sentence in his article about Flaubert, unaware of the immense hidden iceberg of *Contre Sainte-Beuve,* which was not published until 1954. Halévy's defense hit home, since it touched on a delicate issue never addressed by Proust: Sainte-Beuve's influence on the poetic language of the nineteenth century, the relation between Sainte-Beuve's epithet and Baudelaire's correspondences, and hence Proust's debt to Sainte-Beuve in the matter of the "transposed sensation," which is the basis for the poetics of the entire *Recherche.* Is the "gentle yellow ray" that concludes "Chant d'automne" and that Proust alludes to so frequently not itself a reminiscence of Sainte-Beuve's "Rayons jaunes," of which—along with *Volupté*—Baudelaire claimed to be "hopelessly enamored" in a January 1862 letter to Sainte-Beuve?[34] Moreover, Proust's leniency in dealing with Sainte-Beuve's poetry is in contrast to his general indictment in *Contre Sainte-Beuve:*

> Periodically I wonder whether the best part of Sainte-Beuve's work is not his poetry. Here the subtle contrivances come to a halt. Things are no longer approached sideways, with a thousand clever bowings and scrapings. . . . Appearance, the *Lundis.* Reality, these few lines of poetry. A critic's poetry is the weight on the scale of eternity that will measure his entire work. (CSB 232–32)

Unless he is perhaps being ironic, Proust appears genuinely touched by the "paltry means of expression" in "Les Rayons jaunes," just as he praises Baudelaire's recourse to "the most ordinary" of words (CSB 257).

It is true that there is a passage in *Contre Sainte-Beuve* where the hero, speaking to his mother, admits there are in Baudelaire's work—although he does not quote a single one—lines "that you could easily mistake for Sainte-Beuve" (CSB 259); it is also true that Proust does recognize Sainte-Beuve to be among those with the greatest understanding of Baudelaire (CSB 261). And the only things he really condemns are superficial aspects of the style of Sainte-Beuve's criticism, its oral character, its conversational tone, as artificial as "those, so to speak, purely physical remarks, which, in the writer who stoops so low as to transcribe them, are accompanied always by, for instance, the little smile, the little grimace which at every turn disfigures the spoken phrase of a Sainte-Beuve" (3:934; 4:476). Proust's repudiation of Sainte-Beuve as a critic is not enough to free him from *Joseph Delorme* or *Volupté,* both of which promoted the transposed epithet. Thus in June 1905, Proust congratulates Madame de Noailles for a characteristic of her style that is particuliarly reminiscent of Sainte-Beuve: "Sometimes what held my attention was an unbelievable adjective, like 'the *favored* flower' " (*Corr.* 5:195). And he compares *Les Eblouissements* to certain lines of Baudelaire on the grounds that "the irregularity of the images adds a certain beauty" ("*Les Eblouissements,* par la comtesse de Noailles," CSB 543).

In a 1910 draft for *Le Temps retrouvé,* Proust defines style as a synthesis of separate sensations that "beats them together on the anvil and takes out of the forge an object in which the two things are attached to each other"—the surrealist images of Reverdy or Breton come to mind—and he makes note of and comments on an example of an adjective particularly reminiscent of Sainte-Beuve that he himself used:

> In the preface of *Sesame and Lilies* I speak of certain Sunday cakes I speak of "their idle sugary aroma."[35] I could have described the shop, the shuttered houses, the fine aroma of the cakes, their wonderful taste, there would have been no style, . . . would have been

> nothing. . . . Paltry style, paltry impression, but at least for a few months, style.[36]

It is thus beyond question that in Proust's mind, style is related to the transposed epithet, and this is instantly confirmed by yet another descriptive adjective: "When discovering a Turner painting which depicts a monument to speak of the importance of the lighting I say that it makes the monument appear '*instantaneous.*' There is reality of style."[37] But adjectives like these, which do not reach the boiling point, will not stand the test of time, as Proust himself recognizes. So what is the use?

The second of Sainte-Beuve's reservations about the Goncourt brothers' unusual epithets of which Halévy reminds Proust was also decisive, and this one was developed further: "What's more, the unusual epithet is not everything. . . . The epithet, always the epithet! Why not also mention the noun? Why not the verb sometimes? Why not the turn of phrase, or the harmoniousness of the language?"[38] In a note Sainte-Beuve gave an example from Virgil, "Si nox pluviam ne colligat ante" (If we fear that the night might *gather* the rain): "Here is an *unusual* verb indicating the author's talent just as much as an epithet would." The critic seems yet again to be pleading his own cause, the "endless deviation of expression" that Proust, as we saw earlier in this chapter, characterized as "charming" but "second-rate" in a note to *Sesame and Lilies.* The former adjective comes to his mind again in 1921, when he is writing about Virgil's use of the verb: "It is charming, but there is no reason to make such a fuss over a simple observation" ("A propos de Baudelaire," CSB 639).

Indeed, a recurrent idea in Proust is that originality of style does not derive from the unusual use of a word, whether the adjective as practiced by the Goncourt brothers, or Sainte-Beuve's verb, or even Victor Hugo's noun, in spite of his authority and the "importunity of sinister birds" in *Les Contemplations* (harking back to Virgil's "importunaeque volucres") that Proust cites in 1906 (and once again in 1921) as a line worthy of praise, not for the unusual use of the substantive, but for the poet's "all-powerful freedom" in his allusions to antiquity.[39] "In theory I am in favor of calling things by their names and against making originality and innovation consist of altering those names" (*Corr. gén.* 3:148), Proust wrote in 1919 to Jacques-Emile Blanche, in his discussion of the style of his preface to *Propos de peintre*. This principle has all the impact of another, equally important *Contre Sainte-Beuve*.

Nevertheless, in his 1921 postscript to "A propos de Baudelaire," Proust appears unable—or perhaps unwilling—to understand Sainte-Beuve's observations about the Goncourt brothers' style that Halévy's article set forth. Proust modifies the notion of "unusual epithet" explicitly discussed by Sainte-Beuve and Halévy by using the less widely accepted phrase *descriptive adjective*, which blurs the terms of the debate and totally avoids the question of the relation between Sainte-Beuve's transposition and Baudelaire's correspondences. Moreover, Proust manages to confuse the discussion further and to bring it back to familiar ground by attributing to Halévy a criticism he never voiced: "Among the comments I have omitted, one of them agrees with Monsieur Halévy's criticism—following Sainte-Beuve's lead in this—that I used the term 'descriptive adjective,' as if a verb could not also be descriptive" (Halévy had never said that, but rather had emphasized that Sainte-Beuve criticized the Goncourt brothers for limiting to adjectives alone the unusual use of words that reveals the true writer) "and by the same token also agrees with those who do not understand that in my opinion there is only one way to depict a given thing" (CSB 638). "By the same token" the debate is conveniently redirected toward an idea that has long preoccupied Proust. He expressed it, as we have seen, in the preface to *Tendres Stocks*—"he sometimes has images that are not inevitable images"—and criticized Péguy as a caricature of this fault, with his way of "trying out ten different ways of saying something, even though there is only one" (CSB 616).

Proust's obsession with finding the right word, like Baudelaire's, is inextricably linked to his obsession with the unified work. Faulty words, like those of the Goncourt brothers, for example, are indicative of a work in which a sense of construction and wholeness is lacking. In the indictment of decadentism, the autonomy of detail and the absence of composition are, as we have seen, two synonymous charges (see chapter 1). Thus, in a letter of January 1913 to Louis de Robert, Proust opposes Péguy's style, characterized by "a kind of indolence which makes you imagine one word in the place of another word and because of which you don't have the strength to give up this process of trial and error" (*Corr.* 12:38), to the epithet of Francis Jammes, who manages to salvage something even from the disorder of his works:

> Even if he did not know how to put his feelings in order, or how to write a book, even a story, or a paragraph, or a sentence, he would still have the cell or the atom, that is to say his epithets and his images have a depth and a precision that nobody else can reach.
> (*Corr.* 12:37)

Proust has much less of a preference for composed works in which words are imprecise—"we splendidly arrange things that are sloppily expressed"—than for Jammes' talent for expressing things effectively, although with a certain amount of disorder. What is at stake once again is the unity and the wholeness of the organic work, but between Jammes and Péguy, as between Sainte-Beuve and Fromentin or between Mesdames de Cambremer Senior and Junior, the choice is a difficult one. In the great work that is supposed to reveal the real world, finding the right word will go along with finding an inevitable structure: the two ideals are inseparable in the *Recherche,* for here word and book are united, the relation between word and book demanding that the work be united. In his January 1914 response to Henri Ghéon, whose review of *Du côté de chez Swann* in *La Nouvelle Revue Française* irritated him (see chapter 1), Proust lights into "a certain writer who is in vogue these days"—he is probably thinking of Romain Rolland, who had just been awarded the Grand Prix de Littérature by the Académie française, beating out Péguy—and who, he observes, "comes out with one volume after another . . ., but with each sentence is at a loss to discover the right metaphor, and so takes the long way around because he can never manage to jump over the ditch" (*Corr.* 13:24–25). Jammes' effectiveness at the level of the individual word is thus paradoxical, since it does not go along with the unity of the book, as it does in the case of Anna de Noailles, whom Proust congratulates around the same time, comparing her to the very symbol of organicism: "You grow like a tree" (letter of February 1913, *Corr.* 12:70).

As early as *Contre Sainte-Beuve,* Proust already had the same bone to pick, first with Nerval, then with Baudelaire:

> It might even be said—and this is obviously something one can reproach him for, one of the things that show him up to be an author who is not necessarily second-rate but certainly has no really definite genius, creating his artistic form at the same time as his thought—that his poetry and his novellas are nothing more (like Baudelaire's *Petits Poèmes en prose,* or *Les Fleurs du mal,* for example) than different attempts to express the same thing. (CSB 234)

At the time Proust was excessively hard on Nerval and Baudelaire, on the grounds that they wrote the same thing twice, the first time in verse and the second time in prose. "One can compare this with the compulsion which continually draws the criminal to the scene of the crime," Walter Benjamin would later write.[40] Proust diagnosed rather "an infirmity of will or lack of definite instincts"—precisely the diagnosis that was for a long time to be offered for the hero's malaise in the *Recherche*. Proust's criticism looks ahead to the passage in *La Prisonnière* that will take all the great works of the nineteenth century to task for being imperfectly mastered, for lacking a preconceived plan or a predetermined form (3:157–59; 3:666–68; see chapter 1). There the figures mentioned are Balzac, Michelet, and Wagner, but Baudelaire and Nerval could just as well have been on the list. Even the example not to be followed remains identical, from the 1909 draft to the 1921 article: "In Baudelaire we find a line, 'The pure sky in which eternal heat shivers,' and in the corresponding 'petit poème en prose,' 'a pure sky in which eternal heat sprawls.' "[41] Indeed, as early as 1908, in Carnet 1 we read: "What reassures me is that Baudelaire wrote the *Poèmes en prose* and *Les Fleurs du mal* on the same topics. . . . In fact these are defects, when we read great writers, we allow them to fall short of our ideal, which was better than their work."[42] But when Proust responds to Daniel Halévy in 1921, he has softened his stance, or perhaps he has recognized that his judgment of *Le Spleen de Paris* as a double of *Les Fleurs du mal* is erroneous. He concedes more than his adversary asked for: "So there are two equally beautiful versions, and both times the epithet is a verb" ("A propos de Baudelaire,"

CSB 638). Whereas at the time of *Contre Sainte-Beuve* duplication practically made Baudelaire and Nerval second-rate writers—and the "ten different ways" Péguy tried out without hitting on the right one probably made him a tenth-rate writer—from here on in Baudelaire is saved from mediocrity, for his two ways of expressing are one and the same, unique. Baudelaire's epithet is doubly beautiful, and it is a verb; or perhaps we should say, *because* it is a verb.

Epithet and Syntax

What Proust favors in place of the Goncourt brothers' "unusual" usages, Sainte-Beuve's "deviation," or the "alteration of the noun" that he criticized in Jacques-Emile Blanche is the *alteration of syntax*. He characterizes Bergotte's way of writing as "those alterations of syntax and accentuation which bear a necessary relation to originality of mind" (1:598; 1:545), and Flaubert's as "immutable peculiarities of a deforming syntax" ("A propos du 'style' de Flaubert," CSB 593); "As he spent so much time and effort on his syntax, that is where he stored his originality for all times. He is a grammatical genius" ("A ajouter à Flaubert," CSB 299). The most eloquent testimony to the fact that Proust equated originality of style with boldness of syntax is the wonderful angry letter he wrote to Madame Straus in November 1908. Here he pokes fun at the epithets of Louis Ganderax, the editor-in-chief of *La Revue de Paris:*

> Why, when one refers to 1871, should one add "that abominable year of years?" Why is Paris immediately qualified as "the great city," Delaunay as "the master painter." Why should emotion always be automatically "discreet," benevolence "smiling," mourning "cruel." The only people who really defend the French language (like the Army during the Dreyfus affair) are those who "attack" it. . . . [Writers] don't start writing well unless they are original and create their language themselves. There is such a thing as correctness, even perfection of style, but only on the other side of originality, after one has made one's way across the dangers of error, and not on the safe side of it. Correctness that stays on the safe side—"discreet emotion," "smiling benevolence," "that abominable year of years"—there is no such thing. The only way to defend our language is to attack it, yes Madame Straus! (*Corr.* 8:276–77)

To illustrate this principle, Proust traditionally quotes lines of Racine: "Je t'aimais inconstant, qu'aurais-je fait fidèle!" As early as the translation of *Sesame and Lilies,* Proust allowed himself the following commentary:

> The charm one usually finds in this line from *Andromaque,* "Pourquoi l'assassiner? Qu'a-t-il fait? A quel titre? / Qui te l'a dit?" comes precisely from the fact that the usual syntactic link has been purposely broken. . . . The best-known of Racine's lines are actually famous because their charm comes from some colloquial boldness of language thrown out like a daring bridge between two gentle, compliant banks.[43]

The lesson given to Madame Straus is as forceful as the only given young Santeuil by Monsieur Beulier. Proust made it into his own lesson, and the adjective, it would appear, is found guilty without any possibility of appeal: unusual or stultified, what is the difference? In his analysis of Flaubert's "eternal imperfect" in his 1920 article, Proust adds this ironic parenthetical comment:

> (I hope I shall be allowed to call an indefinite past tense "eternal," even though three times out of four, journalists use the word to refer not to love—they are right in this—but rather to a neckerchief or an umbrella. With his *eternal neckerchief*—at least we can console ourselves at having been spared *legendary neckerchief*—is a "consecrated" phrase). ("A propos du 'style' de Flaubert," CSB 590)

But journalistic style is not the only one in question here. Nothing becomes bogged down as a cliché more quickly than the unusual or transposed epithet. Witness Montesquiou, or the elder Madame de Cambremer, who once again provides a caricature of this fatal flaw in *Sodome et Gomorrhe:*

> Mme de Cambremer had acquired the habit of substituting for the word "sincere" (which might in time begin to ring false) the word "true." And to show that it was indeed by sincerity that she was impelled, she broke the conventional rule that would have placed the adjective "true" before its noun, and planted it boldly after. Her letters ended with: "*Croyez à mon amitié vraie*"; "*Croyez à ma sympathie vraie.*" Unfortunately, this had become so stereotyped a formula that the affectation of frankness was more suggestive of a polite

> fiction than the time-honoured formulas to whose meaning one no longer gives a thought. (2:978; 3:336–37)

Once again, like Sainte-Beuve, she reinforces the impact made by the novelty of the adjective by an unexpected reordering of words. But this still leaves us the highly unpleasant task of choosing between the unusual epithet and the natural epithet.

Thus the adjective is acquitted of the charges leveled against it only to the extent that it is an infraction against syntax; the term *alliance* of words must reassume its true meaning, a bold and broken syntactic turn: "linguistic zigzags," Proust will say of Racine's sentence, whereas Boileau called it a "small poetic license in syntax." An epithet that condenses syntactic boldness into a stylistic effect of blending or dissolving: such is Proust's idea of a beautiful epithet, the epithet of Baudelaire, of course, but also the epithet of Flaubert. In "A propos du 'style' de Flaubert," Proust calls *L'Education sentimentale* "a wonderful title because of its solidity—in fact it could just as well fit *Madame Bovary*—but grammatically incorrect" (CSB 588). Indeed, what exactly is a "sentimental education," or for that matter a "sentimental journey"? Neither the journey nor the education are sentimental; does that make the phrases into examples of improper alliance or transferred epithet, ellipsis or hypallage? "And as in the game wherein the Japanese amuse themselves by filling a porcelain bowl with water and steeping in it little pieces of paper" (1:51; 1:47) which will unfold to reveal an entire universe, Flaubert's title suggests the existence of a sentence in which the adjective would modify a different substantive; it contains the kernel of an entire story, the sketch of an entire novel.

Grand style always resides in understatement, euphemism, and litotes. Here Proust is proving faithful to a poetics of *brevitas* or brevity. This does not mean that he makes short work of things—on the contrary, he is known for the length of his sentences—but rather that he is brief, that is, that he does not repeat himself at regular intervals. He avoids both abundance and obscurity, *ubertas* and *obscuritas,* to which he gave a rigorous definition in a note to his translation of *Sesame and Lilies* in 1906:

> To give one's thought a brilliant form, more accessible and seductive to the public, diminishes it, and this is what makes for a facile

> writer, a second-rate writer. But to wrap one's thought up so that it can be seized only by those who take the trouble to lift the veil is what makes for a difficult writer who is also a second-rate writer.[44]

These are the terms of a classical debate that has been going on since the time of the ancient Greeks. Between the opposition of the two terms, or perhaps beyond them, resides *brevitas,* which presupposes that the writer has access to a cornucopia of words from which he can always find the right one: "First-rate writers are those who make use of the very words dictated to them by an inner necessity." But those who give in to the urge to be pleasing "will produce second-rate books composed of everything that is not said in beautiful books and that goes to make up their noble atmosphere of silence, that marvelous veneer shining with the sacrifice of everything that has not been given voice. Instead of writing *L'Education sentimentale,* they write *Fort comme la Mort.*" Proust certainly wrote a great deal. But he did not say everything he had to say. One has only to think of the countless versions of the first sentence of "Combray" to have some idea of what remained stored in his head.

But what about the "sun radiating forth over the sea"? Did we really need all these developments to explain a line that, in the end, has an almost childish simplicity, like a mountain giving birth to a molehill? It is not the most indispensible line of *Les Fleurs du mal;* nevertheless, no other line better crystallizes Proust's theory of style. The epithet is inevitably connected to syntax, since it is itself a present participle: a verbal adjective or a true present participle, an adjective or a verb, a "radiant sun" or a "sun that radiates": the choice remains. The definite article and the complement weigh on the side of reading the word as a determinative present participle, that is, a verb: not "a radiating sun," but rather "the sun that radiates over the sea." The past participle and the present participle, which are related both to the verb and to the adjective, form a privileged locus in which to observe the wrinkles and creases of language: Sainte-Beuve was one of the first to make full, systematic use of their ability to alter syntax. But the "sun radiating out over the sea" is not separable from the phrase on which it is syntactically dependent, *I value nothing* ("rien ne me vaut"):

> And I value nothing, neither your love, nor the
> boudoir, nor the hearth,
> As much as the sun radiating out over the sea.

The status of the personal pronoun is not immediately clear, as one hesitates whether to give the verb "valoir" a transitive meaning, "procure something for someone," or an intransitive one, "to cost, to correspond to, to equal." The transitive meaning is the more common one with the personal pronoun—as in the phrase *Qu'est-ce qui me vaut cet honneur?*" ("To what do I owe this honor?")—whereas the intransitive meaning is more usual without the pronoun—"Tout cela ne vaut pas . . ." ("None of this is as good as . . ."). But the two constructions meet here, enmeshed in a turn of phrase that comes from Latin syntax, the *dativus ethicus* or pronoun of personal interest, which is colloquially used in French as well and indicates a close relation between the action and the person speaking, as in Molière's "Qu'on me l'égorge tout à l'heure."

The disconcerting pronoun and the boldness—as well as the charm—of the syntax are thus a result of a borrowing from Latin. This sort of thing is not out of the ordinary in Baudelaire, and it justifies Proust's insistence on seeing in him a classicist. If we needed further proof, we could find it in the original prepublication version of "Chant d'automne," in the only important variant in the poem: built around a banal epithet and minus the ethical dative construction, by the same token it reveals the striking beauty of the line and, by making clear its syntactic lopsidedness, it shows that the beauty of the line cannot be separated from its syntactic lopsidedness. Baudelaire had first written, and published in the *Revue Contemporaine* in 1859:

> And nothing, even love, the narrow room and the hearth,
> Is as good as the ardent sun radiating out over the sea
> [Ne vaut l'ardent soleil rayonnant sur la mer].
> (OC 1:935 [1:57, var. b])

"L'ardent soleil rayonnant sur la mer" has no magic. Even if the "ardent sun" were not a cliché, the qualifying adjective preceding the noun would have a congealing effect on the combination of words and would result in a natural epithet rather than suggesting a subjective impression. "Ardent" looks ahead to "rayonnant" and reduces it to a redundant synonym. The natural epithet preceding the noun draws the substantive, which marks the caesura, back toward the first hemistiche; the present participle following the noun is immobilized in the second hemistiche, which suggests an explicative value for the participle. In the absence of the personal pronoun, "valoir" has no ambivalence, the meaning being limited to "None of this is as good as . . .," a postcard message. But the elimination of the adjective and the addition of the pronoun, without any change to the second hemistiche which remains as it was, will shift the break and place it between the basically monosyllabic rhythmical beating of the first hemistiche and the solemn procession of the participle in the second. Between the version in the *Revue Contemporaine* and the line in *Les Fleurs du mal*—between 211 degrees Fahrenheit and 212, the boiling point of water—the contrast is so striking that it is in itself a good illustration of Proust's conception of the originality of style as a syntactic unevenness, perfectly blended in Baudelaire's epithet.

Old Madame de Cambremer "upset all the alliances between words, [altered] any expression that was at all habitual." We have seen how strange it is for Proust to use the phrase *alliance between words* as a synonym of a fixed grouping of words rather than in the sense of a daring epithet. We may well wonder if this is a mistake in French, but whether it is or not, it is a marvelous illustration of the paradox of the unusual or unexpected epithet—improper or transposed—that feels belabored and contrived and remains external, that from the very first has an element of predictability and instantly gives a feeling of being a cliché.

Proust only barely avoids evoking alliances of words another time in the *Recherche,* at a decisive moment, when he is speaking about ideal style in *Le Temps retrouvé:*

> [The writer] can describe a scene by describing one after another the innumerable objects which at a given moment were present at a particular place, but truth will be attained by him only when he takes two different objects, states the connexion between them—a connexion analogous in the world of art to the unique connexion which in the world of science is provided by the law of causality—and encloses them in the necessary links of a well-wrought style;

> truth—and life too—can be attained by us only when, by comparing a quality common to two sensations, we succeed in extracting their common essence and in reuniting them to each other, liberated from the contingencies of time, within a metaphor. (3:924–25; 4:468)

This crystallization of the poetics the narrator finally comes to is a transformation of the theory of involuntary memory into an aesthetic dogma. What Proust first wrote down for this passage was much more succinct: "states the connexion between them and fuses them together using the indestructible link of an alliance of words" (4:1265 [4:468, var. a]). What Proust's novel first aimed to achieve was the "alliance of words"; only later did its goal become metaphor. In one of the earliest drafts for *Le Temps retrouvé,* written in 1910, Proust defined style from the very outset as an alliance, with the illustration, discussed above, of the "idle sugary aroma" of Sunday cakes:

> For the [last *crossed out*][IV *corrected*] part (criticism)
>
> As artistic reality is a *relation,* a *law,* bringing together different facts (for example different sensations which are revealed by the synthesis of the impression) reality is given only when there is [has been *added*] style that is alliance of words.[45]

"The indestructible link of an alliance of words" was nearly used to designate the absolute of literature. Probably Proust is still using the notion improperly here; perhaps he discarded it because of the redundancy, "link of an alliance." Nevertheless, it is still more expressive than metaphor, less scholarly; it makes one think of the old and the new alliance, and there is no more insistent example of it in all of Proust's work—no example greater or simpler—than the "sun radiating forth out over the sea." It haunts his whole life and work from *Les Plaisirs et les jours* all the way up to *Le Temps retrouvé.* It is the ultimate Baudelairean epithet, the mystery of an adjective.

8

Brichot: Etymology and Allegory

The theme of etymology that runs through *A la recherche du temps perdu* is one of the novel's most notable curiosities, and one of its most disconcerting. More than a few readers have undoubtedly skipped Brichot's lengthy onomastic speeches in *Sodome et Gomorrhe,* finding them useless and fussy. Joseph Vandryes' judgment of Proust's weakness for linguistics is particularly apt: "In the long run, it is tiresome and irritating for the reader; in a word, it is an error in taste."[1] Jean Cocteau dubs these long speeches "zigzags," and chalks them up to the writer's exhaustion.[2] Even those readers who find them fascinating and delicious, like weird figures on a carpet, are no less perplexed for all that; they hesitate over the function, the value, and the meaning of these pieces, like lost objects one might happen upon, or pasted-on bits of paper.[3] Here once again I will be combining facts of history with facts about the genesis of the work in the goal of interpreting Proust's etymologies.

Etymology, and in particular onomastics—that is, the study of the origins and evolution of place-names (toponymy) and names of people (anthroponymy)—was in fashion around the turn of the century, like other forms of scientific knowledge whose presence is felt in the *Recherche*. But these branches of French philology, seeking to establish their autonomy from the Germans after 1870, undoubtedly had a greater tendency toward a kind of caricature of ideology than other discourses like Darwinism or medicine, and that is perhaps why they are parodied in the novel. Toponymy, which gets the greatest exposure in the *Recherche,* is quite a new field, a subdiscipline of history, connected to historical geography.[4] As such, it is represented in Vidal de la Blache's "Tableau de la géographie de France," which opens Lavisse's famous *Histoire de France.*

People have always been fascinated by the meaning of names, especially proper names, at least as far back as Plato's *Cratylus* and the tradition stemming from that dialogue. But the philologists of this period claim that up until then, the explanations of place-names were generally nothing more than flights of fancy, with names being divided up into as many parts as they had syllables. Ernest Renan, they say, was one of the last people to delve into the realm of philology without much concern for method, as Maurice Barrès in his 1886 pamphlet, *Huit jours chez M. Renan,* points out with no little irony: "He has a fondness for a certain number of etymological considerations—about the name of *Tomé* island, for example, which he claims comes from the Greek *Stoma,* or from the Spanish *San Tome*—which, I must confess, bore me to tears."[5]

Arthur Giry's *Manuel de diplomatique,* a monument to the fledgling turn-of-the-century French science, devoted a long chapter to place-names and quoted four scientists who had recently been particularly illustrious in their analyses: Jules Quicherat, Hippolyte Cocheris, Auguste Longnon, and Henry d'Arbois de Jubainville.[6] But Quicherat and Cocheris are rank amateurs compared to Longnon, who devoted his life to laying the groundwork for the study of toponymy and searching through archives to find the earliest forms of place-names. In 1891 he published the topographical dictionary of the Marne in a collection of departmental topographical dictionaries begun in 1861 and never completed, and also many provincial church records that are, along with church deeds, the principal sources of toponymy, as Brichot well knows. Longnon, the true founder of French historical toponymy—a German scientist, Hermann Gröhler, was his great rival—specialized in establishing collections of place-names rather than in studying historical phonetics, which accounts for linguistic evolution. He put an end to the fanciful musings and speculations about the meanings of proper names in themselves that had previously been indulged in.

The Curé of Combray

In *Du côté de chez Swann*, several place-names are explained by the curé of Combray when he is visiting Tante Léonie. The theme is a latecomer: it is not found on either the manuscript or the typescript, and does not appear until the summer of 1913, in handwritten additions to the second proofs. The source Proust was using at the time was a little book by Jules Quicherat, *De la Formation française des anciens noms de lieu.*[7] But if Proust made use of Quicherat's book for those few etymologies given in "Combray," the source for the interminable ramblings in *Sodome et Gomorrhe* is not the same, as we shall see.

In "Combray," then, the curé shores up his lessons about the history of the region with etymological proofs: *Roussainville* is assimilated to *Rouville*, from *Radulfi villa*, by analogy to Quicherat's derivation of *Châteauroux* from *Castrum Radulfi* (1:112; 1:103).[8] *Saint Hilaire, Illiers, Hélier,* and *Ylie*, in the Jura region, are all interpreted as corruptions of *Sanctus Hilarius* (1:113; 1:103); Quicherat classified *Saint-Illiers* (Seine-et-Oise) and *Saint-Ylie* (Jura) as examples of "names that have been completely disfigured."[9] And just as Quicherat lists *Sancta Eulalia* and *Saint-Eloi* (Ain) as examples of "names whose gender has changed,"[10] the curé also mentions the transformation of *Sancta Eulalia* into *Saint-Eloi* in Burgundy, leading up to the humorous conclusion: "Do you hear that, Eulalie—after you're dead they'll make a man of you!" (1:113; 1:103). The derivation of *Thiberzy* from *Theodeberciacus* (1:113; 1:104) and of *Jouy-le-Vicomte* from *Gaudiacus vice comitis* (1:114; 1:105) are based on the models of *Thiberzey* (from *Theudeberciaco*)[11] in the first case and *Jouy* (from *Gaudiacus*) and *La Chaize-le-Vicomte* (from *Casa vice comitis*)[12] in the second. In a slightly later passage, the example of *Champieu*, derived from *Campus Pagani* (1:159; 1:144), conforms to Quicherat's derivation of *Champien* (in the department of the Yonne), a shortening of *Champayen*, also from *Campus Pagani.*[13]

These few etymologies added to the text at a late stage may seem inconsequential, but they do fit into the long list of references in "Combray" to various nineteenth-century scientific discourses, and also to the text's predilection for the Middle Ages, ranging from Augustin Thierry's *Récits des temps mérovingiens* (1840), to Ruskin, to Emile Mâle's *L'Art religieux du XIIIè siècle en France* (1898), which all contribute to its numerous allusions to the medieval period. Yet an important distinction must be made here: Proust read Augustin Thierry as a child, voraciously; he discovered the works of Emile Mâle and Ruskin before 1900 and never stopped being fascinated by them. These works, then, are examples of the kind of mythical, intimate, subjective references that tell us less about the works themselves than they do about the state of mind a person was in when he or she read them. This is not the case with etymologies, which represent the other aspect of reading for Proust: erudition. The sort of knowledge embodied by the curé of Combray is immediately presented as slightly ridiculous. External, deterministic, and related to events, it pales in significance beside the rich imaginary potential of names. The curé is a pastiche of another historian of Combray, Canon Joseph Marquis, the dean of Illiers, who devoted an entire work to the village in 1904. Proust owned a copy of this book.[14] This kind of monograph, the height of traditional erudition, also contains a number of etymologies, and Proust makes use of them for street names in Combray, like the Rue de l'Oiseau: "The inn, 'L'Oiseau fléché' [The Pierced Bird], gave its name to a street, in the heart of Illiers. The sign had a picture of a bird struck by an arrow."[15]

Following the latest fashions in etymologies, the curé shamelessly paraphrases Canon Marquis, who wrote: "The Vicomte de Châteaudun, Geoffroy, early in life lost his father, and he wielded power with the independence and arrogance of a man who has not been subjected to discipline in his youth."[16] Here is Proust's version: Charles the Stammerer, Gilbert's brother, "having early in life lost his father, . . . wielded the supreme power with all the arrogance of a man who has not been subjected to discipline in his youth" (1:113; 1:104). Geoffroy de Châteaudun took up arms against the bishop of Chartres, Fulbert, and King Robert II (the Pious); he destroyed the farmlands of the bishopric and was excommunicated.

In all these actions, he is the model for Gilbert le Mauvais, even in the circumstances of his death:

> Geoffroy visited Chartres Cathedral in 1040, convinced that the devastation and the fires he had once brought to this region had been forgotten. Unfortunately, his hateful name had remained etched in the memories of the local people. As he was coming out of the holy service, he was set upon and massacred by residents of Chartres.[17]

Proust echoes this passage: the residents of Combray "fell upon him as he was coming out from mass, and cut off his head" (1:114; 1:104).

In its interweaving of Quicherat and Canon Marquis, the curé's discourse reaffirms the ambiguity of the theme of etymology, even as early as "Combray." This theme is connected to local lore and scholarship rather than to a symbolic system of forms like Emile Mâle's iconography or Ruskin's aesthetics, which are the source of the hero's conception of the church in Combray. The description of the church (1:63–72; 1:58–66), which is given before the curé manages to spoil its charm, does in fact borrow elements from Emile Mâle and Augustin Thierry. The local color and the historical anecdotes fossilized in place-names and street names have nothing like the universality of symbols perpetuated in stone. There is no illustrated Bible to be found in a name. If, in the final pages of "Combray," Canon Marquis is once again repeatedly put to use, the point is merely to decorate the Guermantes way with picturesque touches.

The curé's etymological trivia are also quite distinct from the poetic onomastics set forth at the beginning of "Place-Names: The Name." Names stir up associations in one's imagination, and they kindle the hero's desire to see the corresponding places: "Names present to us—of persons, and of towns which they accustom us to regard as individual, as unique, like persons—a confused picture, which draws from them, from the brightness or darkness of their tone, the colour in which it is uniformly painted" (1:421; 1:380). This phenomenon may take the form of hearing "in color" (with sounds instantly evoking colors, as Gérard Genette has suggested[18]) or associating names with certain words (as Claudine Quémar has shown, proper nouns evoke images related to common nouns that are homophones or are brought to mind by assonance[19]), but at any rate it rests on the premise that names can express meaning in quite a different way than is usually thought: "Bayeux, so lofty in its noble coronet of russet lacework, whose pinnacle was illumined by the old gold of its second syllable; Vitré, whose acute accent barred its ancient glass with wooden lozenges; gentle Lamballe, whose whiteness ranged from egg-shell yellow to pearl grey" (1:422; 1:381). Other examples are given: Coutances, Lannion, Questambert, Pontorson, Benodet, Pont-Aven, Quimperlé . . . Balbec is first mentioned in the context of these names, their charm and their mysteriousness emanating from the way they sound. Etymology is the search for the significance of a name in its origins, that is, in the realm of meaning; the reduction of the name to something historically determined in a way that is quite distinct from its phonetic evolution; a rational process dealing in terms of laws, of cause and effect. Poetry, which opens the name up to the infinite field of feeling and sensation and peers inside the name, is quite the opposite.

But the "Age of Things" will destroy the illusions of the "Age of Names." Neither things nor people—Balbec and the Guermantes particularly come to mind—will live up to their names. Thus the narrator states, as soon as he arrives in Normandy in *A l'ombre des jeunes filles en fleurs:* "As for Balbec, no sooner had I set foot in it than it was as though I had broken open a name which ought to have been kept hermetically closed" (1:710; 2:21). In the course of his apprenticeship, the hero gives up Cratylus' hypothesis and opts for Hermogenes': the name, which does not contain the truth of the thing it names, is arbitrary. That is the novel's true antithesis, the antithesis of the "Age of Names" and the "Age of Things," of Cratylus and Hermogenes, of childhood and adulthood. The history of place-names is not identified with either term in these pairs; its hypothesis is that names are motivated, but that motivation has nothing essential about it. Toponymy is a heterogeneous genre, a mixture of science and poetry; it is yet another form of the "in-between" that characterizes *A la recherche du temps perdu.*[20]

This ambiguity is brought out by several passages in "Combray" that straddle historical toponymy and poetic onomastics, positivism and the imaginary. Anatole France's prose, particularly *Pierre No-*

zière, is a good example of this mixture in Proust's novel. Legrandin gives one of the first examples of poetic onomastics, one of the very first times Balbec is mentioned:

> Balbec! the most ancient bone in the geological skeleton that underlies our soil, the true Ar-mor, the sea, the land's end, the accursed region which Anatole France—an enchanter whose works our young friend ought to read—has so well depicted, beneath its eternal fogs, as though it were indeed the land of the Cimmerians in the Odyssey. (1:142; 1:129)

"Armor," meaning "on the sea," is the Celtic name for Brittany, whereas the Cimmerians, encountered in Book 11 of the *Odyssey,* are the former inhabitants of what is now known as Crimea. But Ernest Renan compared Brittany to the land of the Cimmerians in his "Prière sur l'Acropole," and Anatole France picked up on that idea in *Pierre Nozière,* after his hero reads the *Odyssey* at the Pointe du Raz.

Renan was mocked by Barrès, whereas Anatole France was one of the models for Bergotte; the presence of these two figures at the intersection of etymology and poetry establishes the ambiguity of both, especially since these words are spoken by Legrandin, one of the most equivocal characters in the entire novel.[21] In counterpoint to Emile Mâle's system of symbolic forms, and also to the poetic onomastics of the "Age of Names," Proustian toponymy, following in the footsteps of the curé of Combray and Legrandin, the positivist and the snob, seems a shady business even before it is associated with Brichot.

The Curé Disproven

As early as the beginning of his second visit to Balbec in *Sodome et Gomorrhe,* the hero shows a keen interest in the particularities of Norman place-names: Gonneville, Amfreville, Graincourt, Franquetot, and Cambremer, to name a few examples. On a death announcement, they seem to ring out with their "joyous endings in *ville,* in *court,* or sometimes on a duller note (in *tot*)" (2:814; 3:182). Once again we find the theme of the "Age of Names": the names of the Norman aristocracy are evocative of villages, castles, and churches.

Later, when the two Cambremer ladies visit Balbec, true etymology is brought in over the question of the name of the property the Cambremers rent from the Verdurins for the season: *La Raspelière,* it is claimed, comes from *Arrachepel,* the name of the previous owners (2:837; 3:204). Here again Proust takes his inspiration from Canon Marquis' monograph, which states that the Arrachepel family—the name apparently means "Post-puller" ("Arrache-pieux")—gave their name to La Rachepelière, or La Raspelière, in the area around Illiers. Young Madame de Cambremer immediately mentions the curé of Combray, whom she once invited to Normandy but who left almost as soon as he got there: "But he amused himself while he was our neighbour in going about looking up all the old charters, and he compiled quite an interesting little pamphlet on the place-names of the district" (2:837; 3:204). This passage is a handwritten addition on an insert. It brings back into *Sodome et Gomorrhe,* by means of a fictional book, a character from "Combray," thereby retrospectively giving his first appearance the impact of a kind of preparation. Proust did not in fact have this sudden revival in mind when he published *Du côté de chez Swann;* nevertheless, it serves as an organic link between the toponymy of *Sodome et Gomorrhe* and the toponymy of "Combray," since the way Brichot appropriates the theme of onomastics is to take exception to the etymologies of the curé of Combray.

Apart from a few isolated etymologies, there are basically three large etymological groupings in *Sodome et Gomorrhe,* three great lessons taught by Brichot:

1. The first lesson takes place in the train going to La Raspelière, when the hero takes his first trip with the "faithful" (2:916–21; 3:280–84). When he learns that Madame de Cambremer will be attending the party, he mentions that he can finally ask her for a copy of the curé's brochure. At this point, Brichot sets out to disprove the curé's etymologies. The whole passage appears on an insert in the manuscript;[22] two fragments are added to the typescript.[23]

The insert contains a list of refutations: *Bricq* does not come from the Celtic word *briga* ("height"), but rather from the old Norse word *bricq* ("bridge"). *Fleur* does not come from the Scandinavian words *floi* or *flo,* nor is it from the Irish words *ae* and *aer,* but from the Danish *fjord* ("port"). *Hon* ("home") and *holm* do not come from *holl, hullus* ("hill"), but rather from the old Norse *holm* ("island"). In the place-name *Carquethuit,* the curé is correct in his analysis of the first element, *carque* (German "Kirche," English "church"), but he is mistaken about *thuit,* which does not come from *toft* ("building"), but from *thveit* ("reclaimed land"). In *Clitourps* he correctly identifies the Norman word *thorp* ("village"), but the beginning of the name does not come from *clivus* ("slope"), but rather from *cliff* ("precipice"). In *Montmartin-en-Graignes,* he figured out the Latin *grania* and the Greek *krene* ("ponds"), but *Montmartin* comes from the Roman god Mars rather than from St. Martin.

When *Sodome et Gomorrhe* was published in 1922, some of these etymologies were held to be correct and others thought to be spurious, but all of them have the weight of scholarship behind them. The examples used to support them go into some detail, as do the anecdotes illustrating the curé's tendency to find Christian and French roots in Norman place-names that are actually of non-Christian, Scandinavian origin.

The etymologies added to the typescript are evidence of the pleasure these accumulations of examples gave to Proust. Starting with the simple goal of refutation, he moves on to more complex reasoning. *Saint-Martin-le-Vêtu* does not come from *vetus* ("old"), or even from *vadum* ("ford"), but rather from *vastatus* ("a place that is devastated"). *Saint-Mars* is in fact a name of Christian origin, but *Mars* and *Jeumont* are not, whereas *Loctudy* and *Sammarcoles,* despite what one might expect, are.

As for *carque,* the "church" element in *Carquethuit* (as well as *Querqueville* and *Dunkerque*), we find the insertion of a lengthy elaboration of the Celtic word *dun* ("high ground"), including the most complex twists and turns of this entire first lesson. The curé had first connected it to *Douville* but then changed his mind, deriving it from *Domvilla* (from *domino abbati* ["belonging to the abbot"]). But according to Brichot, the true derivation is *Eudonis Villa* ("the village of Eudes"), which he justifies with a particularly detailed anecdote:

> Douville was formerly called Escalecliff, the steps up the cliff. About the year 1233, Eudes le Bouteiller, Lord of Escalecliff, set out for the Holy Land; on the eve of his departure he made over the church to the Abbey of Blanchelande. By an exchange of courtesies, the village took his name, whence we have Douville to-day.
>
> (2:919; 3:282–83)

But Brichot further adds that *Douville* might also come from *Ouville* ("the Waters"), since *ai* (from *aqua*) can be changed to *eu* or *ou*. The professor can no longer take a firm stance. Doubt has entered the field of etymology.

2. Brichot gives his second lesson in the course of the dinner hosted by the Verdurins (2:953–69; 3:314–29). This passage is included in its entirety in the first manuscript version,[24] except for the wonderful explanation of *Pont-à-Couleuvre,* which appears on an insert,[25] and Proust did not add anything to the typescript. Because this lesson is not about Norman place-names, it is not very specialized. These are the first etymologies to find their way into *Sodome et Gomorrhe,* first the etymologies of place-names that derive from the names of animals: *Chantepie* ("Magpiesong"), the forest where Monsieur de Cambremer hunts, allows Brichot to draw attention to himself by asking him if the place is worthy of its name, and then *Chantereine* ("Frogsong") and *Renneville* ("Frogtown"). On the manuscript insert that analyzes *Pont-à-Couleuvre* ("Snakebridge") in detail, mention is made of the curé of Combray, who saw snakes in that place even though the name actually comes from *Pont-à-Quileuvre* (Latin *pons cui aperit,* "bridge that opens"). Then we find names of people—politicians, academics, and diplomats, all prominent under the Third Republic—whose family names are derived from the names of plants: *Saulces de Freycinet* ("Willow and Ash"), *Houssaye* ("Holly"), *d'Ormesson* ("Elm"), *de la Boulaye* ("Birch"), *d'Aunay* ("Alder"), *de Bussière* ("Box-Tree"), *Albaret* ("Sapwood"), *de Cholet* ("Cabbage"), and *de la Pommeraye* ("Appletree"). They are followed by *Saint-Frichoux* ("Sanctus Fructuosus") and *Saint-Fargeau* ("Sanctus Ferreolus"), *Saint-Martin-du-Chêne* and *Saint-Pierre-des-Ifs. Saint-Martin-du-Chêne* is simply *Saint-Martin-by-the-Oak,* but *If* ("Yew"), on the other hand, is actually *ave* or *eve* ("water"), as in *évier* ("sink"), *ster* in Breton.

Finally—this is the climax of the passage—Brichot, questioned by the hero, discusses the origins of *Balbec,* a corruption of *Dalbec,* and from there he gradually makes his way toward pseudo-Norman etymologies in preparation for a very learned anecdote:

> Balbec was a dependency of the barony of Dover, for which reason it was often styled Balbec d'Outre-Mer, Balbec-en-Terre. But the barony of Dover itself came under the bishopric of Bayeux, and, notwithstanding the rights that were temporarily enjoyed in the abbey by the Templars, from the time of Louis d'Harcourt, Patriarch of Jerusalem and Bishop of Bayeux, it was the bishops of that diocese who collated to the benefice of Balbec. (2:968; 3:327–28)

Balbec purportedly comes from *bec* ("stream")—as in *Mobec* (from *mor* or *mer* ["marsh"]), or *Bricquebec* (from *briga* ["fortified place"], or *brice* ["bridge"])—and *dal* or *thal* ("valley").

This grouping of etymologies culminating in *Balbec,* the oldest in all of *Sodome et Gomorrhe,* has an easily identifiable source, as we shall see.

3. Brichot's last set of etymologies, which are also present as early as the manuscript version but on an insert glued to the page, are given near the end of the second visit to Balbec, when memories linked to the stops along the local train line are evoked (2:1135–37; 3:484–86). The curé is no longer mentioned; toponymy has been completely taken over by Brichot. Indeed, toponymy is quite distinct from poetry, since Brichot's lessons have "humanized" the names of the stations: because they have "lost their strangeness" and are reduced to facts of history and language, they no longer fire the hero's imagination. Thus etymology contributes to disillusionment in the same way that discovering the reality of places does. But it gives birth to a different kind of wonder. The associations with *flower* (*fleur*) and *ox* (*boeuf*) are certainly removed from names ending in *-fleur* and *-boeuf* when the endings are revealed to be the Norman words *fiord* ("harbor"), and *budh* ("hut"). In "Pennedepie," the hero says, "I was disappointed to find the Gallic *pen* which means mountain" (2:1135; 3:484). But when Albertine says in speaking of the village Marcouville-l'Orgueilleuse, " 'Yes, I love that *orgueil,* it's a proud village,' " Brichot supports her intuition, and in a whole series of station names sees "the ghosts of the rude Norman

invaders" (2:1135; 3:484): *Marcovilla* ("the domain of Merculph"); *Herimundvilla* ("the domain of Herimund"); *Incarville* ("the village of Wiscar"); *Tourville* ("the village of Turold"). Next we find place-names derived from the names of various groups of people: *Aumenancourt,* from *Alemanicurtis (Alemanni* ["Germans"]); *Sissonne,* from *Saxons; Mortagne,* from *Mauretania* ("Moors"); *Gourville,* from *Gothorumvilla* ("Goths"); *Lagny,* from *Latiniacum* ("Latins"). Here there is another letdown: Monsieur de Charlus thinks he sees *man (homme)* in *Thorpehomme,* but Brichot breaks the name up into *holm* ("island") and *thorp* ("village"). Then we come back to individuals who gave their names to villages, like *Orgeville* ("the domain of Otger"), *Octeville-la-Venelle,* named for the Avenel family, *Bourguenolles,* along with *Chaise-Baudoin,* named for Baudoin de Môles. The series is brought to a close with *Doncières,* a synonym of *Saint-Cyr,* both names coming from *Dominus Cyriacus.*[26]

To sum up, the first appearance of the theme from the reader's point of view is one that was added to the manuscript version and elaborated on the typescript; it is essentially about Norman names and is highly specialized. The second appearance, which was actually written earlier as part of the original manuscript version, is basically general until we get to the analysis of the name *Balbec;* this series of etymologies starts off with place-names deriving from the names of animals and plants. The third appearance, which was also in the manuscript version, mixes together place-names deriving from names of individuals and populations with a few Norman names.

The second appearance, at the Verdurins' dinner, is actually the earliest in terms of the writing of the novel. From a marginal addition on the manuscript that has been crossed out, we may conclude that Proust had not yet thought up what was to be the first appearance from the reader's point of view, in the train going to La Raspelière, when he wrote the passage that includes the second appearance:

> "Monsieur, I cannot express how much you have sparked my interest," I said to Brichot. "Where we used to live in the country we had an old priest who knew a whole bunch of etymologies. Afterward I

> was sorry I never took full advantage of his knowledge. I am awfully eager to ask you the meaning of certain names in that part of the country." (3:1521 [3:316, var. a])[27]

In the manuscript version, Brichot did not go into any etymologies before dinner with the Verdurins. Then, in a process that we often find repeated in the genesis of the novel, Proust hit upon the idea of bringing back the curé of Combray, thereby setting up a symmetry between the priest and Brichot. He incorporated the suggestion given on this marginal addition by inventing Brichot's first etymology lesson; the addition itself was then crossed out.

The third appearance from the reader's point of view, at the end of the Balbec sequence, was the second one to be written. This is proven by a memo Proust wrote to himself in the margin of the manuscript version; it brought up the possibility of moving the third appearance back to the train trip to La Raspelière, before the Verdurin dinner: "It would be better if the etymologies were discussed on the way there at each station, with Albertine asking Brichot about them and adding names like Marcouville which are not stations" (3:1611 [3:484, var. b]).[28] Proust followed his own advice by inventing the first lesson, which is thus actually the last of the three to be written. But he did not get rid of the third one, and this leads to the occasional repetition. Finally, as the memo indicates, in the manuscript version it was Albertine rather than the hero who was interested in etymologies and questioned Brichot about them: she was present in the train going to La Raspelière and the Verdurin dinner party. A trace of this remaining in the third lesson is the inconsistency whereby we are told that names have lost their charm "since the evening when Brichot, at Albertine's request, had given us a more complete account of their etymology" (2:1134–35; 3:484); in the novel, this is not the way things happen.

A second, perhaps more disconcerting fact is that the etymologies in *Sodome et Gomorrhe* are no longer taken from Quicherat's book, which Proust used for "Combray." Proust's source for the general etymologies of *Sodome et Gomorrhe,* and even for the first etymologies of Norman names, is in fact another of the pioneers of historical toponymy mentioned by Arthur Giry: Hippolyte Cocheris, a school inspector and the author of *Origine et formation des noms de lieu.*[29]

Longnon was to say of this book that it was "seemingly more comprehensive and more methodical" than Quicherat's work, but that "everything that comes directly from its author must be taken with a large grain of salt."[30] Brichot will not be taken with a grain of salt. Once again the information Proust uses dates back to when he was a young man, and even to his childhood; it is out-of-date when his novel is published, although we must concede that it does fit the beliefs of Brichot's generation. But as for the later set of Norman etymologies, the problem cannot be so easily resolved.

Mysteries of Proustian Erudition

The final pages of chapter 3 of *Sodome et Gomorrhe* are quite nostalgic in their reminiscences about the area around Balbec, which has lost much of its magic since the narrator's first trip to the seashore in *A l'ombre des jeunes filles en fleurs*: "So that it was not merely the place-names of this district that had lost their initial mystery, but the places themselves. The names, already half-stripped of a mystery which etymology had replaced by reasoning, had now come down a stage further still" (2:1145; 3:494). It so happens that things are somewhat more complicated than the narrator's reconstruction of the entire process after the fact, since these places had already been emptied of their mystery even as early as the first trip to Balbec, and in fact the etymologies gave them back a bit of their power of seduction—the power of the Norman conquest—but habit subsequently erased it yet again. Shadowy forms come up to the train during the nighttime return-trip to Balbec, and "Brichot, who could see nothing at all, might perhaps have mistaken [them] in the darkness for the ghosts of Herimund, Wiscar and Herimbald" (2:1145–46; 3:494), but the hero knows they are nothing more mysterious than Monsieur de Cambremer or some other seaside acquaintance: "And so Hermenonville, Harambouville, Incarville no longer suggested to me even the rugged grandeurs of the Norman Conquest, not content with having entirely rid themselves of the unaccountable melancholy in which I had seen them steeped long ago in the moist evening air" (2:1147; 3:495). Thus, the explanations Proust gives of the role of etymology in the process of disillusionment do not really hold water, which is understandable once we realize that the development of the theme had not been planned out much ahead of time. The theme reinforces the hero's disenchantment but at the same time postpones it; in fact it upsets the fine symmetry of the "Age of Names" and the "Age of Things," and more generally the entire system of symmetries on which the novel was supposed to be based.

The genesis of the theme supports the idea that the theme opens up a breach in the novel, a gap within the gap already created by *Sodome et Gomorrhe*. The few etymologies given in "Combray," which date from 1913 and belong to a different part of the country, do not suggest in the least that Proust intended at the time to pick up on this theme later on, but then a first set of place-names appears in the drafts dating from the beginning of the war. In Carnet 2, Proust recorded a few names coming from Canon Marquis,[31] and *Bricquebec* is written on the back at the end of the notebook,[32] but these notations may well date back to 1913; at any rate they are nothing more than details.

A much more important piece of evidence is found in Cahier 54, which, immediately after the departure and death of Alfred Agostinelli in the spring of 1914, lays the groundwork for the novel of Albertine. Here we see that starting with this point, Proust began to think about coming back to the theme of etymology:

> N.B. In the last part of Combray I will read in the curé's book the etymologies *Bricquevilla Superba Eudonis villa* belonging to a certain Bigot and *Radulphi villa* from *Calvo loco* [*marginal addition*: that is to say the barren place and not the hot place]. As for Saint Martin le Vêtu, the abbé will say that it is not a deformation of *vetus* (Saint Martin le vieux) but a variation on *vestitus*, covered with pasture, as opposed to Saint Martin le Gast (that is to say *vastatus*, barren).[33]

This memo did not foresee that the theme would be taken up by a character who was not the same as the one who introduced it in "Combray," nor, of course, that Brichot would disprove the curé's theories.[34] Probably what Proust calls "the last part of Combray" refers to the visit with Gilberte at Tansonville, which presently closes *Albertine disparue;* here he seems to consider the possibility of making the hero himself read a book by the curé about the etymologies around the area of Combray rather than around Balbec.

As for the source of these lines, it would not appear to be exclusively Cocheris. On the other hand, in Carnet 4 we find a dozen etymologies,[35] only one of which was used in the novel (*Saint-Fargeau,* 2:963 and 1028; 3:323 and 384), but all of which are taken from Cocheris. Consequently, Proust must have consulted Cocheris' book at the beginning of the war, and there isn't the shadow of a doubt that the book is the source for the earliest etymologies in *Sodome et Gomorrhe.*

Proust continued to use this work for the draft and the manuscript of *Sodome et Gomorrhe.* In the 1915 draft notebook that sketched out the end of the second stay in Balbec, Cocheris is the sole inspiration—starting with the description of the faithful in the little train—for Cahier 72, including the etymologies that form the framework for Brichot's second lesson, the original one at the Verdurin dinner party, with its connection of proper names to plants and animals, and the analysis of the name *Balbec.* Further on, Cahier 72 also comprises lists of place-names that Proust thought of using for the stops on the little train. The source is the same, but here Proust's inventiveness already begins to show a certain degree of freedom (3:1612 [3:485 n. 1]).[36]

Proust again made use of Cocheris' book when he wrote the manuscript of *Sodome et Gomorrhe* in 1915. In one of the margins he recorded several names and, more important, a page number, "p. 164": all the names but two are found in Cocheris' book on or near page 164 (3:1564 n. 2 [3:383, var. a]).[37]

Matters become more complicated when we look at the etymologies added to *Sodome et Gomorrhe* at the end of the war. These more scholarly etymologies, made up of additions and inserts to the manuscript and the typescript, deal with place-names of Scandinavian origins in Normandy, mostly in the Cotentin and Avranchin regions. Unlike the earlier etymologies, they apparently cannot be traced back to a single source.

The question of the Scandinavian influence in Normandy after its transfer by the terms of the Treaty of Saint-Clair-sur-Epte in 911 was much studied in the nineteenth century. The renewed interest in Normandy dates back to Augustin Thierry's *Histoire de la conquête de l'Angleterre par les Normands* (1825), which was reprinted many times. The most important names associated with the scholarly study of Norse contributions to Norman place-names are Estrup, a Dane whose work began as early as the 1820s, and later Depping, Le Prévost, Petersen, Duméril,[38] Gerville,[39] Fabricius,[40] Le Héricher, and Joret. These learned men are mostly amateurs of local trivia. But the topic had already become popularized by the time Proust became interested in it.[41] After a great number of rather fanciful works, the most systematic synthesis can be found in Longnon's book, *Les Noms de lieu de la France, leur origine, leur signification, leur transformation.* It has been claimed by some that Proust got his etymological information from Auguste Longnon. As we have seen, this is not the case for "Combray." But might it be true for *Sodome et Gomorrhe,* and even for toponymy in general, at least Norman toponymy? The hypothesis is a peculiar one and needs to be disproven. Even the mystery shrouding the sources of Proust's knowledge of onomastics is an illustration of the theme's ambiguity. Proust spent so much time and energy on his etymologies that his infatuation can be seen as a reflection of a strange, almost perverse intention.

Longnon died in 1911. The fundamentals of his work were published posthumously, between 1920 and 1929.[42] Proust came out with *Sodome et Gomorrhe II* in 1922, the same year as the second volume of Longnon, which contains Saxon and Norman etymologies: for Proust to have made use of it, he would have had to have been familiar with it before its publication. This is a complicated issue, but Longnon, who became head of instruction at the Ecole pratique des Hautes Etudes in 1886 and a professor at the Collège de France in 1889, had regularly presented his theories in his classes from the late 1880s until his death, and more particularly during a cycle of courses he gave during the period 1889–1893. It has been pointed out that Proust studied at the Sorbonne during this period, but the connection seems somewhat gratuitous. Some of the etymologies given in *Sodome et Gomorrhe* are indeed discussed by Longnon. But is there anything surprising in this, given that his work is the first compendium on the topic? In fact, other etymologies contradict what Longnon says.

Might Proust perhaps have known one of Longnon's sons? A letter he wrote to Louis Martin-Chauffier, dating from late 1919, brings up the possibility, but simultaneously appears to dismiss it: "Sir, some time in the future I may perhaps ask your advice about etymologies. I asked Monsieur Dimier (whom I do not know) about it, and he kindly replied by offering to put me in touch with Monsieur Longnon. As far as that goes, there is no dearth of people who could tell me about any and all etymologies" (*Corr. gén.* 3:298). Who were these learned "people"? Louis Dimier, to whom, according to the same letter, Proust had sent a list of names to explain, and Henri Longnon, Auguste's son, were both Renaissance specialists.[43] Another of Longnon's sons, Jean, wrote a guidebook to Normandy as part of a collection edited by this very same Louis Dimier.[44] In late 1920 he marked the posthumous publication of his father's work with an article on toponymy.[45] Neither the guidebook nor the article were useful to Proust, but the beginning of the article is noteworthy: "The war has revived France's taste for geography. . . . Can it not be said, first of all, that war is first and foremost an understanding of territory? Have certain writers not revealed themselves to be first-rate military critics because they were eminent geographers and topographers?" There is nothing to indicate that Longnon is speaking of Proust, whose *Le Côté de Guermantes I,* which had just come out in October of 1920, includes lengthy expositions on the military arts; nevertheless, an important link is established between the two parasitical forms of knowledge that invaded the novel during the war years: military strategy and toponymy. Did Proust have an "informant" about toponymy? Will internal analysis of his work give us the answer to this question?

Proust's knowledge of Normandy is heterogeneous; it is older and less methodical than Longnon's. The writer to whom it is most closely akin is Edouard Le Héricher, a professor of rhetoric at the secondary school in Avranches, a man of local learning rather than a scholar from Paris and the author of numerous papers that appeared in the *Mémoires de la Société des Antiquaires de Normandie,*[46] and in particular a *Philologie topographique de la Normandie.*[47] But the elements of Proust's knowledge that do not come from Cocheris are also not completely contained in Le Héricher's volume, which was not Proust's sole, direct source, since the information he uses can sometimes be found scattered throughout the works of Le Héricher. Sometimes Proust even distances himself from Le Héricher and goes back to Longnon, for example in his discussion of *tuit, toft,* and *thveit* (2:920; 3:283). But the work of Longnon that Proust is faithful to is not the posthumous work of the 1920s, but rather a single short passage about Norman place-names of Scandinavian origin, perhaps all Proust knew of Longnon, in a book of popularization, *Origines et formation de la nationalité française,* with a preface by Charles Maurras.[48]

By his knowledge of the topic, Proust is somewhere between Le Héricher, whose work dates back to the 1860s, and Longnon, whose work was published after 1920. The middle term between the two is Charles Joret: his two works, *Des Caractères et de l'extension du patois normand,*[49] and *Les Noms de lieu d'origine non romane et la colonisation germanique et scandinave en Normandie,*[50] mark the transition between local trivia and the more methodical work being done in Paris and Germany. But it would appear Proust did not consult these works; his knowledge of Normandy thus remains to some extent mysterious.

Nevertheless, a notation from Cahier 60 (a notebook of additions from the end of the war) that the novel did not make use of demonstrates that Proust intended to draw his knowledge of Normandy from learned societies rather than from the Sorbonne, from the Collège d'Avranches rather than from the Collège de France. In this notation Proust gives an explanation for Monsieur de Cambremer's curiosity about Brichot's etymologies at the Verdurin dinner:

> When the Princesse de Parme speaks to Monsieur de Charlus about Mademoiselle d'Oloron add extremely important.
> The name Cambremer was familiar to Monsieur de Charlus long before Balbec, what ever people might have believed. The father of the current marquis, grandfather of the potential bridegroom, had in fact had a nasty, almost legendary reputation that had not been limited to the area around Avranchin, all the more so as his name had quite often been quoted by learned men in Paris because he had been president of the Société des Etudes normandes. (Retrospectively when Brichot gives etymologies at the Verdurin dinner-party at La Raspelière Monsieur de Cambremer will say: "My father would have found you fascinating. Oh! he loved things like that more than

anything else," an imperceptible smile creases Monsieur de Charlus' lips.)[51]

It was the Société des Antiquaires de Normandie, founded in 1824, and not the Société des Etudes normandes that published the *Mémoires* in which Le Héricher's works appeared. Moreover, the association of learned trivia and sexual inversion is quite remarkable. It is reminiscent of the allusions in *Sodome et Gomorrhe I* to inversion as a kind of refined taste of the sort found in "collectors of old snuffboxes, Japanese prints or rare flowers," the atmosphere of the inverts' gatherings being compared to meetings of learned societies, "as in a stamp market" (2:641; 3:20).[52] Inverts take refuge in erudition; etymology, like inversion, is a return to one's roots. Perhaps this helps to explain why Albertine, in the draft for the second stay in Balbec in Cahier 72, was so curious about etymologies, why she attended the Verdurin dinner party and pelted Brichot with questions. At the time she was the one, rather than the hero, who originated the etymological theme of *Sodome et Gomorrhe*. Given this affinity between inverts' search for other inverts and the search for etymologies, we may find the complicity that is quickly established between Brichot and Charlus quite easy to understand.

In March 1922, just before the publication of *Sodome et Gomorrhe II*, Proust wrote to Martin-Chauffier: "Don't worry about those awful etymologies I was supposed to ask you about. I figured them out all by myself as well as I could, which is to say rather badly. Whatever is fanciful or erroneous about them will be chalked up to the ignorance of my characters" (*Corr. gén.* 3:304). As early as July 1921 he used more or less the same terms in a letter to Jacques Boulenger: "I figured them out all by myself come what may" (*Corr. gén.* 3:279). Even if we assume he did not have an informant but rather used several books straddling the nineteenth and twentieth centuries,[53] his fascination with etymologies has even more astonishing ramifications for the destruction of the novel that they bring about.

Destroying the Novel

Here, then, is a remarkable example of the insertion into the novel of an immense body of knowledge that is gathered together, removed from its historical and geographical function, undermined, and finally transformed into a veritable mania. This in itself is probably more important than the sources of Proustian toponymy, but to appreciate it fully we must be able to evaluate Proust's use of his sources. Indeed, this is not an isolated example; it is similar to the plethora of sometimes tedious teachings that Monsieur de Charlus takes from the Gotha Almanac and Saint-Simon's *Mémoires,* also in *Sodome et Gomorrhe.* For Brichot and Charlus, etymologies and genealogies play an analogous role in the names of places and people; they are both halfway in between names and things. What we need to evaluate is this upsetting of the antitheses of the novel.

As we have seen, the gap is enormous between the etymologies in "Combray," which date back to 1913, and the etymologies in *Sodome et Gomorrhe,* from the war years and the period after the war. The idea of bringing back the curé of Combray, which came to Proust afterward, provides a link between the two sets of etymologies in terms of the plot, but their sources are not the same, and when he was working on the occasional etymologies found in "Combray," Proust had no plans to come back to the theme later on. In "Place-Names: The Name," Balbec and its name are evoked in a purely poetic way; there is no hint of the precise philological explanation that will be given later on, long after visiting the place has emptied its name of all mystery. Thus the usual typological structure of the *Recherche,* based on preparation and reminiscence, or prefiguration and fulfillment, is not operative with the name of Balbec and onomastics in general; it is not dispensed with, but rather temporarily breaks down.

All the etymological notes for *Sodome et Gomorrhe* not only come from a period after the writing and even the publication of *Du côté de chez Swann,* but it would appear they are also later than the composition of *A l'ombre des jeunes filles en fleurs.* The setting for this second part of the cycle is the area around Balbec, and a whole set of place-names is mentioned, but the etymological theme is not foreshadowed here either. The names of the stops on the local railway line—Incarville, Marcouville, Pont-à-Couleuvre, Arambouville, Saint-Mars-le-Vieux, Hermonville, Maineville, which are all unquestionably taken from Cocheris—simply sound peculiar to the hero. They do not have the same evocative richness as names around the area of Combray, because it is not his grandmother who pronounces the names; they do not belong to his personal history. Consequently, they do not have much of an air of mystery to be dispelled by etymology:

> Nothing could have reminded me less than these dreary names, redolent of sand, of space too airy and empty, and of salt, out of which the suffix "ville" emerged like "fly" in "butterfly"—nothing could have reminded me less of those other names, Roussainville or Martinville. (1:711–12; 2:22)

The etymological theme does not really make an appearance until Cahier 72 is elaborated in 1914 or 1915, and it would be difficult to reduce it to an unpleasant bursting of the bubble, a rude awakening to reality from an onomastic daydream. In fact the theme basically uses names that did not appear in the original daydream.

The emergence of the theme may have been facilitated by two motifs that coincide with its two appearances in Cahier 72: the idea of giving a meaning to the name *Balbec*, and the wish to trace the line of the little local railway. It is quite likely that the analysis of the name *Balbec* came before the list of the names of the stops on the railway line, but it would be difficult to say which of the two motifs was more important in facilitating the insertion of the theme. At any rate the two motifs, which both expand by leaps and bounds, work together to make the geography of Balbec so unrealistic that trying to compile a map of the stops on the little local railway would be utterly ridiculous: Proustian geography is historical in nature; it is a form of onomastics.

We know that Balbec was called *Querqueville* until 1913, and then *Criquebec* and *Bricquebec* in the proofs of *Du côté de chez Swann* in 1913. The name *Criquebeuf* was analyzed by Cocheris, and *Querqueville* and *Bricquebec* are mentioned by Le Héricher.[54] It would appear that *Criquebec* was a name synthesized by Proust, as was *Balbec*. The role that *Balbec* may have played in the early stages of the theme is suggested by the importance of the name of the resort town in the novel, and also by the lengthy passages devoted to the roots *bec, bricq,* and *carque* among the various etymologies in *Sodome et Gomorrhe*.

But whether the theme originates in the explanation of the name

Balbec or in the railway line of the little local train, why, and how, does it take on the extraordinary breadth that it does, as if an initial concern for historical and geographical realism had paradoxically given rise to one of the most fanciful and subversive variations in the entire work? To begin with, the explanation of *Balbec* is attributed to Brichot in Cahier 72. He has been a professor of ancient literature at the Sorbonne and, as we saw in chapter 5, the character was modeled after Victor Brochard, a professor of ancient philosophy. One of Proust's reasons for expanding on etymologies may have been to sketch out this character, to make him ridiculous; toponymy is his only unquestionable claim to competence as a philologist in the novel. Toponymy was apparently not a neutral science from an ideological point of view. As we have seen, Maurras wrote a preface to one of Longnon's essays. Brichot himself takes umbrage against the Sorbonne, where the modern humanities emerged triumphant at the time the law was passed separating Church and State: "He was out of sympathy with the modern Sorbonne, where ideas of scientific exactitude, after the German model, were beginning to prevail over humanism" (2:897; 3:261).[55] Etymology is a national—indeed, a nationalistic—theme.

The novel has evolved in other respects since "Combray," and the dream of poetic prose is not to be found in *Sodome et Gomorrhe*. In some sense toponymy is substituted for poetic prose, and etymology takes over where daydreams about place-names left off, just as genealogy forms a web of relations between names of people that were at first thought to be unique and incomparable entities. Bodies of knowledge pervade the novel, as does strategy, starting with *Le Côté de Guermantes I*. Knowing how to manipulate bodies of knowledge is one of the conditions of novelistic prose. The reason not all readers are completely put off by Brichot's etymologies is that the etymologies are a parody of one of the novel's requirements: the attempt to synthesize bodies of knowledge. But readers are nonetheless disappointed and deceived. How can they react when they are drowning in a flood of references to a body of knowledge they have no mastery of? What does it mean to try to evaluate a body of knowledge without having any criterion of truth or falsehood at one's disposal? Truth becomes a matter of indifference, the reader a victim of an authority over which there is no control. Is it true that

Balbec is a corruption of *Dalbec,* or that *Torpehomme* combines *thorp* and *holm?* Readers who cannot put up with being victims finally give up and skip over Brichot's ravings; they cannot accept the idea that a body of knowledge can become an object of ridicule, or that it can become completely separated from the world of things. Riled up by a discourse they cannot see as anything but padding or filler, as a literary eyesore, they rise up in protest against analyses lacking in any function, generally dealing with names of places that do not even enter into the novel, piling up without being integrated into the work; these analyses are endless. The expectation of a synthesis of this body of knowledge is nothing more than a carrot on a stick.

Thus Brichot's etymologies represent the most violent challenge in the entire *Recherche* to the model of the organic, coherent, autonomous work in which the part and the whole are necessarily interconnected. They are a kind of list or catalogue rather than forming part of a plot or a development. They can be lengthened or shortened on a whim, and Proust actually does this. Their arbitrary construction is a form of montage rather than a form of composition, and the etymologies themselves are also a product of montage. Proust puts together Cocheris' analyses of *vadum, vetus,* and *vastatus;* he swipes an anecdote here and an anecdote there in explaining such and such a name; he manufactures novel place-names by combining Celtic and Norse roots. The provocative effect achieved is inseparable from the form of montage.

Toponymy results from the grafting of a foreign body onto the novel. This grafting is arbitrary; it is a question of chance. Nowhere else can we see so clearly that Proust's work belongs to a universe of probability in spite of its claims for a higher determinism. It mimics or parodies great laws, in this case the laws of historical phonetics. Etymologies, isolated from the system in which they have a meaning, history, and philology, are mere fragments detached from an organic whole, trivia. As such, they become empty signs, and they illustrate once again the tension to be found throughout the entire novel between irreducible intermittencies and reminiscences governed by the law of involuntary memory; between empty detail and organic whole; between forgetfulness and memory.

Montage, the juxtaposition of detached fragments, establishes, or at least suggests, a new meaning, as we find in Picasso's and Braque's "papiers collés" and Duchamp's "ready-mades." This is how Walter Benjamin defines *allegory,* as opposed to *symbol,* in the romantic or organic work.[56] The unity of the allegorical work is not given, but suspended; it is put together, if at all, by the reader. Probably that is why the reception of toponymy is actually depicted in the novel itself, with people like Albertine in the drafts and the hero and Charlus in the novel begging for more and more etymologies.

An important element in Benjamin's definition of the allegorical work is also brought into play by the etymological fragments: the melancholy that goes along with a fascination for the isolated, meaningless fragment. The meaning that was originally present for those who heard "Eudes le Bouteiller" in *Douville* or "stream of the valley" in *Balbec* has been lost. History is experienced as a loss of meaning, a falling off. The hero's personal lesson as he moves from the "Age of Names" to the "Age of Things" is matched by a historical lesson. History is a primordial, petrified landscape. *A la recherche du temps perdu* is presented as a circular, typological work, but in the distance between the great arc that stretches between "Combray" and *Le Temps retrouvé,* the reader may not always have the opportunity to move between the parts and the whole, to see through the hermeneutic circle and constitute meaning. Interpretation stumbles over these intermittencies, for example, these rough patches created by etymologies. Etymologies constitute some of the most melancholic moments in the novel, with the massive intrusion of an indeterminate kind of knowledge, a sort of equivalent of the long series of clauses introduced by "whether it be . . ." that unravel Proust's sentences in their exhaustive search for the motives of an action, in the meeting place between a world of extreme determinism and one of generalized probability, a world of absolute indeterminism. Etymological analysis is like psychological investigation in that it crumbles into small details, separating itself from any form of conclusiveness because of its obsessive and inevitably disappointed concern for origins. Thus etymologies, which grow like a kind of tumor inside the novel, by the same token reaffirm its functioning, with law eroding into coincidence and the intermittencies brought about by forgetfulness presented as facts of memory.

Vetus, vadum, or *vastatus: A la recherche du temps perdu* is a novel of forgetfulness rather than a novel of memory, as Benjamin also points out.[57]

One final thought, perhaps, to provoke the reader: the pages dealing with toponymy in *Sodome et Gomorrhe* undermine the idea that aesthetic originality is strictly opposed to convention, just as linguistic creativity is opposed to clichés. Indeed, the etymologies of place-names reduce linguistic creativity to a kind of conformity. After the journey through the "Age of Names" and the "Age of Things," in the course of which the dialectic of illusion and disillusionment forms the basis of learning, toponymy gives proof of an absolute lack of faith in language. If *Balbec* can be reduced to *dal* and *bec,* it is not simply reality that is not on a par with language, but language itself that is devalued.

The link between erudition and sexual inversion seems to be another factor in the theme's amplification. The learned society is a sect, like the sect of inverts, and sometimes, as we have seen, it is even the same sect, as in the case of old Monsieur de Cambremer, in a fragment that was not used in the definitive text. Whence, in the drafts, Albertine's original curiosity about etymologies, which is continued in the novel by Monsieur de Charlus. Both of them want to know the origins of words, what motivates them historically, how the past is forgotten in the present, and life in language. Proust's only true etymological invention, along with *Balbec,* is *Thorpehomme,* which Charlus questions Brichot about. The invert and the learned man, Charlus and Brichot, will be linked by a growing complicity, culminating in their impressive conversation in *La Prisonnière.*

The novel's basic curiosity about the origins of names goes far beyond Quicherat and Cocheris, the essential sources for the toponymy of "Combray" and *Sodome et Gomorrhe.* Etymology represents an "in-between" connecting the "Age of Names" and the "Age of Things," illusion and disillusionment. An unspoken pact exists between historical toponymy and nationalism, as we have suggested, and Proust uses place-names derived from the names of plants to show that academics all have very French names: indeed, this is the first use of Cocheris in Cahier 72, even before Balbec and the stops on the little local train. This, then, brings to mind one last etymology given in the *Recherche*. It is all by itself, neither in "Combray" nor in *Sodome et Gomorrhe,* far from the novel's large groupings of etymologies; it is isolated, but it keeps coming back. It is the etymology not of a place-name but rather of the name of a person, one of those people whose names are also place-names, like academicians whose names are rooted in the earth. In *Le Côté de Guermantes I,* Saint-Loup makes an arrangement at Boucheron's about a necklace for Rachel: no one besides him will be able to give it to her if he decides against it. Rachel is furious about this tactic:

> "So that's it! You wanted to blackmail me, so you took all your precautions in advance. It's just what they say: Marsantes, *Mater Semita,* it smells of the race," retorted Rachel, quoting an etymology which was founded on a wild misinterpretation, for *Semita* means "path" and not "Semite," but one which the Nationalists applied to Saint-Loup on account of the Dreyfusard views for which, as it happened, he was indebted to the actress. (2:182; 2:476)

There was not a trace of Jewishness to be found in Saint-Loup's mother, Proust counters, "apart from her kinship with the Lévy-Mirepoix family" (2:182; 2:477). Nevertheless, the suspicion of Judaism hangs over Saint-Loup's head from this point on, and because where there's smoke, there's fire (at least in novels), Saint-Loup will turn out to be, if not a Jew, an invert.

Is this simply a sign of a writer running out of steam? The witticism, based on an etymology discussed by Quicherat,[58] is echoed later on in the same volume by the Duc de Guermantes speaking about Saint-Loup's pro-Dreyfus stance, where it is followed by the same allusion to the Lévy-Mirepoix family (2:246; 2:535–36), and yet again in *Albertine disparue* by Gilberte speaking about her marriage to Saint-Loup: "In my case, however, it's my pater" (3:680; 4:243). In his *Avranchin monumental et historique,* Le Héricher did a census of the popular names of small rural settlements. The last one listed was "Sodome, Gomorrhe, Marcelet."[59]

9

Madame de Cambremer, Née Legrandin; or, the Avant-Garde in Reverse

"A thoroughgoing distinction can no longer be made between originality and tradition," Maurice Barrès opined in his *Cahiers* in June 1896.[1] "Ideas, like organic seeds, are carried off in all directions; but they take root only where the soil is propitious, and there they rise up to superior forms." From here on in, originality and tradition cannot be conceived independently of each other, for together they make up the movement of history: this does not appear to be an earth-shattering concept. But let us pay closer attention to the organic image borrowed from Darwinian biology: original ideas are seeds, tradition a favorable soil. And let us not overlook the implicit warning in Barrès' statement: "can no longer be made," as if, up to the present, a distinction had been possible between originality seen as a liberation from tradition and tradition defined as an absence of originality. Barrès is thinking of Greek philosophy: "The true originality of Greek philosophy comes only when it is perfected, not when it is starting out." Barrès is wise to go against the "genetic illusion" perpetrated by positivism and Darwinism; he refuses to reduce the complex to the simple, the phenomenon to its origins. He rejects the notion of explaining things purely by their causes and instead emphasizes process: "tradition" and "being perfected." This is not surprising: Barrès may be a thinker interested in tradition, a conservative, but he is not a reactionary.[2] He never gave his support to l'Action française, which Maurras thought should try to return France to its prerevolutionary state. Barrès accepted the fact that history has a continuity that prevents one from denying what has been; against the Revolution, he accepts the Revolution, that is, he accepts it as a fact and not as a right, because it happened, not because it had to happen. He recognizes the Revolution, so to speak, in the name of evolution. In his mind history is a whole, and 1789 did not shatter the whole; Maurras' way of thinking seems as abstract, as false, and as dangerous to him as Rousseau's.

Thus Barrès' remark implies a basic stance about the Revolution that is a model or a myth for all perception of change in the nineteenth century, especially in the sciences and the arts. Members of the avant-garde, partisans of originality for its own sake, and reactionaries, partisans of tradition for its own sake, are disarmed in the name of a doctrine of continuity that valorizes the organic. "Mallarmé is an innovator in one area. Rimbaud in another. As for the rest of their work, neither one is innovative, but rather traditional," Valéry was to say as late as 1917.[3] Tradition and originality, innovation and imitation: this dilemma was rehashed again and again throughout the nineteenth century. A contrast made by Barrès will be useful as we attempt to zero in on Proust's position in this regard. In the Dreyfus affair, Barrès sees the clash of "two revolutions . . . : the first one to upset everything, the second one to reestablish it";[4] that is, two illusions. What is visible behind any stance on the role of tradition and originality and the relation between them is the French Revolution, whether a refusal of it, a glorification of it, or a paradoxical acceptance of it in the name of its opposite. In 1929 Valéry explains how this obsession took hold: "In the Nineteenth Century, the notion of revolution-rebellion quickly stopped representing the idea of violent Reform—because of the sorry state of things—and came to express the upsetting of what exists as such, *whatever that might be*. The recent past becomes the enemy. Change in itself becomes what is important, etc."[5] In expressing a point of view on tradition and originality, I am implicitly taking a stance on the validity of applying a political metaphor to cultural affairs. Let us look more closely at what is involved in this issue.

The revolutionary model defines any change as a new beginning, a violent break with the past.[6] This was not the meaning of the word before 1789. On the contrary, *Revolution,* as Copernicus, for example, used the term, referred to a cyclical movement characterized by the regular return to an earlier state. In its metaphorical meaning, Revolution originally had to do with restoration and not at all with impatience for new things. Thus the term *Glorious Revolution* is used to describe the act of bringing the monarchy back to power in England in 1688. As has often been observed, since Tocqueville, about the French Revolution, the first revolutionaries were not innovators; they did not want to destroy the Ancien Régime, but rather to restore it by reforming the abuses of the absolute monarchy. They were onlookers, or rather laggards, in terms of the way the Revolution unfolded. At least this is the way it looks after the fact, and here we may find an explanation of why—to quote the well-known phrase of Vergniaud, a member of the Gironde faction—the Revolution devoured its own children, who basically were not revolutionary enough for it. The Revolution was history's triumph over the actors of history, and this is what inspired Hegel to come up with the concept of historical necessity that is the one we have to this day, the concept of a history conceived by spectators rather than by actors, seen from the outside, retrospectively. The historical avant-garde—or avant-gardes, as they have been called in art since the beginning of the twentieth century—maintains the illusion that from now on the actors' extempore or even prophetic point of view and the spectators' retrospective point of view will overlap. In its claims to inform the course of history and its agenda of changing forms, the avant-garde conceives of art using terms taken from politics, and it conceives of politics using terms taken from Hegel's definition of history.

Political metaphors are useful in helping us to conceptualize aesthetic changes; this is true to such an extent that one wonders whether aesthetic changes could be conceived as anything but revolutions, avant-gardes, decadent movements, and so forth.[7] These metaphors started to become prevalent at the beginning of the nineteenth century, after the French Revolution; in 1829, for example, Benjamin Constant criticized the alterations he himself brought to Schiller's tragedy, *Wallenstein,* when in 1809 he adapted it to the classical, or neoclassical tastes of the French public of the Empire period: "I should have foreseen that a political revolution would bring with it a literary revolution."[8] The phrase "literary revolution" is quite remarkable, as is the immediately deterministic notion used to conceptualize the link between "political revolution" and "literary revolution."

But here we are instantly confronted with a paradox that illustrates the inadequacy of these metaphors, a paradox that was best described by Baudelaire. Our fetish about originality, developed during the course of the nineteenth century, identifies what is modern with what is revolutionary or subversive. Yet the political left and innovators in the field of aesthetics have never seen eye to eye, and this is something Benjamin Constant is well aware of:

> From our very earliest times of unrest, the most revolutionary politicians have always had a tendency to advertise their attachment to and their respect for the most humdrum doctrines of seventeenth-century literature, and for the rules recommended by the titular head of the French Parnassos.[9]

In short—and this holds good for the entire nineteenth century—nothing could be further from literary revolution than the humdrum routine of revolutionaries. Constant suggests this rather dull explanation: revolutionaries are trying to give proof of their good taste to "*la bonne compagnie,* a pretentious and stuffy clique that prefers to forget duty rather than forms."

The notion of avant-garde originated in several milieux: among proponents of socialism, and among followers of Saint-Simon and Fourier. It took off from the idea that art must be on the cutting edge of society, and that the artist—along with the engineer a new heroic figure—belongs to an elite, those who show the way to the rest of society. Avant-garde art is thus socialist art, art in the service of socialism, and not at all new art. Avant-garde literature is subordinated to the political avant-garde.[10] But after 1870, the concept changes and comes to refer to the idea that certain artists are ahead of others, and that these are precisely the ones who are resented by their contemporaries. Being misunderstood to begin with becomes a sign of quality, the mark of a promising future for an artist. "All great creators met heavy resistance at the beginning of their careers—this is an absolute rule, a rule with no exceptions," exclaims Zola in his "Salon de 1879," and he then goes on to give Bastien-Lepage as an unfortunate example: "He's very popular. That is a bad sign."[11] Nevertheless, Zola's judgment can be interpreted as yet another expression of the eternal conflict between solitary genius and the blindness of the masses, or, as Proust will say somewhat less brutally in speaking of Vinteuil: "The reason why a work of genius is not easily admired from the first is that the man who has created it is extraordinary, that few other men resemble him" (1:572; 1:522). In a similar way, the impressionists striking out against academicism do not attribute a historical sense to the dispute, but rather see it as the usual contradiction between two conceptions of art. On the other hand, a few years later neoimpressionism, as Félix Fénéon dubbed it, defined itself historically, as something that went beyond impressionism. In June 1886, in his article in *La Vogue* about the eighth impressionist exhibit, which included Seurat's "Grande Jatte," Fénéon first emphasizes that compared to Monet, Gauguin, and so forth, "Messieurs Pissarro, Seurat and Signac are innovators,"[12] and then concludes with a word of regret about Dubois-Pillet's absence: "He is, along with the four artists we have just mentioned [Seurat, Signac, Camille and Lucien Pissarro], in an avant-garde at the forefront of impressionism."[13] Even before "neoimpressionism" has a name, it is conceived of as being at the forefront of impressionism, and the spirit of competition is so keen that the painter Guillaumin, mentioned along with Monet and Gauguin, misunderstands Fénéon, who he erroneously believes is saying that Dubois-Pillet is in an avant-garde ahead of Seurat and Signac: "Dubois-Pillet is no more in the avant-garde *than you and Signac,*" he is reported to have said to Seurat, who then repeated his words to Signac.[14]

There is a double confusion of politics and aesthetics here. On the one hand, Seurat and Signac themselves want to be considered revolutionaries in politics, as well as in painting, and believe that the same scientific doctrine of progress is the basis for all their practices. On the other hand, Fénéon in a note to "Les Impressionnistes en 1886" alludes to Théodore Duret, who was both a political journalist and an art critic, and to his work entitled *Critique d'avant-garde,* published in 1885 and dedicated "to the memory of [his] friend Edouard Manet." Starting with his "Salon de 1870," Duret's chronicles are consecrated "to those who are still being contested or misunderstood."[15] The controlling idea is the evolution of art and taste; the theme that comes up again and again is "the long persecution inflicted on the truly original and creative artists of this century."[16] And avant-garde criticism comes before avant-garde art. It is true that the term *avant-garde* used as a substantive had not yet made its appearance with the historical meaning it was destined to take on during the twentieth century, and all we find at this point are the phrase *in the avant-garde* and the use of the term as an adjective;[17] nonetheless, the concept changed with neoimpressionism, and with symbolism in literature: Duret and Fénéon are important evidence of that.[18]

Baudelaire had already long before pointed out that the idea of revolutionary art was a paradox, whereas equating revolutionary art and revolutionary politics—or perpetrating the illusion caused by confusing political and aesthetic revolution—was absurd. Like Barrès later on, he was not fooled by the common illusion because he did not believe in progress. If there is nothing much to be expected from the movement of history, why make movement in art dependent on it? Granted that before 1848, in the "Salon de 1846," Baudelaire still describes Delacroix's 1822 painting "Dante et Virgile aux Enfers" as the "true mark of a revolution" (Baudelaire, OC 2:428), and that a little further on he presents the painter as "the final expression of progress in art" (2:441). But there is nothing preconceived about the revolution and the progress Baudelaire speaks of; they are not elements in a platform. When the Duc de La Rochefoucauld, the head of the Ecole des Beaux-Arts, asked Delacroix to "modify his style," the latter replied that "if he painted in this way, it was because that was necessary, and because he could not paint in any other way" (2:430). Baudelaire stresses Delacroix's naïveté, and opposes it to Hugo's more conscious technique; Valéry is wrong to see the author of *Les Fleurs du mal* as a worshiper of novelty:

> It is admirable to see a being as original as Poe carrying lucidity and rigorousness so far that they are almost turned against him, and even questioning the sacred cow of originality. Unlike Baudelaire, he would not have considered novelty as having a value in itself; that shows a lack of discernment. He knew that novelty must not be sought out, for it is created of itself in the midst of antiquities.[19]

The cult of novelty understood in this way presupposes a belief that the present endlessly goes beyond the past, a faith in the perpetual movement of fashion, but in Baudelaire novelty is not identified with revolution and progress, but rather with what is original, inhabitual, and modern; novelty "draws the eternal from the transitory"; by a heroic effort, it wrests beauty away from temporality as an eternal return of sameness.[20] Considering Baudelaire to be an activist of novelty would be confusing him with Breton, who is often taken to task by Valéry; it would mean not recognizing the melancholy in the last line of "Le Voyage": "Au fond de l'Inconnu pour trouver du *nouveau!*"

"Belief in progress is a lazy man's doctrine, a doctrine for *Belgians,*" Baudelaire will write in the same vein in "Mon coeur mis à nu" (OC 1:681). The political metaphor in art is not artistic. It is in speaking about Wagner that Baudelaire makes his clearest statements about the obstacles blocking the artist's path and the illusions they engender: "Embittered by so many letdowns, disappointed by so many dreams, he was forced, at a particular moment, as the result of an error that was understandable in a sensitive and exceedingly high-strung spirit, to establish an ideal complicity between bad music and bad governments" ("Richard Wagner et 'Tannhäuser' à Paris," OC 2:787). Baudelaire speaks out against identifying a reactionary regime with an academic form of art, as well as the corollary illusion of a revolutionary regime being open to new forms of art. Since Baudelaire's time there is no dearth of examples to disprove these equations: "Possessed by the supreme desire to see the ideal in art take precedence over the ordinary and humdrum once and for all, he may have wished (it is an essentially human illusion) that revolutions in the political order would favor the cause of revolution in art." This "essentially human illusion," which Baudelaire observed as early as the mid-nineteenth century, is basically the illusion of all the historical avant-gardes of the twentieth century, in Germany and France, in Italy as well as Russia; moreover, the alliance between a so-called revolutionary art and a so-called reactionary regime that Baudelaire had just witnessed in his own time allowed him to foresee this: "Wagner's own success undermined his hopes and expectations; for in France the order brought by a *despot* was needed to carry out the work of a revolutionary." This case is not unusual. Baudelaire immediately draws an analogy with the academicism of the Left: "Similarly, in Paris we have already seen the evolution of romanticism favored by the monarchy, whereas the liberals and the republicans remained stubbornly attached to the humdrum routines of so-called classical literature." The classicism Benjamin Constant was thinking of was the classicism of the writers of the Empire period, but the two statements are very close indeed.

Let us not be too hasty in using these two examples to establish a rule that would itself be illusory, a rule that would see the absence of political freedom as encouraging aesthetic innovation: what Baudelaire is defending is precisely the separation of the political and aesthetic orders, of history and art. Let us simply say that long before the birth of historical avant-gardes, Baudelaire, by taking note of the misunderstanding that persisted throughout the entire century and accounting for the lack of understanding that greets the work of most innovative artists, clearly spoke out against the "futurist illusion." In "Mon coeur mis à nu," he drew up a list of "military metaphors" that the French hold dear, among which are "militant literature," "militant press," "combat poets," and "literary vanguard." Clearly, we are still dealing with a form of literature that depends on an ideal of political progress: "These ways of thinking are indicative of minds made for discipline, that is, conformity" (OC 1:690–91). Once the avant-garde, under the influence of theories of evolution or permanent revolution, replaces decadence as a definition of modernity, "avant-garde literature" in the service of progress will become a "literary avant-garde" ahead of its time, and this literary avant-garde will be identified with a breathtaking rejection of the commonplace. The real issue for the avant-garde is when to stop. As soon as it takes a breather, it is overwhelmed from its "left." What the avant-garde cannot escape is the forward rush of time.

Proust, who saw the dawning of the myth of the historical avant-garde, made the misunderstanding that initially greets an artist's work into a sign of its prophetic nature. Neither Manet nor Gauguin made any such claim; they would have been happier to be appreciated, as Zola says of Manet in 1884 in his preface to the catalogue of the Manet retrospective: "He did what he could, and he could not have done otherwise. Indeed, he did not take sides: he wanted to be appreciated."[21] But it is difficult to escape falling into the trap of conceptualizing art in terms of the categories passed down from Hegel and Darwin, revolution and evolution. Proust, like Baudelaire before him, is more successful than Barrès—that misguided student of the Third Republic who finds absolute continuity and complete determinism once he has dismissed Hegel and Darwin—at escaping this trap.

We will begin with Proust's conception of inversion, then move on to his conception of art using the model of inversion; finally, we will examine his critique of the avant-garde. I will attempt to demonstrate that in finding a way to explain inversion, Proust comes up with a model of history that is neither evolutionary nor revolutionary, and that this profoundly nondeterministic model informs a theory of art as memory, a theory that is not reactionary or belonging to the "old guard," but classical in the sense that Valéry uses the term: "A classic is not something one *is*. It is something one *becomes*."[22]

Inversion and Invention

Every time Proust mentions perversion in *A la recherche du temps perdu*—and it happens often—he speaks in terms of outbursts of emotion, eruptions, and attacks. All the episodes of sadism and homosexuality, with Charlus being the main character after Mademoiselle Vinteuil has introduced the theme into the novel, are described as seizures: they are short-lived and recurrent. For example, when Morel teases out the fantasy of deflowering Jupien's niece and then dropping her, Charlus experiences an acute sexual enjoyment: "The idea of Morel's 'ditching' without compunction a girl whom he had outraged had enabled him to enjoy an abrupt and consummate pleasure" (2:1042; 3:398).

Moreover, the eruption of sadism or homosexuality is invariably depicted as a very particular kind of seizure, almost like being possessed or in a trance:

> From that moment his sensual appetites were satisfied for a time and the sadist (a true medium, he) who had for a few moments taken the place of M. de Charlus had fled, handing over to the real M. de Charlus, full of artistic refinement, sensibility and kindness.

Charlus has two personalities, or a double personality. There is the "real" baron, kind, sensitive, noble, and generous; and then there is the other one, the spirit that is substituted for him and takes control of his body in these unusual moments: a violent and vulgar beast. The case of Dr. Jekyll and Mr. Hyde was in fashion: Stevenson's story, published in 1886, was translated into French in 1890. "It wasn't me, . . . I was out of my mind" (3:264; 3:766), as the narrator claims Mademoiselle Vinteuil would have been justified in saying about the torments she put her father through. And as early as the scene at Montjouvain Proust wrote: "perpetually, in the depths of her being, a shy and suppliant maiden entreated and reined back a rough and swaggering trooper" (1:176; 1:159). As for Albertine, this is how she is described when desire takes hold of her: "Like a medium whose body is inhabited by another being, she would change personalities, almost instantly she would stop having her usual voice and would take on the voice of another person, a hoarse, bold, almost debauched voice" (3:1573 [3:403, var. e]). Even when the narrator meets Charlus as an old man in *Le Temps retrouvé,* he once again points out: "There were, however, two M. de Charluses, not to mention any others," and he calls them "the intellectual one" and "the subconscious one" (3:893; 4:440). Sadists are inflicted with a split personality, which means they are inhabited by a split temporality, regularized temporality and the temporality of crisis. The latter could also be called *intermittent*—a term dear to Proust's heart—to emphasize the relation between perversion and the psychology of the "Intermittencies of the Heart" so basic to the *Recherche*.

What's more, these attacks of perversion or "intermittencies" of sadism and homosexuality, defined as being periodically taken over by the other or the double, in fact correspond to an underlying permanence, an essential continuity; they bear witness to the complex and critical intermingling of event and structure within the individual. Charlus' laugh, the bizarre sporadic chuckle that reveals his split personality—for example, in the scene with the strawberry juice at the Verdurins' (2:999; 3:356; see chapter 5)—what is its nature? Where does it come from? The invert's voice, a commonplace of the *Recherche* (see chapter 5), provides the most obvious evidence of Proust's conception of inversion and the finest illustration of the theory of women-men, which says that the body of a man can house the soul of a woman.

Under the appearance of a man, the invert is a woman. The woman inside of him expresses herself in seizures. In *Sodome et Gomorrhe I,* the discovery of Monsieur de Charlus' true nature is summed up by the exclamation "He's a woman!" This is what allows the hero to figure him out in one fell swoop: "Although in the person of M. de Charlus another creature was coupled, as the horse in the centaur, which made him different from other men, although this creature was one with the Baron, I had never perceived it" (2:637; 3:16). The centaur is another image—evocative, like the woman-man, of Gustave Moreau—of Charlus' duality, the coexistence of man and beast or man and other that is here expressed in almost sexual terms. What the hero had never perceived before witnessing the meeting between Charlus and Jupien was the baron's split personality. And yet, as early as their first meeting in Balbec, what struck him about the baron was his voice, "like certain contralto voices in which the middle register [médium] has not been sufficiently cultivated, so that when they sing it sounds like an alternating duet between a young man and a woman," a voice that seems to shelter a "bevy of young girls" (1:820; 2:122–23). It is as if the word *médium,* which is both a musical term and one belonging to the vocabulary of spiritualism—"middle register" or "medium"—made the voice into the very place of possession.

The theory of the woman-man and the generic explanation of homosexuality through the presence of a feminine temperament inside the body of a man probably come from contemporary medical discourse. André Gide stressed the relation between the theory and the discourse in his preface to the new edition of *Corydon* in 1924:

> Certain books—Proust's in particular—have accustomed the reading public to being less easily shocked and to daring to contemplate with a certain detachment what they once pretended not to know or preferred not to know. . . . But by the same token these books have also contributed, I am afraid, to certain common misconceptions. The theory of the woman-man, of the "Sexuelle Zwischenstufen" (intermediate degrees of sexuality) that was proposed by Dr. Hirschfeld in Germany quite some time before the war and apparently subscribed to by Marcel Proust, may well have some truth to it; but it explains and touches upon only certain cases of homosexuality, exactly the cases I do not deal with in this book—cases of inversion, effeminacy, and sodomy. And today I am well aware that one of my book's greatest flaws is precisely that I do not deal with them—and they are turning out to be much more widespread than I first thought.
>
> But even if we do believe that Hirschfeld's theory satisfactorily accounts for these cases, this theory of the "third sex" is completely incapable of explaining what is usually called "Greek love," or pederasty, in which neither party is the slightest bit effeminate.[23]

Long before Hirschfeld, Krafft-Ebing had conceived of degrees of inversion in his 1886 *Psychopathia sexualis:* in ascending order, hermaphroditism (or bisexuality), homosexuality, effeminacy, and androgyny. This demonstrates yet again that Proust's notions belong to the end of the nineteenth century and are an anachronism by the time the novel is published. In a series of volumes published twenty years before Krafft-Ebing, from 1864 to 1869, a learned jurist who defended inversion, Karl Heinrich Ulrichs, maintained that inversion was inborn and that in the invert the soul of a woman was locked into the body of a man. Many works of psychiatry and forensic medicine dealt with the subject after 1870.[24] The term *inversion* is actually French, whereas *homosexuality,* which was coined by the Hungarian Károly Mária Benkert in 1869, is German: "In France, this phenomenon is referred to, following Charcot and Magnan, by the name of inversion of the sexual instinct."[25] Charcot and Magnan had translated the German phrase introduced by Westphal in 1870, "die conträre Sexualempfindung," "reverse sexual sense," as "inversion," but they did not particularly associate it with effeminacy—that is, with the higher degrees in Krafft-Ebing's classification—as Gide and Proust appear to do.

Thus, the hypothesis of the woman-man seems to conform to the medical discourse of Proust's adolescence. In the previous quarter of a century, the medical establishment no longer considered pederasty as an unnatural vice or a monstrosity of the will and began to define it, along with Krafft-Ebing, as a "morbid congenital abnormality": Proust will call it a "defect of the nerves." In one of the most important treatises of French forensic medicine, Ambroise Tardieu's work published in 1857, pederasty was still seen as a vice, and only once was mention made of the hypothesis linking it to a form of insanity.[26] But a whole group of German authors, beginning with Casper, consider it to be inborn and attribute it to instinct: "In most people who are addicted to it, it is there from birth and constitutes so to speak a kind of moral hermaphroditism."[27] In fits of inversion or perversion, what is coming to light would appear to be an innate instinct.

But we must take things one step further and at last distinguish between Proust's point of view and the point of view of the medical establishment of his time. The woman that takes possession of "a Charlus"—as Proust dubs the invert for lack of a better word—the woman who controls him as if he were a medium in a trance, this woman is not just any woman: she is an ancestor, the voice of the tribe, the secret of the blood, the reincarnation of the race. Monsieur de Charlus' chuckle has been around for centuries, and has been handed down to him from generation to generation:

> And he gave a little laugh that was all his own—a laugh that came down to him probably from some Bavarian or Lorraine grandmother, who herself had inherited it, in identical form, from an ancestress, so that it had tinkled now, unchanged, for a good many centuries in little old-fashioned European courts, and one could appreciate its precious quality, like that of certain old musical instruments that have become very rare. (2:973–74; 3:332–33)

This is reminiscent of the concept of degeneracy so dear to Zola's heart, a degeneracy that is passed on to the entire Rougon-Macquart family and explains their neuroses in terms of heredity. Proust actually describes the Guermantes as a "perverted family" suffering from a "hereditary disease" (3:705; 4:265) in an attempt to explain the inversion of both the uncle and the nephew. And this is how he accounts for the Princes de Foix—father and son—both sharing a weakness for men: "For the Prince de Foix had succeeded in preserving his son from the external influence of bad company but not from heredity" (3:857; 4:407).

Nevertheless, it is better to keep the term *intermittency,* for Proust conceives of heredity as a kind of intermittency applied to a given race: "Through these selves that were so different certain particularities, however rare or intermittent they might be, persist, perhaps for an even longer time than the individual's life, in the course of an entire ascendency" (3:1485 [3:253, var. a]). This is how Proust explains Saint-Loup's indiscretions when he repeats what someone has confided to him after swearing him to secrecy, this being "something absolutely eccentric to his character that was perhaps the character—residing in him—of a relative whom he took after just as one might have one's uncle's nose." Moreover, Proust generalizes these notions to such a great extent that they lose all medical value: "In fact the human race is too old, flaws have multiplied through heredity, and if we examined the most reasonable people impartially, we would recognize that there is perhaps not a single one of whom we could not say at one moment or another, to excuse him in such and such a circumstance, or when we observe one of his manias: 'He is a madman.' " Sadism and inversion, like some of Saint-Loup's faults, which are widespread among inverts and which he shares with Vaugoubert, are revealed only in brief seizures or spells, but these seizures are signs of a centuries-old secret, traces of the most durable transmission that can be found: heredity.

In his explanation of inversion, Proust adds a curious and idiosyncratic conception of Darwinism to elements drawn from psychiatry, forensic medicine, and theories of degeneracy. In *Sodome et Gomorrhe I,* as he draws out the image of the orchid and the bumblebee borrowed from Darwin as an extended metaphor in counterpoint to the meeting between Charlus and Jupien, he even goes beyond the notion of the tribe and attributes inversion to a return to origins, to an "initial hermaphroditism of which certain rudiments of male organs in the anatomy of women and of female organs in that of men seem still to preserve the trace" (2:653; 3:31). The myth of Aristophanes, taken from Plato's *Symposium,* is reinforced by Darwin's work, according to which the separation of the sexes was a late development in the evolution of species. Ontogenesis and phylogenesis, heredity and evolution appear to intermingle. Similarly, Proust describes Legrandin's homosexuality as "a sort of return, however circuitous, towards nature" (3:683; 4:246).

In *Sodome et Gomorrhe,* when Charlus is first introduced to the Verdurins at La Raspelière, at what Proust calls a "critical moment," his firm intention of appearing cold and virile is undermined by his double, by the "resources of the subconscious" (2:937; 3:299). This is what Proust calls a "sentiment of instinctive and atavistic politeness" that takes possession of the baron—and of all other "Charluses"—at a critical moment when his will is caught off guard. When timidity gains the upper hand, "it is always the spirit of a relative of the female sex, attendant like a goddess, or incarnate as a double, that undertakes to introduce him." (2:937; 3:299). The double unconsciously mimicked by the invert in this way is a female relative, a cousin or an aunt, a sister or a mother. The passage leads the narrator to evoke "desecrated mothers" after giving other examples of undignified mimicking:

> Thus a young painter, brought up by a godly, Protestant, female cousin, will enter a room, his trembling head to one side, his eyes raised to the ceiling, his hands clutching an invisible muff, the remembered shape of which and its real and tutelary presence will help the frightened artist to cross without agoraphobia the yawning abyss between the hall and the inner drawing-room.
>
> (2:937; 3:299)

The emphasis placed on desecration is obvious, ranging from the adjectives used to describe the cousin, "godly" and "Protestant," to the strange allusion to the "real presence" of the muff, as if inversion were also doing a parody of the sacrifice in the Mass: "By virtue of the same law, which ordains that life, in the interests of the still unfulfilled act, shall bring into play, utilise, adulterate, in a perpetual prostitution, the most respectable, sometimes the most sacred, occasionally only the most innocent legacies of the past," Madame

Cottard comes back to life in one of her nephews "who distressed his family by his effeminate ways and the company he kept." In a roundabout way—a function of "his unconscious heredity and his misplaced sex"—the aunty [tante] is reincarnated in the fairy [tante]. By the same token, Charlus makes his entrance "with a fluttering, mincing gait and the same sweep with which a skirt would have enlarged and impeded his waddling motion" (2:938; 3:300), and when he smiles at Madame Verdurin,

> One might have thought that it was Mme de Marsantes who was entering the room, so salient at that moment was the woman whom a mistake on the part of Nature had enshrined in the body of M. de Charlus. Of course the Baron had made every effort to conceal this mistake and to assume a masculine appearance. But no sooner had he succeeded than, having meanwhile retained the same tastes, he acquired from this habit of feeling like a woman a new feminine appearance, due not to heredity but to his own way of living.
> (2:938; 3:300)

When the hero first met Madame de Marsantes at a social gathering, he was already astonished that "melancholy, pure, self-sacrificing women, venerated like ideal saints in stained-glass windows, had flowered from the same genealogical stem as brothers who were brutal, debauched and vile" (2:258; 2:546–47). This time the reasoning is more complicated: when Charlus manages to stymy heredity, habit once again takes the upper hand, like a kind of second nature. His body, Proust concludes, "displayed, to such an extent that the Baron would have deserved the epithet *ladylike,* all the seductions of a great lady" (2:938; 3:300). When in *Le Temps retrouvé* Charlus finds himself in the midst of a harem of young men at Jupien's hotel, the narrator again recognizes in him "graces inherited from some grandmother whom I had not known," generally covered up by the virility of his appearance but revealed "when circumstances made him anxious to please an inferior audience, by the desire to appear a great lady" (3:853; 4:403).

If we began with the outward expression of Charlus' inversion in intermittent seizures, here we come to see it as the product of heredity at work over the course of several centuries. But far from being conceived of as a form of degeneracy, this heredity is a kind of resurrection, and this shift away from the medical establishment—as well as from its literary expression in writers like Zola—gives an adequate explanation of why Proust rejected the German term *homosexuality* which he was still using in the prewar drafts, in favor of "inversion":

> Indeed, there is a slight difference. Homosexuals take great pride in not being inverts. According to the theory I am sketching out here—however fragmentary it might be—there are in fact no such things as homosexuals. However masculine the appearance of a fairy might be, his feelings of attraction to virile men come from an underlying femininity, although it may be hidden. If this is true, a homosexual is what an invert claims to be, what an invert believes himself in all good faith to be. (3:955, Esquisse IV)[28]

Unlike Krafft-Ebing and Gide, who both distinguish several different varieties of "the love that dares not speak its name," Proust reduces it to one single physiology. In *Sodome et Gomorrhe I,* different behaviors of inverts are enumerated and classified. They depend—to return to the distinction Proust makes about Charlus' pose in meeting Madame Verdurin—on the inverts' "own ways of living" and not on "heredity"; they are acquired, not inborn. But faced with the diversity of individual manifestations of inversion, we must not lose sight of the fact that according to Proust, inversion belongs to a single species. If his doctrine of the woman-man makes do with the single term *inversion,* the term is not used to mean an inversion of the object—which might in some cases be purely contingent—but rather an inversion that is absolutely congenital, an inversion of desire itself, an inversion determined by the incorporation of a feminine soul in a masculine body, the reincarnation of a distant female ancestor.

Inversion is described as something that has existed for all eternity. The chance meeting between Charlus and Jupien in *Sodome et Gomorrhe I* has all the appearance of the consummation of an omnipotent act of fate:

> This Romeo and this Juliet may believe with good reason that their love is not a momentary whim but a true predestination, determined by the harmonies of their temperaments, and not only by their own personal temperaments but by those of their ancestors, by their most distant strains of heredity, so much so that the fellow-creature who

> is conjoined with them has belonged to them from before their birth, has attracted them by a force comparable to that which governs the worlds on which we spent our former lives. (2:651; 3:29)

Probably this is an illusion on the invert's part, as Proust already suggested in Carnet 1: "The peder[ast] when he finds another one finds a kind of predestination that the person in love does not find. Would like a nonfairy but quickly believes when he likes a fairy that he is a half-fairy."[29] And the hero of *Sodome et Gomorrhe* is quick to learn that the "race of fairies" is much more numerous than he had first suspected; he even has a tendency to see them everywhere. This does nothing to change the fact that the eruption of perversion and the fit of inversion that are first described as a spiritualist phenomenon, like going into a trance, has proven to be deeply rooted in congenital essentialism. The doctrine of the woman-man, an amalgam of psychiatry and Darwinism that conceives of inversion as the reincarnation of a female relative, is more radical than any other contemporary theory on the topic.

Indeed, this is a key to Proust's recurrent equating of inversion and Judaism, one he never explains. Both are passed on by women, constituted by a female lineage. The analogy is extended throughout *Sodome et Gomorrhe I,* the chosen members of the "accursed race," "having finally been invested, by a persecution similar to that of Israel, with the physical and moral characteristics of a race" (2:639; 3:18), being "excluded even, save on the days of general misfortune when the majority rally round the victim as the Jews rallied round Dreyfus, from the sympathy—at times from the society—of their fellows" (2:638; 3:17). When he refers to Monsieur de Charlus' typically inverted voice at the party given by the Princesse de Guermantes, Proust wonders if it is not rather a voice that comes from the Guermantes way, only to conclude in the end that everything is related to everything else:

> If one wishes to see a Jewish nose on the face of the son of a Jewish woman and a Catholic man, one has only to realize that the son has the hooked nose of his father. Whether in the shadowy course of the long mysterious history of heredity—as a furtive bird brings a flower the fortuitous gift of a different pollen and hence a new characteristic that will make an appearance from time to time—one of the female ancestors of the Catholic family might not in the past have had a fling with a Jewish man remains to be seen; or in the Middle Ages

> did a Guermantes that was an invert not perhaps indelibly imprint on his descendents the particular characteristics of inversion which even those not inflicted by it will pass on, if only in their facial expression, their gait, and the sound of their voices?
>
> (3:1317 [3:34, var. b])

At any rate the idea of intermittency persists, and it makes of Monsieur de Charlus one of those "hybrids that could probably be found at least every sixty years in every family."

Inversion constitutes a race; it is the product of a selection process. The critical moment and the short-lived seizure are the distant result of a tradition that goes back many centuries. Meetings like the one between Charlus and Jupien are tinged with the "elective character of such a select conjunction." They are extraordinary even if they are not quite as out of the ordinary as the hero first believed. The race of Sodom is so numerous that this verse from Genesis fits it quite well: "If a man can number the dust of the earth, then shall thy seed also be numbered" (Genesis 13:16, quoted 2:655; 3:33). But God's promise to Abraham was repeated to Jacob (Genesis 28:14), so once again Proust is conflating the descendants of Sodom and the children of Jacob, that is, the children of Israel.

Charlus is known for his anti-Semitic seizures as much as for his endless and irrepressible allusions to inversion, "just as a Jew is eager to tell Jewish jokes," Proust points out.[30] Charlus is the only one who can joke about inversion and Judaism, because being an invert he is also in some sense a Jew. His violent anti-Semitic speech at the end of *Sodome et Gomorrhe* is motivated by his desire for Bloch, so that the narrator can conclude that his speech, "anti-Jewish or pro-Hebrew—according to whether one pays attention to the overt meaning of its sentences or the intentions that they concealed" (2:1144; 3:492)—is ambiguous, as are all seizures once we see that they are the result of a split.

Art and Memory

Why should we put so much emphasis on Proust's definition of inversion as the reincarnation of an ancestor or the resurgence of the race within the individual, as a resurrection of the past in the present, a memory of the origin, a nondeterministic intermittency rather than a form of degeneracy or hereditary determinism? The reason is that yet another polarity is destroyed—or at least muddled—by this definition. Beyond the whimsical or aberrant explanation of inversion that we find in the woman-man or the third sex—an explanation that in fact Théophile Gautier was already using as early as *Mademoiselle de Maupin*[31]—and in spite of what Proust borrows from popularized medicine, what we have here is yet another form of the "in-between" so characteristic of the revelation of truth in the *Recherche*. The novel first created an opposition between tradition and a break with tradition, between history and event, but now they are reconciled, or rather they begin to merge as the crisis, always unique and yet at the same time basically the same, causes them to mesh within a kind of intermittency that is a memory of the origin. Inversion remains the finest model in Proust's work of the intersection between the two heterogeneous forms of temporality, race and moment, that Taine speaks of; or, to return to Darwin and social Darwinism, imitation and innovation. The vocabulary of spiritualism, medicine, and even Darwinism that Proust is so fond of and that he uses to depict outbursts, eruptions, and attacks is overdetermined by a doctrine of transmigration.

Now Proust conceives of other temporal "in-betweens" in the same terms as inversion, in particular the time of art, and this allows us to understand the paradoxical situation of his own novel between the two centuries. The evolutionary model, applied to physical and social life, assimilates the moment of adaptation to the moment of originality, the interplay of tradition and the break from tradition to the interplay of imitation and innovation. By the same token, evolution becomes synonymous with progress; those who triumph over the endless struggles of natural selection are held to be the best. In France, the sociologist Gabriel de Tarde adapted this framework for his analysis of social evolution. Emile Hennequin and particularly Ferdinand Brunetière adapted it for use in the literary domain. But Proust rectifies the positivists' confusion of evolution and progress, both in its positive, artistic aspect and in its negative aspect having to do with inversion. Between evolutionary and revolutionary temporality, he believes in the intermittent temporality of art, a critical temporality that is, in the final analysis, nondeterministic.

If the pervert's outburst is the equivalent of a trance, one could say as much about the artistic act, particularly for music. On the very same page of *Sodome et Gomorrhe* that was our starting point, the passage in which Charlus' sadistic pleasure is presented as an act of momentary possession by a double, what leads to the analogy between art and inversion is a criticism of Morel's style of piano playing. Charlus scolds the young man for neglecting the "mediumnistic aspect" involved in performing a piece of music (2:1042; 3:398). The pianist must behave as if he were a medium who has placed himself completely at the composer's disposal, as if he were himself a reincarnation of the composer: "You ought to play it as though you were composing it." As he gives this advice—the word *it* refers to the piano transcription of Beethoven's Quartet No. 15—Charlus, overcome with delight, imagines Morel in a trance and describes him in this way:

> "The young Morel, afflicted with a momentary deafness and with a non-existent genius, stands motionless for an instant; then, seized by the divine frenzy, he plays, he composes the opening bars; after which, exhausted by this trance-like effort, he collapses, letting his pretty forelock drop to please Mme Verdurin, and, moreover, giving himself time to restore the prodigious quantity of grey matter which he has drawn upon for the Pythian objectivation; then, having regained his strength, seized by a fresh and overmastering inspiration, he flings himself upon the sublime, imperishable phrase which the virtuoso of Berlin" (we suppose M. de Charlus to have meant Mendelssohn) "was to imitate unceasingly. It is in this, the only truly dynamic and transcendent fashion, that I shall make you play in Paris." (2:1042–43; 3:398)

There are many terms here that are taken from the domain of spiritualism, just as when the hero observes Monsieur de Charlus at the Princesse de Guermantes' enthusiastically contemplating Madame de Surgis' two sons, his gaze "like the eyes of a Pythian priestess on her tripod" (2:714; 3:87). Whether Charlus is an artist or a pervert, it amounts to the same thing.

In "Un Amour de Swann," when Swann hears Vinteuil's sonata at Madame de Saint-Euverte's, the musical ecstasy experienced by the violinist is depicted in similar terms. The interplay of piano and violin is reminiscent of a mating dance: "the piano complained alone, like a bird deserted by its mate; the violin heard and answered it, as from a neighbouring tree" (1:382; 1:346). Starting with this first image, the text shifts toward a more mysterious metaphor: "Was it a bird, was it the soul, as yet not fully formed, of the little phrase, was it a fairy—that being invisibly lamenting?" The little phrase—bird, fairy, woman, like Baudelaire's "passante" when it is heard for the first time at Madame Verdurin's—soon comes to possess the violinist: "Its cries were so sudden that the violinist must snatch up his bow and race to catch them as they came. Marvellous bird! The violinist seemed to wish to charm, to tame, to capture it. Already it had passed into his soul, already the little phrase which it evoked shook like a medium's the body of the violinist, 'possessed' indeed" (1:382–83; 1:346). Music, which according to Schopenhauer is supposed to allow access to the contemplation of essences, is best expressed, like inversion, in the vocabulary of spiritualism, whether in a serious vein, as in this passage, or in a burlesque mode, as when the Comtesse de Monteriender, even before the end of the sonata, leans over toward Swann in a desire to make him share her admiration: "It's astonishing! I've never seen anything to beat it . . . since the table-turning!" (1:384; 1:347). Swann smiles at her naïveté, but "perhaps also found an underlying sense, which she herself was incapable of perceiving, in the words that she used," as if the music gave even someone like Madame de Monteriender an inkling of truth.

In a fragment about poetic inspiration that is contemporary to *Jean Santeuil,* Proust has no compunctions about comparing the poet's split personality when he is invaded by the "mysterious energy" of enthusiasm to the schizophrenia of Stevenson's hero: "as soon as he reappears, the other is no longer to be found; like when you used to try to figure out what Hyde did with Jekyll; when you saw Jekyll, there was no sign of Hyde, and when you saw Hyde, there was no sign of Jekyll" ("[La poésie et les lois mystérieuses]," CSB 420). The physiology of inspiration is really the same as the physiology of inversion.

The similarity between fits of perversion and musical climaxes is accentuated by the fact that in the *Recherche,* musical genius often coincides with the kind of congenital flaw that characterizes inversion. Even if, in *Sodome et Gomorrhe I,* Proust pokes fun at inverts who "regard homosexuality as the appurtenance of genius and the great periods of history" (2:643; 3:22), the artistic nature of inverts is another commonplace that the novel exploits as shamelessly as the cliché that they are betrayed by their voices, their laughs, or their gestures, a cliché that is also mentioned in a fragment from Cahier 49:

> For Charlus, . . . now I fully realized that intelligence is so closely linked to certain physiological conditions that probably the principle that distinguishes him from his brother, the Duc de Guermantes, probably came from the little finishing touch that his homosexuality had put on the machinery of his nervous system, simultaneously putting it out of order.
>
> At Balbec he must play Chopin well, and Saint-Loup will tell me that he is quite superior to the rest of the family, one should wonder why. (3:954–55, Esquisse IV)[32]

The twist of fate that distinguishes Charlus' desires from his lady-killing brother's by the same token explains his literary and musical sensitivity, when he accompanies Morel in Fauré's Sonata No. 1 at La Raspelière:

> I thought with curiosity of this combination in a single person of a physical blemish and a spiritual gift. M. de Charlus was not very different from his brother, the Duc de Guermantes. . . . But it had sufficed that nature should have upset the balance of his nervous system enough to make him prefer, to the woman that his brother the Duke would have chosen, one of Virgil's shepherds or Plato's disciples, and at once qualities unknown to the Duc de Guermantes and often combined with this lack of equilibrium had made M. de Charlus an exquisite pianist, an amateur painter who was not devoid of taste, and an eloquent talker. Who would ever have detected that the rapid, nervous, charming style with which M. de Charlus played the Schumannesque passage of Fauré's sonata had its equivalent—one dare not say its cause—in elements entirely physical, in the Baron's nervous weaknesses? (2:985–86; 3:343–44)[33]

Many works published in the last third of the nineteenth century similarly linked genius and madness, from Moreau de Tours to Lombros and Max Nordau.[34] "Genius is sometimes akin to madness," Dr. Cottard exclaims in speaking of the coexistence in Charlus of intelligence and "sexual abnormality" (2:1074; 3:428).

An artistic nature is the end result of a heredity similar to the heredity that produces the invert, that is, the product of a form of decadence. The medical establishment was quick to see the artist as a neurotic or a degenerate. But in the *Recherche,* the aesthetic moment—not only the moment of interpretation, but also the moment of creation—is described as a time of crisis, for example in the initiating episode of the three steeples of Martinville at the end of "Combray," when the hero seated in the carriage starts to write "to appease [his] conscience and to satisfy [his] enthusiasm" (1:197; 1:179). Crises of desire and crises of inspiration are intermittencies of the same type. Originality or greatness—if not innovation—have "their correspondents—one is tempted to say their cause"—in the past, the race, tradition. The fractured temporality of art is deceptive, for its breaks, its moments of crisis are in truth examples of the past resurgent. Tradition and originality, imitation and innovation merge in art in the same way that inversion combines a short-lived seizure with the heredity of many centuries. Modernity draws its resources from the "unconscious," in the sense Proust gives to that word. Perhaps, then, by examining Proust's murky relation to modernity and classicism, we may close the circle we opened in the first chapter.

Let us recall what Proust said about the pitched battled waged around Baudelaire, who was attacked after *Les Fleurs du mal* appeared, and Manet, whose painting, "Olympia," created a scandal (see chapter 1). A generation later they had become classics: "These great innovators are the only true classics, and they form an almost continuous series" ("[Classicisme et romantisme]," CSB 617). At the time people complained bitterly about the crisis in poetry and painting—or took great pleasure in it—but, retrospectively, Baudelaire and Manet clearly belong to tradition, and their kinship to Racine and Goya is obvious:

> It is the case for all the great artistic inventors, at least in the nineteenth century, that at the very same time the aesthetes were showing their relation to the past, the public found them vulgar. However often one repeats that Manet, Renoir—who is being buried tomorrow—and Flaubert were not initiators but rather the latest descendents of Velasquez, Goya, Boucher, Fragonard, Rubens, the

ancient Greeks even, Bossuet and Voltaire, their contemporaries found them somewhat common.

("A propos du 'style' de Flaubert," CSB 593–94)

Vulgar and common—that is how they seemed, Baudelaire and Flaubert, Manet and Renoir, like Charlus when his double takes over. Far from being the first, they were the last, or rather they were both the last and the first; two temporal orders overlap in them, as they do in the invert. Proust does not trust avant-gardes, servants of progress, worshipers of novelty, trailblazers or prophets any more than Baudelaire does; he does not believe in aesthetic revolutions declared by manifesto. His position is closer to that of Brunetière, whom we have already discussed in speaking of Racine, and to whom we must now return.

Brunetière has long been discredited. Perhaps his use of Darwin's theory has done him less disservice than his militant pro-Catholic and anti-Dreyfus stance. In imitation and innovation he saw the two principles of the evolution of genres, a way of conceptualizing the relations between the old and the new in literature. He was a defender of the classical tradition. Nevertheless, after the work of Sainte-Beuve and Taine, he reacted against biographical and sociological determinism by conceiving of the great work, the classical work, as a work of crisis: inevitably clumsy, uneven and provisional, always disconcerting. As we saw in chapter 3, Racine represented the finest example of the classical writer: the nineteenth century had seen him as a man of the court and a Jansenist, thus making his theater fit in with his times, as the harmonious expression of an individual and his society. But Brunetière made a naturalist out of him. One might well have assumed—particularly in light of Hegel, but even without reference to his work—that classical writers were ones whose authority had transcended history, writers who carried their own interpretation within themselves. But Brunetière traced this new image of Racine he was inventing to a split within the public when it first received Racine's work in the seventeenth century. The conflicts within the history of interpretation correspond to the ambiguity of the work itself, and can be seen in the split dividing its first audiences: "They recoiled in astonishment and indignation when suddenly, in *Andromaque* or *Bajazet,* they saw passion explode with such violence, love reaching the ecstasies of crime, in short, all that blood showing up underneath the flowers. . . . That eminently polite century never forgave Racine the truth, the audacity, the frankness of his depictions."[35] At this point we need to explain in some detail the meaning of the reevaluation in question here: it was not only because of the contents of his tragedies that Racine was so controversial. In Brunetière's mind, form and content are inseparable from the point of view of the effect Racine makes and the hostility of his first audiences. The caesura between form and content is associated with a caesura inherent to the form: Brunetière is thinking of the same bold turns of phrase of Hermione in *Andromaque* that Proust will latch on to and that give Racine's style an extraordinary tension (see chapter 7). Brunetière points out that Racine's expressions are fluid and familiar, his syntax broken: *concordia discors*. Finally, Racine's originality resides in his archaism. Tomorrow's tradition is innovative today when it brings yesterday back to life.

Brunetière analyzed Flaubert's style in the same way. He is not a fan of Flaubert's, but he does recognize that he is a master, if only because of the lasting impression he has made on literature. Flaubert defines the rhetoric of naturalism, in particular when he transposes sentiment into sensation. As in the case of Racine, the procedure was not a new one—Chateaubriand had already made use of it—but Flaubert alters its effect by attributing it to the characters themselves. Flaubert, Brunetière concludes, "derived novel effects from a familiar procedure; is literary invention anything else but that?"[36] Innovation throws imitation off balance, shifting the position of the model being used without throwing it overboard; it modifies a system of equivalences between forms and functions. The procedures Flaubert uses are not new—they come out of romanticism—but Flaubert organizes them into a different kind of system. This is why readers feel somewhat disoriented, why they have an impression of disquieting recognition when they simultaneously feel themselves to be on familiar ground and elsewhere.

Innovation and modernity are always a parody, a reincarnation, like Charlus. Brunetière makes an astute comparison between the relation of *Madame Bovary* to romanticism and the relation of *Don*

Quixote to novels of chivalry. Flaubert and Cervantes undermine the romantic novel and the novel of chivalry; they do not make a clean break, but rather shift particular details, turning isolated and localized features upside down at different levels. What they are doing is reacting. Innovative works are parodies, reactions; quite the opposite of avant-gardes, manifestos, and platforms, they swim against the current. If they innovate, it is by resisting. The original work faces backward; the gesture that will be retrospectively judged innovative is a deliberate gesture of restoration. Literature progresses against the current, or, more precisely, it walks sideways, obliquely, like a crab.

Brunetière misunderstood Baudelaire, but what Proust would subsequently have to say about the classical tradition, from Racine to Baudelaire and probably going all the way up to include himself, is reminiscent of Brunetière's conception of literary movement, which is not Hegelian or dialectical—that is why it is original—or basically Darwinian—since it cannot be assimilated to either progress or decadence, but only to tradition. The classical work, that is, the work that becomes attached to a tradition after the fact, is a work of breaking away, not because it has a particular historical intention, or is the product of a revolutionary, or tries to make a clean break, but rather because it is neither stable nor harmonious. It is a work defined by crisis, just as Charlus' nature is defined by crisis: split, precarious, paradoxical. *Phèdre, Les Fleurs du mal,* and *A la recherche du temps perdu* are works that last for a long time, perhaps forever, because of their essential vacillation. Great works are always amphibious.

The Futurist Illusion

To tell the truth, the only character in the *Recherche* who has faith in the avant-garde—beside Rachel, who performs an avant-garde, symbolist scene (1:841–42; 2:142)—is the young Madame de Cambremer in *Sodome et Gomorrhe:* "Because she considered herself 'advanced,' because (in matters of art only) 'one could never be far enough to the Left,' she maintained not merely that music progressed, but that it progressed along a single straight line, and that Debussy was in a sense a super-Wagner, slightly more advanced again than Wagner" (2:843; 3:210). Her maiden name is Legrandin, she lives in the provinces, she subscribes to all the high-brow Paris magazines, and she imitates the Goncourt brothers' unusual epithet. No hesitant stammerer she, she babbles endlessly without making any sense. For her, and also for her guest, a fan of Le Sidaner, to take up arms for a painter is to take sides, as in politics, "to fight the good fight." Art is conceived as a battleground, a permanent struggle for life; if one does not come up with something new every second, one is instantly "old-fashioned." In their eyes a painter goes downhill as soon as he stops striving to go higher: "Elstir was gifted, indeed he almost belonged to the avant-garde, but for some reason or other he never kept up, he has wasted his life" (2:839; 3:205–206).

When Proust has Madame de Cambremer use the phrase *avant-garde* before the turn of the century, he is committing an anachronism; at any rate he applies so many political and military metaphors to art that he starts to sound like Stendhal, who wrote at the beginning of his *Salon de 1824*: "My opinions, in painting, are *extremely left-wing*."[37] We might add that as in the case of Madame de Cambremer this applies only to Stendhal's opinions about painting, and he was careful to keep them distinct from his political ideas, which "are *left-center*, as they are for the overwhelming majority of people."[38] If we recall Benjamin Constant's statement about revolutionaries being defenders of aesthetic conformism, it is clear that this awareness of a chiasmus between aesthetics and politics goes back to the early part of the nineteenth century, long before Manet's bemused comment: "It is peculiar how reactionary republicans become when they are speaking about art;"[39] he also found it puzzling that the royalist Durand-Ruel promoted the impressionists, who had been branded as supporters of the Commune.

The younger Madame de Cambremer is a fan of everything that lays any claim to being modern: in her we see the birth pangs of the snobbery of the avant-garde observed by Proust. When the hero, "because of the level of mere 'medium' to which social conversation reduces us" (2:836; 3:203), speaks to her in the voice of her brother, Legrandin, comparing the seagulls in Balbec to Monet's water lilies and the light to a painting by Poussin, he is smartly dressed down with this raging retort:

> In heaven's name, after a painter like Monet, who is quite simply a genius, don't go and mention an old hack without a vestige of talent, like Poussin. I don't mind telling you frankly that I find him the deadliest bore. I mean to say, you can't really call that sort of thing painting. Monet, Degas, Manet, yes, there are painters if you like!
> (2:839–40; 3:206)

Similarly, in her opinion Chopin "was not music" (2:843; 3:209) and she "despised nobody so much as the Polish composer" (2:842; 3:209). Still, her mother-in-law, old Madame de Cambremer, plays Chopin wonderfully, and she even illustrates the "mediumnistic" conception of performance so dear to Proust's heart: "Chopin's only surviving pupil declared, and with justice, that the Master's style of playing, his 'feeling,' had been transmitted, through herself, to Mme de Cambremer alone" (2:842; 3:209). But the young Madame de Cambremer's progressive views on art history prevent her from feeling the slightest appreciation for her mother-in-law's talent, which is the incarnation of tradition in the sense of a transmission of origins. One art takes the place of another and makes it old-fashioned. After Manet has come along, Poussin is no longer a painter; after we have heard Wagner, Chopin no longer sounds like music: the theme reappears in a thousand different forms. Not only has impressionism had to struggle with academicism, but neoimpressionism has already replaced impressionism, gone beyond it. There was a time when the young Madame de Cambremer adored Manet, but nowadays she prefers Monet. Wagner put Chopin to death, Debussy in turn laid Wagner low, and the hero predicts that it will not be long before Debussy will sound to him like just another Massenet, with Mélisande taking the place of Manon. As Valéry was to say in 1929, speaking of the avant-garde and its rhetoric of ending: "Thus the work must be such that what is most interesting about it evaporates as soon as one disregards the work it is replacing and abolishing, as soon as it is considered to be merely *the work of tomorrow*."[40] This is what Valéry calls "self-contained novelty."

The hero seems skeptical; he describes the ups and downs, seemingly ruled by the whim of fashion, that affect the Stock Exchange of aesthetic values: "theories and schools, like microbes and corpuscles, devour one another and by their warfare ensure the continuity of life" (2:844; 3:210). Proust avoids confusing selection and evolution, evolution and progress. Artistic movement seems like a form of anarchy, with the evolution of aesthetic judgments not responding to any kind of determinism, but rather dependent on contingency. The struggle for life assures continuity but not progress, and Proust once again prods Darwinism into becoming a doctrine that resurrects the past in the present. Not only is Debussy not independent of Wagner, "because an artist will after all make use of the weapons he has captured to free himself finally from one whom he has momentarily defeated," but he is reacting against Wagner; he "sought . . . to satisfy an opposite need" (2:843; 3:210).

It cannot be said that Proust denies the existence of the history of art, with its changes and even its breaks, and we see this in his cautious judgment of Elstir: "in so far as art brings out certain laws, once an industry has taken those laws and popularised them, the art that was first in the field loses retrospectively a little of its originality" (1:896; 2:194). But the point of view here is the reception of the work of art, which Proust clearly distinguishes from its creation. Beethoven's late quartets, he says, took fifty years to gather an audience, "thus marking, like every great work of art, an advance if not in the quality of artists at least in the community of minds" (1:572; 1:522). On the other hand, Proust dismisses historical explanations that connect artists to their precursors and their heirs, grounded in the need to equate aesthetic ontogenesis with phylogenesis. A break with the past cannot be the object of a platform, for all artists must start all over again from the beginning; only retrospectively and not prospectively can art have been original, that is, become classical. Even if earlier painters lose their originality after Elstir, Proust judges "that there can be no progress, no discovery in art, but only in the sciences, and that each artist starting afresh on an individual effort cannot be either helped or hindered therein by the efforts of any other" (1:896; 2:194). This doctrine conforms to the idea that the artist must "divest himself of intelligence" in order to create, an idea that was expressed with clarity even as early as *Contre Sainte-Beuve:*

> Now in art there is no initiator or precursor (at least in the scientific sense). Everything [is] within the individual, each individual starts

> the artistic or literary enterprise all over again for himself; and the works of his predecessors do not constitute, as they do in the sciences, an acquired truth that all those who come later will take advantage of. For a writer of genius today, everything remains to be done. He is not any more ahead of the game than Homer.
>
> (CSB 220)

This was already Victor Hugo's hypothesis in *William Shakespeare.*

The paradox, if you will, is that this purely individual effort still comes back to a form of continuity, or that ontogenesis meets phylogenesis. This is a movement we also saw in Barrès' work, as early as *Le Culte du moi,* until "The Earth and the Dead" turned into a doctrine, with Barrès' anti-Dreyfus stance and his support for the Ligue de la Patrie française. Rather than being a theory of progress stating that followers and survivors are the best, the theory of evolution can be interpreted as a doctrine of reincarnation, the return of the old within the new. In 1899 Barrès wrote: "I am the continuity of my parents. That is true from an anatomical point of view. They think and they speak through me. . . . I make no claims to being a better thinker, to feeling greater feelings, to having broader knowledge than my father and mother; I am them."[41] Similarly, the "Masked Ball" at the end of *Le Temps retrouvé* is completely based on atavistic resemblances. Just as Swann looked like his father, Gilberte looks like Swann, and also like Odette: " 'You take me for my mother,' Gilberte had said to me. It was true."[42] In the opposite direction, Legrandin looks like his nephew, Léonor de Cambremer (3:987; 4:520–21). These resemblances come out with the passage of time, as the hero comments when he observes Monsieur de Charlus going up to Morel at the Doncières train station: "Starting from a certain age, and even at the same time as other evolutions are taking place in all of us, the features that make one look like certain members of one's family become more and more striking" (3:1488 [3:256, var. c]). The hero thinks his mother looks like his grandmother after the latter's death, while the hero himself is an amalgam of all his relatives. He points out the phrases he gets from his mother and his grandmother, and worries about the weather just as his father does: "Little by little, I was beginning to resemble all my relations, . . . not my father only, but, more and more, my aunt Léonie" (3:72; 3:586). Aunt Léonie, "transmigrated into me," as he puts it, is given as the cause of his fondness for lounging around in bed. The peculiar result of these reincarnations is that the way the hero speaks to Albertine resembles both the way he used to speak to his mother as a boy and the way his grandmother used to speak to him as a boy.

Here is Proust's version of "La Terre et les morts," yet another intersection of ontogenesis and phylogenesis:

> When we have passed a certain age, the soul of the child that we were and the souls of the dead from whom we sprang come and shower upon us their riches and their spells, asking to be allowed to contribute to the new emotions which we feel and in which, erasing their former image, we recast them in an original creation. . . . We have to give hospitality, at a certain stage in our lives, to all our relatives who have journeyed so far and gathered round us.
>
> (3:73–74; 3:587)

Original creation is conceived of as a memory of ancestors, as was the case for the supposedly Celtic belief alluded to in the prelude to the madeleine episode at the very beginning of "Combray." The souls of our dear departed take refuge in a lower being and there we are given the chance to be with them: "Delivered by us, they have overcome death and return to share our life" (1:47; 1:44). The past recaptured is also the reincarnation of the race. Art carries out this transmigration without the aid of Barrès' cult of the dead—that atheistic form of Catholicism that Proust seems to adhere to in his 1904 article, "La mort des cathédrales" (CSB 141–49)—and for this reason it is important to stress the essential difference between them. On the one hand, Barrès concludes that the past defines the present through a form of determinism, an absolute continuity; in Proust's mind, on the other hand, the present reincarnates the past through a fortuitous discovery. In *Contre Sainte-Beuve,* the moments of the past were similarly hidden inside of some material object—"as happens to the souls of the dead in certain popular legends"—and Proust lays even greater emphasis on the coincidental nature of reminiscence. The same might be said of childhood summers brought back by soaking a piece of toast in a cup of tea: "There was every likelihood that they would remain dead for me for all time. Their resurrection, like all resurrections, was the product of a simple coincidence" (CSB 211). It is true that in *Le Temps retrouvé* Proust will give art the value of a quest for laws, but his thought, especially by comparison with Barrès', remains fundamentally nondeterministic.

When in *A l'ombre des jeunes filles en fleurs* Proust distinguishes between "Bergotte's ways" and the style of his followers, he wonders about the property of this man of genius that prevents every new form of beauty he creates from being reducible to his past work and yet still makes it recognizable as belonging to him, hence inimitable: "So it is with all great writers: the beauty of their sentences is as unforeseeable as is that of a woman whom we have never seen" (1:593; 1:541). An imitator of Saint-Simon "might at a pinch give us the first line of his portrait of Villars: 'He was a rather tall man, dark . . . with an alert, open, expressive physiognomy,' but what law of determinism could bring him to the discovery of Saint-Simon's next line, which begins with 'and, to tell the truth, a trifle mad'?" (1:593; 1:541). Proust still conceptualizes the interplay of imitation and originality in terms inspired by Darwin, as we see in the metaphor that immediately follows this passage: "The true variety is in this abundance of real and unexpected elements, in the branch loaded with blue flowers which shoots up, against all reason, from the spring hedgerow that seemed already overcharged with blossoms." But this Darwinism remains unpredictable; originality will always be something unexpected.

In *Sodome et Gomorrhe,* the news from Paris that the hero tells the young Madame de Cambremer merely in an attempt to keep her in check is nevertheless of some consequence: "M. Degas affirms that he knows nothing more beautiful than the Poussins at Chantilly" (2:841; 3:208), whereas "Chopin, so far from being out of date, was Debussy's favourite composer" (2:845; 3:212). The poor woman goes all to pieces; she vows to take a closer look at Poussin and to give Chopin a second hearing. The great artist recognizes what he owes to tradition; it is the public hungry for modernity that chalks up the misunderstanding that greets the works of a great artist to his being ahead of his time. Just as there is a genetic illusion, we might well call this a "futurist illusion." In *A l'ombre des jeunes filles en fleurs,* Proust takes Vinteuil's sonata to task for the same things he criticizes about the illusion that is analogous to it:

> No doubt it is easy to imagine, by an illusion similar to that which makes everything on the horizon appear equidistant, that all the revolutions which have hitherto occurred in painting or in music did at least respect certain rules, whereas that which immediately confronts us, be it impressionism, the pursuit of dissonance, an exclusive use of the Chinese scale, cubism, futurism or what you will, differs outrageously from all that has occurred before.
>
> (1:573; 1:522–23)

The great artist, Vinteuil or Elstir, projects his work into the future, that is, he sees it not so much in time as out of time. The original work is assimilated in time, but not because it tried to be ahead of its time.

Thus, the fact that Vermeer's genius was not recognized for a long time has nothing to do with his modernism, and if Chopin and Poussin both underwent a reevaluation at the turn of the century, its context was perhaps not so much aesthetic as political. The examples Proust chooses are telling ones. Chopin was indeed out of fashion in the latter part of the nineteenth century. Maurice Rollinat dedicated a poem to him in his collection *Les Névroses* in 1883. About the same time, Camille Bellaigue, the music critic for the *Revue des Deux Mondes,* wrote: "For an elegant or touching phrase, and even surrounding that phrase, what a flood of notes, what useless chatter, what an unbearably fussy ornamentation frames every melody." Chopin, the critic concludes, whose style is reminiscent of Brichot, would have put "pompons on the Venus de Milo."[43] But Marguerite Long points out that Debussy took Chopin to be his main model—he supposedly owed his familiarity with Chopin's work to his first piano teacher, Madame Mauté, Verlaine's mother-in-law, who was purported to be a student of Chopin's. Debussy edited a collection of Chopin's works during the war, when German editions of it were no longer available; in 1915 he dedicated his twelve *Etudes* to Chopin's memory, and the link between the two musicians has been amply demonstrated.[44] Thus Chopin came back into fashion later than Proust suggests, during the war, and in the context of an appreciation of French music.

As for Degas, who in 1870 had done a copy of "L'Enlèvement des Sabines" in the Louvre, he helped bring Poussin back into fashion in the 1890s. In addition to him, Cézanne, who also took an anti-Dreyfus position, was associated with this reevaluation. In his *Journal,* Gide quotes a significant juxtaposition found in an 1896 letter from his friend Athman to Degas: "What I am pleased about is that you don't like Jews, you read *La Libre Parole,* and you agree with me that Poussin is a great French painter."[45] In the course of the Dreyfus affair, Degas severed contact with his great friends, the Halévys. The examples Proust chooses to convince the anti-Dreyfus, nationalistic Madame de Cambremer—who, let us recall, "could never be far enough to the Left," but "in matters of art only"—are thus particularly appropriate.

Proust suggests a number of reasons for the transformation of artistic values, but they are bad reasons, ones that are not themselves artistic, "theories . . . like those theories which, in politics, come to the support of the laws against the religious orders, or of wars in the East (unnatural teaching, the Yellow Peril, etc., etc.)" (2:843; 3:210). The only one that is artistic—and it may even have played a role in Degas' and Debussy's changes in position—is this one:

> Certain artists of an earlier generation have in some fragment of their work achieved something that resembles what the master has gradually become aware that he himself wanted to do. Then he sees the old master as a sort of precursor; he values in him, under a wholly different form, an effort that is momentarily, partially fraternal.
> (2:844; 3:211)

Here once again is the fraternity—the intemporal and mystical kinship linking Racine to Baudelaire and Baudelaire to Proust—that goes to make up tradition, the "almost continuous"—that is to say, intermittent—tradition, as Proust puts it, which he distinguishes from the ideology of limitless and continuous progress. What we are dealing with here are not premeditated imitations or sources, but rather intersections that come to light after the fact. The earlier artist and the later one are alike in that neither one wishes to give himself precursors, but in the earlier artist the later one retrospectively recognizes what Proust in *Contre Sainte-Beuve* calls "forward-looking 'reminiscences' of the same idea, of the same sensation, of the same artistic effort that we are presently expressing" (CSB 311). Thus, in *Le Côté de Guermantes II,* Elstir admires, in the work of Chardin or Perronneau, "anticipatory fragments, so to speak, of works of his own" (2:435; 2:713). And in *Le Temps retrouvé,* when he decides to make the "transposed sensation" into his aesthetic dogma, the hero feels "reassured to find [it] akin to characteristics, less marked but still perceptible and at bottom not at all dissimilar, of certain well-known writers" (3:958; 4:498).

The new is a fragment of the old. Proust's "anticipatory recognitions" recall Walter Benjamin's "dialectical images," the wrecks that float toward us from the past, "flashing up momentarily" "in the 'now' of [their] recognisability,"[46] the ruins of history that chance saves from catastrophe. They are the elements of a work that have not "already become part of its influence," its "rough outcrops" and "jagged prongs," failures from the point of view of progress, unfulfilled promises and forgotten hopes.[47] But young Madame de Cambremer is incapable of grasping the backward, inward movement of art; she cannot "brush history against the grain," as Benjamin defines the historian's task.[48] A victim of the Darwinian illusion in its genetic and futuristic form, she is the exact opposite of Charlus who, like old Madame de Cambremer, is "natural": Stimati, his piano teacher, forbade him from going to hear Chopin, who would have exerted too great an influence on him (2:1042; 3:397). The young Madame de Cambremer is not stupid, as Proust points out; indeed, she has more intelligence than she knows what to do with, but it is a useless intelligence because it is misplaced, applied to artistic concerns. She is not stupid but she is a snob, that is, she claims to have made a break with her ancestors. Her interest in the avant-garde and her snobbery are one and the same thing. In this respect her brother is a monster of schizophrenia, for his snobbery shuns his forebears while his inversion brings them back to life. But she herself has forgotten that her maiden name is Legrandin, as Proust points out (2:849; 3:215). In a strange but in some sense inevitable way, this remark is followed by a comment about the wife and the son of the lawyer who is a fan of Le Sidaner, a comment that appears completely unrelated: "The wife had a round face like certain flowers of the ranunculus family, and a large vegetable growth, which might have helped towards the classification of a variety of the species, protruded below the eye of the son" (2:849; 3:215–16). No one can escape tradition, whether it be the young Madame de Cambremer whose maiden name is Legrandin or the son of the fan of Le Sidaner, or Bloch who, in *Le Temps retrouvé,* thinks he can cover up his origins underneath the pseudonym Jacques du Rozier (3:995; 4:530), like the Rue des Blancs-Manteaux in Paris, whose Christian associations do not prevent Charlus from calling it "the Judengasse of Paris" (2:1143; 3:491). But the young Madame de Cambremer's snobbery prevents her from realizing that art is not dialectic, that it is essentially critical. She speaks of it in terms of evolution, that is, progress and obsolescence, thereby confusing the evolution of her own taste, the development of her artistic culture, with the movement of art itself. Once again the history of art, beholden to Hegel or Darwin, is written from the perspective of the viewer, not the actor; it is a sociology of reception rather than the truth of creation. Creators have no use for history; they recognize themselves in the present. As Proust puts it as early as his preface to Ruskin's *Sesame and Lilies:* "The romantics . . . are the only ones who know how to read classical works, because they read them as they were written, romantically" ("Journées de lecture," CSB 190).

The illusion of the avant-garde is that the point of view of the spectator is taken for the point of view of the creator. It is the illusion of a break with tradition and of a tradition formed without breaks, whereas in fact crisis in art is not merely an outward manifestation but the thing itself: what first appeared as a break in the present—after Debussy, Wagner and Chopin no longer sound like music; soon there would be no apparent difference between Debussy and Massenet—is in time revealed to have been inseparable from tradition. Often it would be more apt, rather than speaking of obsolescence, to speak of archaisms: "There are bits of Turner in the work of Poussin, phrases of Flaubert in Montesquieu" (2:844; 3:211), Proust writes as a counter to the young Madame de Cambremer's modernism. This is an idea he holds dear, one also found in the 1920 article on Flaubert: "Flaubert was always delighted to find an anticipation of his own writing in writers of the past, for example Montesquieu's sentence, 'Alexander's vices were extreme, as were his virtues; he was terrifying when he was angry; anger made him cruel.' " ("A propos du 'style' de Flaubert," CSB 587). In a 1913 letter to Antoine Bibesco, Proust judged the same sentence of Montesquieu to resemble Flaubert, and the sentence is immediately compared to a line from Racine which is the prototype of syntactical gymnastics: "Why kill him? What did he do? For what reason? / Who told you to? [Pourquoi l'assassiner? Qu'a-t-il fait? A quel titre? / Qui te l'a dit?]" (*Corr.* 12:34). Once again an archaism is the very principle of innovation, an archaism embedded within the old, an "anticipatory reminiscence."

Let us emphasize that this questioning of the avant-garde is not at all the same as a defense of the old guard. On the contrary, what we are dealing with here is a refusal to identify the modern either with decadentism or with futurism, but rather an attempt to associate it essentially with the critical. I have alluded to Barrès. But Proust does not share his determinism, which claims there is no beginning that is not the continuation of the past, history being an indivisible whole. The work is never made obsolete if it is critical, in its present and in our time. Tradition and the break with tradition: tradition is made up of broken works; not of breaks with tradition but rather with works that are themselves broken. Or, as Proust himself puts it in one of the last positions he took, in a July 1922 response to a questionnaire about the renewal of style:

> 1. The continuity of style is not compromised but rather guaranteed by the perpetual renewal of style. . . .
> 2. I do not "give my support" (to borrow the phrase you used in your questionnaire) to those writers who might feel "preoccupied by originality of form." (CSB 645)

Here, in a nutshell, are the two propositions I have attempted to demonstrate. Proust's defective sense of history is what saved him from the nineteenth century—and also from the twentieth.

Conclusion

In 1956 Nathalie Sarraute made the following statement: "For most of us, the works of Joyce and Proust already appear in the distance, as witnesses to an era that is no longer." She went on to make this prediction: "It will not be long before we visit these historic monuments only with the help of a guide, amidst groups of schoolchildren, with a respectful silence and a somewhat gloomy admiration."[1] Thirty-five years have gone by since then. Sarraute fell victim to the same futurist illusion as Madame de Cambremer, née Legrandin: after Manet, Poussin can no longer be considered painting; after Wagner, Chopin is no longer music; after Robbe-Grillet, Proust is no longer literature. The ravages brought by an activist conception of art are not over yet. But the point is not to replace them with an essentialist conception—Racine will always be Racine—or a good-natured one—today's romantics are tomorrow's classics, "just as the worst cads, or so the saying goes, make the best family men," Brunetière would have added (see chapter 3). It is true that Baudelaire, the father of the decadent movement before 1900 and Brunetière's pet peeve, himself became the classic of the twentieth century.

I hope I have demonstrated that a work remains present and

alive through its flaws and disparities, that its defects are indications of the way it is rooted in time. A work elicits renewed interpretations because it does not give answers to the questions it raises, questions that remain irreducible. Racine is neither classic nor baroque; Baudelaire is neither decadent nor rhetorical; Proust is neither reactionary nor futuristic. And, quite against the current predicted by Nathalie Sarraute, in our times we continue to read *A la recherche du temps perdu* as a modern work. But "modern" does not mean "modernistic," in the sense of the artistic militancy of the twentieth century, ranging from Apollinaire through surrealism to the Nouveau Roman. It does not mean "in favor of progress," in the sense of the Enlightenment, positivism, and Darwinism. It means unclassifiable, essentially ambiguous, divided. At the beginning of *Le Peintre de la vie moderne,* Baudelaire states that "the beautiful is always, inevitably, of a double composition" (OC 2:685), and he then goes on to say it is composed of two distinct elements, one eternal, one circumstantial. Literature is paradoxical: modernity includes a resistance to modernity.[2] As Baudelaire later points out, "The duality of art is an inevitable consequence of the duality of man" (OC 2:685–86).

In Proust's terms, let us think back to idolatry and allegory: the idolatry that he condemns in Montesquiou and that is embodied by Swann in the novel; the allegory that he praises in Giotto and that his hero is supposed to reach at the end of his apprenticeship. Ruskin is somewhere between the two, indefinable. In the first long note to his translation of *Sesame and Lilies,* Proust accuses Ruskin of idolatry because of the epigraph he borrows from Lucian: "You shall each have a cake of sesame,—and ten pound." Ruskin is playing with the different meanings of the word *sesame:* "It is my belief that Ruskin, perhaps because of the idolatry I have often spoken of, simply indulged his adoration for a particular word by admiring it in every fine passage by a great author in which it is to be found."[3] But at the same time, this epigraph instantly introduces the key word of the book, its allegory, which ties together all its meanings and becomes clear only at the conclusion: it is simultaneously a sesame seed, Ali Baba's magic password, and reading that opens up the doors of wisdom. Allegory reveals the existence of a "superior logic" beyond the apparent disorder that reigns in Ruskin's work:

"It turns out that he obeys a kind of secret outline which, finally unmasked, retrospectively gives a kind of order to the whole and makes it appear to be magnificently tiered or terraced all the way up to the final apotheosis."[4] Retrospectively at least, we certainly have the impression that here Proust is unveiling the "secret outline" and the "superior logic" that he is destined, some years hence, to try to carry out in the *Recherche,* between the centuries. Behind all the dualities, behind all the disharmonies that make up *A la recherche du temps perdu,* the perpetually uncertain struggle between idolatry and allegory, decadence and modernity is reborn again and again.

Every one of Proust's sentences bears the traces of this tension, including this one, perhaps the most famous: "To think that I've wasted years of my life, that I've longed to die, that I've experienced my greatest love, for a woman who didn't appeal to me, who wasn't even my type" (1:415; 1:382). Those who do not notice the tension here are the very same people who read the beginning and the end of the *Recherche* without paying any attention to the middle; many are those who go directly from "Combray" to *Le Temps retrouvé* and heap praise on the work's completeness, as if "Combray" were actually the book announced in *Le Temps retrouvé.* But the entire *Recherche* is the product of an enormous act of procrastination by the hero, who does not so much wait around for the final moment of revelation as he puts off—after the revelation and in spite of it—starting the book that might accomplish the ideal of *Le Temps retrouvé.* After all, where is it written that the book we have in our hands is that book? The book we have is rather the postponement of that other one; it takes the place of that other book. Only the narrator's bad faith can bring off the substitution of one for the other.

The hero of *A la recherche du temps perdu* leads us to believe that he is telling the truth about himself, that he is digging down deep into the unconscious of the person he has seen with as much perceptiveness as he shows in exploring the psychology of his other characters. But this is untrue. The hero lies about his past. Between the hero and himself, or between the narrator and the hero, that is the path along which the underlying fault of *A la recherche du temps perdu* runs. And that fault is Proust himself, his duplicity, or his duality, to speak in Baudelaire's terms: it is what the novel hides or what its author wants to forget. Proust's decadentism, Proust's sadism, Proust's homosexuality, Proust's snobbery, Proust's positivism: in truth, are these not the objects of previous studies? Allegories always wind up becoming clichés. As Benjamin said of Baudelaire's relapses, the murderer always comes back to the scene of the crime. And as André Breton puts it at the beginning of *Nadja,* tell me who you hang out with (and I'll tell you who you are) . . .

If the doctrine behind *A la recherche du temps perdu* is hard to put one's finger on, is this not because the novel is more protective and indulgent of the hero than of anyone alse? He is not the one who recites lines from *Esther* and *Athalie* as he ogles embassy employees at the Princesse de Guermantes' or bellboys at the Grand Hotel in Balbec, or if he does, he is merely imitating Monsieur de Charlus. He is not the one who has a mania for etymologies. He is never the one who does wrong. For example, he does not ask himself even once whether he is not responsible to some extent for his family's feud with Uncle Adolphe. He sees Mademoiselle Vinteuil and her friend profaning the musician's memory; he observes Rachel in the brothel; he witnesses the meeting between Charlus and Jupien. But he never questions the meaning of his recurrent voyeurism. When Forcheville humiliates Saniette at the Verdurins', Odette, we are told, darts him a "look of complicity in the crime" (1:302; 1:272). But we are told nothing about the observer's look, the narrator's look, nothing about the cruelty of the hero himself in his extreme sensitivity to pain. The narrator lies, he keeps the hero under cover instead of exposing his "vices." Since the hero is riddled with vice and the narrator hides it from the reader, the novel is based on a lie. The search for truth is a disguise imposed on the reader: it is the most important transposition in the entire novel.

If the narrator were faithful to the doctrine he develops in *Le Temps retrouvé,* he would be forced to exclaim: "To think that I've wasted years of my life for a book that wasn't even my type." But the narrator would never have written a book that conformed to the model set forth in *Le Temps retrouvé,* just as Swann would never have fallen in love with a woman who was his type. And we would have found a book like that—and a woman like that—boring. Here is the last word on Proustian indeterminism. We hypothesize the existence of laws—an ideal book, an ideal woman—but they are never the ones we love. And we love the others precisely because that is not what they are.

Notes

Introduction

1. *Le Temps,* December 10, 1913; *Marcel Proust* (Paris: Kra, 1927), 11.

2. Letter of December 1919, *Correspondance générale de Marcel Proust,* ed. Robert Proust, Paul Brach, and Suzy Mante-Proust (Paris: Plon, 1930–36), 3:72. Subsequent references to this work (abbreviated *Corr. gén.*) will be given in the body of the text.

3. Marcel Proust, *A la recherche du temps perdu,* ed. Jean-Yves Tadié (Paris: Gallimard, Pléiade, 1987), 1:5. English translation in *Remembrance of Things Past,* trans. C. K. Scott Moncrieff and Terence Kilmartin (New York: Random House, 1981), 1:5. All subsequent quotations from the *Recherche* will refer to these editions, and references will be given in the body of the text in the following order: English edition, French edition.

4. Charles Baudelaire, "Le Soleil," line 7, in *Oeuvres complètes,* ed. Claude Pichois (Paris: Gallimard, Pléiade,1975–76), 2 vols., 1:83. This edition will hereafter be abbreviated OC, and references will be placed in the body of the text.

5. Walter Benjamin, *Charles Baudelaire: A Lyric Poet in the Era of High Capitalism,* trans. Harry Zohn (London: NLB, 1973), 118.

6. Roland Barthes, *Critique et vérité* (Paris: Seuil, 1966), 54–55. This and all translations from the French, unless otherwise noted, are those of the translator of this book.

7. Barthes, *Critique et vérité,* 56.

8. Paul Valéry, *Cahiers,* ed. Judith Robinson (Paris: Gallimard, Pléiade, 1974), 2:1204.

9. See Hans-Georg Gadamer, *Truth and Method,* trans. and revis. Joel Weinsheimer and Donald Marshall (New York: Continuum, 1988) (German title *Wahrheit und Methode*).

10. See my "La démocrasserie moderne," *La Troisième République des lettres, de Flaubert à Proust* (Paris: Seuil, 1983), 269ff.

11. See Hans Robert Jauss, *Toward an Aesthetic of Reception,* trans. Timothy Bahti, intro. Paul de Man (Minneapolis: University of Minnesota Press, 1982), in Theory and History of Literature series, vol. 2.

12. Jacques-Emile Blanche, Preface to *Propos de peintre: De David à Degas* (Paris: Emile-Paul, 1919), in Marcel Proust, *Contre Sainte-Beuve,* preceded by *Pastiches et Mélanges* and followed by *Essais et articles,* ed. Pierre Clarac and Yves Sandre (Paris: Gallimard, Pléiade, 1971). References to this edition, hereafter abbreviated CSB, will be placed in the body of the text.

13. Quoted in Jauss, *Toward an Aesthetic of Reception,* 71. See Jean Starobinski, *La Relation critique* (Paris: Gallimard, 1968).

14. Arthur Rimbaud, *Oeuvres,* ed. Suzanne Bernard and André Guyaux (Paris: Garnier, 1981), 351, letter of May 15, 1871, to Paul Demeny.

15. Louis Althusser, "Du *Capital* à la philosophie de Marx," in Louis Althusser, Jacques Rancière, and Pierre Macherey, *Lire le capital* (Paris: Maspero, 1965), vol. 1.

16. Jacques Derrida, *De la grammatologie* (Paris: Editions de Minuit, 1967); English translation *Of Grammatology,* trans. Gayatri Chakravorty Spivak (Baltimore: Johns Hopkins University Press, 1974).

17. Marcel Proust, *Correspondance,* ed. Philip Kolb (Paris: Plon, 1970–), 16 vols. to present covering the period 1880–1917. This edition will hereafter be abbreviated *Corr.* and references will be given in the body of the text.

18. Charles Baudelaire, Feuillet 20, OC 1:662.

19. Gustave Flaubert, *Correspondance,* ed. Jean Bruneau (Paris: Gallimard, Pléiade, 1973), 1:389, letter of October 14, 1846.

1. The Last Writer of the Nineteenth Century and the First Writer of the Twentieth

1. See Lucchino Visconti and Suso Cecchi D'Amico, *Alla ricerca del tempo perduto. Sceneggiatura dall'opera di Proust* (Milan: Mondadori, "Teatro e cinema," 1986).

2. Blaise Pascal, *Pensées,* ed. Dominique Descotes (Paris: Garnier-Flammarion, 1976), 150; Brunschvicg 353, Lafuma 681.

3. Jacques Rivière, "Marcel Proust et la tradition classique" (February 1, 1920), *Nouvelles Etudes* (Paris: Gallimard, 1947), 150; *Quelques progrès dans l'étude du coeur humain* (1926), ed. Thierry Laget (Paris: Gallimard, "Cahiers Marcel Proust," 1985), 61.

4. Marcel Proust, *Contre Sainte-Beuve,* ed. Pierre Clarac and Yves Sandre (Paris: Gallimard, Pléiade, 1971), 641 and note 6. References to this edition, hereafter abbreviated CSB, will be placed in the body of the text.

5. 3:917–18 and 928–31; 4:466–67 and 471–73. This passage is sketched out in Cahier 58: see *Matinée chez la princesse de Guermantes,* ed. Henri Bonnet and Bernard Brun (Paris: Gallimard, 1982), 114–18.

6. Jean-Jacques Nattiez recently published an interesting analysis of the same passage in *Proust musicien* (Paris: Christian Bourgois, 1984), 35ff. He demonstrates that Proust's idea about Wagnerian composition—fragments brought together into a whole only after the fact—is based on the erroneous hypothesis that the Good Friday Spell was conceived before *Parsifal,* as Proust remarked as early as the essay on Sainte-Beuve: "The Good Friday Spell is a piece which Wagner wrote before thinking of doing *Parsifal* and which he subsequently incorporated into it. But the additions, the beautiful elements which are carried over, the new interrelations which the genius suddenly perceives between the separate parts of his work and which join up, come to life, and can no longer be separated, are they not among his finest intuitions?" ("Sainte-Beuve et Balzac," CSB 274). Proust was already comparing Wagner and Balzac: "Certain parts of his great cycle were joined onto it only after the fact." Proust probably got this dubious information about the composition of *Parsifal* from one of the classics of Wagnerism at the turn of the century, Albert Lavignac's *Le Voyage artistique à Bayreuth* (Paris: Delagrave, 1897) (English title: *The Music Dramas of Richard Wagner and His Festival Theatre in Bayreuth,* trans. Esther Singleton [New York: Dodd, Mead, 1906]), which said in speaking of the Good Friday Spell: "It was written long before the rest of the score" (quoted by Nattiez, 42; *Music Dramas,* 467n.1). If this is the case, Proust's reflection about the unity of the work of art thus stems from an erroneous description of Wagner's characteristic method of composition.

7. Cahier 49, fols. 42v–45v and 40v–41v; Esquisse IV, var. b.

8. Cahier 49, fols. 42r–46r; Esquisse IV.

9. Cahier 49, fol. 44r; Esquisse IV.

10. Charles Baudelaire, *Correspondance,* ed. Claude Pichois and Jean Ziegler (Paris: Gallimard, Pléiade, 1973), 2:196.

11. Paul Souday, *Le Temps,* December 10, 1913; *Marcel Proust,* (Paris: Kra, 1927), 11.

12. Henri Ghéon, *La Nouvelle Revue Française,* January 1, 1914; *Du côté de chez Swann,* ed. Antoine Compagnon (Paris: Gallimard, Folio, 1988), Document VIII, 454.

13. Désiré Nisard, *Etudes de moeurs et de critiques sur les poètes latins de la décadence* (1834; 3d ed. [Paris: Hachette, 1867]), 2:286.

14. Joris-Karl Huysmans, *A rebours,* ed. Marc Fumaroli (2d ed. [Paris: Gallimard, Folio, 1983]), 116.

15. Paul Bourget, "Charles Baudelaire," *Essais de psychologie contemporaine* (Paris: Lemerre, 1883), 3–32.

16. Ibid., 25.

17. Ibid., 9.

18. Friedrich Nietzsche, *Fragments posthumes. Automne 1887–mars 1888,* French trans. Pierre Klossowski (Paris: Gallimard, 1976). See, in particular, 242–44.

19. Bourget, *Essais de psychologie contemporaine,* 9.

20. See Anne Henry, *Marcel Proust. Théories pour une esthétique* (Paris: Klincksieck, 1981), 81ff.

21. Charles Baudelaire, *Oeuvres complètes,* ed. Claude Pichois, 2 vols. (Paris: Gallimard, Pléiade, 1975–76), 2:431–33. References to this edition, abbreviated OC, will hereafter be given in the body of the text.

22. Gabriel Séailles, *Essai sur le génie dans l'art* (Paris: G. Baillière, 1883), 244.

23. Paul Valéry, *Cahiers,* ed. Judith Robinson, 2 vols. (Paris: Gallimard, Pléiade, 1973–74), 2:1099.

24. Letter of October 1913, *Corr.* 12:278.

25. Letter of November 1913, *Corr.* 12:295.

26. Letter of January 1913 to Louis de Robert, *Corr.* 12:38.

27. Letter of June 1913, *Corr.* 12:214.

28. Letter of February 1913, *Corr.* 12:82.

29. Letter of July 1913, *Corr.* 12:230–31.

30. Friedrich Nietzsche, *The Case of Wagner,* in *The Case of Wagner. Nietzsche contra Wagner. Selected Aphorisms,* trans. Anthony M. Ludovici; *We Philologists,* trans. J. M. Kennedy (New York: Russell and Russell, 1964), 13. The second phrase, given in French in Nietzsche's text, means "Wagner is a neurosis."

31. Nietzsche, *The Case of Wagner,* 19–20.

32. Nietzsche, *The Case of Wagner,* 20.

33. Nietzsche, *The Case of Wagner,* 20.

34. Nietzsche, *The Case of Wagner,* 24.

35. Paris: Librairie Albert Schulz.

36. *Le Postillon de Longjumeau* is a famous comic opera by Adam that dates from the July Monarchy.

37. Cahier 49, fol. 44v.

38. Nietzsche, *The Case of Wagner,* 1.

39. Nietzsche, *The Case of Wagner,* 1–2.

40. Paris: Calmann-Lévy, 1909.

41. Nietzsche, *The Case of Wagner,* 37.

42. A similar comment can be found in Carnet 2, under a different fragment dated between April and August 1913: "For Franck / It is not a musical motif which was repeated, it is an attack of neuralgia starting up again, difficult to pinpoint, vague and ganglionic" (fol. 25r).

43. Nietzsche, *Selected Aphorisms,* in *The Case of Wagner,* 96. The fragment dates from the summer of 1878, or ten years after the composition of *The Case of Wagner.*

44. Paul Bourget, *Etudes et Portraits* (Paris: Lemerre, 1889), 1:256.

45. Nietzsche, *The Case of Wagner,* 5. Proust will use the same phrase, in *Le Temps retrouvé,* in designating his own work: "my book being merely a sort of magnifying glass like those which the optician at Combray used to offer his customers" (3:1089; 4:610).

46. Nietzsche, *The Case of Wagner,* 21.

47. Quoted by Henri Bonnet, *Marcel Proust de 1907 à 1914,* 2 vols. (1959; rpt. [Paris: Nizet, 1971]), 1:181.

48. Lyof N. Tolstoï, *What is Art?*, trans. Aylmer Maude, in *The Works of Lyof N. Tolstoï* 6 (New York: Charles Scribner's Sons, 1929), 114. A whole chapter is devoted to Wagner who is once again brought to task over the lack of organic unity in his works: "Wagner's new music lacks the chief characteristic of every true work of art; namely, such entirety and completeness that the smallest alteration in its form would disturb the meaning of the whole work" (*What is Art?*, 113). Here again we can perceive the dogma that structuralism shares with organicism, and that is passed from one to the other by the mediation of Saussure; this explains that they are both incapable of fathoming deranged works, which are, unfortunately, the great works.

49. Anne Henry, who has this kind of tendency to assimilate the *Recherche* to an exercise of applied philosophy, transfers to Proust one of the complaints formulated by Nietzsche against decadence: along with "the decline of all organising power" and "excessive vitality in small details," "the counterfeit imitation of grand forms" (*The Case of Wagner*, 44). On the other hand, Paul Ricoeur emphasizes the gap implied by the writing of the novel in relation to the theory. *Temps et Récit II: La Configuration dans le récit de fiction* (Paris: Seuil, 1984), 194–225.

50. Cahier 49, fol. 42r; Esquisse VIII. Querqueville will become Balbec in the novel.

51. In a February 1913 letter to René Blum, Proust uses the same ambiguous image about Maeterlinck's essay, *La Mort* (Paris: Fasquelle, 1913), which had just come out (*Corr.* 12:82).

52. Letter of July 1913 to Louis de Robert (*Corr.* 12:230). The writer is also compared to a carrier pigeon or the needle of a compass at the time of *Contre Sainte-Beuve* ("Notes sur la littérature et la critique," CSB 311).

2. Fauré and Unity Recaptured

1. Proust's work has been compared to many different kinds of music. Its relation to Fauré's music—certainly among the most important—has been given an excellent analysis by a Fauré scholar: Jean-Michel Nectoux, "Proust et Fauré," *Bulletin de la Société des amis de Marcel Proust* 21 (1971): 1102–20.

2. Cahier 46, fols. 74v–75v; Esquisse XVII. The allusion is to Fauré's Opus 5, No. 1 (1871). For *Chant d'automne*, both the poem and the melody, see chapter 7.

3. The allusion is to Fauré's Opus 23, No. 1 (1879). The melody is entitled *Les Berceaux*, but it is a setting of "Le Long du quai," another poem from Sully Prudhomme's first collection of poetry, *Stances et Poèmes*. See *Poésies de Sully Prudhomme. Stances et Poèmes. 1865–1866* (Paris: Lemerre, 1872). "Les Berceaux" is on 23, and "Le Long du quai" on 163. Fauré writes in a letter of July 1879 to Madame Camille Clerc: "I have just received a very flattering letter from Sully Prudhomme. Monsieur Gaston Paris had mentioned to him that I was concerned about the title of my latest melody, *Le long du quai*. The poet has authorized me to call it *Les Berceaux*." Gabriel Fauré, *Correspondance*, ed. Jean-Michel Nectoux (Paris: Flammarion, 1980), 88. Proust is thus alluding to Fauré's melody and not Sully

Prudhomme's poem, which has a different title. This example confirms the fact that Proust knows the poem through the melody.

4. *Corr.* 1:340. The allusions are to Fauré's Opus 51, No. 2, based on a poem by Jean Richepin, and to Opus 7, No. 1, based on a poem by Romain Bussine.

5. *Corr.* 1:375. The "serenade pleasers" refer to *Mandoline,* Fauré's Opus 58, No. 1 (1891), the first of the *Cinq Mélodies* known as the "Venice" melodies, based on poems by Verlaine. The Reynaldo Hahn melody based on the same poem is entitled *Fêtes galantes* (April 1892). See *Mélodies* (Paris: Heugel, 1893), 1:47.

6. Letter of July 1907 to Reynaldo Hahn, *Corr.* 7:211–12.

7. See George D. Painter, *Marcel Proust: A Biography,* 2 vols. (1959; rpt. [New York: Random House, 1978]), 2:243. See also an April 1916 letter to the violinist Raymond Pétain, *Corr.* 15:77; and a May 1916 letter to Gaston Poulet, *Corr.* 15:83. Cf. Gabriel Fauré, *Correspondance,* 209–10.

8. Carnet 3, fol. 43v. Like the Quatuor Poulet, the Quatuor Capet, which specialized, among other things, in Beethoven's late quartets, came to play at Proust's apartment on the Boulevard Haussmann during the war.

9. Cahier 49, fol. 21r; Esquisse VIII.

10. Fauré, *Correspondance,* 96.

11. Jean-Michel Nectoux, *Fauré* (Paris: Seuil, "Solfèges," 1972), 38.

12. Jean-Michel Nectoux, *Fauré,* 40.

13. Vladimir Jankélévich, *Fauré et l'Inexprimable* (Paris: Plon, 1974), 110.

14. *Matinée chez la princesse de Guermantes. Cahiers du "Temps retrouvé,"* ed. Henri Bonnet and Bernard Brun (Paris: Gallimard, 1982), 292; Cahier 57, fol. 3r.

3. *"Racine is more immoral!"*

1. In Cahier 49 from 1910–1911, only Walter Scott and Baudelaire are cited (fol. 53r); Sully Prudhomme and Musset are then invoked, and the invert finds equal solace. In another context (fols. 56–57r), inverts "interpret the great books of the past in the light of their obsession, and they find in Montaigne, Gérard de Nerval [Molière is crossed out], and Stendhal a sentence about a rather warm friendship, and are convinced that in them they had a brother" (3:950; Esquisse IV).

2. The two hemistiches are inverted.

3. On the corrected typescript one can read: "lines of Racine that I had quoted in quite a different sense."

4. N.a.fr. 16728, fols. 43–46.

5. Cahier II, fol. 54r.

6. This passage is from an insert missing from the manuscript and belonging to the Reliquat du Fonds Marcel Proust at the Bibliothèque Nationale.

7. Cahier II, fol. 33r.

8. Cahier II, fols. 33r–34r.

9. Proust attended the dress rehearsal on February 13, 1910; see letter of February 15 to Georges de Lauris, *Corr.* 10:49–50.

10. The last sentence quoted introduces lines 101–6 of *Esther*. Lines 122, 124,

and 125 are added in the margin. Lines 90 and 92 belong to another addition. Except for the switching of lines 123 and 125, these are the lines that were to appear in the definitive version of the episode.

11. Cahier IV, fol. 43r.

12. N.a.fr. 16739, fol. 42. In this back-and-forth movement there is obviously a reticence on Proust's part to attribute to his protagonist the parallel between the Grand Hotel and Racine's choruses; further evidence for this comes in this late notation from Cahier 61 (fol. 42r): "[It would probably be better (*crossed out*)] [It would perhaps be (?) (*interlinear addition crossed out*)] [to attribute the whole (*crossed out*)] piece from Cahier IV *bis* where I compare the hotel in Balbec to Solomon's Temple to Monsieur de Charlus, for example when I chat with him at the Princesse de Guermantes' when he says to me 'Here are Esther's superb gardens' he could say: 'By the way you did not return to Athalie's temple.' For once he condescended to explain what he meant. 'You know, the hotel in Balbec.' 'Indeed,' I said to him, 'I noticed the performance aspect when the public is allowed in (as in Cahier IV *bis*).' 'But especially this whole "tribe of lovers," this whole "young and timid" troupe of page boys. I find that really awful. They look like little girls. They put on a thousand affectations. But in the end the decorative aspect is interesting.' Then would come the piece from Cahier IV *bis* attributed to Charlus." Cahier IV *bis* is Cahier IV of the manuscript in an earlier numbering system; it is meant to go at the end of Cahier III. Proust thus proposes getting rid of the second appearance of the theme in Cahier IV, in which the hero is responsible for the analogy, and joining it to Charlus' initial comparison of his cousin's gardens and Esther's.

13. N.a.fr. 16739, fols. 99–103; see 3:1473 (3:236, var. b).

14. Cahier IV, fols. 139–41.

15. N.a.fr. 16740, fol. 120. A first version of this marginal addition is found in Cahier 61, fol. 41r, a notebook of additions from the end of the war. This dates the moment when the Nissim Bernard episode is dissociated from the Charlus episode.

16. Cahier VI, fol. 6. The insert was torn out, but it can be found in the Reliquat du Fonds Marcel Proust in the Bibliothèque Nationale.

17. The transition leading back to the Baron was this on the manuscript insert: "But at this evening hour Monsieur Nissim Bernard was not there, but among his own, like a good kinsman, and Monsieur de Charlus would have been able to seduce the lover of his brother-in-law Marsantes' old friend. This competition with Monsieur Bernard might have made him pay more attention to the young Jew. But being unaware of it, he found the young man too feminine; this was not what Monsieur de Charlus desired but rather men, fully grown men" (3:1561 [3:375, var. d]). This same objection already followed the description of the young Hippolyte, before the Nissim Bernard episode, which shows that the narrative is an addition to the addition. Moreover, the allusion, in this context, to Nissim Bernard's friendship with Monsieur de Marsantes, Saint-Loup's father, mentioned only twice in the definitive text (1:831–32; 2:133–34 and 2:286; 2:573), gives a particular meaning to this relationship.

18. See 1:758–59; 2:66, which I shall discuss below.

19. On the Vaugoubert insert lines 101–6, 122, 124, 125, and 90–92 of *Esther* were quoted. Lines 122–25 and 112 are on the Charlus and Nissim Bernard insert.

20. Jacques Nathan, *Citations, références et allusions de Proust dans "A la recherche du temps perdu"* (1953; 2d ed. [Paris: Nizet, 1969]), 23. On Proust and Racine, see René de Chantal, *Marcel Proust, critique littéraire* (Montreal: Presses de l'université de Montréal, 1967); François Kessedjian, "Proust et Racine," *Europe* (February–March 1971).

21. Cahier 49, fol. 46r; Esquisse IV.

22. Carnet 3, fol. 2r–2v.

23. Edwin E. Williams, *Racine depuis 1885. Bibliographie raisonnée* (Paris: Belles-Lettres, 1940).

24. Marcel Proust, *Contre Sainte-Beuve* suivi de *Nouveaux Mélanges,* ed. Bernard de Fallois (Paris: Gallimard, 1954), 127–28.

25. See Henry Bidou, "*Esther* au Théâtre Sarah-Bernhardt," *L'Année dramatique, 1911–1912* (Paris: Hachette, 1912), 32–40.

26. See A. Hermant, "Odéon: *Esther, princesse juive,*" *Essais de critique* (Paris: Grasset, 1912), 262–66. Jeanne Dieulafoy, the well-known French archaeologist, brought back the "bowmen's frieze" (which is now in the Louvre) from digs she conducted in Persia between 1881 and 1886.

27. Henry Bordeaux, "Odéon: *Esther,* drame en quatre actes et en vers," *La Vie au théâtre, 1911–1913,* 3d series (Paris: Plon-Nourrit, 1913), 126.

28. Emile Deschanel, *Le Romantisme des classiques,* 2d series, *Racine* (Paris: Calmann-Lévy, 1884), 2 vols, 1:39. Cf. Brunetière, "De l'interprétation du répertoire tragique," *Revue des Deux Mondes,* April 15, 1880.

29. *Jean Santeuil,* précédé de *Les Plaisirs et les jours,* ed. Pierre Clarac et Yves Sandre (Paris: Gallimard, Pléiade, 1971), 240. Subsequent references to this work, abbreviated JS, will be given in the body of the text.

30. See also *Recherche* 1:97; 1:90.

31. Paul de Saint-Victor, *Les Deux Masques,* vol. 3, *Les Modernes* (Paris: Calmann-Lévy, 1884), 3:393.

32. Jules Lemaitre, *Racine* (Paris: Calmann-Lévy, 1908), 279.

33. Saint-Victor, *Les Deux Masques* 3:399. Cf. Jules Lemaitre, *Racine,* 283.

34. Henry Bidou, *L'Année dramatique, 1911–1912,* 38.

35. A.-E. Marty, "*Esther* à l'Odéon et chez Sarah-Bernhardt," *Comoedia illustré* (March 15, 1912): 454–55.

36. *Contre Sainte-Beuve,* ed. Fallois, 129.

37. In Stendhal, *Oeuvres complètes,* ed. P. Martino (Paris: Cercle du bibliophile, 1970), 37:40.

38. Ibid., 37:39.

39. For Stendhal's role in defining our concept of modernity, see Hans Robert Jauss, "Literarische Tradition und gegenwärtiges Bewusstsein der Modernität: Wortgeschichtliche Betrachtungen," in *Aspekte der Modernität,* ed. Hans Steffen (Göttingen: Vandenhoek and Ruprecht, 1965).

40. See Jean-Jacques Roubine, *Lectures de Racine* (Paris: Armand Colin, 1971).

41. Proust-Rivière, *Correspondance, 1914–1922,* ed. Philip Kolb (Paris: Gallimard, 1976), 166–67.

42. Proust-Rivière, *Correspondance,* 169 and 172.

43. As Gilbert Lély points out in his *La Vie du Marquis de Sade* (Paris: Jean-Jacques Pauvert, 1965), "The twenty-two lines of *Britannicus* (act 2, scene 2) in which the emperor recites to Narcisse the birth of his love for Junie offer us, without our being aware of it, a gripping portrait of sadomasochistic inspiration" (115 n. 1).

44. Quoted by Jean Pommier, *Aspects de Racine* (Paris: Nizet, 1954), 341.

45. Victor Stapfer, *Racine et Victor Hugo* (Paris: Armand Colin, 1887). In *A l'ombre des jeunes filles en fleurs,* Saint-Loup, a defender of Victor Hugo, squabbles with his uncle, Charlus, who sides with Racine (1:819–20; 2:122)

46. Ferdinand Brunetière, "La tragédie de Racine" (*Revue des Deux Mondes,* 1884), *Histoire et Littérature* (Paris: Calmann-Lévy, 1884), vol. 2.

47. Ferdinand Brunetière, "Les Ennemis de Racine au XVIIe siècle" (*Revue des Deux Mondes,* 1879), *Etudes critiques,* 1st series (1880; 4th ed., Paris: Hachette, 1896). The review is of Félix Deltour, *Les Ennemis de Racine au XVIIe siècle* (Paris: Didier, 1859 and 1865), published by Hachette in 1879 and reprinted in 1884, 1892, and 1898.

48. André Ferré, *Les Années de collège de Marcel Proust* (Paris: Gallimard, 1959), 180. Reynaldo Hahn was to say years later, "Since I had no voice, I spent my days reading *Les Ennemis de Racine,* an amusing book and a useful one for all those who are involved in the field of theatrical production." *Notes (Journal d'un musicien)* (Paris: Plon, 1933), 108.

49. Brunetière, *Etudes critiques,* 1st series, 165.

50. Ibid., 171.

51. Brunetière, "Le Naturalisme au XVIIe siècle," *Etudes critiques,* 1st series, 318.

52. Ferré, *Les Années de collège de Marcel Proust,* 185.

53. Ibid., 187.

54. Ibid., 185.

55. Ibid., 186.

56. Lemaitre, *Racine,* 248.

57. Charles Baudelaire, "Mon coeur mis à nu," in OC 1:677.

58. Louis Veuillot, *Les Odeurs de Paris* (Paris: Palmé, 1867).

59. Joseph Joubert, *Carnets* (Paris: Gallimard, 1938), 2 vols., 2:679.

60. Ibid., 2:740–41.

61. See Lemaitre, *Racine,* 323–24.

62. Lemaitre, *Racine,* 314.

63. Gustave Lanson, *Histoire de la littérature française* (1895; rpt. [Paris: Hachette, 1951]), 546–47.

64. Brunetière, *Histoire et littérature* 2:1–2.

65. Ibid., 17.

66. Ibid., 11–12.

67. Ibid., 12.

68. Ibid., 14.

69. André Suarès, *Sur la vie* (Paris: Collection de la Grande Revue, 1909), 1:144.

70. Charles Péguy, *Victor-Marie, Comte Hugo* (1911), in *Oeuvres en prose, 1909–1914* (Paris: Gallimard, Pléiade, 1961), 777 and 781.

71. Ibid., 774.

72. Ibid., 789.

73. Ibid., 777.

74. Proust subscribed to Péguy's *Cahiers de la Quinzaine*, but he found it such a "hodge-podge" that he probably did not read very much of it. (Letter of April 1921 to Jacques Boulenger, *Corr. gén.* 3:238.)

75. Quoted by Pommier, *Aspects de Racine*, 210.

76. Letter of April or May 1905 to Madame Fortoul, *Corr.* 5:127.

77. *Le Temps*, April 14, 1889. *La Vie littéraire*, 1891, 3d series; in Anatole France, *Oeuvres complètes* (Paris: Calmann-Lévy, 1926), 7:32–39.

78. *Revue des Deux Mondes*, June 1, 1887, 697.

79. France, *Oeuvres complètes*, 33.

80. Ibid., 36.

81. Ibid., 39.

82. Letter of November 1920, *Corr. gén.* 3:86.

83. André Gide, *Journal, 1889–1939* (Paris: Gallimard, Pléiade, 1951), 692.

84. This is Claude Pichois' thesis; see Baudelaire, OC 1:793–94.

85. This harsh judgment of Morel turns out to be more nuanced and ambiguous in the novel.

86. Letter of January 4, 1921, to Charles Bugnet, *Bulletin de la Société des Amis de Marcel Proust* 3 (1953):13.

87. Baudelaire, "Mon coeur mis à nu," OC 1:678.

4. Huysmans, or Reading the Italian Renaissance Perversely

1. See Mario Praz, *The Romantic Agony*, trans. Angus Davidson (1933; rpt. [London: Oxford University Press, 1954]), 339.

2. "Bianchi," *Certains* (1889; rpt. 3d ed. [Paris: Stock, 1898]), 220; subsequent references to this work will be given in the body of the text. In his review of *Certains*, Jean Lorrain draws attention to this final chapter: "The whole book is crowned by the most disturbing piece of literature which has perhaps ever been written since d'Aurevilly and Baudelaire, about a painting in the Louvre by Bianchi." *Du temps que les bêtes parlaient. Portraits littéraires et mondains* (Paris: Courrier français, n.d. [1911]), 222.

3. Francesco Marmitta, *Virgin and Child between St. Benoît and St. Quentin*, Louvre Museum, Inventory no. 116. Huysmans attributes the painting to Francesco Bianchi, as does Théophile Gautier who, in spite of his sensitivity to androgyny, describes it quite blandly: "The saint is bare-headed, with a juvenile, proud head, and he looks more like a knight errant than one blessed by God." *Guide de l'amateur du musée du Louvre* (Paris: Charpentier, 1882), 81.

4. Preface to Abbé J.-C. Broussole, *La Jeunesse du Pérugin et les origines de l'école ombrienne* (Paris: Oudin, 1901), vii.

5. Preface to *La Jeunesse du Pérugin,* iv.

6. Preface to *La Jeunesse du Pérugin,* vii.

7. Reported by Gustave Coquiot, *Le Vrai J.-K. Huysmans* (Paris: Bosse, 1912), 91.

8. Huysmans, "Noëls du Louvre," *L'Echo de Paris,* December 28, 1898; in *De tout* (Paris: Plon-Nourrit, 1901), 138.

9. In Elstir's mythological works, the poet similarly belongs to a race "characterised by a certain sexlessness" (2:437; 2:714–15).

10. Gustave Moreau, copy of Francesco Marmitta, but classified according to the attribution of the times "Biancho dei Frari G. M.," no. 4715, *Catalogue des dessins de Gustave Moreau. Musée Gustave Moreau,* established by P. Bittler and P.-L. Mathieu (Paris: Réunion des Musées nationaux, 1983).

11. Cahier 46, fols. 58v and 94r; Esquisse XVII.

12. Cahier 46, fol. 58v, insert; Esquisse XVII.

13. Cahier 46, fol. 58v, marginal addition; Esquisse XVII, var. a.

14. See Gérard Genette, "Métonymie chez Proust," *Figures III* (Paris: Seuil, 1972).

15. Cahier 71, fol. 9v; Esquisse XVI.

16. K.-J. Huysmans, *A rebours,* ed. Marc Fumaroli (2d ed., Paris: Gallimard, Folio, 1983), 153. Further references to *A rebours* will be given in the body of the text.

17. J.-K. Huysmans, *Curieuse* (Paris: Laurent, 1886), 6.

18. Ibid., 7–8.

19. Ibid., 7.

20. Ibid., 49.

21. J.-K. Huysmans, *A coeur perdu* (Paris: Edinger, 1888), 26.

22. Honoré de Balzac, *La Maison Nucingen,* in *La Comédie humaine,* ed. Pierre-Georges Castex (Paris: Gallimard, Pléiade, 1976–81), 6:348.

23. Honoré de Balzac, *La Comédie humaine,* 6:344–45.

24. Honoré de Balzac, *Les Secrets de la princesse de Cadignan,* in *La Comédie humaine,* 6:953.

25. "Over the nakedness of her firm and luminous breasts, just below the neck, there is passed a band as of metal." The description immediately suggests the image of Medusa: "Her hair, close and curled, seems ready to shudder in sunder and divide into snakes." Algernon Charles Swinburne, "Notes on Designs of the Old Masters at Florence," *Essays and Studies* (London: Chatto and Windus, 1875), 319–20. See Praz, *The Romantic Agony,* 239–41.

26. J.-K. Huysmans, "Le Salon officiel de 1880," *L'Art moderne* (Paris: Charpentier, 1883), 136–37.

27. There are in fact several heroines with this name.

28. Quoted by Praz, *The Romantic Agony,* 320.

29. Cahier 43, fol. 56v; Esquisse VI.

30. Cahier 24, fols. 8r–9r; Esquisse IX.

31. Cahier 47, fol. 23r; Esquisse XI.

32. Cahier 46, fol. 97r, marginal addition; Esquisse XVII, var. a.

5. *Tableaux Vivants* in the Novel

1. Cahier 60, fols. 70–74. Typescript: N.a.fr. 16739, fols. 1–2.

2. Quoted by Jean-Denis Bredin, *L'Affaire* (Paris: Julliard, 1983), 248.

3. For the manuscript, see Cahier 3, fol. 9. For the typescript, see N.a.fr. 16728, fol. 108.

4. George D. Painter, *Marcel Proust: A Biography,* 2 vols. (1959; rpt. [New York: Random House, 1978]), 1:101–4.

5. Cahier 24, fols. 3–7.

6. Cahier 47, fols. 22r–35r; Esquisse XI.

7. Abel Hermant, *La Mission de Cruchod* (Paris: Dentu, 1885), reprinted under the title *Le Disciple aimé* (Paris: Ollendorff, 1895).

8. Cahier 47, fols. 12r–15r; Esquisse XI.

9. Carnet 1, fol. 51r; Esquisse XII; *Le Carnet de 1908,* ed. Philip Kolb (Paris: Gallimard, Cahiers Marcel Proust, 1976), 120. Cahier 51, fol. 7r; Esquisse II; *Matinée chez la princesse de Guermantes. Cahiers du "Temps retrouvé,"* ed. Henri Bonnet and Bernard Brun (Paris: Gallimard, 1982), 51.

10. Cahier 47, fols. 22r -23r; Esquisse XI.

11. Cahier 46, fol. 97r; Esquisse XVII.

12. Cahier 57, fol. 40r; *Matinée chez la princesse de Guermantes,* 377.

13. Cahier 49, fol. 49v; Esquisse IV. For the resemblance between Madame de Marsantes and her other brother, the Duc de Guermantes, see *Le Côté de Guermantes I* (2:258; 2:547).

14. For the manuscript, see Cahier 1, fols. 58–59. For the uncorrected carbon copy of the first typescript, see N.a.fr. 16738, fol. 46. For the second typescript: N.a.fr. 16738, fol. 74.

15. French trans. and preface E. Heckel (Paris: Reinwald, 1878).

16. Darwin, *Des différentes formes de fleurs,* trans. and preface E. Heckel, xxxiii.

17. Cahier 6, fol. 41r; Esquisse I.

18. Victor Hugo, *Les Voix intérieures,* XI; quoted 2:650; 3:28. Reynaldo Hahn composed his melody at the age of fourteen, in 1888, under the title *Rêveries,* in *Mélodies* (Paris: Heugel, 1892), 1:1. Fauré had also set this poem to music (Opus 10, No. 1 [1874]). Proust also quotes the poem in a sketch for "The race of fairies" in *Contre Sainte-Beuve:* 3:938, Esquisse II; Cahier 51, fol. 7v; *Matinée chez la princesse de Guermantes,* 54.

19. Cahier 43, Esquisse VI; and Cahier 49, Esquisse VIII.

20. Cahier 49, fols. 12r–13r; Esquisse VIII.

21. Letter of September 1921 to Gaston Gallimard. In *Lettres à la NRF* (Paris: Gallimard, 1932), 158.

22. See Kazuyoshi Yoshikawa, "Marcel Proust en 1908," in *Etudes de langue et littérature françaises* 22 (1973).

23. Carnet 1, fol. 10v; *Le Carnet de 1908,* 60.

24. Carnet 1, fol. 11r; *Le Carnet de 1908,* 61.
25. Carnet 1, fol. 12r; *Le Carnet de 1908,* 63.
26. Carnet 1, fol. 2r; *Le Carnet de 1908,* 47; Esquisse XII.
27. Cahier 50, fol. 15r; Esquisse XIII.
28. Carnet 1, fol. 3v; *Le Carnet de 1908,* 50; Esquisse XII.
29. Cahier 48, fols. 50v–51v; Esquisse XIII.
30. Carnet 1, fol. 4r; *Le Carnet de 1908,* 50–51; Esquisse XII.
31. Cahier 50, fols. 31r–34r; 3:1045–46, Esquisse XIII.
32. Carnet 1, fol. 5v; *Le Carnet de 1908,* 53.
33. Carnet 1, fols. 50r–51v; *Le Carnet de 1908,* 118–20; Esquisse XII.
34. Carnet 1, fol. 54r; *Le Carnet de 1908,* 124.
35. Carnet 50, fol. 23v; Esquisse XIII.
36. Cahier 50, fol. 26r; Esquisse XIII.
37. Cahier 48, fols. 48r–49r; Esquisse XIII.
38. N.a.fr. 16739, fol. 28.
39. N.a.fr. 16711, fol. 33.
40. *Le Carnet de 1908,* 69.
41. Paris, Lemerre, 1877.
42. Letter to Henri Ghéon, January 1914, *Corr.* 13:26; letter to Paul Souday, November 1919, *Corr. gén.* 3:69.
43. Liliane Fearn, "Sur un rêve de Marcel," *Bulletin de la Société des Amis de Marcel Proust* 17 (1967): 535–49.
44. Cahier 26, fols. 15–21. See *Du côté de chez Swann,* ed. Antoine Compagnon (Paris: Gallimard, Folio, 1988), 437.
45. Alain Roger, *Proust. Les plaisirs et les noms* (Paris: Denoël, 1985), 85.
46. Gérard Genette, *Figures III* (Paris: Seuil, 1972), 199.

6. *"This shuddering of a heart being hurt"*

1. Maurice Sachs, *Le Sabbat* (1946; rpt. [Paris: Gallimard, 1960]), 198. André Gide apparently heard Proust himself speak of the role played by "chasing rats" when he was trying to reach orgasm. *Ainsi soit-il,* in *Journal, 1939–1949. Souvenirs* (Paris: Gallimard, Pléiade, 1954), 1223. For the testimony of a male prostitute later frequented by Marcel Jouhandeau, see Henri Bonnet, *Les Amours et la sexualité de Marcel Proust* (Paris: Nizet, 1985), 79ff.
2. Paris: Doin, 1888.
3. Mario Praz, *The Romantic Agony,* trans. Angus Davidson (1933; rpt. [London: Oxford University Press, 1954]), 142–43.
4. On the subject of Proust and evil, see especially Henri Massis, *Le Drame de Marcel Proust* (Paris: Grasset, 1937).
5. Cahier 50, fol. 19r; Esquisse XIII.
6. Charles Baudelaire, letter of March 17, 1862. In *Correspondance,* ed. Claude Pichois and Jean Ziegler, 2 vols. (Paris: Gallimard, Pléiade, 1973), 2:234.
7. See two books by Georges Blin, *Baudelaire* (Paris: Gallimard, 1939) and *Le Sadisme de Baudelaire* (Paris: José Corti, 1948). On Proust and Baudelaire, see

especially René Galand, "Proust et Baudelaire," *PMLA* 65 (1950): 1011–34; and René de Chantal, *Marcel Proust, critique littéraire* (Montreal: Presses de l'Université de Montréal, 1967), particularly 2:438–58.

8. This is reminiscent of a scene from Ernest Feydeau's *Fanny,* in which the heroine seduces her husband while her lover watches from the balcony. *Fanny* (Paris: Amyot, 1858), 227–28.

9. Marcel Proust, *Contre Sainte-Beuve* followed by *Nouveaux Mélanges,* ed. Bernard de Fallois (Paris: Gallimard, 1954), 282.

10. Georges Blin, *Le Sadisme de Baudelaire,* 16.

11. Letter of 1865 to Louis Marcelin, *Corr.* 2:465.

12. Proust is probably alluding to an anecdote about Nero told by Emile Mâle in his demonstration of the influence of *La Légende dorée* on medieval iconography. Nero "married one of his freedmen, and he is absolutely insistent that his doctors must find a way to allow him to have a baby; and indeed, by means of a potion, he gave birth to a frog that he had brought up in his palace." Emile Mâle, *L'Art religieux du XIIIème siècle en France* (Paris: Ernest Leroux, 1898), 379.

13. Cesare Lombroso, *L'Homme de génie,* French translation [of the sixth Italian edition] by François Colonna d'Istria (Paris: Alcan, 1889), 92–95. See Philippe Roger, "Au nom de Sade," in *Obliques* 12–13 (1977): 23–27. Given the variety of meanings that Proust gives to the words *sadisme* and *sadique,* the author concludes that Proust goes beyond Krafft-Ebing's definitions and begins to move toward modern polymorphism. But Proust often and willingly identifies sadism with perverted sensitivity; this larger definition of sadism, which includes masochism and fetishism, among other concepts, is not, of course, true to Sade, but it does actually conform to the current medical beliefs at the turn of the century.

14. Carnet 1, fol. 12v; *Le Carnet de 1908,* 63.

15. Ferdinand Brunetière, *Revue des Deux Mondes,* June 1, 1887, 696–97.

16. Georges Bataille, *Oeuvres complètes* (Paris: Gallimard, 1979), 10:267. Bataille's discussion is taken from his article "Marcel Proust et la mère profanée," in *Critique* 7 (December 1946): 601–11.

17. Cf. "Préface de *Tendres Stocks*" and "A propos de Baudelaire," in CSB 609 and 627.

18. Georges Blin, *Le Sadisme de Baudelaire,* 38.

7. "The sun radiating out over the sea"; or, the Uneven Epithet

1. Charles Sainte-Beuve, *Volupté,* ed. André Guyaux (Paris: Gallimard, Folio, 1986), 209.

2. John Ruskin, *Sesame and Lilies,* French trans. *Sésame et les Lys,* trans. Marcel Proust (Paris: Mercure de France, 1906), 94 n. 1.

3. "Critique du roman de M. Gustave Flaubert sur l''Affaire Lemoine' par Sainte-Beuve," *Pastiches et Mélanges,* CSB 16. Proust did two pastiches of Sainte-Beuve, one published (CSB 16–20), the other in the form of a draft in Carnet 1 (CSB 195–96). See Jean Milly, *Les Pastiches de Proust* (Paris: Armand Colin, 1970), 108–10.

4. Cahier 46, fols. 74v–75v; 3:1084, Esquisse XVII. About the quotation of Sully Prudhomme, see chapter 2 above.

5. John Ruskin, *Sesame and Lilies: Three Lectures* (Philadelphia: Henry Altemus, 1893), 56. Proust's translation, "un plus petit nombre fera le travail," can be found in *Sésame et les Lys,* 90.

6. Ruskin, *Sesame and Lilies,* trans. Proust, 90 n. 1.

7. Opus 5, No. 1 (1875).

8. Thanks to André Bon for his help in this analysis.

9. *Les Chants du crépuscule,* XXVII. This is Fauré's first melody: Opus 1, No. 1 (1862). See chapter 5.

10. Opus 8, No. 3 (1877).

11. Opus 58, No. 1 (1891), *Mandoline,* first of the *Cinq Mélodies* ("Venise"), based on poems by Verlaine.

12. *Fêtes galantes* (April 1892), *Mélodies* 1:47.

13. George D. Painter, *Marcel Proust: A Biography,* 2 vols. (1959; rpt. [New York: Random House, 1978]), 1:166.

14. The first line of the second stanza, "Tout l'hiver va rentrer dans mon être," is also quoted in a letter to Léon Yeatman in December 1893 (*Corr.* 1:265).

15. The sentence is reminiscent of Sainte-Beuve; Proust noted several similar expressions of his in Carnet 1 in 1908. See *Le Carnet de 1908,* 71, 81, 91.

16. In August 1905, Proust quotes in its entirety the fifth stanza of the poem in a letter to Louisa de Mornand, who is in Trouville (*Corr.* 5:331). A letter from June 1914 to Henry Bordeaux again juxtaposes the Verlaine line and a variation of the first line of the second stanza of "Chant d'automne," "The whole winter is entering my being" (*Corr.* 13:243).

17. Cahier 38, fol. 3v; Esquisse XXXIV.

18. Cahier 46, fol. 74v; Esquisse XVII.

19. Carnet 1, fol. 10v; *Le Carnet de 1908,* 60.

20. The poem was not divided up in the prepublication version that appeared in the *Revue Contemporaine* in 1859. See OC, 1:934.

21. There are in fact occasions when Proust quotes lines from "Chant d'automne" that are not used in Fauré's song, for example, "The whole winter is entering my being" (*Corr.* 1:265), or "the gentle yellow ray of autumn's end" (*Corr.* 4:349). For other quotations from stanzas 2 and 7 of the poem not used in Fauré's song, see the section "September Poetry" earlier in this chapter.

22. *La Minerve Française,* February 1, 1920, 291–96.

23. These words of Rosny aîné, reported by Jules Renard, are a fine example of the fashion for unusual adjectives: "In *Les Corneilles,* . . . I said 'the dichotomous moon' so as to avoid saying 'the half-moon,' which is a disgusting image" (Jules Renard, *Journal* [Paris: Gallimard, Pléiade, 1960], 127).

24. Sainte-Beuve, *Nouveaux Lundis* (Paris: Michel Lévy, 1868), 10:410. Quoted in Halévy's article about Sainte-Beuve for *La Minerve Française,* 294.

25. Quoted by André Guyaux, *Volupté,* 14.

26. *Volupté,* 329. For an analysis of the language of *Volupté,* see Charles Bruneau, *L'Epoque romantique,* in Ferdinand Brunot, *Histoire de la langue française*

des origines à nos jours (Paris: Armand Colin, 1948), 12:330–36. See also Yves Le Hir, *L'Originalité littéraire de Sainte-Beuve dans "Volupté"* (Paris: SEDES, 1953).

27. George Sand, *Correspondance,* ed. Georges Lubin (Paris: Garnier, 1966), 2:713.

28. *Volupté,* 276. The same references to Homer appear in Raphaël Molho, ed., *Le Cahier vert, 1834–47* (Paris: Gallimard, 1973), 143 and 237.

29. *Volupté,* 63.

30. "Préface à *Tendres Stocks*" and "A propos de Baudelaire" (CSB 609 and 627).

31. *Le Carnet de 1908,* 68.

32. Ibid., 71, 85, 90, 93.

33. Ibid., 93.

34. Baudelaire, *Corr.* 2:219.

35. See "Journées de lecture," *Pastiches et Mélanges,* CSB 169.

36. Cahier 28, fols. 33r–34r; Daniela De Agostini, Maurizio Ferraris, and Bernard Brun, *L'Età dei nomi. Quaderni della "Recherche"* (Milan: Mondadori, 1985), 249.

37. Cahier 28, fol. 34r.

38. *Nouveaux Lundis,* 10:410–11, quoted by Halévy, 294–95.

39. *Sésame et les Lys,* 95 (end of note 1 on 93) (1906); "A propos de Baudelaire," CSB 627 (1921).

40. Walter Benjamin, "Central Park," in *New German Critique* 34 (Winter 1985):40–41.

41. "[Gérard de Nerval]," CSB 235. Cf. "A propos de Baudelaire," CSB 638. The poems quoted are "La Chevelure" and "Un hémisphère dans une chevelure."

42. Carnet 1, fol. 13v; *Le Carnet de 1908,* 65.

43. "Journées de lecture," *Pastiches et Mélanges,* CSB 192. Proust meets Boileau, who used to say of the line, "Je t'aimais inconstant, qu'aurais-je fait fidèle!": "Where would Racine be if we squabbled about this lovely line of poetry . . . ? This kind of small poetic license in syntax, far from being an error, often leads to some of the greatest charms of poetry." Boileau, letter to Brossette, August 2, 1703, quoted in Racine, *Théâtre complet,* ed. Jean-Pierre Collinet (Paris: Gallimard, Folio, 1982), 1:496. Proust will see a classicist in Baudelaire, a brother of Racine, precisely because of this sort of daring line that goes beyond the classical doctrine.

44. *Sésame et les Lys,* 85 n. 1.

45. Cahier 28, fol. 33r; *L'Età dei nomi,* 249.

8. Brichot: Etymology and Allegory

1. Joseph Vendryes, "Marcel Proust et les noms propres" (1940), in *Choix d'études linguistiques et celtiques* (Paris: Klincksieck, 1952), 85.

2. Jean Cocteau, *Le Passé défini, 1951–1952* (Paris: Gallimard, 1983), 1:272.

3. The first work on this topic was André Ferré, *Géographie de Marcel Proust* (Paris: Sagittaire, 1939).

4. For a good bibliography on the subject, see Marianne Mulon, *L'Onomastique française* (Paris: La Documentation française, 1977).

5. Maurice Barrès, *Huit jours chez M. Renan,* in *L'Oeuvre de Maurice Barrès* (Paris: Club de l'honnête homme, 1965–1969), 2:314.

6. Arthur Giry, *Manuel de diplomatique* (Paris: Hachette, 1894), 378. The first three names on this list will be discussed later on. The fourth is the only one to have proposed a real hypothesis: see Henry d'Arbois de Jubainville, *Recherches sur l'origine de la propriété foncière et des noms de lieux habités en France* (Paris: Thorin, 1890).

7. Jules Quicherat, *De la Formation française des anciens noms de lieu* (Paris: Franck, 1867). Jacques Nathan pointed this out. See *Citations, Références et Allusions de Proust,* 17, and "Marcel Proust et Jules Quicherat," *Cahiers de lexicologie* 23 (1973): 118–20. Victor E. Graham is mistaken in contesting this. See "Proust's Etymologies," *French Studies* (July 1975): 300–312.

8. Quicherat, *De la Formation française des anciens noms de lieu,* 61.

9. Ibid., 66.

10. Ibid., 67.

11. Ibid., 38.

12. Ibid., 37 and 57.

13. Ibid., 59.

14. Joseph Marquis, *Illiers,* Chartres, "Archives du diocèse de Chartres," vol. 12, "Monographies paroissiales," vol. 2 (1907). The work first appeared as a volume of the series *Archives historiques du diocèse de Chartres* 111, 10th year (March 25, 1904). Proust mentions it in a June 1913 letter to Max Daireaux (*Corr.* 12:209).

15. Marquis, *Illiers,* 280; cf. "Combray," 1:52; 1:48.

16. Ibid., 28.

17. Ibid., 36.

18. Gérard Genette, "L'âge des noms," in *Mimologiques* (Paris: Seuil, 1976), 315–28.

19. Claudine Quémar, "Rêveries onomastiques proustiennes," in R. Debray-Genette, ed., *Essais de critique génétique* (Paris: Flammarion, 1979), 69–102.

20. On this point my interpretation diverges from Gérard Genette's in "Proust et le langage indirect." In Genette's judgment, Brichot's etymologies, "by reestablish[ing] the disappointing truth of historical filiation, of phonetic erosion, in short of the diachronic dimension of language," fascinate the hero "because they put the finishing touches on the destruction of his earlier beliefs and begin to fill him with the healthy disenchantment brought by truth." *Figures II* (1969; rpt. [Paris: Seuil, "Points," 1979]), 245–46. Brichot's etymologies do indeed come into play after the hero has become disenchanted. Probably they confirm that disenchantment was inevitable, but they also confuse the duality separating names and things, illusion and disillusionment, as we will attempt to demonstrate. They reinstill names with mystery, and give them a different sort of depth.

21. See also what Legrandin says later about the area around Balbec, 1:417; 1:377.

22. Cahier V, fol. 52r.

23. N.a.fr. 16740, fol. 31.

24. Cahier V, fols. 77r–89r.

25. Cahier V, fol. 79r.

26. In addition to these three lengthy developments of this theme, a few isolated etymologies are given here and there in parentheses after the place-name. There are nine in all, only three of them found in the manuscript version, the others having been added to the typescript: "Fervaches," from "fervidae aquae" (2:923; 3:286); "La Sogne," from "Siconia" (2:924; 3:287); "Englesqueville," from "Engleberti Villa" (2:928; 3:291); "Epreville," from "Sprevilla" or "Aprivilla" (2:1026; 3:383); "Saint-Fargeau," from "Sanctus Ferreolus" (2:1028; 3:384); "Parville," from "Paterni villa" (2:1037 and 1147; 3:393 and 495); "Maineville," from "media villa" (2:1112; 3:463); and "Egleville," from "Aquilaevilla" (2:1147; 3:495). Also notable is the passage that forms a sort of coda to the theme: Monsieur de Charlus rails against Jews who commit a kind of sacrilege by living in places with the most Christian of names, like "La Commanderie," "Le Temple" [Protestant Church], "Pont-l'Evêque," and "Pont-l'Abbé" (2:1141–42; 3:490).

27. Cahier V, fol. 79r.

28. Cahier VI, fol. 109r.

29. Librairie de l'Echo de la Sorbonne, 1874 and 1875; Delagrave, 1885. Arthur Giry quotes an undated edition that is in fact from 1869 (*Manuel de diplomatique,* 378).

30. Longnon, *Les Noms de lieu de la France* (Paris: Champion, 1920–1929), 4.

31. Carnet 2, fol. 54r.

32. Carnet 2, fol. 59v.

33. Cahier 54, fol. 34v.

34. Despite Richard Bales' assertions in *Proust and the Middle Ages* (Geneva: Droz, 1975), 141–43.

35. Carnet 4, fols. 51v and r.

36. Cahier 72, fol. 34v and fol. 35, marginal addition.

37. Cahier VI, fol. 7r. This page is torn out of the manuscript and is a part of the Reliquat du Fonds Marcel Proust at the Bibliothèque Nationale.

38. Edélestand and Alfred Duméril, *Dictionnaire du patois normand* (Caen, 1849).

39. Charles de Gerville, "Lettres . . . sur l'origine de quelques noms d'hommes et de lieux," *Mémoires de la Société des Antiquaires de Normandie,* vol. 13, 1842–1843: *Etudes géographiques et historiques sur le département de la Manche* (Cherbourg, 1854).

40. Adam Fabricius, "Recherches sur les traces des hommes du Nord dans la Normandie," *Mémoires de la Société des Antiquaires de Normandie* 22 (1856); *Danske minder i Normandiet* (Danish memories in Normandy) (Copenhagen: 1897).

41. See Henri Prentout, *Essai sur les origines et la formation du duché de Normandie* (Paris: Champion, 1911); and a guidebook, A. H. Bougourd, *Saint-Pair sur la Mer et Granville la Victoire. Abrégé de leur histoire à travers les âges, suivi d'étymologies de noms de pays et de notes antiques très curieuses de la Normandie et de la Bretagne* (Granville, 1912).

42. Established by two disciples, Paul Marichal and Léon Mirot (Paris: Champion, 1920–1929), 5 vols. and index.

43. See Henri Longnon, *Pierre de Ronsard. Essai de biographie. Les ancêtres, la jeunesse* (Paris: Champion, 1912). It is possible Proust consulted this book for the passage in *Sodome et Gomorrhe* in which he says that "the Rumanian estimate of Ronsard's nobility is founded upon an error" (2:933; 3:295).

44. Jean Longnon, *La Haute Normandie* (Paris: Delagrave, "Guides artistiques et pittoresques des pays de France," 1912).

45. Jean Longnon, "Ce que disent les noms de lieu," *La Revue critique des idées et des livres* 179 (December 25, 1920): 30:663–75.

46. Vol. 35, 1863.

47. Caen: A. Hardel, 1863.

48. Paris: Nouvelle librairie nationale, 1912.

49. Paris, 1883; rpt. *Bulletin de la Société des Antiquaires* 12 (1877).

50. Rouen and Paris, 1913.

51. Cahier 60, fol. 110r. When, in *Albertine disparue,* the Princesse de Parme puts pressure on Monsieur de Charlus to support the marriage of Mademoiselle d'Oloron, Jupien's niece, and the Cambremer boy, what Monsieur de Charlus will react to will be the name of Legrandin, the future bridegroom's uncle, but in the same way as he here reacts to the bridegroom's grandfather (3:681; 4:243–44).

52. "To have known the stamp market thoroughly," Proust noted in Carnet 1. *Le Carnet de 1908,* 57.

53. Among other sources, probably indirect and even more peculiar, let us take note of the tracing back of "Douville" to Eudes le Bouteiller, which apparently paraphrases a page of Le Héricher in *Avranchin monumental et historique* (Avranches, 1845), 1:508; or the derivation of "Bourguenolles" and "La Chaise-Baudoin" from the same Baudoin de Môles, this being found in an anonymous study in *Mémoires de la société d'archéologie, littérature, science et arts des arrondissements d'Avranches et de Mortain* (1894–1895): 12:147.

54. Cocheris, *Origine et formation des noms de lieu,* 89; Le Héricher, *Philologie topographique de la Normandie,* 8 and 38.

55. In the manuscript Proust wrote "over the humanities," but this was not how the typist read it.

56. Walter Benjamin, *The Origin of German Tragic Drama,* trans. John Osborne (London: New Left Books, 1977), 159–235.

57. Walter Benjamin, "The Image of Proust," in *Illuminations,* trans. Harry Zohn (New York: Schocken, 1969), 202.

58. Quicherat, *De la Formation française des anciens noms de lieu,* 78.

59. *Avranchin monumental et historique* (Avranches, 1865), 3:150.

9. *Madame de Cambremer, Née Legrandin, or the Avant-Garde in Reverse*

1. Maurice Barrès, *L'Oeuvre de Maurice Barrès,* 13:66.

2. See especially Jean Touchard, "Le nationalisme de Barrès," *Annales de l'Est* 24 (1963); and Zeev Sternhell, *Maurice Barrès et le Nationalisme français* (Paris: Armand Colin, 1972).

3. Valéry, *Cahiers,* 2:1083.

4. *Scènes et doctrines du nationalisme* (1902), *L'Oeuvre de Maurice Barrès,* 5:212, quoted by Zeev Sternell, *Maurice Barrès et le Nationalisme français,* 277.

5. Valéry, *Cahiers,* 2:1213.

6. See Hannah Arendt, *On Revolution* (New York: Viking, 1963). To balance Hannah Arendt's prejudiced view in favor of the American Revolution, see Jacques Ellul, *Autopsie de la révolution* (Paris: Calmann-Lévy, 1969).

7. See Francis Haskell, "Art and the Language of Politics," in *Past and Present in Art and Taste* (New Haven: Yale University Press, 1987).

8. Benjamin Constant, *Mélanges de littérature et de politique* (1829), in *Oeuvres* (Paris: Gallimard, Pléiade, 1957), 915.

9. Ibid., 916.

10. See Renato Poggioli, *The Theory of the Avant-Garde* (1962), trans. Gerald Fitzgerald (Cambridge: Harvard University Press, 1968); Linda Nochlin, "The Invention of the Avant-Garde: France, 1830–1880," in Thomas B. Hess and John Ashbery, ed., *Avant-Garde Art* (New York: Collier, 1967). These authors quote Saint-Simon's *Opinions littéraires philosophiques et industrielles* (1825), and an 1845 work written by a follower of Fourier, Gabriel-Désiré Laverdant, *De la Mission de l'art et du Rôle des artistes.*

11. Emile Zola, *Salons* (Geneva and Paris: Droz and Minard, 1959), 228. See Francis Haskell, "Enemies of Modern Art," in *Past and Present in Art and Taste,* 219.

12. Félix Fénéon, *Oeuvres,* preface by Jean Paulhan (Paris: Gallimard, 1948), 72.

13. This is a sentence that is not incorporated into either the separately published version of the article or Paulhan's edition of Fénéon's *Oeuvres.*

14. *Correspondance de Paul Gauguin,* ed. Victor Merlhès (Paris: Fondation Singer-Polignac, 1984), 1:127. See Francis Haskell, "Enemies of Modern Art," 220–21.

15. Théodore Duret, *Critique d'avant-garde* (Paris: Charpentier, 1885), 3.

16. Ibid., 109.

17. "What the snob wants above all is to be noticed in the avant-garde," Coppée writes in 1895. Quoted by Emilien Carassus, *Le Snobisme et les lettres françaises de Paul Bourget à Marcel Proust, 1884–1914* (Paris: Armand Colin, 1966), 28; and also by Francis Haskell, "Enemies of Modern Art," 220.

18. See also Françoise Nora, "The Neo-Impressionist Avant-Garde," in *Avant-Garde Art.*

19. *Cahiers,* 2:1179–80.

20. See Walter Benjamin, "Central Park," in *New German Critique* 34 (Winter 1985):43.

21. Zola, *Salons,* 261. Zola also puts it in this way: "This painter in revolt, who was extremely fond of high-society life, always dreamed about the kind of success that can spring up in Paris, being fawned on by women and received with open arms in the salons, leading the high life in the midst of the oohs and ahs of the public. . . . But he also had to contend with his temperament, which would not

allow him to make concessions and in spite of everything kept him close to the path he had set out for himself" (259).

22. Valéry, *Cahiers,* 2:1181.

23. Gide, *Corydon* (Paris: Gallimard, 1924), 11 n. 1.

24. See in particular Albert Moll, *Les Perversions de l'instinct génital. Etude sur l'inversion sexuelle,* preface by Richard von Krafft-Ebing, French trans. Dr. Pactet and Dr. Romme (Paris: G. Carré, 1893); and Julien Chevalier, *Une maladie de la personnalité. L'inversion sexuelle* (Lyon: A. Storck, 1893).

25. Moll, *Les Perversions de l'instinct génital,* 54.

26. Ambroise Tardieu, *Etude médico-légale sur les attentats aux moeurs* (1857; rpt. 7th ed. [Paris: J.-B. Baillère, 1878]), 255.

27. Johann Ludwig Casper, *Traité pratique de médecine légale* (1857–1858), French trans. G.-G. Baillère (Paris: G. Baillère, 1862), 1:118.

28. Cahier 49, fol. 60v.

29. Carnet 1, fols. 12r–v; *Le Carnet de 1908,* 63.

30. 3:437, unpublished variant.

31. "I am of a third sex that does not yet have a name"—it is actually a woman speaking here—"I have the body and soul of a woman, the mind and strength of a man." Théophile Gautier, *Mademoiselle de Maupin* (Paris: Garnier, 1966), 352, chap. 15.

32. Cahier 49, fol. 60v.

33. See also a June 1914 letter to Gide: "I am convinced that Monsieur de Charlus' homosexuality is what allows him to understand so many things that are inaccessible to his brother the Duc de Guermantes, and to be more subtle and more sensitive." (*Corr.* 13:246)

34. See A. E. Carter, *The Idea of Decadence in French Literature, 1830–1900* (Toronto: University of Toronto Press, 1958), 64–68.

35. Brunetière, "La tragédie de Racine," *Histoire et Littérature,* 2:18–19.

36. Ferdinand Brunetière, *Le Roman naturaliste* (1882; rpt. [Paris: Calmann-Lévy, 1892]), 171.

37. Stendhal, *Salon de 1824, Mélanges d'art* (Paris: Le Divan, 1932), 6. Quoted by Francis Haskell, "Art and the Language of Politics," 68.

38. Ibid., 8.

39. Quoted by Haskell, "Art and the Language of Politics," 73.

40. Valéry, *Cahiers,* 2:1213.

41. Barrès, *Mes cahiers. L'Oeuvre de Maurice Barrès,* 13:262.

42. Sentences restored to the 1989 Pléiade edition (4:526), but not included in the Moncrieff-Kilmartin translation. Similar words are found on 3:993; 4:529 [translator's note].

43. *Le Figaro,* April 28, 1888, quoted by Christian Goubault, "Frédéric Chopin et la critique musicale française," in Danièle Pistone, ed., *Sur les traces de Chopin* (Paris: Champion, 1984), 162.

44. Louis Laloy pointed it out for the *Preludes:* after Chopin paved the way, "Claude Debussy was able to discover its unique, radiant goal" (*La Grande Revue,*

July 10, 1913, 180, quoted by Goubault, 150). In 1918, Robert Godet and Marie Panthès performed a series of lectures and recitals of Chopin and Debussy and showed the affinities between the *Preludes* and *Etudes* of the two musicians (Lockspeiser, *Claude Debussy,* 307).

45. André Gide, *Journal, 1889–1939,* 77. See Theodore Reff, "Cézanne and Poussin," *Journal of the Warburg and Courtauld Institutes* 23 (1960): 150–74.

46. Benjamin, "Central Park," 49.

47. Ibid., 33.

48. Walter Benjamin, "The Image of Proust," in *Illuminations,* trans. Harry Zohn (New York: Schocken, 1969), 257.

Conclusion

1. Nathalie Sarraute, *L'Ere du soupçon* (1956; rpt. [Paris: Gallimard, Folio Essais, 1987]), 84.

2. See Paul de Man, "Literary History and Literary Modernity," *Blindness and Insight. Essays in the Rhetoric of Contemporary Criticism,* 2d ed. (Minneapolis: University of Minnesota Press, 1983).

3. Ruskin, *Sesame and Lilies,* 62 (end of note 1 on page 61).

4. Ibid., 62–63.

Bibliography

1. *Works by Proust*

A la recherche du temps perdu. 3 vols. Ed. Pierre Clarac et André Ferré. Paris: Gallimard, Pléiade, 1954.

Contre Sainte-Beuve, followed by *Nouveaux Mélanges.* Ed. Bernard de Fallois. Paris: Gallimard, 1954 (*CSB,* ed. Fallois).

Contre Saint-Beuve, preceded by *Pastiches et Mélanges* and followed by *Essais et Articles.* Ed. Pierre Clarac and Yves Sandre. Paris: Gallimard, Pléiade, 1971 (*CSB*).

Jean Santeuil, preceded by *Les Plaisirs et les Jours.* Ed. Pierre Clarac and Yves Sandre. Paris: Gallimard, Pléiade, 1971 (*JS*).

Textes retrouvés. Ed. Philip Kolb and Larkin B. Price. Paris: Gallimard, Cahiers Marcel Proust, 1971.

Le Carnet de 1908. Ed. Philip Kolb. Paris: Gallimard, Cahiers Marcel Proust, 1976 [Carnet 1].

Matinée chez la princesse de Guermantes. Cahiers du "Temps retrouvé." Ed. Henri Bonnet and Bernard Brun. Paris: Gallimard, 1982 [Cahiers 51, 58, and 57].

Sur Baudelaire, Flaubert, et Morand. Ed. Antoine Compagnon. Bruxelles: Complexe, 1987.

A la recherche du temps perdu. 4 vols. Ed. Jean-Yves Tadié et al. Paris: Gallimard, Pléiade, 1987–89 (*RTP*).

Du côté de chez Swann. Ed. Antoine Compagnon. Paris: Gallimard, Folio Collection, 1988.

II. Translations and Prefaces

Ruskin, John. *La Bible d'Amiens*. Trans., notes, and preface by Marcel Proust. Paris: Mercure de France, 1904.

—— *Sésame et les Lys*. Trans., notes, and preface by Marcel Proust. Paris: Mercure de France, 1906; ed. Antoine Compagnon. Bruxelles: Complexe, 1987.

Blanche, Jacques-Émile. *Propos de peintre. De David à Degas*. Preface by Marcel Proust. Paris: Emile-Paul, 1919.

Morand, Paul. *Tendres Stocks*. Preface by Marcel Proust. Paris: Gallimard, 1921.

III. Correspondence

Correspondance. Ed. Philip Kolb. Paris: Plon. 16 vols. printed since 1970, covering the years 1880–1917 (*Corr.*).

Supplementary editions:

Correspondance générale de Marcel Proust. 6 vols. Published by Robert Proust, Paul Brach, and Suzy Mante-Proust. Paris: Plon, 1930–36 (*Corr. gén.*).

Lettres à la NRF. Paris: Gallimard, 1932.

Kolb, Philip. *La Correspondance de Marcel Proust*. Urbana: University of Illinois Press, 1949 (chronology).

Lettres à Reynaldo Hahn. Ed. Philip Kolb. Paris: Gallimard, 1956.

Proust, Marcel and Jacques Rivière. *Correspondance, 1914–1922*. Ed. Philip Kolb. Paris: Plon, 1955; Paris: Gallimard, 1976.

IV. Manuscripts, Typescripts, and Proofs from the Fonds Marcel Proust at the Bibliothèque Nationale (Cited Documents)

Carnets 1–4 N.a.fr. 16637–16640
[4 carnets of notes]
Cahiers 1–62 N.a.fr. 16641–16702
Cahiers 63–75 N.a.fr. 18313–18325
[75 cahiers]

[The numbering system, including folios of Proust's carnets and cahiers, are those of the Bibliothèque nationale.]

Manuscript of *Sodome et Gomorrhe*

Cahiers I–VII N.a.fr. 16708–16714

[the first seven of the twenty cahiers, numbered by Proust, containing the manuscript of the *Recherche,* from *Sodome et Gomorrhe* to the end of *Le Temps retrouvé*]

Corrected Typescripts

Sodome et Gomorrhe I N.a.fr. 16738
Jalousie N.a.fr. 16728

[extract from *Sodome et Gomorrhe II* published in *Les Œuvres libres* in November 1921]

Sodome et Gomorrhe II	N.a.fr. 16739–16741
Reliquat	N.a.fr. 16738

First Proofs

Sodome et Gomorrhe II	N.a.fr. 16766

V. Biographical Works

Albaret, Céleste. *Monsieur Proust.* Paris: Laffont, 1973 (memoires edited by Georges Belmont).

Bonnet, Henri. *Marcel Proust de 1907 à 1914* [1959]. Reprint. 2 vols. Paris: Nizet, 1971 and 1976.

—— *Les Amours et la sexualité de Marcel Proust.* Paris: Nizet, 1985.

Ferré, André. *Les Années de collège de Marcel Proust.* Paris: Gallimard, 1959.

Maurois, André. *A la recherche de Marcel Proust.* Paris: Hachette, 1949.

Painter, George D. *Marcel Proust: A Biography* [1959]. Reprint. 2 vols. New York: Vintage Books, 1978.

Pierre-Quint, Léon. *Marcel Proust, sa vie, son œuvre* [1925]. Paris: Le Sagittaire, 1976.

VI. Studies on the Genesis of Proust's Work

Bardèche, Maurice. *Marcel Proust romancier.* 2 vols. Paris: Les Sept Couleurs, 1971.

Brun, Bernard. Articles in *Etudes proustiennes* (*EP*) 4 and 5; *Bulletin d'informations proustiennes* (*BIP*) 10, 11, 12, 13, and 16.

Bulletin de la société des amis de Marcel Proust et des amis de Combray. 38 vols. published since 1950 (*BSAMP*).

Bulletin d'informations proustiennes. Presses de l'Ecole normale supérieure. 18 vols. published since 1975 (*BIP*).

Compagnon, Antoine. "Sodome 1913," *EP*, 6 (1987).

De Agostini, Daniela, Maurizio Ferraris, and Bernard Brun. *L'Età dei nomi. Quaderni della "Recherche."* Milan: Mondadori, 1985.

Eells-Ogée, Emily. "La Publication de *Sodome et Gomorrhe,*" *BIP* 15 and 16 (1984 and 1985).

Études proustiennes. Paris: Gallimard, "Cahiers Marcel Proust," 6 vols. published since 1973 (*EP*).

Feuillerat, Albert. *Comment Proust a composé son roman.* New Haven: Yale University Press, 1934.

Kolb, Philip. "La Genèse de la *Recherche:* une heureuse bévue." *Revue d'histoire littéraire de la France.* Septembre–Décembre 1971.

Milly, Jean. *Les Pastiches de Proust.* Paris: Armand Colin, 1970.

—— *Proust dans le texte et l'avant-texte.* Paris: Flammarion, 1985.

Quémar, Claudine. Articles in *EP* 1 and 2; *BIP* 3, 6, and 8.

—— "Rêveries onomastiques proustiennes." In R. Debray Genette, ed. *Essais de critique génétique*. Paris: Flammarion, 1979.

Vigneron, Robert. "Genèse de Swann" [1937]. *Etudes sur Stendhal et Proust*. Paris: Nizet, 1978.

Winton, Alison. *Proust's Additions: The Making of* A la recherche du temps perdu. 2 vols. London and New York: Cambridge University Press, 1977.

Yoshida, Jo. *Proust contre Ruskin. La genèse de deux voyages dans la "Recherche" d'après des documents inédits*. 2 vols. Doctoral dissertation, University of Paris IV, 1978.

Yoshikawa, Kazuyoshi. "Marcel Proust en 1908." *Études de langue et littérature françaises* 22 (1973).

—— *Études sur la genèse de "La Prisonnière" d'après des brouillons inédits*. 2 vols. Doctoral dissertation, University of Paris IV, 1976.

—— "Remarques sur les transformations subies par la *Recherche* autour des années 1913–1914 d'après des cahiers inédits." *BIP* 7 (1978).

—— "Vinteuil ou la genèse du septuor." *EP* 3 (1979).

VII. Critical Studies

Autret, Jean. *L'Influence de Ruskin sur la vie, les idées, et l'œuvre de Marcel Proust*. Geneva: Droz, 1955.

Bales, Richard. *Proust and the Middle Ages*. Geneva: Droz, 1975.

Barthes, Roland. "Proust et les noms." *Le Degré zéro de l'écriture*, followed by *Nouveaux Essais critiques*. Paris: Seuil, Points, 1972.

—— et al. *Recherche de Proust*. Paris: Seuil, Points, 1980.

Bataille, Georges. *La Littérature et le Mal*. Paris: Gallimard, 1957; *Œuvres complètes*, vol. 9. Paris: Gallimard, 1979.

Bem, Jeanne. "Le juif et l'homosexuel dans *A la recherche du temps perdu*." *Littérature* 37 (1980).

Brunet, Etienne. *Le Vocabulaire de Proust*. 3 vols. Geneva: Slatkine; Paris: Champion, 1983.

Carassus, Emilien. *Le Snobisme et les lettres françaises de Paul Bourget à Marcel Proust, 1884–1914*. Paris: Armand Colin, 1966.

Chantal, René de. *Marcel Proust, critique littéraire*. 2 vols. Montreal: Presses de l'Université de Montréal, 1967.

Deleuze, Gilles. *Proust et les signes* [1964]. 7th ed. Paris: PUF, 1986.

Descombes, Vincent. *Proust. Philosophie du roman*. Paris: Ed. de Minuit, 1987.

Fearn, Liliane. "Sur un rêve de Marcel." *BSAMP* 17 (1967).

Fraisse, Luc. *Le Processus de la création chez Proust. Le Fragment expérimental*. Paris: José Corti, 1988.

Genette, Gérard. "Proust et le langage indirect." *Figures II* [1969]. Paris: Seuil, Points, 1979.

—— "Métonymie chez Proust" and "Discours du récit." *Figures II*. Paris: Seuil, 1972.

Henry, Anne. *Marcel Proust. Théories pour une esthétique*. Paris: Klincksieck, 1981.

—— *Proust romancier. Le tombeau égyptien.* Paris: Flammarion, 1983.
Massis, Henri. *Le Drame de Marcel Proust.* Paris: Grasset, 1937.
Muller, Marcel. "*Sodome I* ou la naturalisation de Charlus." *Poétique* 8 (1971).
Nattiez, Jean-Jacques. *Proust musicien.* Paris: Christian Bourgois, 1984.
Piroué, Georges. *Proust et la musique du devenir.* Paris: Denoël, 1960.
Raimond, Michel. *Proust romancier.* Paris: SEDES, 1984.
Revel, Jean-François. *Sur Proust* [1960]. Paris: Grasset, 1987.
Rivers, J. E. *Proust and the Art of Love: The Aesthetics of Sexuality in the Life, Times, and Art of Marcel Proust.* New York: Columbia University Press, 1980.
Rivière, Jacques. *Quelques progrès dans l'étude du cœur humain* [1926]. Ed. Thierry Laget. Paris: Gallimard, Cahiers Marcel Proust, 1985.
Roger, Alain. *Proust. Les plaisirs et les noms.* Paris: Denoël, 1985.
Rousset, Jean. *Forme et signification.* Paris: José Corti, 1962.
Tadié, Jean-Yves. *Proust et le Roman* [1971]. Paris: Gallimard, Collection "Tel," 1986.
—— *Proust.* Paris: Belfond, 1983.
Viers, Rina. "Evolution et sexualité des plantes dans *Sodome et Gomorrhe.*" Europe, 49 (1971).

VIII. Other Works

Balzac, Honoré de. *La Comédie humaine.* 12 vols. Ed. Pierre-Georges Castex. Paris: Gallimard, Pléiade, 1976–81.
Barrès, Maurice. *L'Œuvre de Maurice Barrès.* 20 vols. Paris: Club de l'honnête homme, 1965–69.
Baudelaire, Charles. *Œuvres complètes.* 2 vols. Ed. Claude Pichois. Paris: Gallimard, Pléiade, 1975–76 (*OC*).
—— *Correspondance.* 2 vols. Ed. Claude Pichois and Jean Ziegler. Paris: Gallimard, Pléiade, 1973.
Gide, André. *Journal, 1889–1939.* Paris: Galliimard, Pléiade, 1951.
—— *Journal, 1939–1949. Souvenirs.* Paris: Gallimard, Pléiade, 1954.
Huysmans, Joris Karl. *A rebours.* Ed. Marc Fumaroli. 2d ed. Paris: Gallimard, Folio, 1983.
Racine, Jean. *Théâtre complet.* Ed. Jacques Morel and Alain Viala. Paris: Garnier, 1980.
Sainte-Beuve, Charles. *Volupté.* Ed. André Guyaux. Paris: Gallimard, Folio, 1986.
Valéry, Paul. *Cahiers.* 2 vols. Ed. Judith Robinson. Paris: Gallimard, Pléiade, 1973–74.

Index